NEOTOPIA

Contents

NEOTOPIA™

by Rod Espinosa

Creator - Rod Espinosa
Graphic Designer - Rod Espinosa
Cover Design - Guru e-FX
Layout - Wes Hartman

Editor-in-Chief - Jochen Weltjens
President of Sales and Marketing - Lee Duhig
Art Direction - Guru e-FX
Managing Editor - Paul Kilpatrick
Production Manager - Rob Acosta
Publisher - Joe Dunn
Founder - Ben Dunn

Come visit us online at www.antarctic-press.com

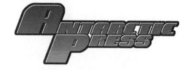

Neotopia Color Manga Volume 3 by Rod Espinosa
An Antarctic Press Color Manga

Antarctic Press
7272 Wurzbach Suite 204 San Antonio, TX 78240

Collects *Neotopia* Vol. 3 issues 1-5
First published in 2004 by Antarctic Press.

Neotopia Color Manga Volume 3, March 2005.

"...Fear of lack causes covetousness and greed; in man also pride which counst it as a glorious thing to surpass and excel others in the superfluous and vain ostentation of things." Sir Thomas More

ISBN: 1-932453-75-X
Printed and Bound in China by REGENT PUBLISHING SERVICES LIMITED.

VOLUME 3

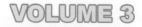

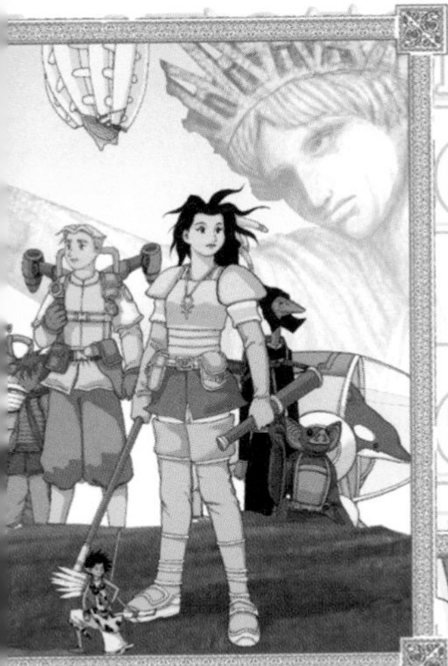

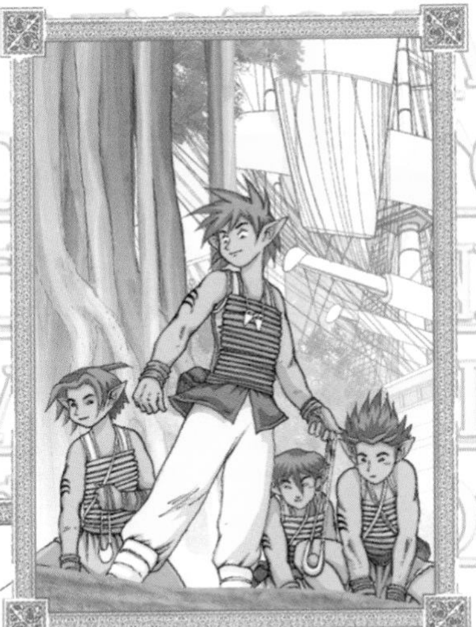

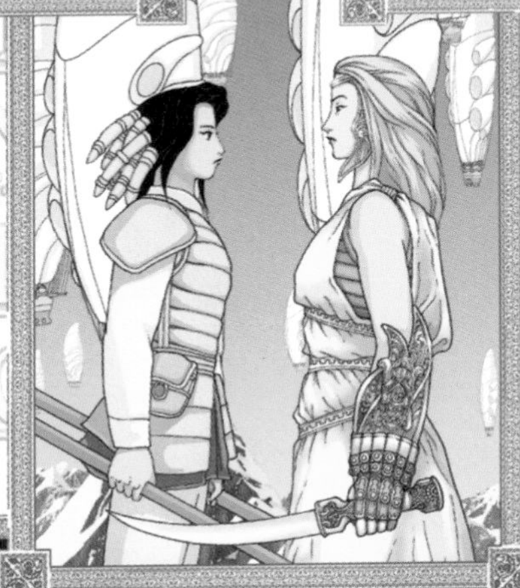

Chapter 1
The Kingdoms Beyond Athanon

Chapter 2
Parting Ways

Chapter 4
Implements of Destruction

Chapter 5
Strength in Unity

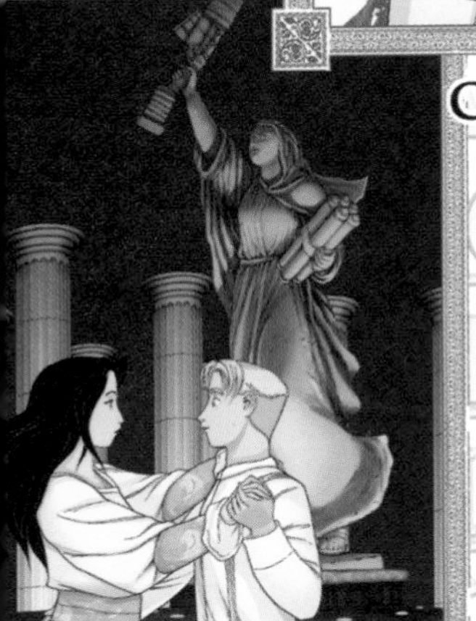

Chapter 3
Kingdom in the Sky

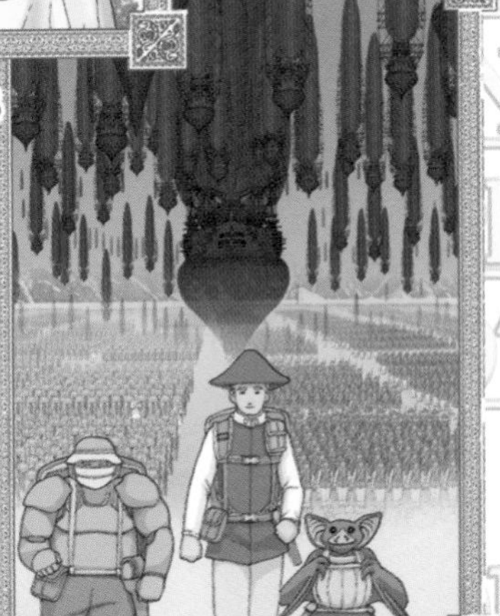

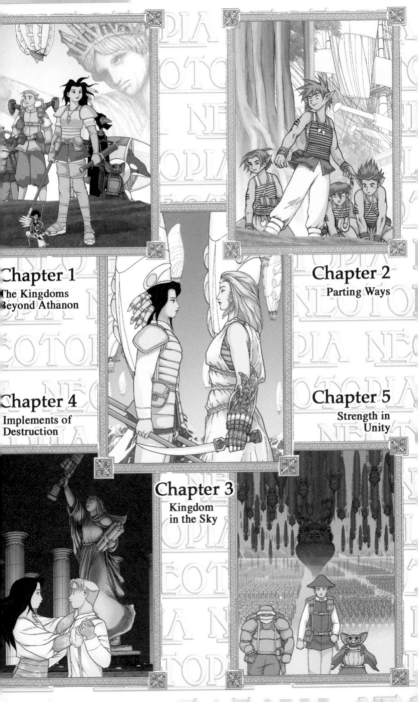

Nalyn

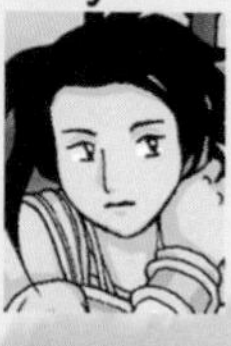

Actually a lowly servant, Nalyn has been posing as the Grand Duchess of Mathenia and has endeared herself to its people in that role. She and Philios get off on the wrong foot when she orders his rocket pack destroyed according to ancient law. Despite this, she has grown fond of the young mechanic. She is about to play the role of her life--that of an army commander!

Philios

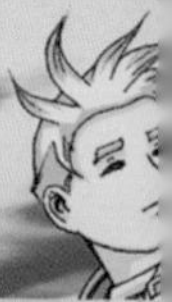

A young inventor who has crossed paths with the "princess." He is Monti's best friend and an expert float ship mechanic. A loyal patriot and Airdiver apprentice, he will do anything to protect his homeland, even if he has to sign up for a war against Krossos.

Ki-Ek

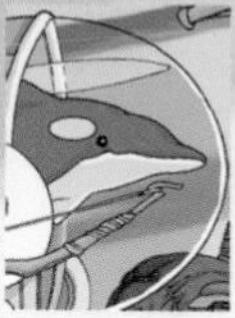

Nalyn's best friend besides Nimn, this intelligent and psionically gifted dolphin is one of only two people who know Nalyn's secret. Part of the rare Dalphinii species, Ki-Ek acts as the navigator on the newly christened Majestic Explorer, a ship he and Nalyn rescued from the scrapyard and now serves as the royal flagship.

Nimn

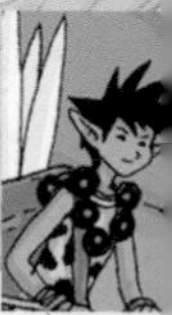

Nalyn's other best friend and brownie companion. When the Age of Heavy Industry came to an end, the world returned to simpler ways of living. Fairies and elves came back to live among people again, and Nimn is but one example. His fairy magic has allowed him to begin to harness mystic ways that were old before the Age of Heavy Industry.

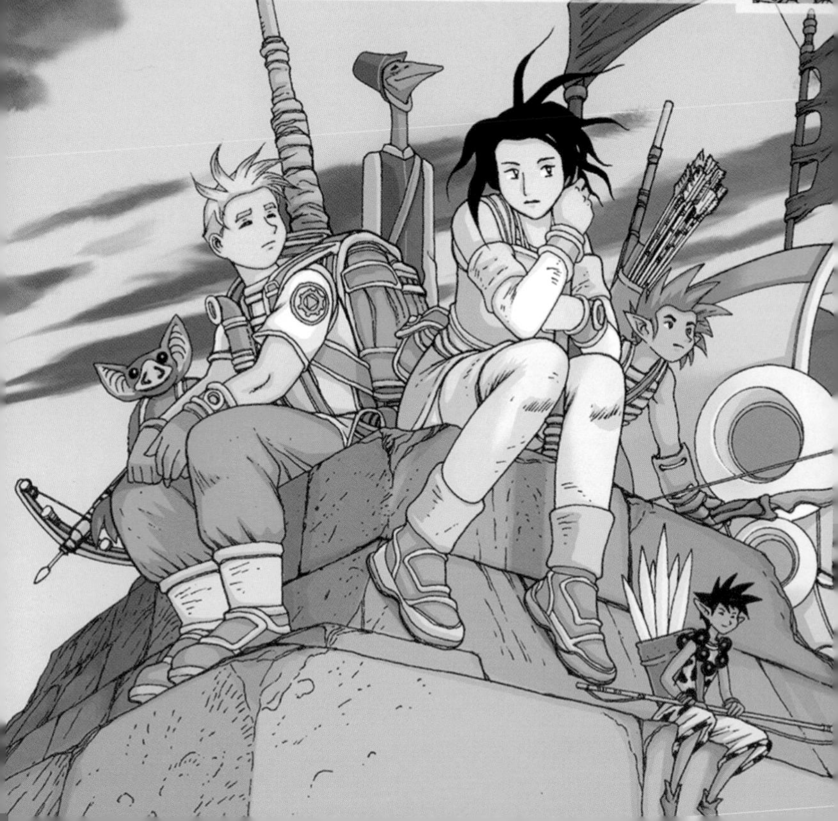

essor Felder

The quintessential Tridactylian, Felder is content with his life, lives peacefully, is highly educated, and can speak many languages. He loyally serves as Nalyn's teacher, butler, and personal secretary without any knowledge of her double identity. He is the Majestic Explorer's Science Officer/First Lieutenant.

Monti

The Chiropterians' superior hearing, acute radar sense, and ability to judge wind behavior and patterns make them the ideal pilots for the float ships of Mathenia. Monti is a young member of his species. As with most Chiropterians, he loves to fly and lives his life with a happy-go-lucky demeanor.

o

An orphan elf raised by humans, he was trained to be a member of the Bodyguard Elite. He is an excellent archer and martial-arts practitioner. The voyage ahead will test his mettle and may well change the way he views his heritage and culture.

Sergeant Tinbolt

A relic from ages past, he is the last functional soldier Orgot. Because of his advancing age, he tends to forget things and is not as alert as he once was. He is a loyal servant of the Grand Duchess and a member of her Bodyguard elite. Aboard the Majestic Explorer, he's the Master of Arms in charge of ship defense. Unfortunately for Nalyn and the rest of the crew was a casualty in the Athanon affair..

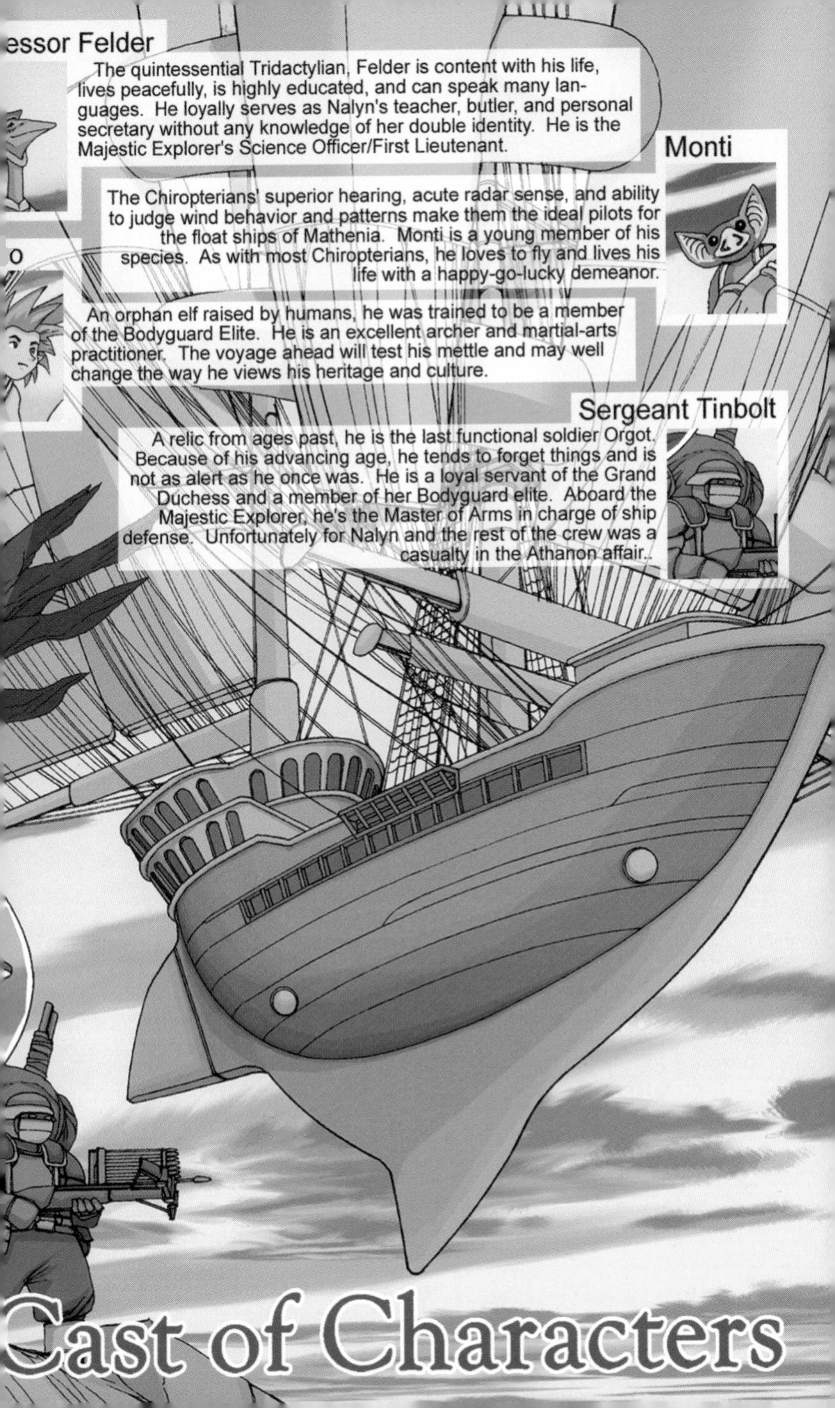

Cast of Characters

In a world where Man has finally learned to exist in harmony with Nature, the citizens of Mathenia live happily under their beloved Grand Duchess. Unknown to them, she is Nalyn, a commoner impersonating Nydia, the real Duchess. When Nalyn is kidnapped by Krossos, an enemy country bent on bringing back the age of technological excess, she is forced to lead her country to war.

Defeated by betrayal, Nalyn flees Mathenia for the open ocean, into the hands of rogue sky pirates. She and her crew gain friendship and freedom, only to fly into the largest storm they've ever seen. Badly damaged, their ship limps to the shore of the island of Eriden, where Nalyn rushes repairs.

Little do they know, the Krossian Emperors have assembled a mighty armada. Their mission: to capture Nalyn and bring her back, dead or alive.

The Krossian armada, led by General Kaizler, arrive on the island. Nalyn and her crew narrowly escape their wrath. With heavy hearts, they leave Eriden in the hands of the enemy.

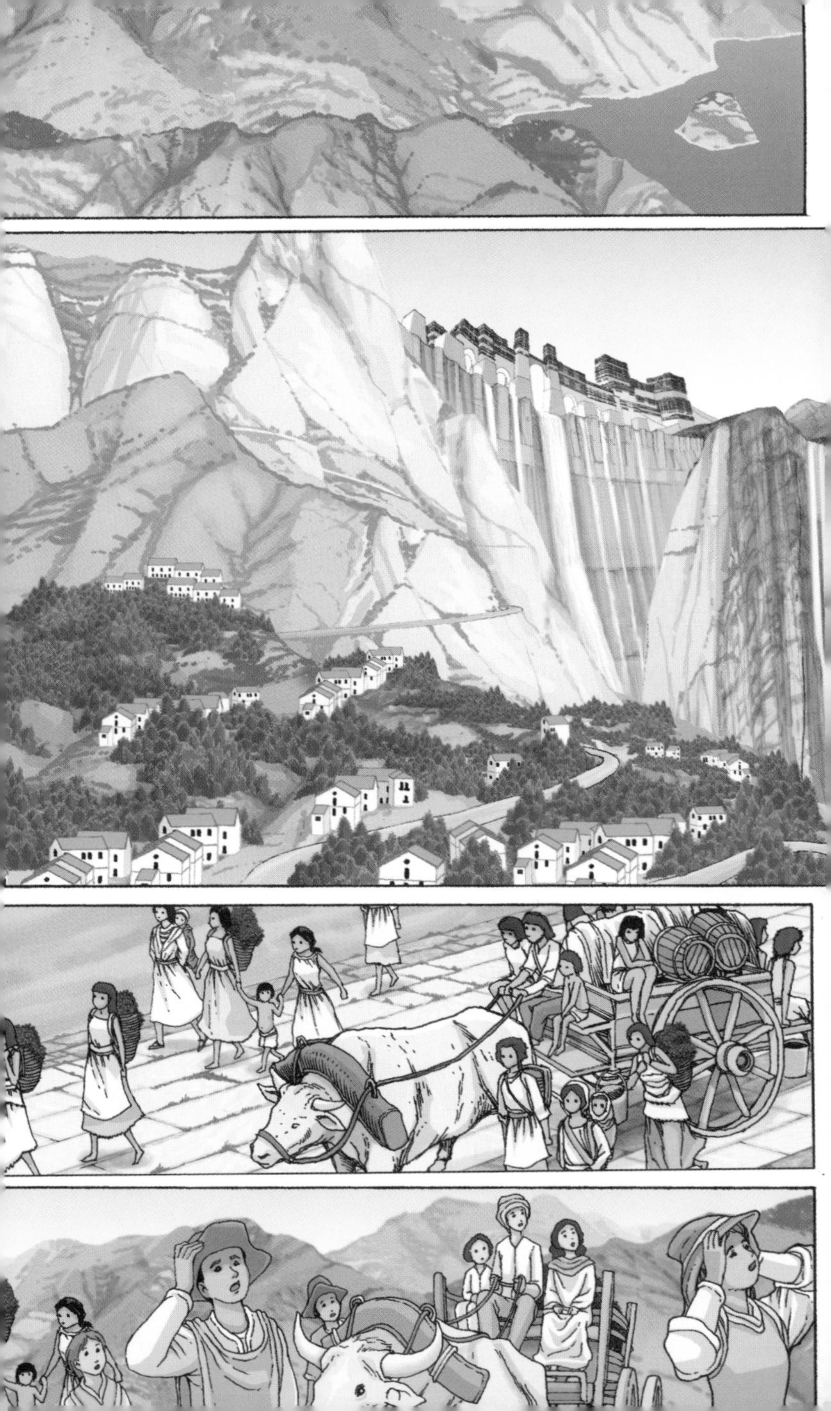

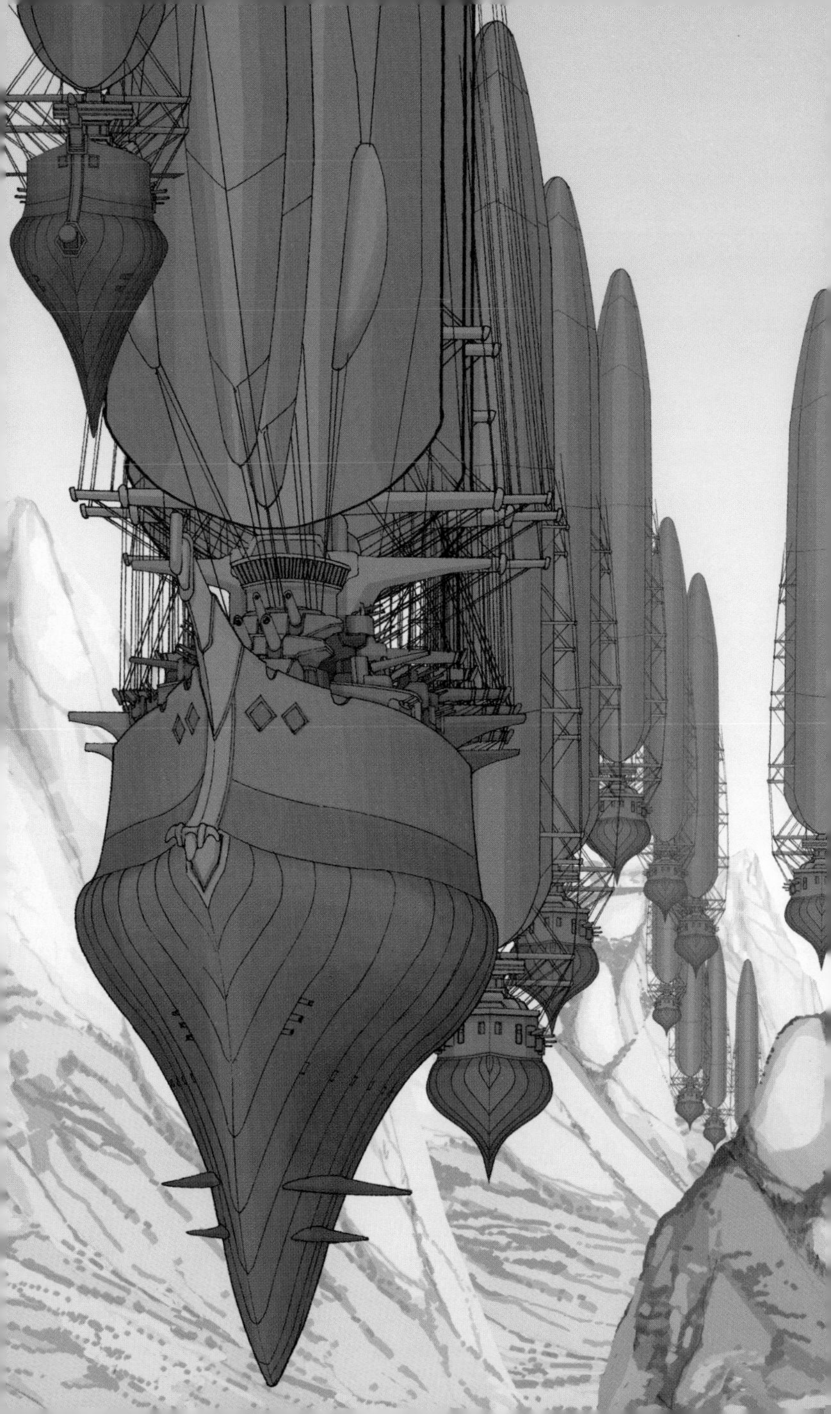

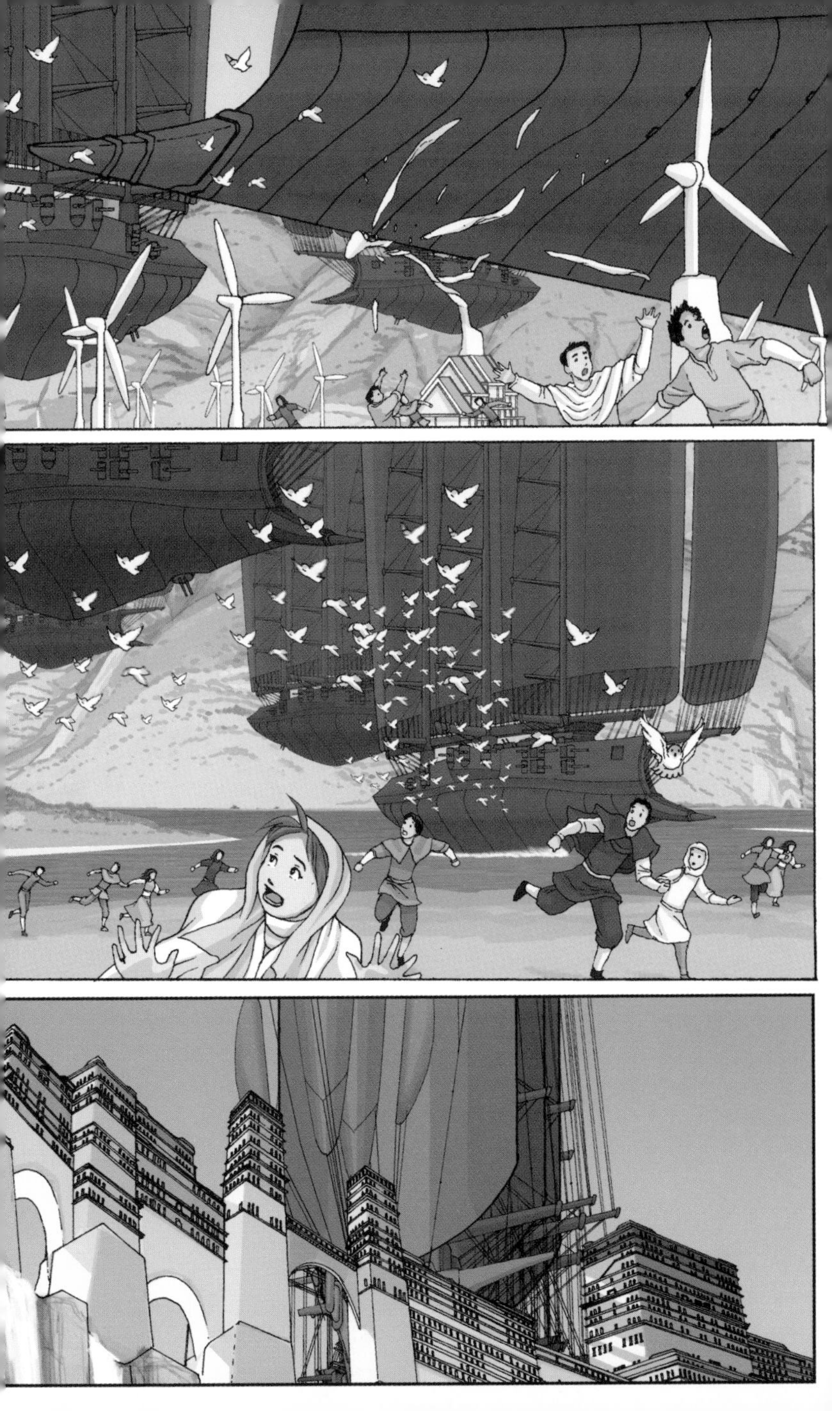

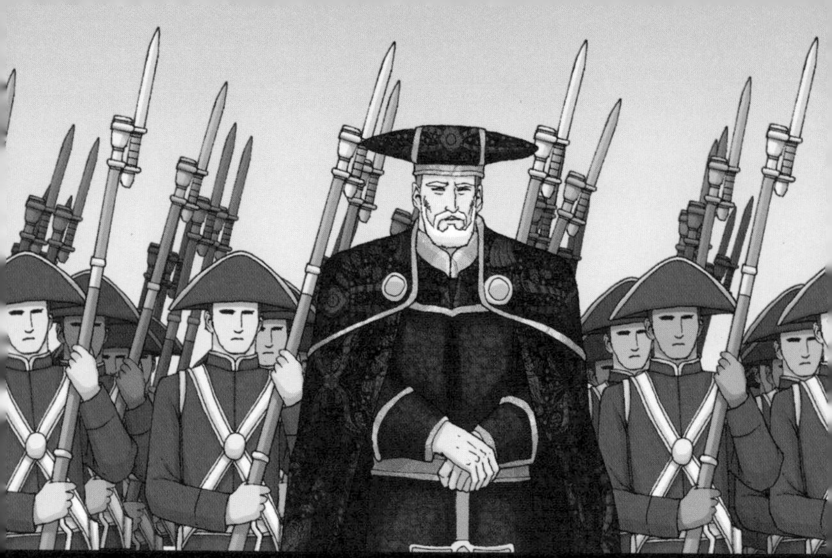

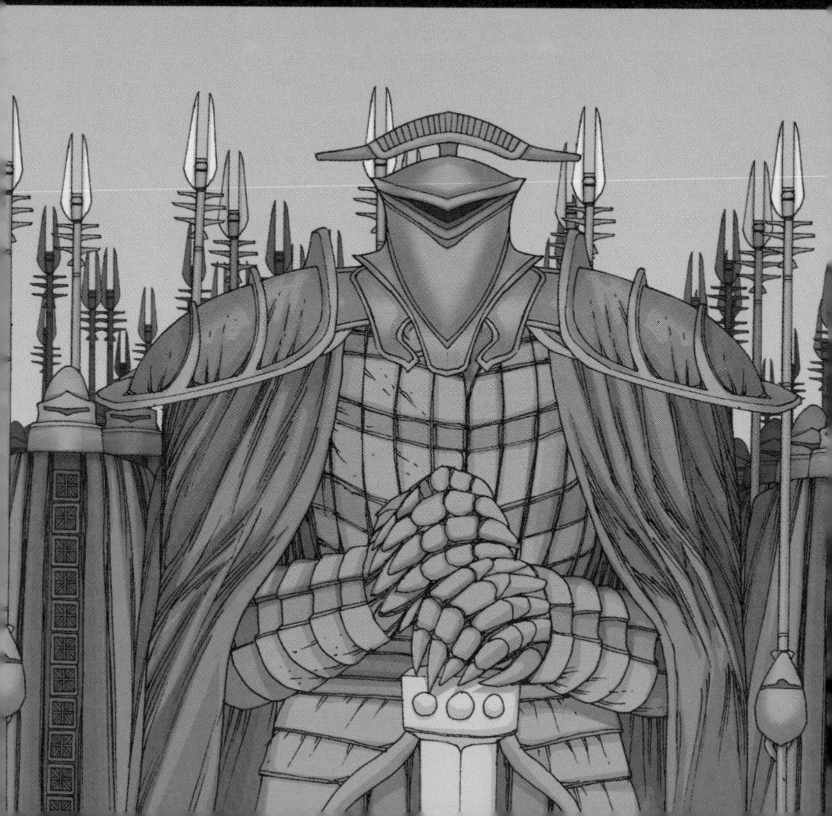

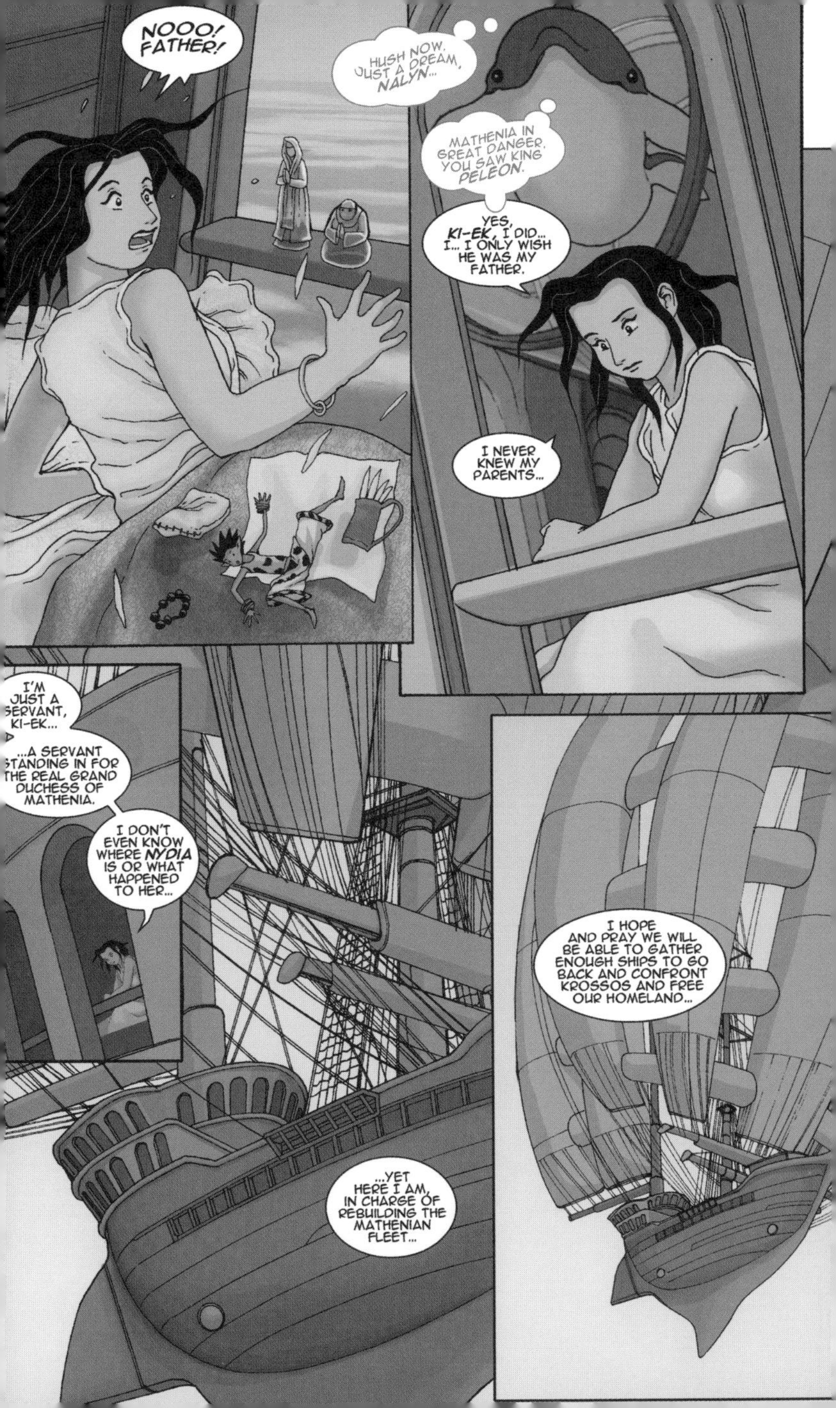
NOOO! FATHER!
HUSH NOW, JUST A DREAM, NALYN...
MATHENIA IN GREAT DANGER. YOU SAW KING PELEON.
YES, KI-EK, I DID... I... I ONLY WISH HE WAS MY FATHER.
I NEVER KNEW MY PARENTS...
I'M JUST A SERVANT, KI-EK...
...A SERVANT STANDING IN FOR THE REAL GRAND DUCHESS OF MATHENIA.
I DON'T EVEN KNOW WHERE NYDIA IS OR WHAT HAPPENED TO HER...
...YET HERE I AM, IN CHARGE OF REBUILDING THE MATHENIAN FLEET...
I HOPE AND PRAY WE WILL BE ABLE TO GATHER ENOUGH SHIPS TO GO BACK AND CONFRONT KROSSOS AND FREE OUR HOMELAND...

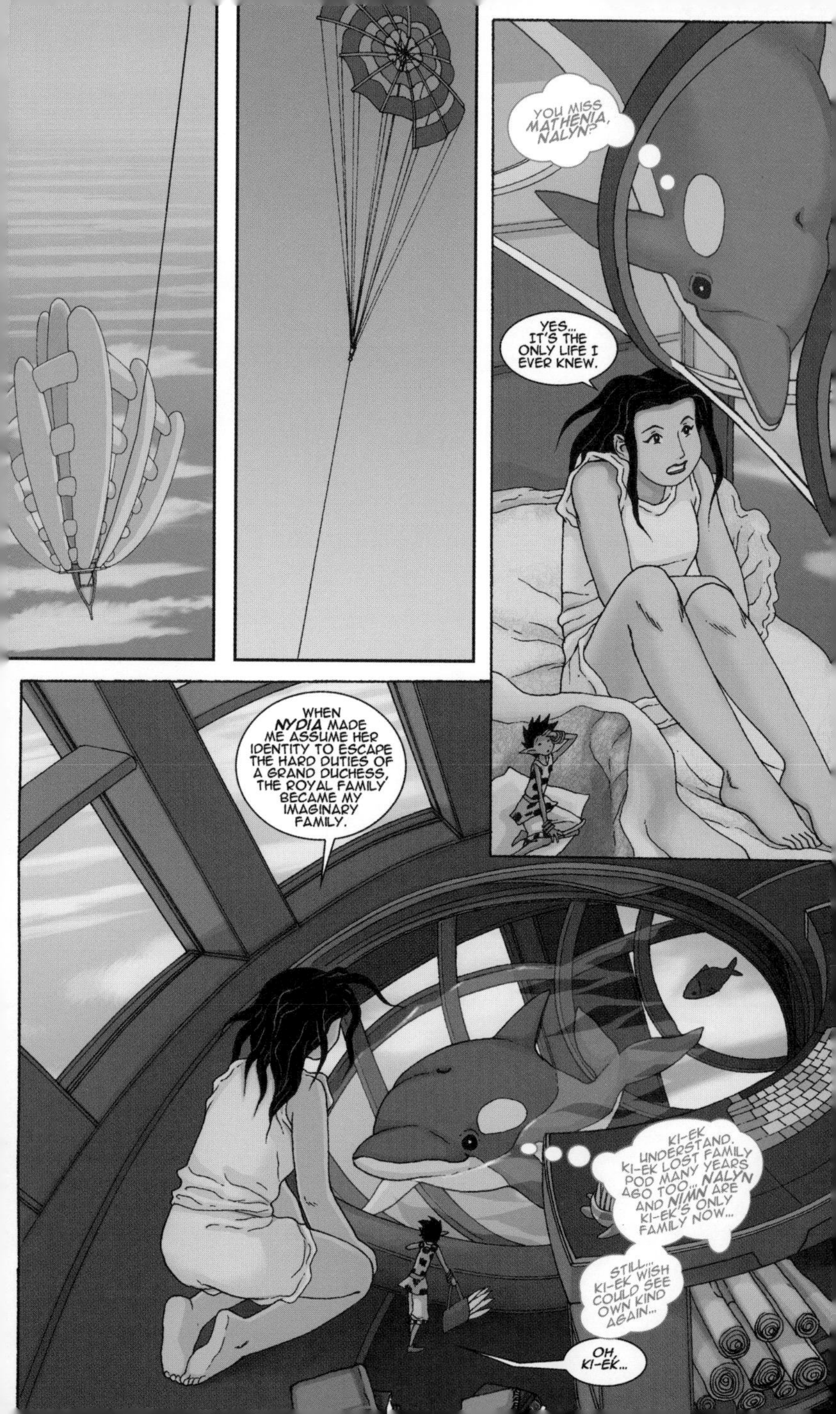
YOU MISS MATHENIA, NALYN?
YES... IT'S THE ONLY LIFE I EVER KNEW.
WHEN NYDIA MADE ME ASSUME HER IDENTITY TO ESCAPE THE HARD DUTIES OF A GRAND DUCHESS, THE ROYAL FAMILY BECAME MY IMAGINARY FAMILY.
KI-EK UNDERSTAND. KI-EK LOST FAMILY POD MANY YEARS AGO TOO... NALYN AND NIMN ARE KI-EK'S ONLY FAMILY NOW...
STILL... KI-EK WISH COULD SEE OWN KIND AGAIN...
OH, KI-EK...

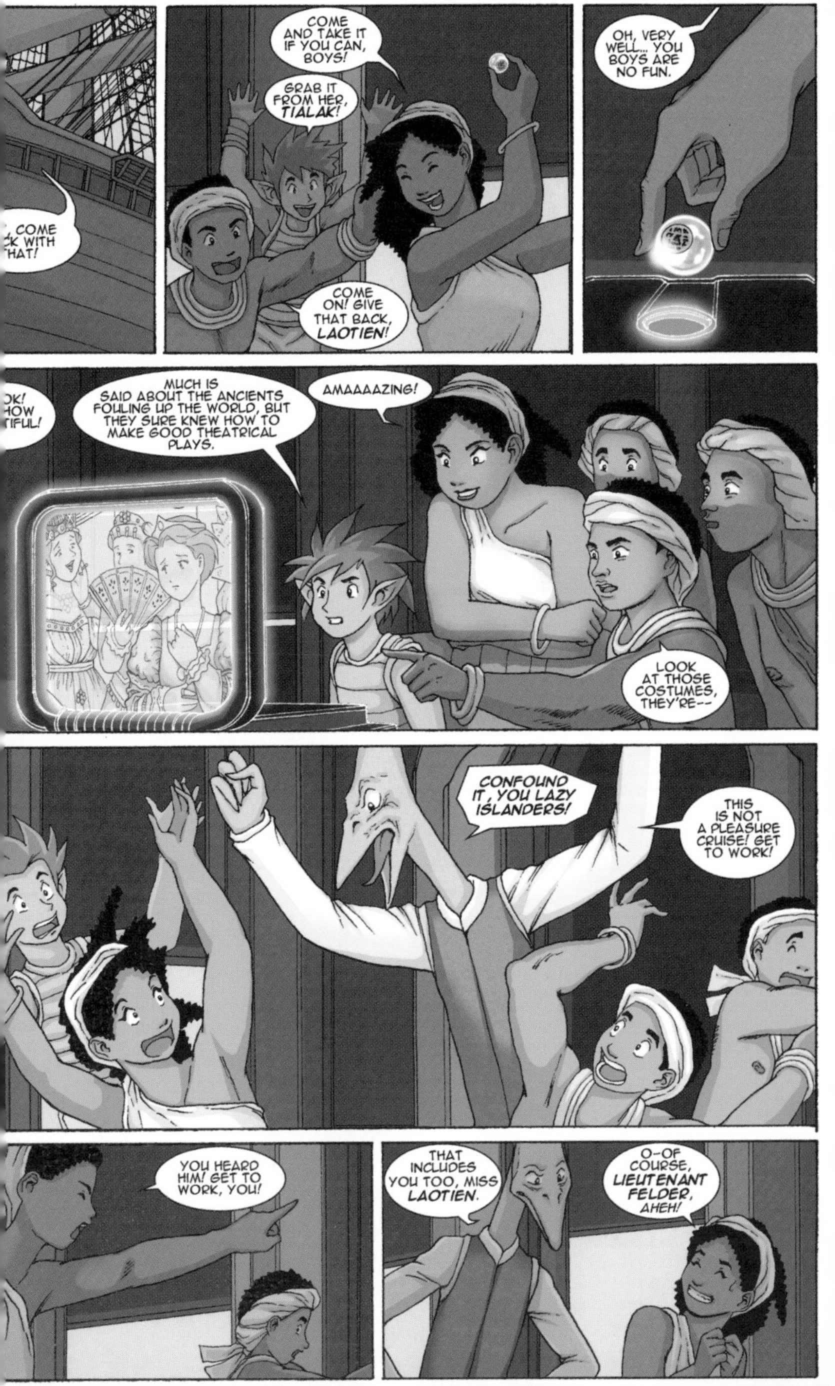

..., COME ...CK WITH ...HAT!
COME AND TAKE IT IF YOU CAN, BOYS!
GRAB IT FROM HER, TIALAK!
COME ON! GIVE THAT BACK, LAOTIEN!
OH, VERY WELL... YOU BOYS ARE NO FUN.
...OK! ...HOW ...TIFUL!
MUCH IS SAID ABOUT THE ANCIENTS FOULING UP THE WORLD, BUT THEY SURE KNEW HOW TO MAKE GOOD THEATRICAL PLAYS.
AMAAAAAZING!
LOOK AT THOSE COSTUMES, THEY'RE--
CONFOUND IT, YOU LAZY ISLANDERS!
THIS IS NOT A PLEASURE CRUISE! GET TO WORK!
YOU HEARD HIM! GET TO WORK, YOU!
THAT INCLUDES YOU TOO, MISS LAOTIEN.
O-OF COURSE, LIEUTENANT FELDER, AHEH!

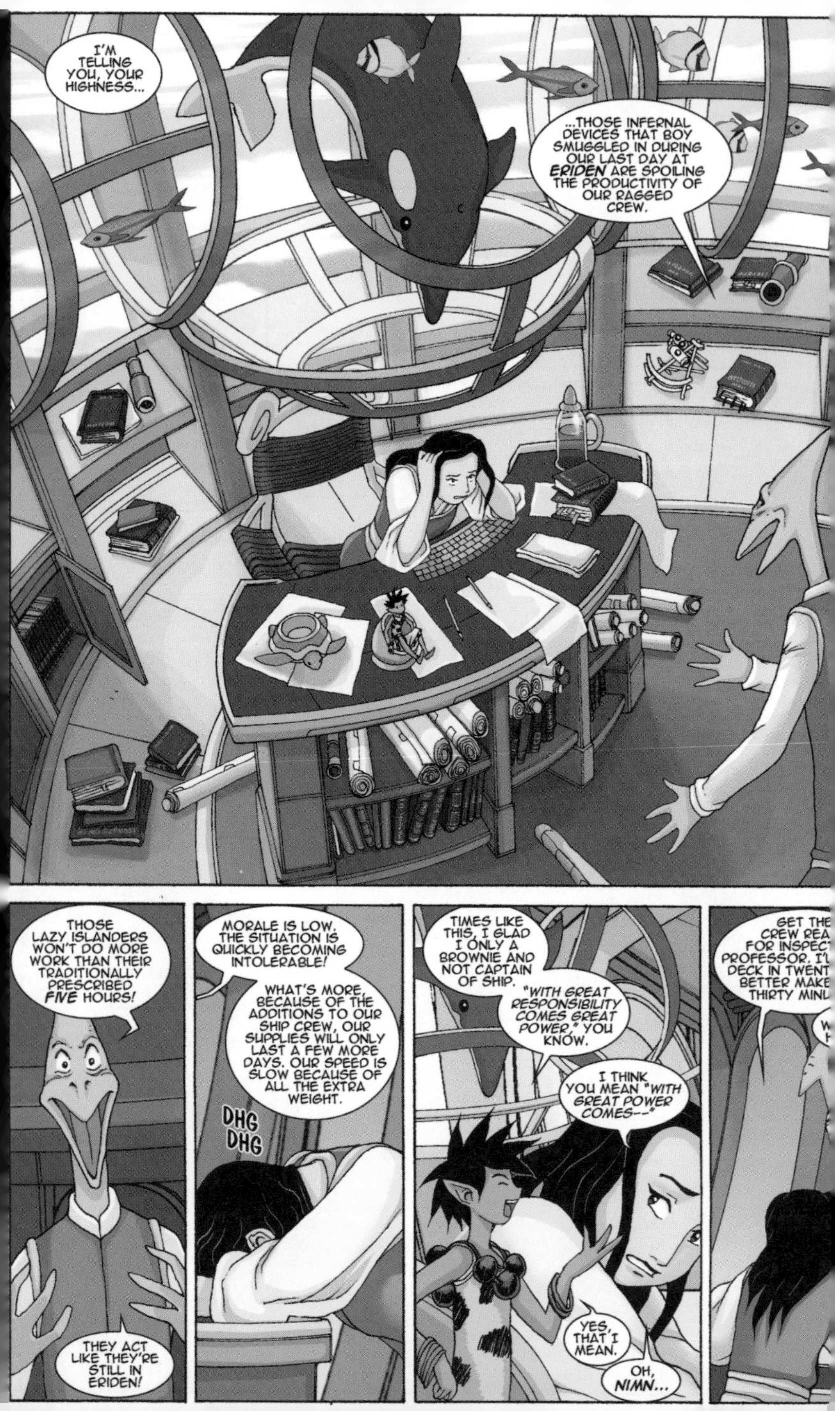
I'M TELLING YOU, YOUR HIGHNESS...
...THOSE INFERNAL DEVICES THAT BOY SMUGGLED IN DURING OUR LAST DAY AT ERIDEN ARE SPOILING THE PRODUCTIVITY OF OUR RAGGED CREW.
THOSE LAZY ISLANDERS WON'T DO MORE WORK THAN THEIR TRADITIONALLY PRESCRIBED FIVE HOURS!
THEY ACT LIKE THEY'RE STILL IN ERIDEN!
MORALE IS LOW. THE SITUATION IS QUICKLY BECOMING INTOLERABLE!
WHAT'S MORE, BECAUSE OF THE ADDITIONS TO OUR SHIP CREW, OUR SUPPLIES WILL ONLY LAST A FEW MORE DAYS. OUR SPEED IS SLOW BECAUSE OF ALL THE EXTRA WEIGHT.
DHG DHG
TIMES LIKE THIS, I GLAD I ONLY A BROWNIE AND NOT CAPTAIN OF SHIP.
"WITH GREAT RESPONSIBILITY COMES GREAT POWER," YOU KNOW.
I THINK YOU MEAN "WITH GREAT POWER COMES--"
YES, THAT I MEAN.
OH, NIMN...
GET THE CREW REA FOR INSPECT PROFESSOR. I'L DECK IN TWENT BETTER MAKE THIRTY MINU

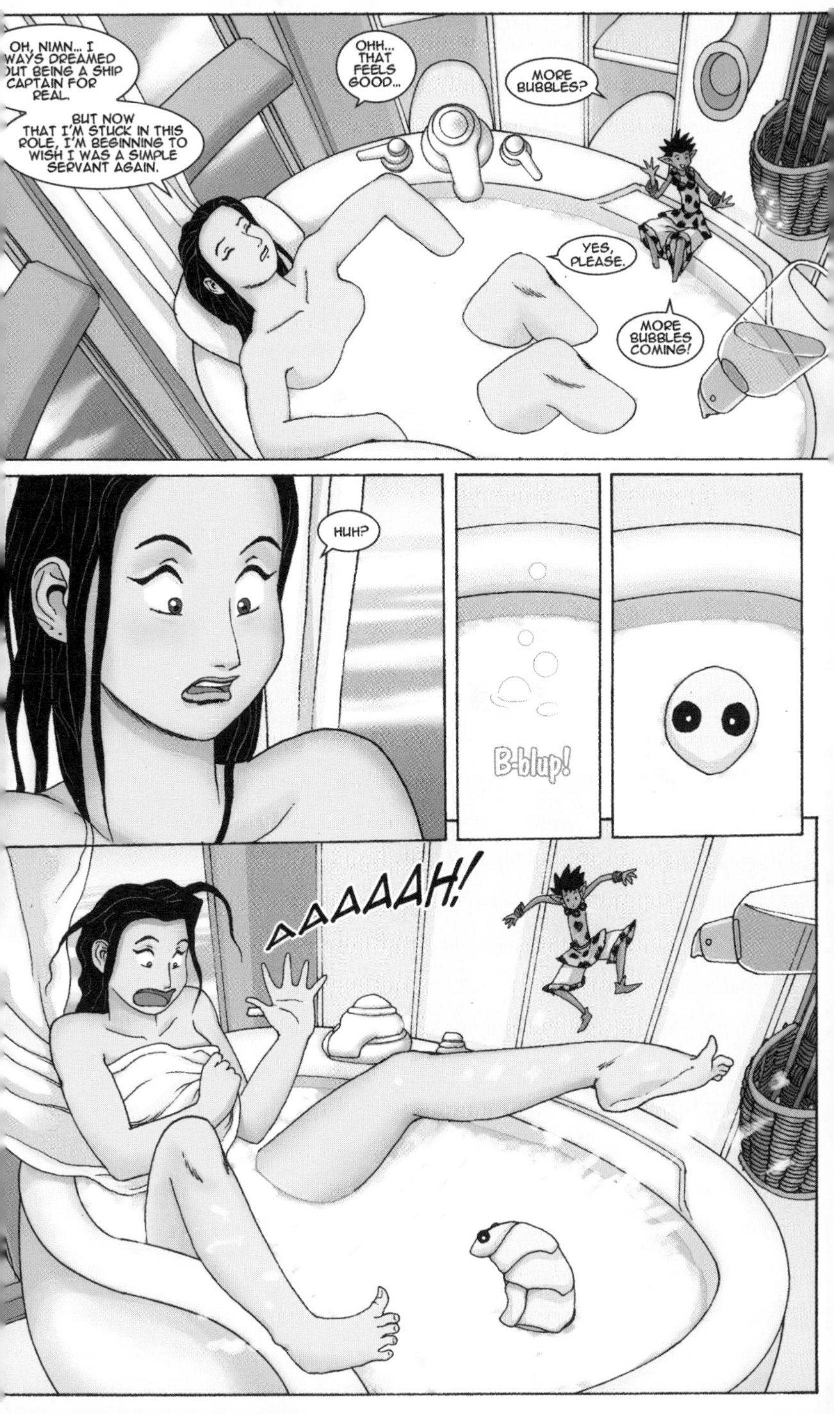
OH, NIMN... I
WAYS DREAMED
OUT BEING A SHIP
CAPTAIN FOR
REAL.
BUT NOW
THAT I'M STUCK IN THIS
ROLE, I'M BEGINNING TO
WISH I WAS A SIMPLE
SERVANT AGAIN.
OHH... THAT FEELS GOOD...
MORE BUBBLES?
YES, PLEASE.
MORE BUBBLES COMING!
HUH?
B-blup!
AAAAAH!

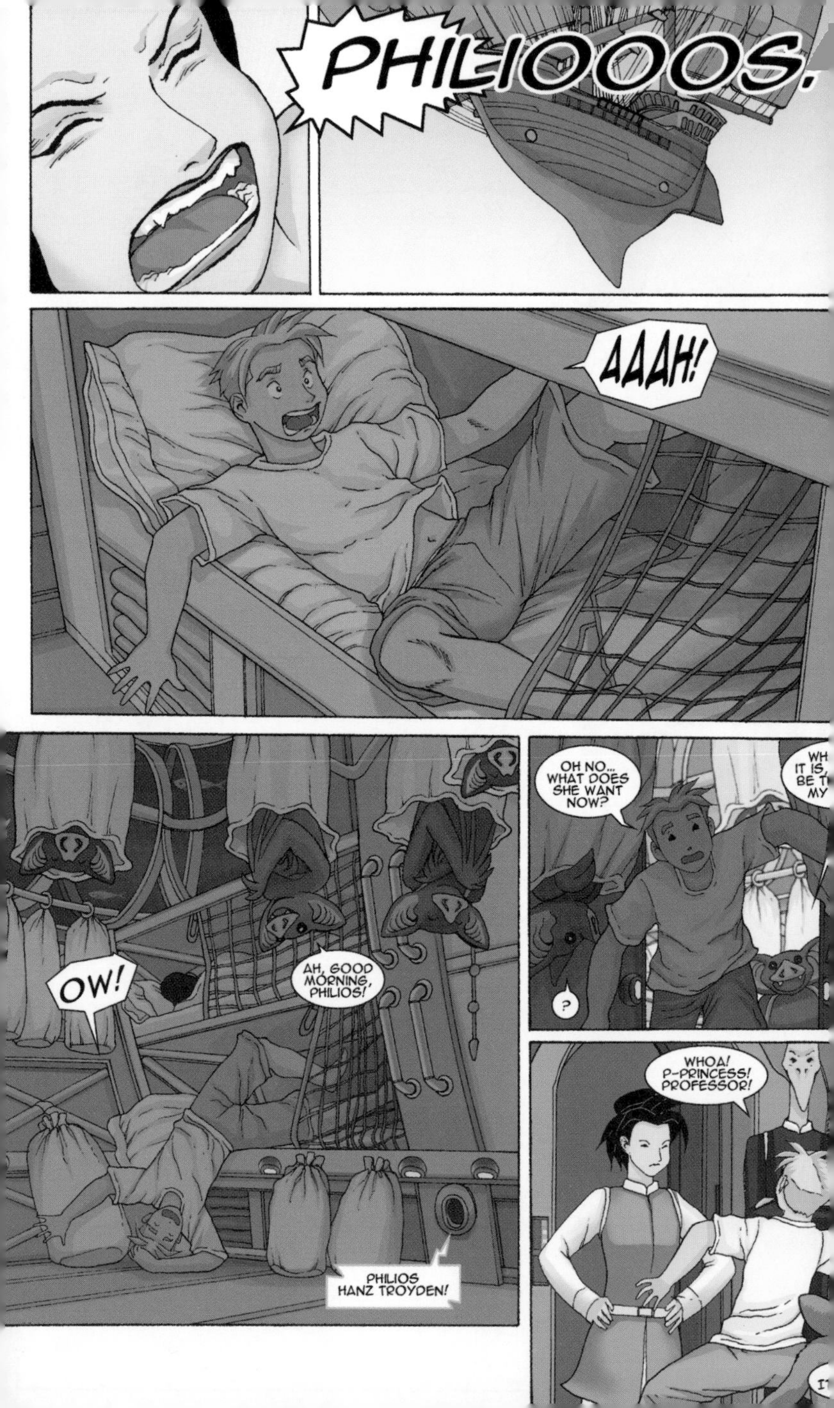
PHILIOOOS.
AAAH!
PHILIOS
HANZ TROYDEN!
OW!
AH, GOOD
MORNING,
PHILIOS!
OH NO...
WHAT DOES
SHE WANT
NOW?
?
WHOA!
P-PRINCESS!
PROFESSOR!

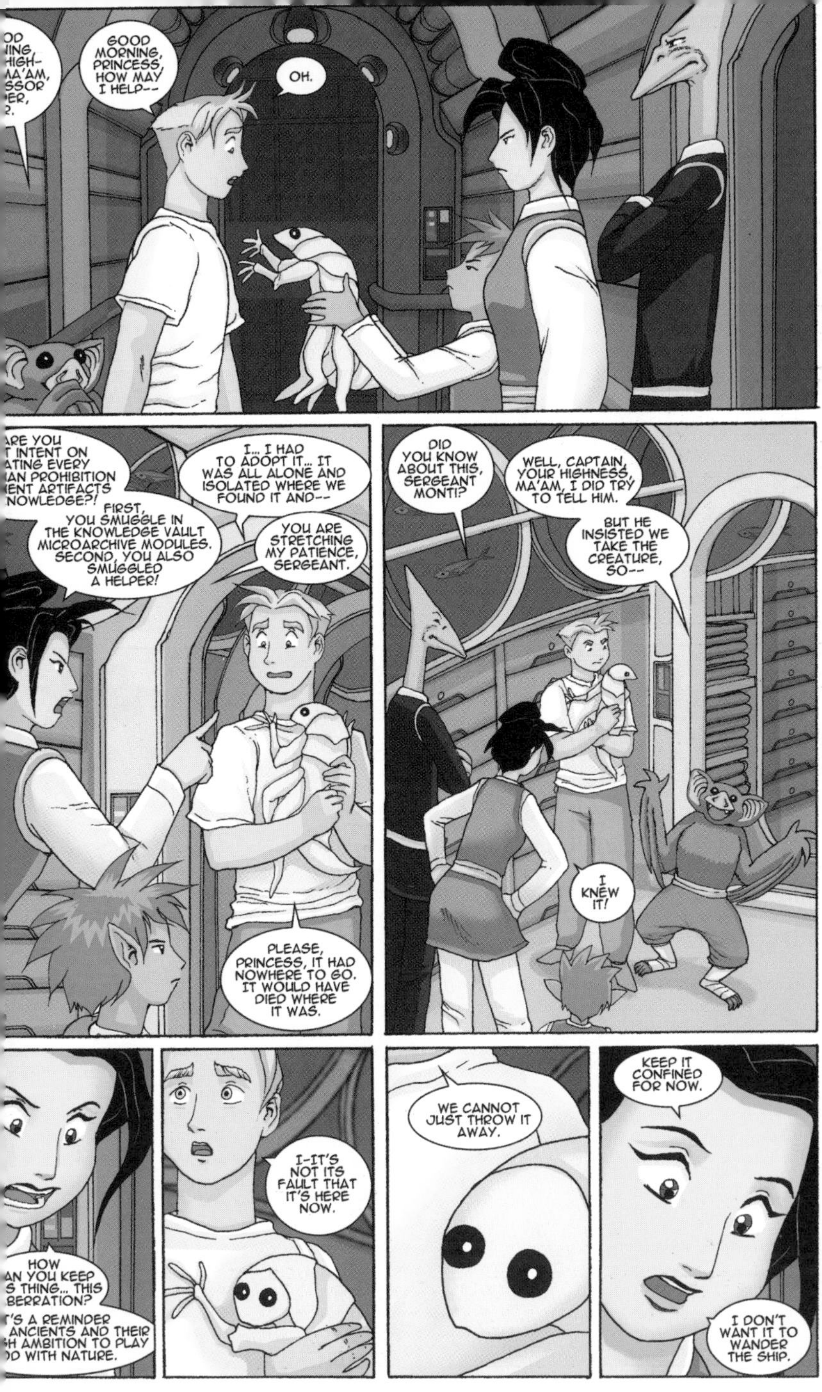
OD NING, HIGH- MA'AM, SSOR ER, R.
GOOD MORNING, PRINCESS, HOW MAY I HELP--
OH.
ARE YOU T INTENT ON ATING EVERY AN PROHIBITION ENT ARTIFACTS NOWLEDGE?!
FIRST, YOU SMUGGLE IN THE KNOWLEDGE VAULT MICROARCHIVE MODULES. SECOND, YOU ALSO SMUGGLED A HELPER!
I... I HAD TO ADOPT IT... IT WAS ALL ALONE AND ISOLATED WHERE WE FOUND IT AND--
YOU ARE STRETCHING MY PATIENCE, SERGEANT.
PLEASE, PRINCESS, IT HAD NOWHERE TO GO. IT WOULD HAVE DIED WHERE IT WAS.
DID YOU KNOW ABOUT THIS, SERGEANT MONTI?
WELL, CAPTAIN, YOUR HIGHNESS, MA'AM, I DID TRY TO TELL HIM.
BUT HE INSISTED WE TAKE THE CREATURE, SO--
I KNEW IT!
HOW AN YOU KEEP S THING... THIS BERRATION?
T'S A REMINDER ANCIENTS AND THEIR H AMBITION TO PLAY D WITH NATURE.
I-IT'S NOT ITS FAULT THAT IT'S HERE NOW.
WE CANNOT JUST THROW IT AWAY.
KEEP IT CONFINED FOR NOW.
I DON'T WANT IT TO WANDER THE SHIP.

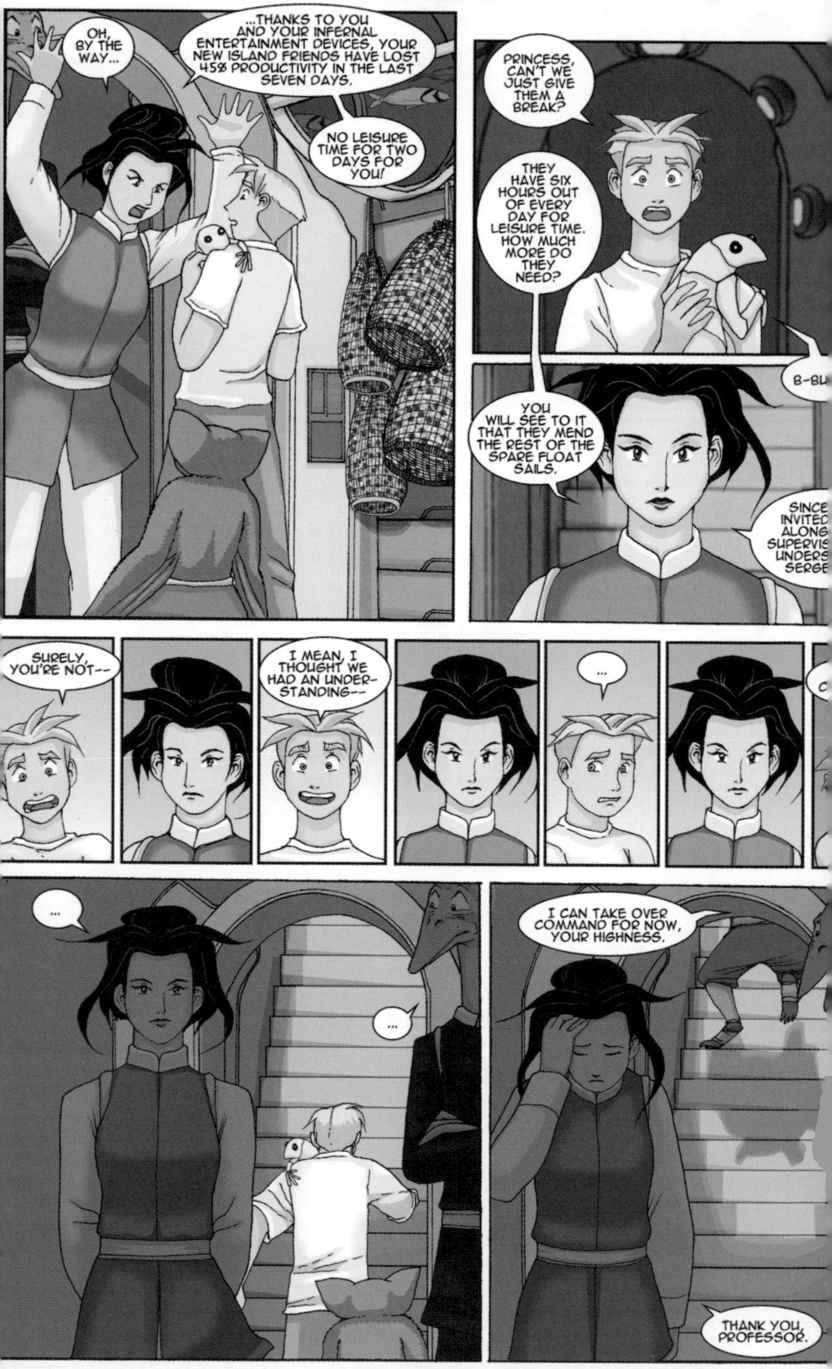
OH, BY THE WAY...
...THANKS TO YOU AND YOUR INFERNAL ENTERTAINMENT DEVICES, YOUR NEW ISLAND FRIENDS HAVE LOST 45% PRODUCTIVITY IN THE LAST SEVEN DAYS.
NO LEISURE TIME FOR TWO DAYS FOR YOU!
PRINCESS, CAN'T WE JUST GIVE THEM A BREAK?
THEY HAVE SIX HOURS OUT OF EVERY DAY FOR LEISURE TIME. HOW MUCH MORE DO THEY NEED?
YOU WILL SEE TO IT THAT THEY MEND THE REST OF THE SPARE FLOAT SAILS.
SURELY, YOU'RE NOT--
I MEAN, I THOUGHT WE HAD AN UNDER-STANDING--
...
...
...
I CAN TAKE OVER COMMAND FOR NOW, YOUR HIGHNESS.
THANK YOU, PROFESSOR.

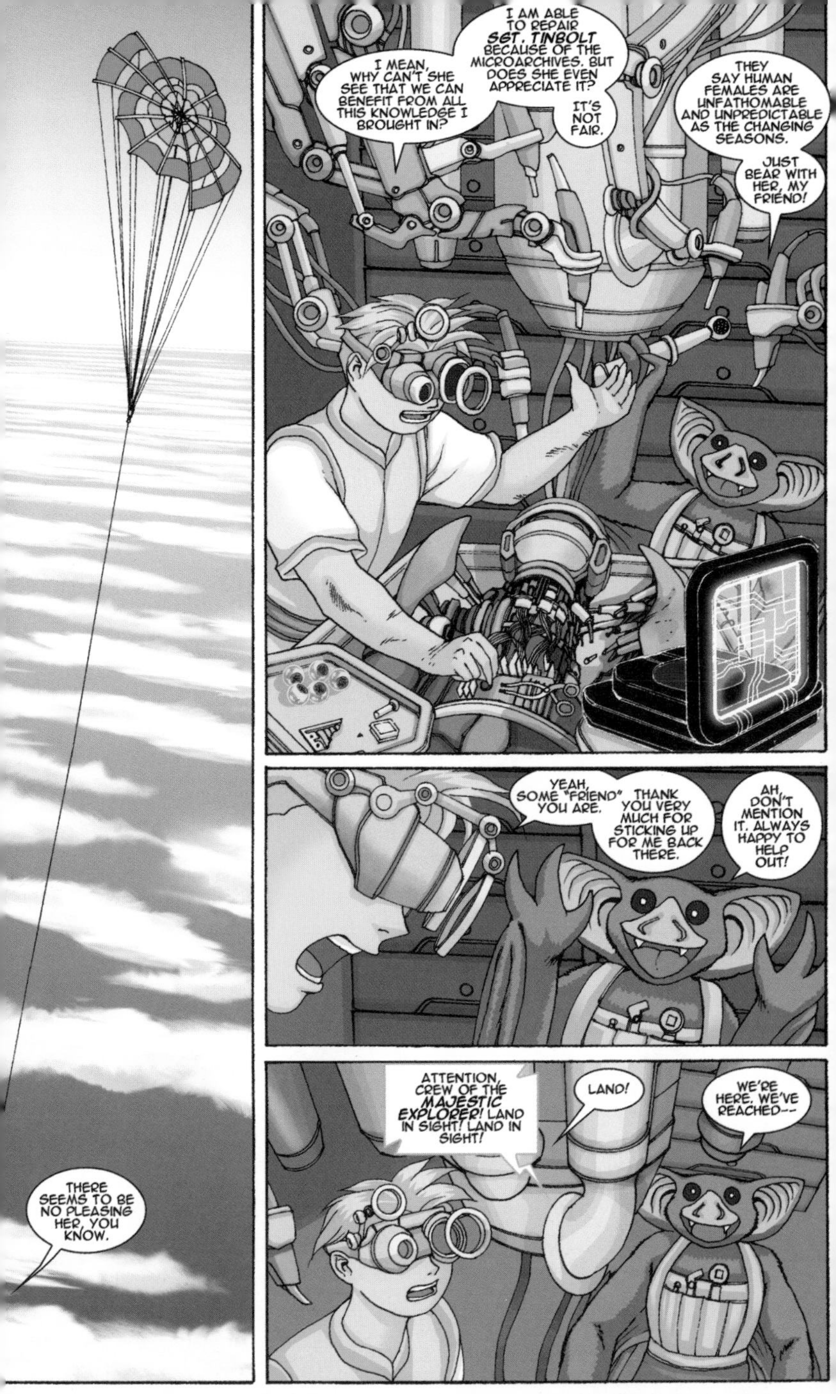
I MEAN, WHY CAN'T SHE SEE THAT WE CAN BENEFIT FROM ALL THIS KNOWLEDGE I BROUGHT IN?
I AM ABLE TO REPAIR SGT. TINBOLT BECAUSE OF THE MICROARCHIVES. BUT DOES SHE EVEN APPRECIATE IT?
IT'S NOT FAIR.
THERE SEEMS TO BE NO PLEASING HER, YOU KNOW.
THEY SAY HUMAN FEMALES ARE UNFATHOMABLE AND UNPREDICTABLE AS THE CHANGING SEASONS.
JUST BEAR WITH HER, MY FRIEND!
YEAH, SOME "FRIEND" YOU ARE.
THANK YOU VERY MUCH FOR STICKING UP FOR ME BACK THERE.
AH, DON'T MENTION IT. ALWAYS HAPPY TO HELP OUT!
ATTENTION, CREW OF THE MAJESTIC EXPLORER! LAND IN SIGHT! LAND IN SIGHT!
LAND!
WE'RE HERE. WE'VE REACHED--

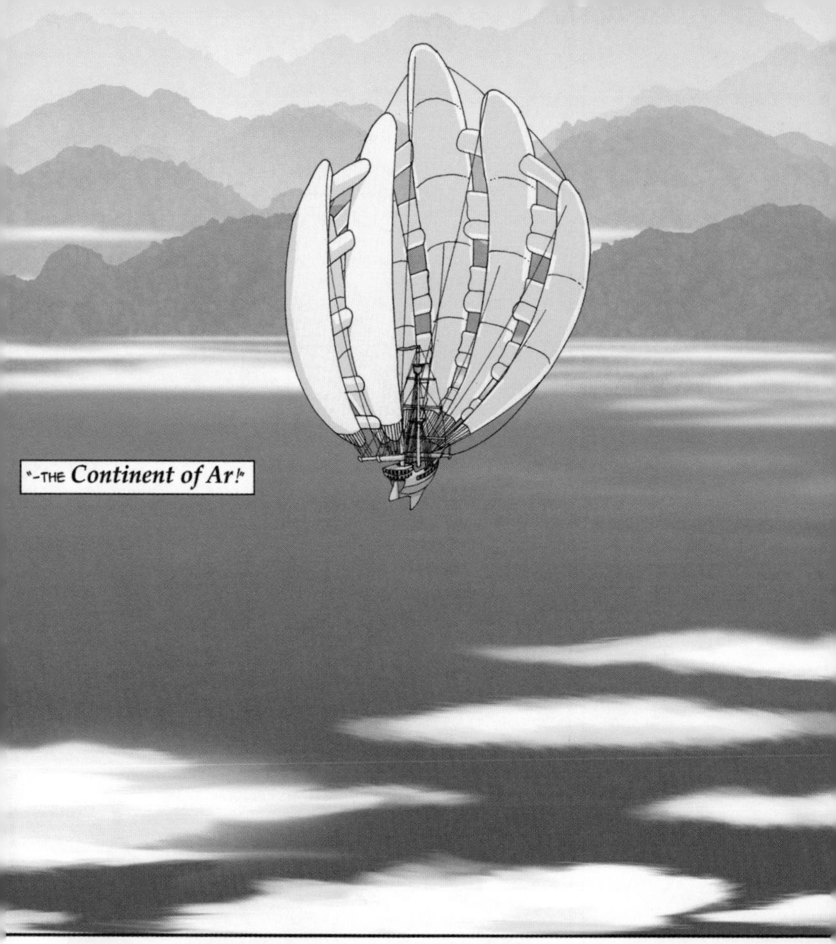
"-THE Continent of Ar!"

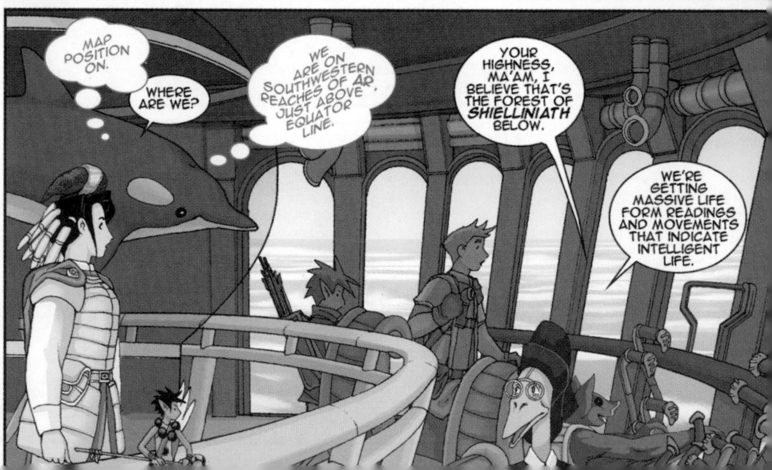
MAP POSITION ON.
WHERE ARE WE?
WE ARE ON SOUTHWESTERN REACHES OF AR, JUST ABOVE EQUATOR LINE.
YOUR HIGHNESS, MA'AM, I BELIEVE THAT'S THE FOREST OF SHIELLINIATH BELOW.
WE'RE GETTING MASSIVE LIFE FORM READINGS AND MOVEMENTS THAT INDICATE INTELLIGENT LIFE.

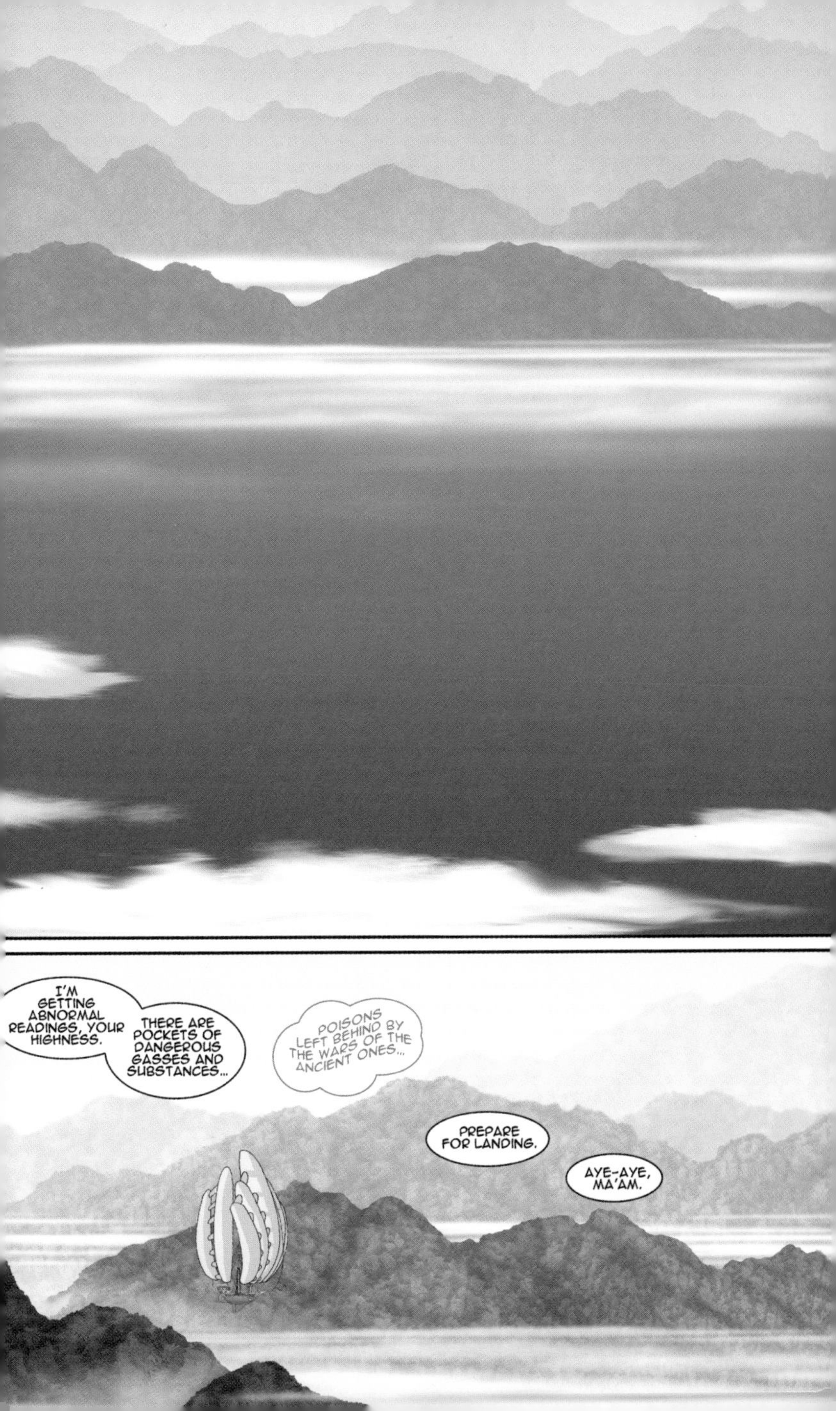
I'M GETTING ABNORMAL READINGS, YOUR HIGHNESS.
THERE ARE POCKETS OF DANGEROUS GASSES AND SUBSTANCES...
POISONS LEFT BEHIND BY THE WARS OF THE ANCIENT ONES...
PREPARE FOR LANDING.
AYE-AYE, MA'AM.

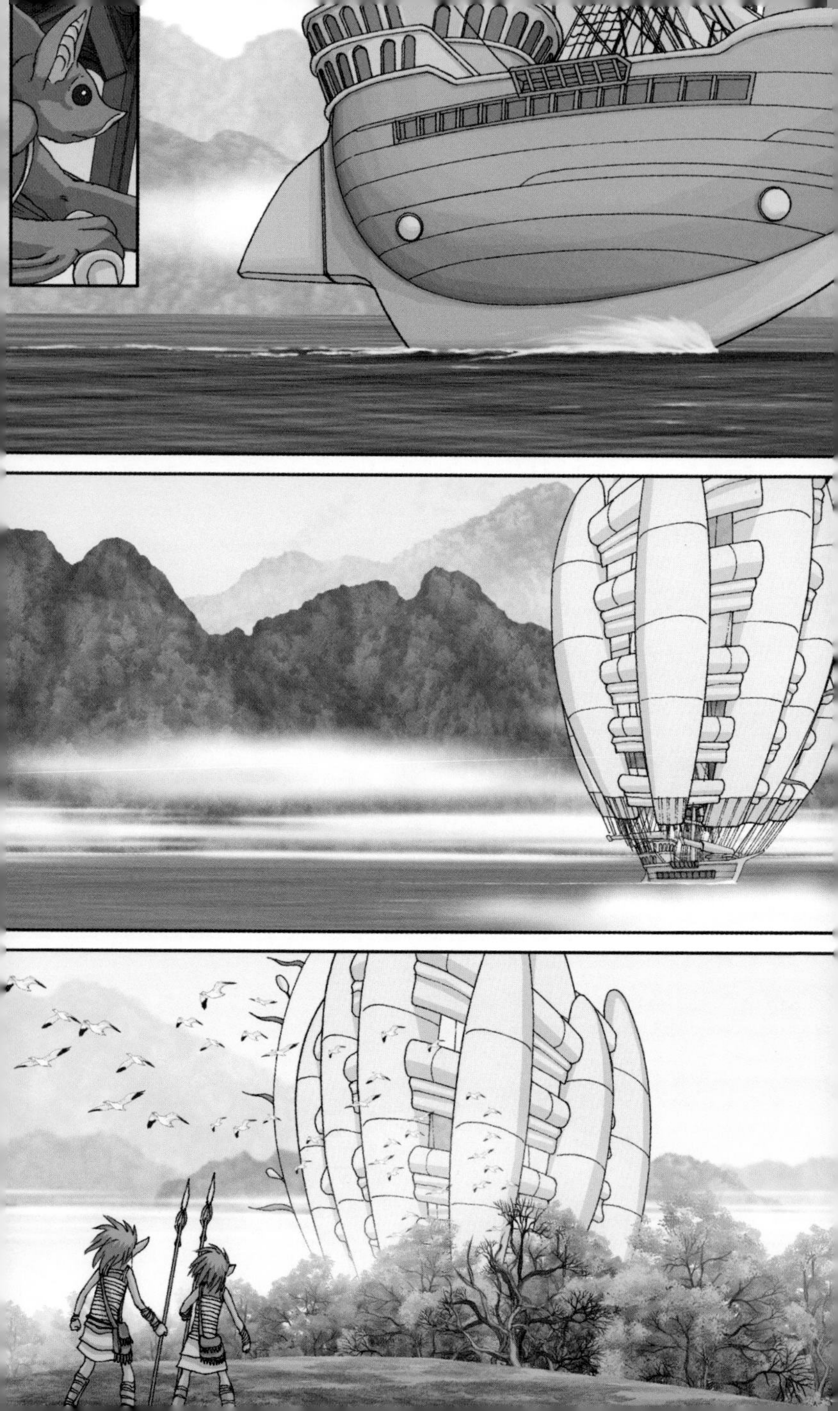

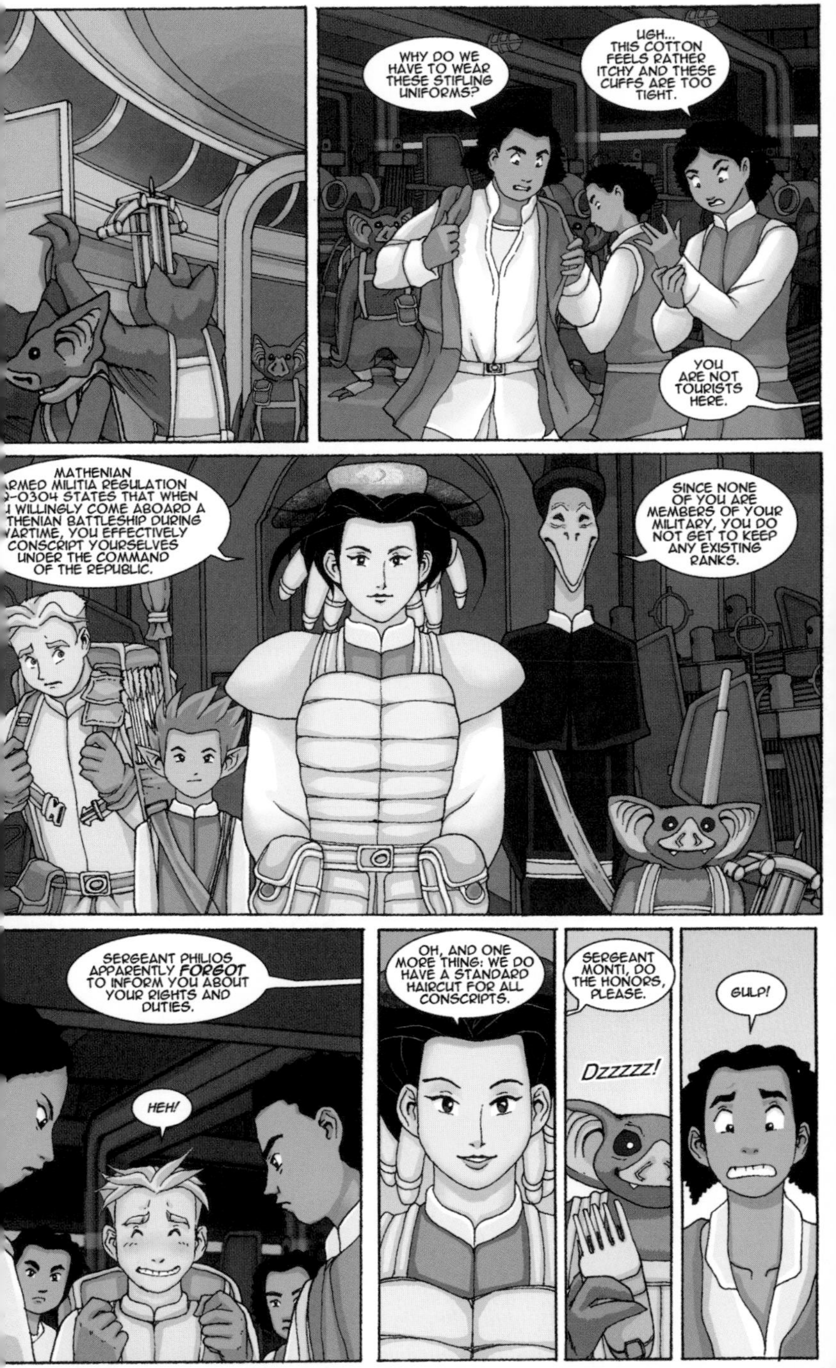
WHY DO WE HAVE TO WEAR THESE STIFLING UNIFORMS?
UGH... THIS COTTON FEELS RATHER ITCHY AND THESE CUFFS ARE TOO TIGHT.
YOU ARE NOT TOURISTS HERE.
MATHENIAN ARMED MILITIA REGULATION -0304 STATES THAT WHEN WILLINGLY COME ABOARD A THENIAN BATTLESHIP DURING WARTIME, YOU EFFECTIVELY CONSCRIPT YOURSELVES UNDER THE COMMAND OF THE REPUBLIC.
SINCE NONE OF YOU ARE MEMBERS OF YOUR MILITARY, YOU DO NOT GET TO KEEP ANY EXISTING RANKS.
SERGEANT PHILIOS APPARENTLY ***FORGOT*** TO INFORM YOU ABOUT YOUR RIGHTS AND DUTIES.
HEH!
OH, AND ONE MORE THING: WE DO HAVE A STANDARD HAIRCUT FOR ALL CONSCRIPTS.
SERGEANT MONTI, DO THE HONORS, PLEASE.
DZZZZZ!
GULP!

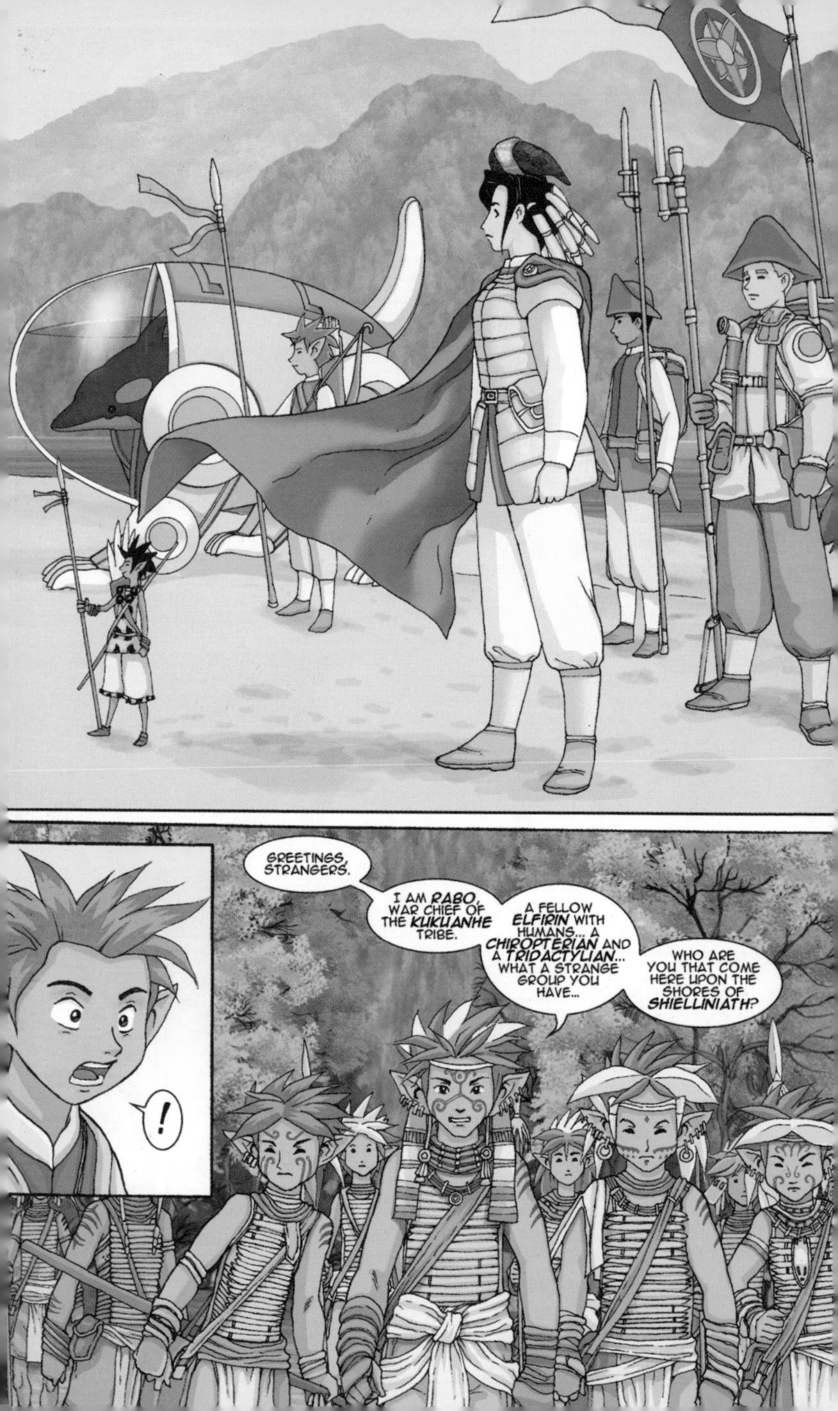
GREETINGS, STRANGERS.
I AM RABO, WAR CHIEF OF THE KUKUANHE TRIBE.
A FELLOW ELFIRIN WITH HUMANS... A CHIROPTERIAN AND A TRIDACTYLIAN... WHAT A STRANGE GROUP YOU HAVE...
WHO ARE YOU THAT COME HERE UPON THE SHORES OF SHIELLINIATH?
!

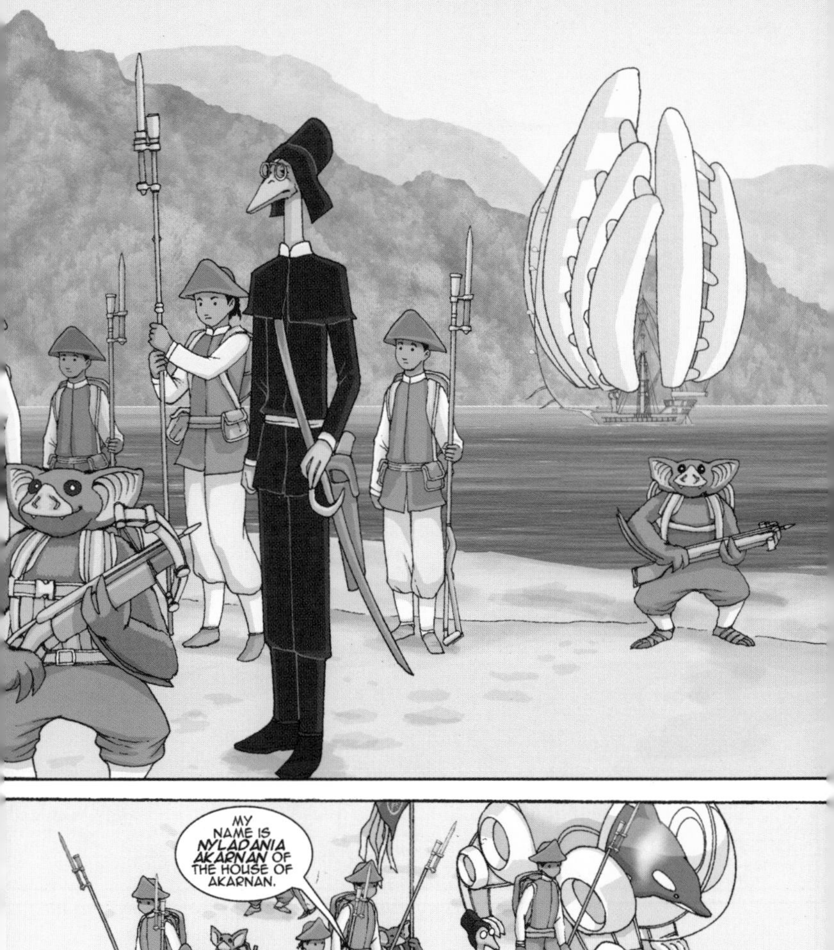

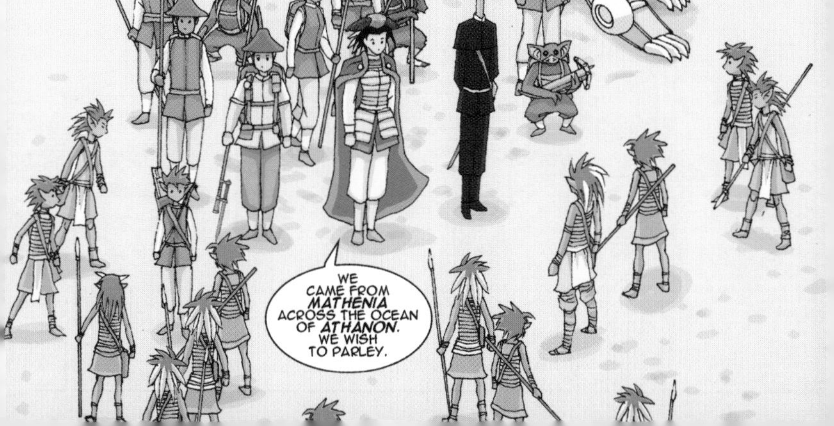
MY NAME IS NYLADANIA AKARNAN OF THE HOUSE OF AKARNAN.
WE CAME FROM MATHENIA ACROSS THE OCEAN OF ATHANON. WE WISH TO PARLEY.

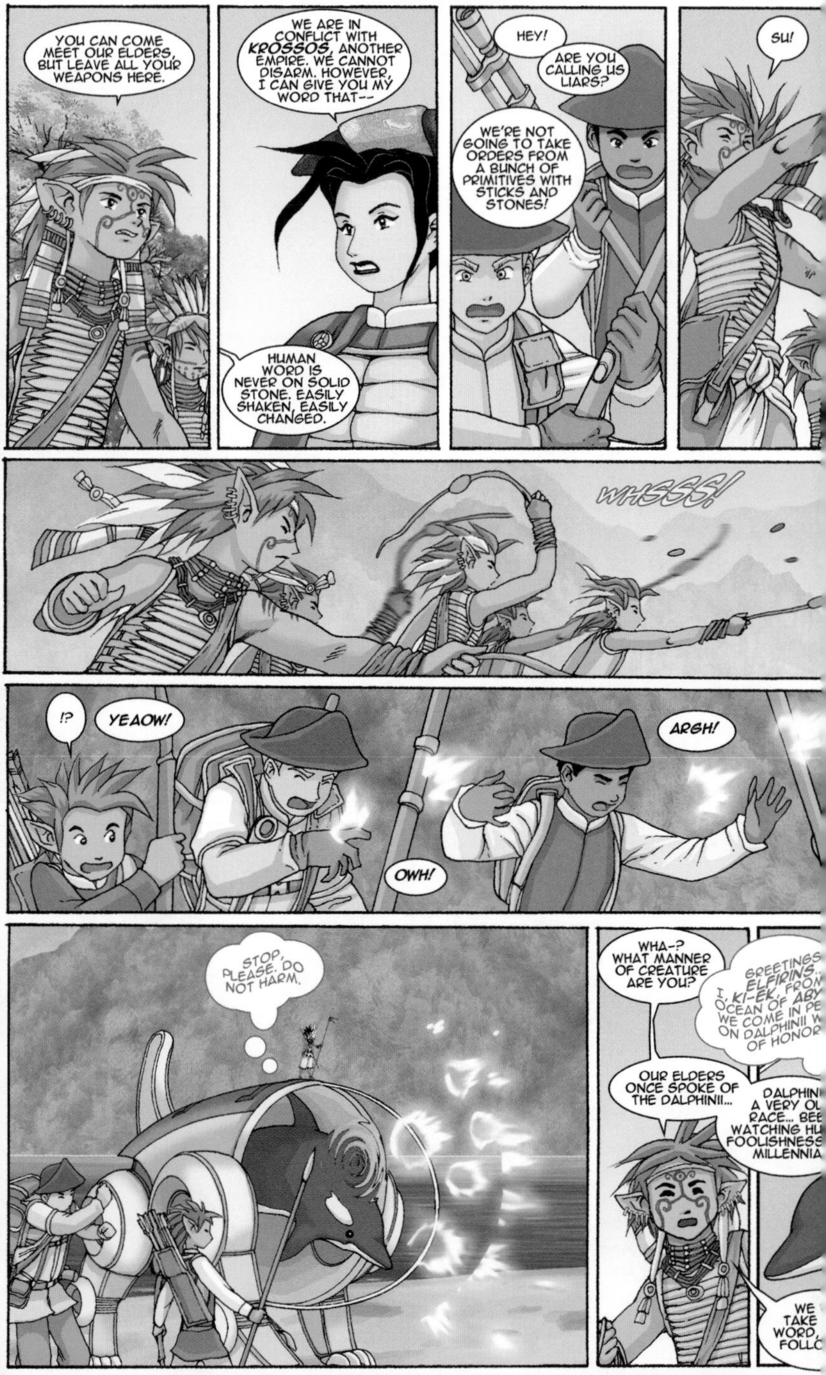

YOU CAN COME MEET OUR ELDERS, BUT LEAVE ALL YOUR WEAPONS HERE.
WE ARE IN CONFLICT WITH KROSSOS, ANOTHER EMPIRE. WE CANNOT DISARM. HOWEVER, I CAN GIVE YOU MY WORD THAT--
HUMAN WORD IS NEVER ON SOLID STONE. EASILY SHAKEN, EASILY CHANGED.
HEY!
ARE YOU CALLING US LIARS?
WE'RE NOT GOING TO TAKE ORDERS FROM A BUNCH OF PRIMITIVES WITH STICKS AND STONES!
SU!
WHSSS!
!?
YEAOW!
OWH!
ARGH!
STOP, PLEASE. DO NOT HARM.
WHA-? WHAT MANNER OF CREATURE ARE YOU?
GREETINGS ELFIRINS. I, KI-EK, FROM OCEAN OF ABY WE COME IN PE ON DALPHINII W OF HONOR
OUR ELDERS ONCE SPOKE OF THE DALPHINII...
DALPHIN A VERY OL RACE... BEE WATCHING HU FOOLISHNESS MILLENNIA
WE TAKE WORD, FOLLO

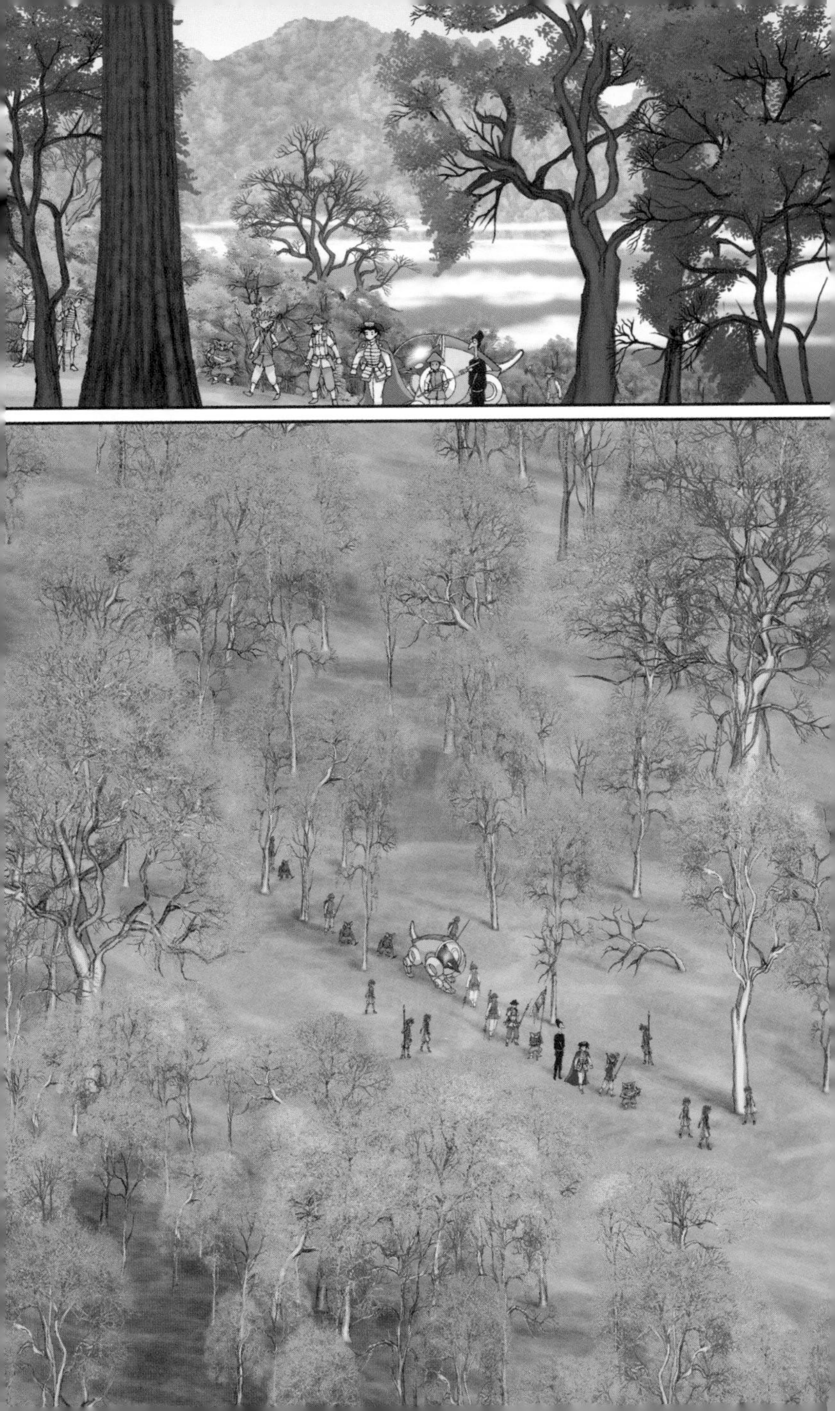

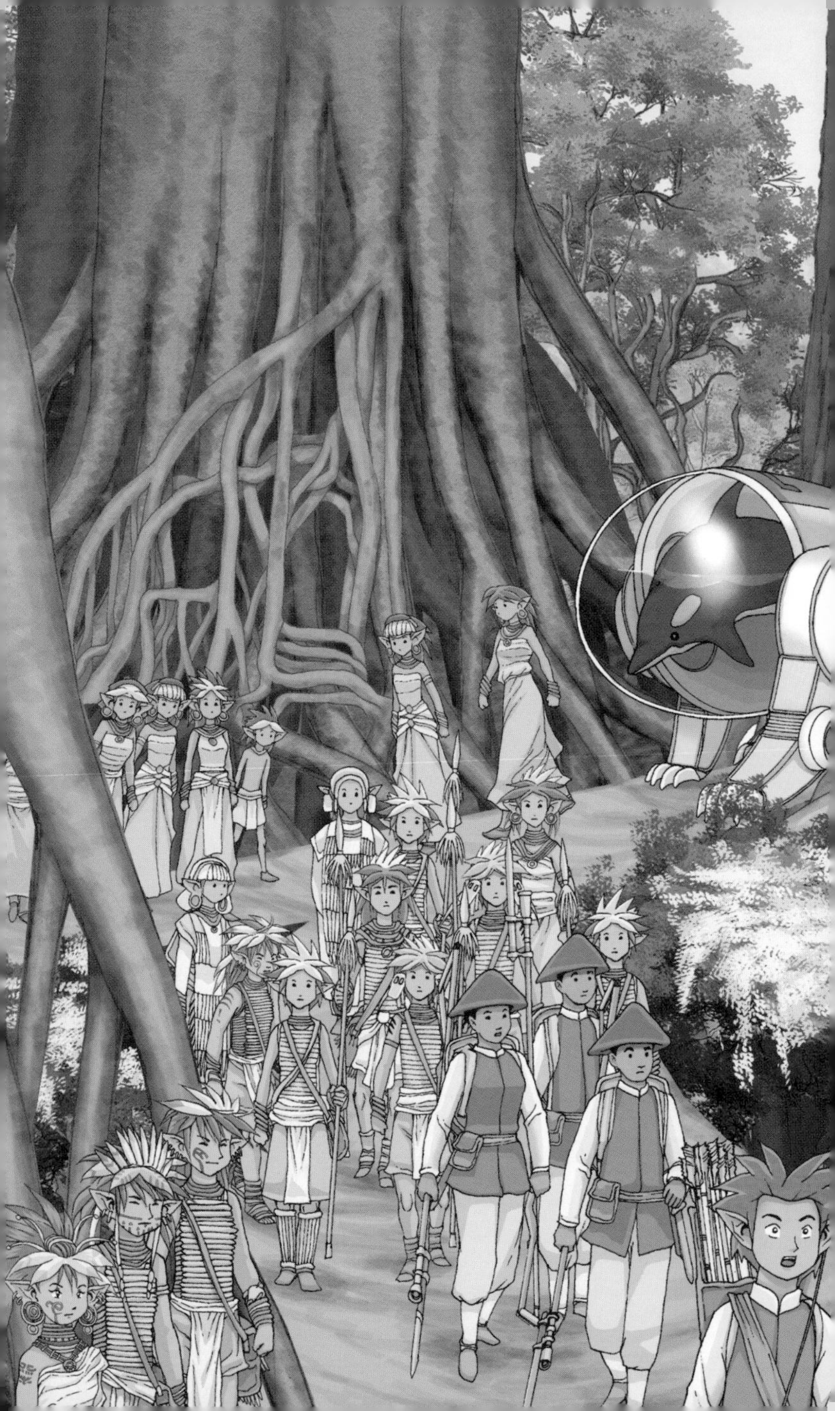

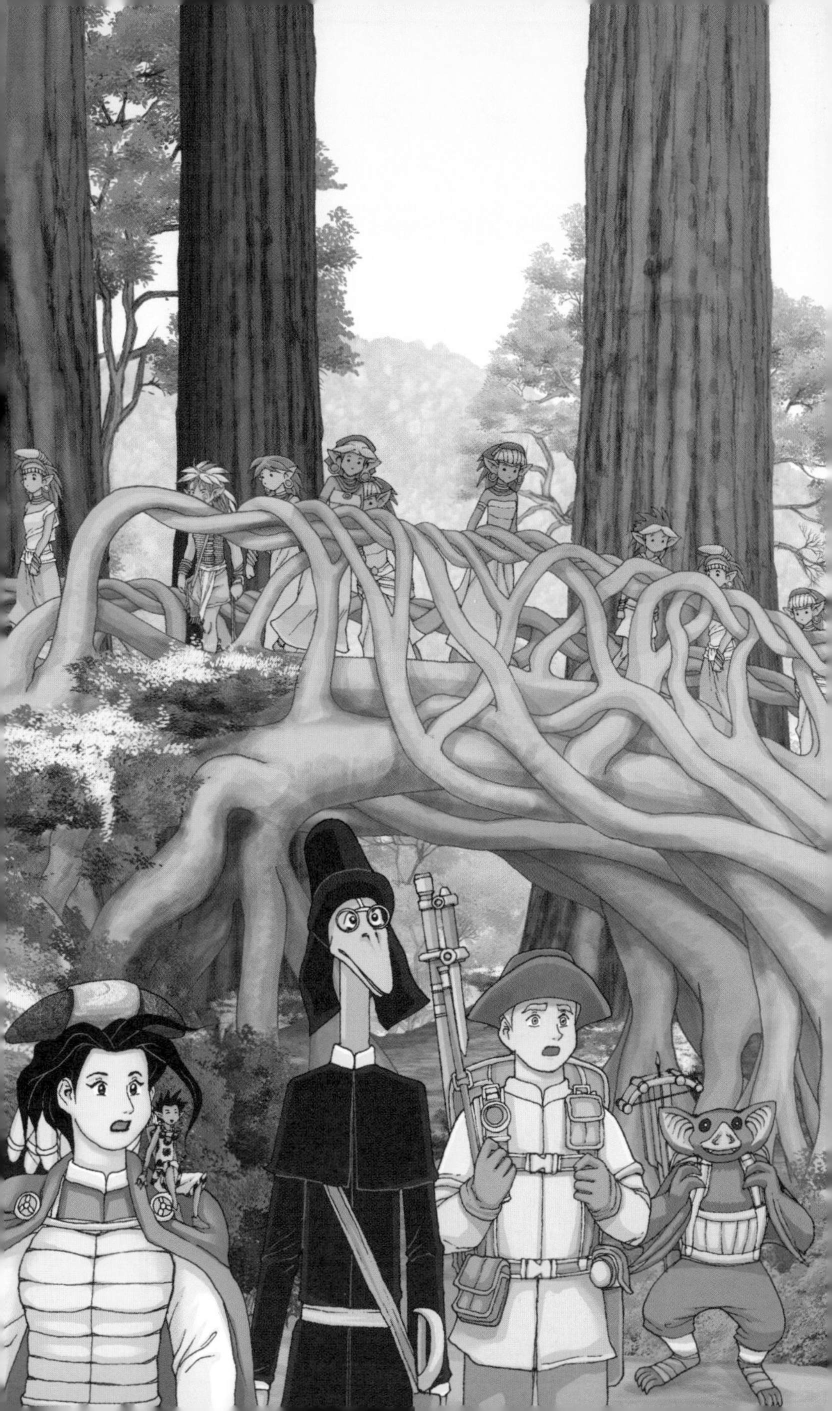

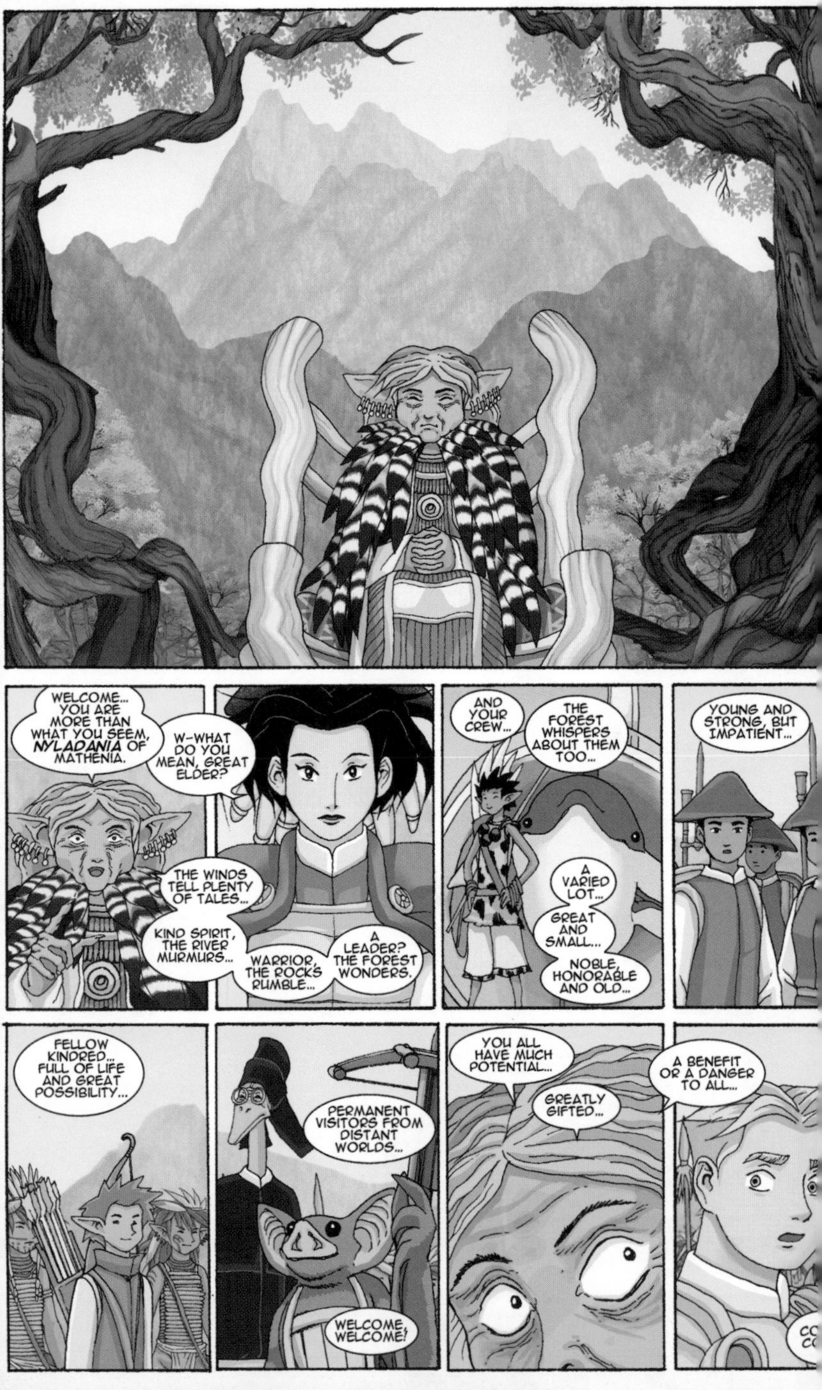
WELCOME... YOU ARE MORE THAN WHAT YOU SEEM, NYLADANIA OF MATHENIA.
W-WHAT DO YOU MEAN, GREAT ELDER?
THE WINDS TELL PLENTY OF TALES...
KIND SPIRIT, THE RIVER MURMURS...
WARRIOR, THE ROCKS RUMBLE...
A LEADER? THE FOREST WONDERS.
AND YOUR CREW...
THE FOREST WHISPERS ABOUT THEM TOO...
A VARIED LOT...
GREAT AND SMALL...
NOBLE, HONORABLE AND OLD...
YOUNG AND STRONG, BUT IMPATIENT...
FELLOW KINDRED... FULL OF LIFE AND GREAT POSSIBILITY...
PERMANENT VISITORS FROM DISTANT WORLDS...
WELCOME, WELCOME!
YOU ALL HAVE MUCH POTENTIAL...
GREATLY GIFTED...
A BENEFIT OR A DANGER TO ALL...

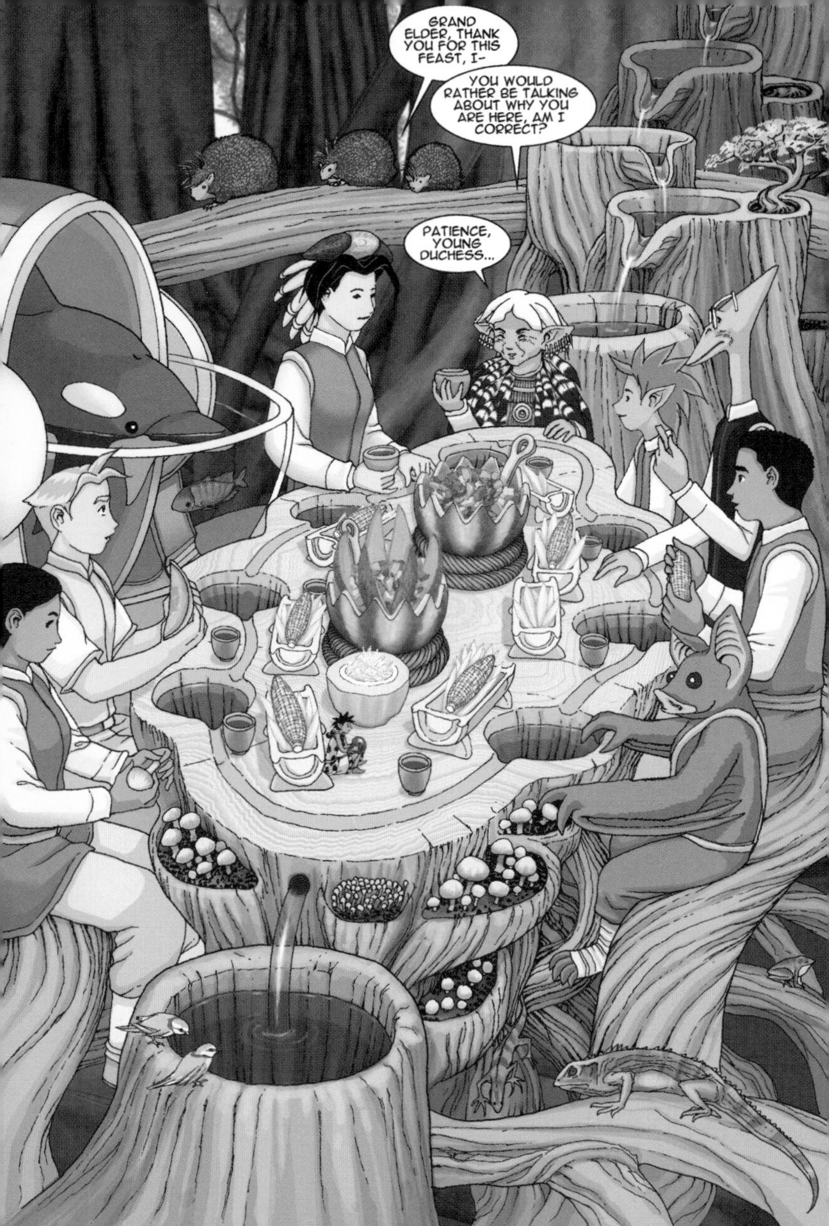
GRAND ELDER, THANK YOU FOR THIS FEAST, I-
YOU WOULD RATHER BE TALKING ABOUT WHY YOU ARE HERE, AM I CORRECT?
PATIENCE, YOUNG DUCHESS...

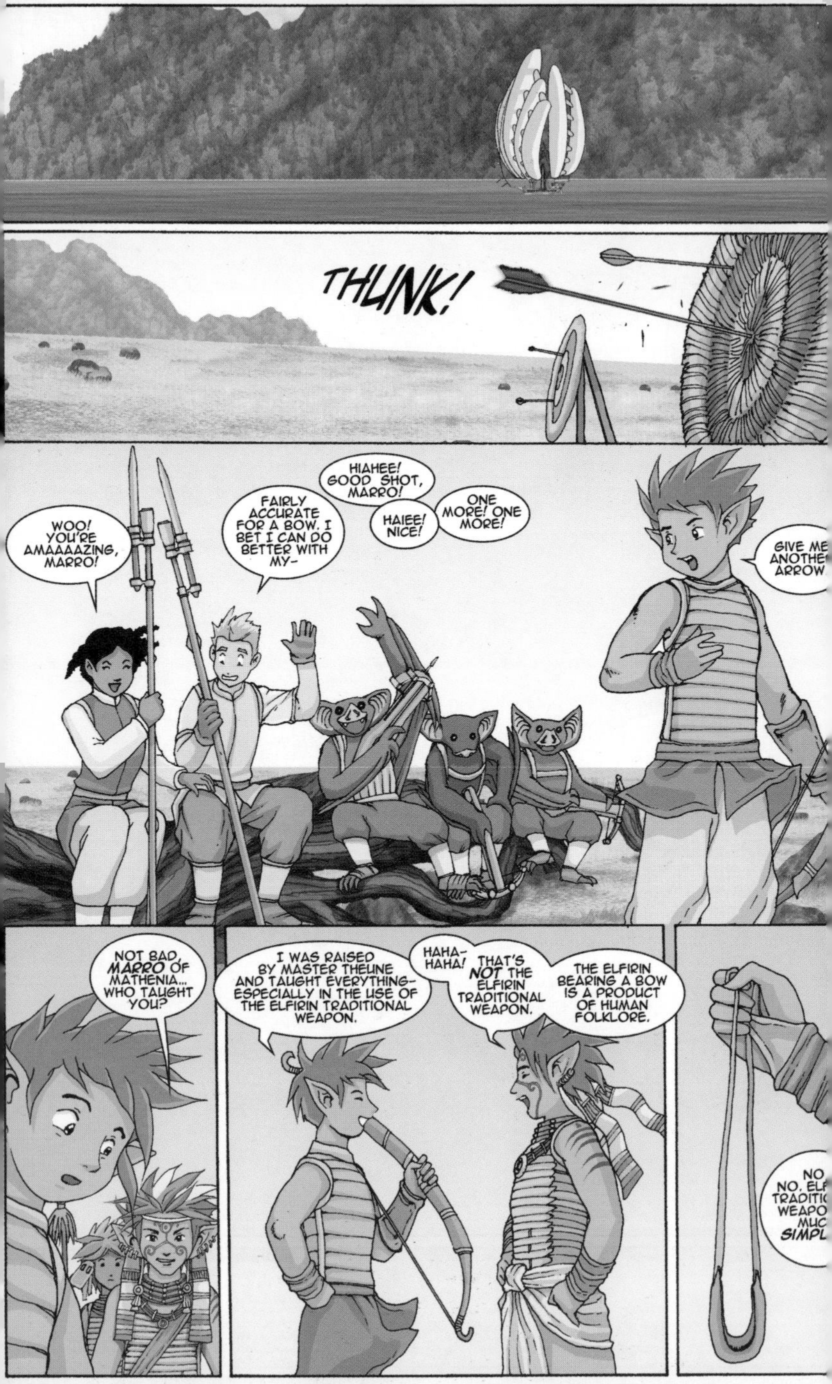
THUNK!
WOO! YOU'RE AMAAAAZING, MARRO!
FAIRLY ACCURATE FOR A BOW. I BET I CAN DO BETTER WITH MY-
HIAHEE! GOOD SHOT, MARRO!
HAIEE! NICE!
ONE MORE! ONE MORE!
GIVE ME ANOTHE ARROW.
NOT BAD, MARRO OF MATHENIA... WHO TAUGHT YOU?
I WAS RAISED BY MASTER THEUNE AND TAUGHT EVERYTHING- ESPECIALLY IN THE USE OF THE ELFIRIN TRADITIONAL WEAPON.
HAHA-HAHA!
THAT'S NOT THE ELFIRIN TRADITIONAL WEAPON.
THE ELFIRIN BEARING A BOW IS A PRODUCT OF HUMAN FOLKLORE.
NO NO. EL TRADITI WEAPO MUC SIMPL

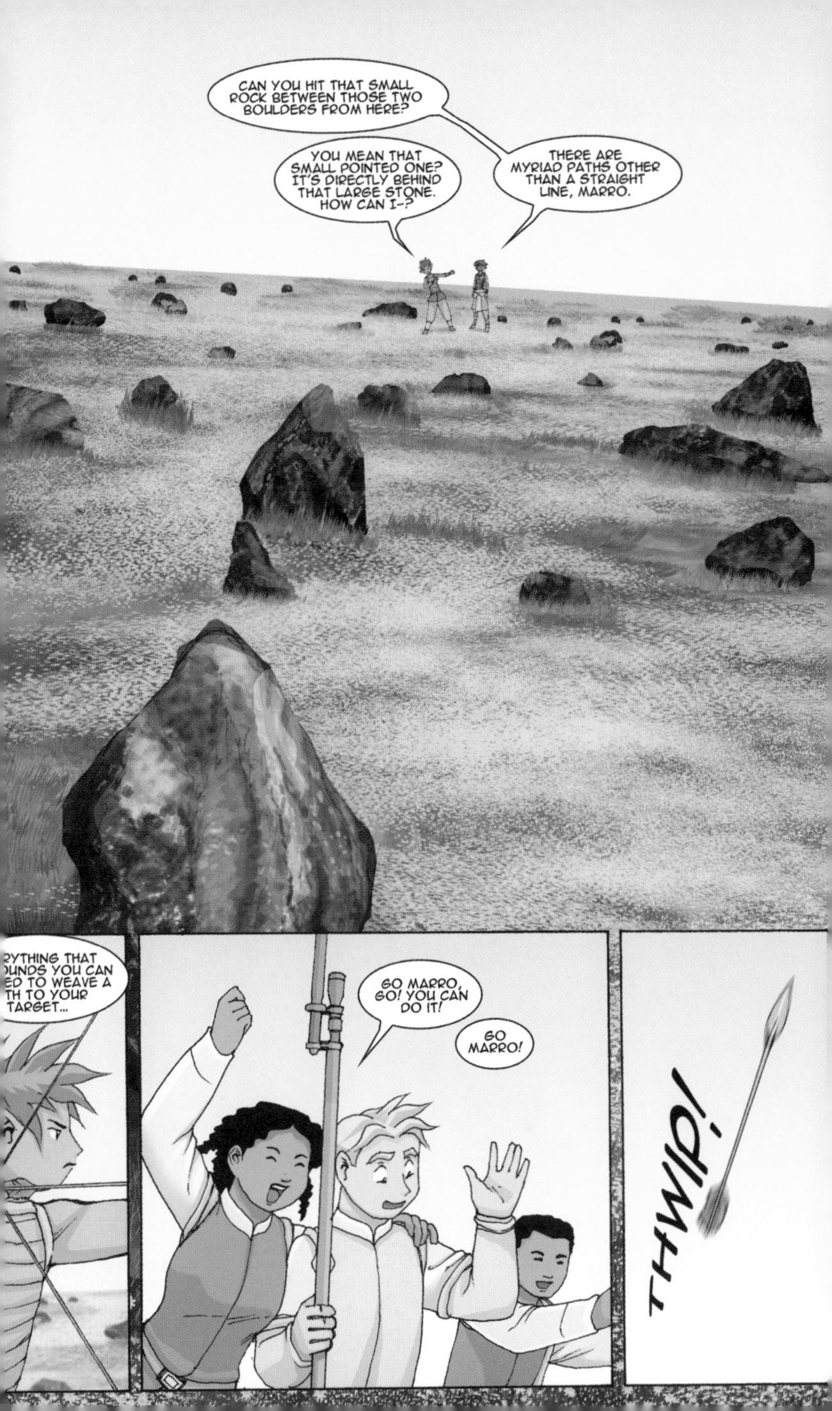
CAN YOU HIT THAT SMALL ROCK BETWEEN THOSE TWO BOULDERS FROM HERE?
YOU MEAN THAT SMALL POINTED ONE? IT'S DIRECTLY BEHIND THAT LARGE STONE. HOW CAN I-?
THERE ARE MYRIAD PATHS OTHER THAN A STRAIGHT LINE, MARRO.
RYTHING THAT OUNDS YOU CAN ED TO WEAVE A TH TO YOUR TARGET...
GO MARRO, GO! YOU CAN DO IT!
GO MARRO!
THWIP!

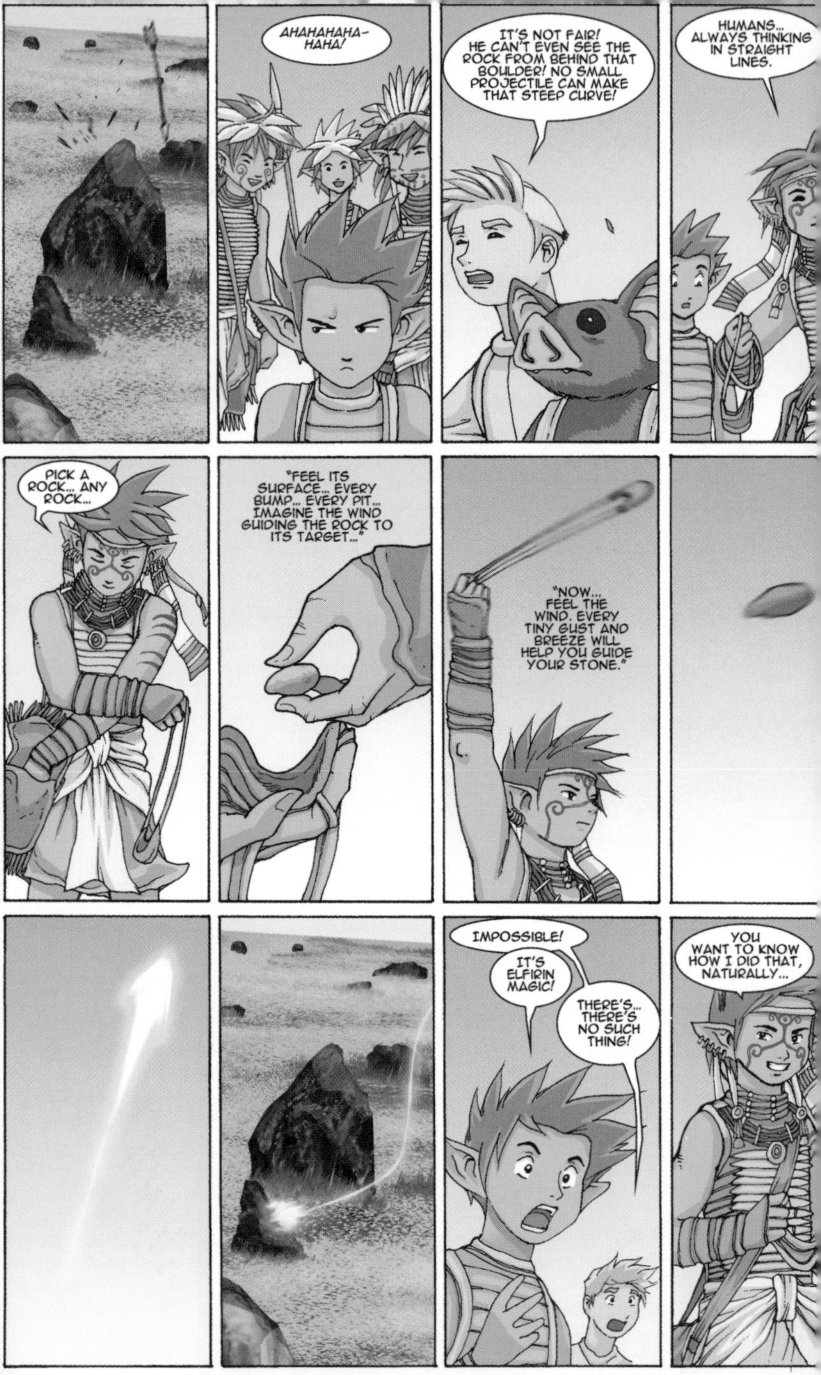
AHAHAHAHA-HAHA!
IT'S NOT FAIR! HE CAN'T EVEN SEE THE ROCK FROM BEHIND THAT BOULDER! NO SMALL PROJECTILE CAN MAKE THAT STEEP CURVE!
HUMANS... ALWAYS THINKING IN STRAIGHT LINES.
PICK A ROCK... ANY ROCK...
"FEEL ITS SURFACE... EVERY BUMP... EVERY PIT... IMAGINE THE WIND GUIDING THE ROCK TO ITS TARGET..."
"NOW... FEEL THE WIND. EVERY TINY GUST AND BREEZE WILL HELP YOU GUIDE YOUR STONE."
IMPOSSIBLE!
IT'S ELFIRIN MAGIC!
THERE'S... THERE'S NO SUCH THING!
YOU WANT TO KNOW HOW I DID THAT, NATURALLY...

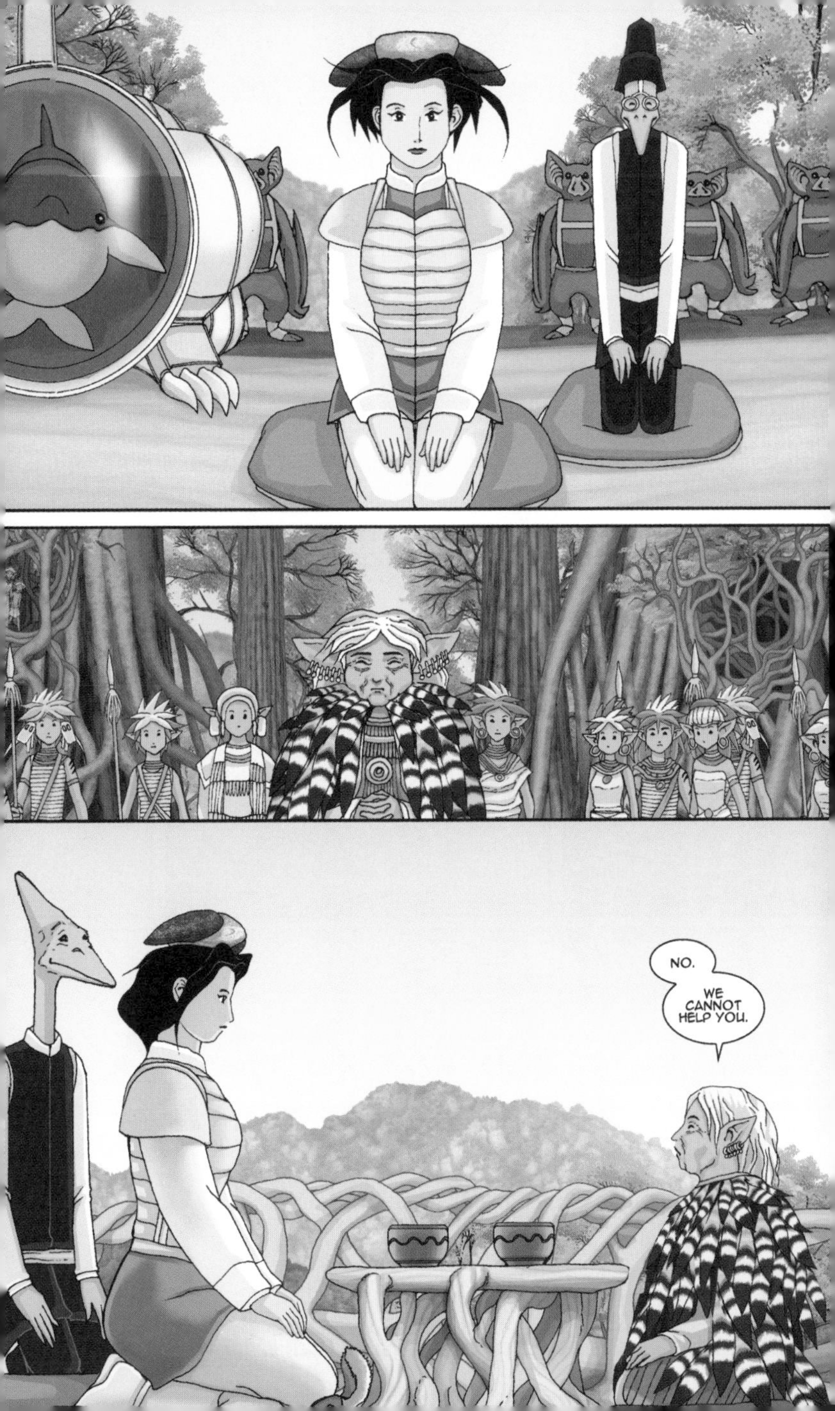
NO.
WE CANNOT HELP YOU.

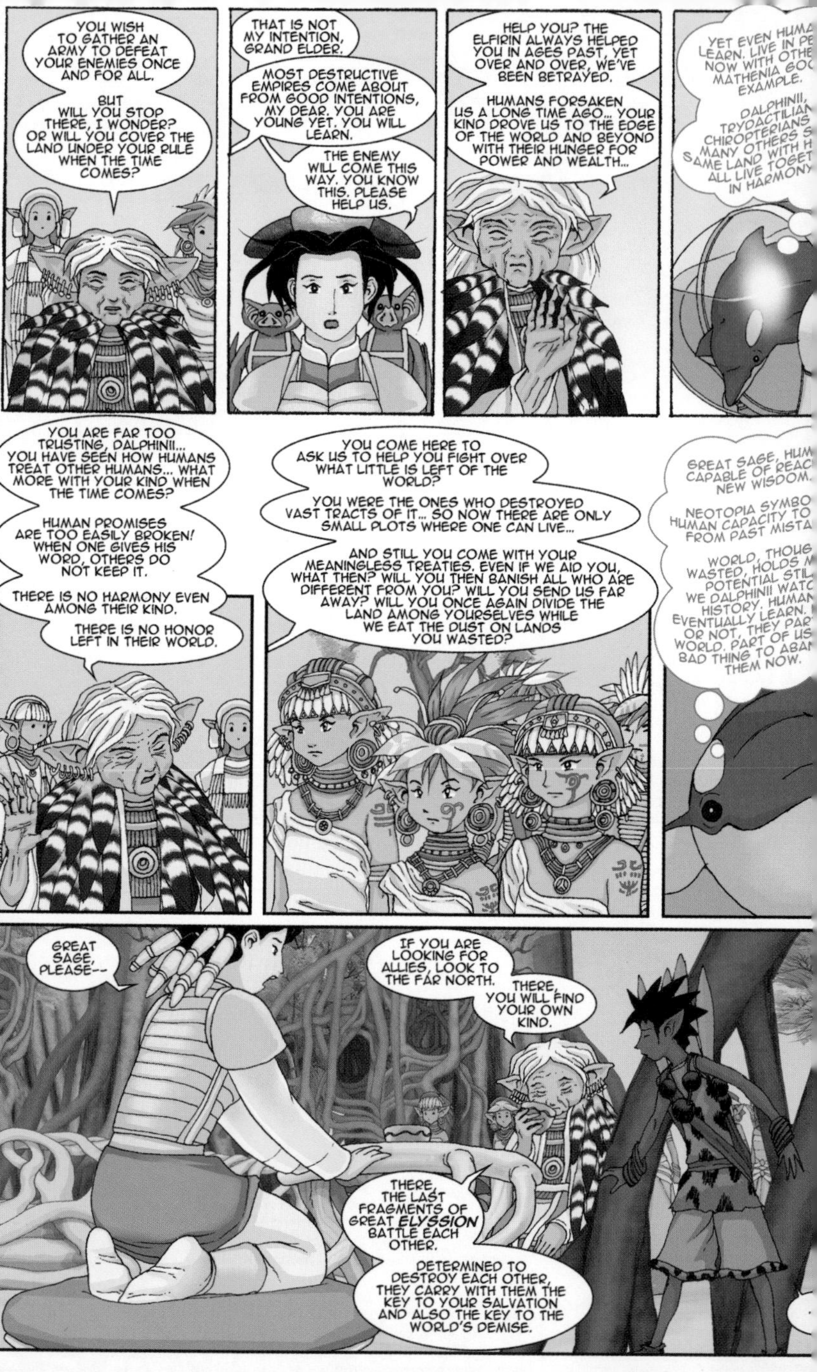

YOU WISH TO GATHER AN ARMY TO DEFEAT YOUR ENEMIES ONCE AND FOR ALL.
BUT WILL YOU STOP THERE, I WONDER? OR WILL YOU COVER THE LAND UNDER YOUR RULE WHEN THE TIME COMES?
THAT IS NOT MY INTENTION, GRAND ELDER.
MOST DESTRUCTIVE EMPIRES COME ABOUT FROM GOOD INTENTIONS, MY DEAR. YOU ARE YOUNG YET. YOU WILL LEARN.
THE ENEMY WILL COME THIS WAY. YOU KNOW THIS. PLEASE HELP US.
HELP YOU? THE ELFIRIN ALWAYS HELPED YOU IN AGES PAST, YET OVER AND OVER, WE'VE BEEN BETRAYED.
HUMANS FORSAKEN US A LONG TIME AGO... YOUR KIND DROVE US TO THE EDGE OF THE WORLD AND BEYOND WITH THEIR HUNGER FOR POWER AND WEALTH...
YET EVEN HUMA LEARN. LIVE IN PE NOW WITH OTHE MATHENIA GO EXAMPLE.
DALPHINII, TRYDACTILIAN CHIROPTERIANS MANY OTHERS S SAME LAND WITH H ALL LIVE TOGET IN HARMONY
YOU ARE FAR TOO TRUSTING, DALPHINII... YOU HAVE SEEN HOW HUMANS TREAT OTHER HUMANS... WHAT MORE WITH YOUR KIND WHEN THE TIME COMES?
HUMAN PROMISES ARE TOO EASILY BROKEN! WHEN ONE GIVES HIS WORD, OTHERS DO NOT KEEP IT.
THERE IS NO HARMONY EVEN AMONG THEIR KIND.
THERE IS NO HONOR LEFT IN THEIR WORLD.
YOU COME HERE TO ASK US TO HELP YOU FIGHT OVER WHAT LITTLE IS LEFT OF THE WORLD?
YOU WERE THE ONES WHO DESTROYED VAST TRACTS OF IT... SO NOW THERE ARE ONLY SMALL PLOTS WHERE ONE CAN LIVE...
AND STILL YOU COME WITH YOUR MEANINGLESS TREATIES. EVEN IF WE AID YOU, WHAT THEN? WILL YOU THEN BANISH ALL WHO ARE DIFFERENT FROM YOU? WILL YOU SEND US FAR AWAY? WILL YOU ONCE AGAIN DIVIDE THE LAND AMONG YOURSELVES WHILE WE EAT THE DUST ON LANDS YOU WASTED?
GREAT SAGE, HUM CAPABLE OF REAC NEW WISDOM.
NEOTOPIA SYMBO HUMAN CAPACITY TO FROM PAST MISTA
WORLD, THOUG WASTED, HOLDS M POTENTIAL STIL WE DALPHINII WATC HISTORY. HUMAN EVENTUALLY LEARN. OR NOT, THEY PAR WORLD. PART OF US BAD THING TO ABAN THEM NOW.
GREAT SAGE, PLEASE--
IF YOU ARE LOOKING FOR ALLIES, LOOK TO THE FAR NORTH.
THERE, YOU WILL FIND YOUR OWN KIND.
THERE, THE LAST FRAGMENTS OF GREAT *ELYSSION* BATTLE EACH OTHER.
DETERMINED TO DESTROY EACH OTHER, THEY CARRY WITH THEM THE KEY TO YOUR SALVATION AND ALSO THE KEY TO THE WORLD'S DEMISE.

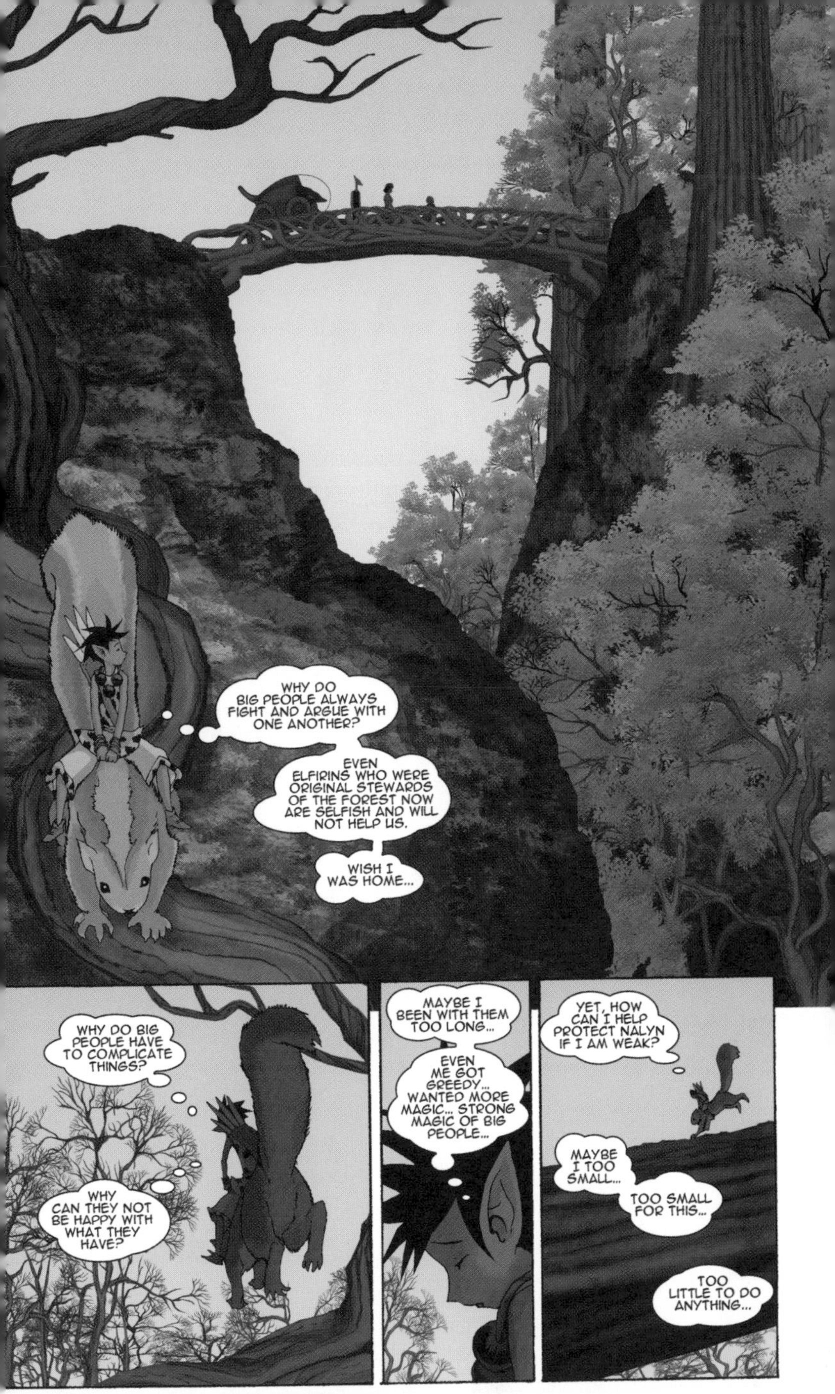

WHY DO BIG PEOPLE ALWAYS FIGHT AND ARGUE WITH ONE ANOTHER?
EVEN ELFIRINS WHO WERE ORIGINAL STEWARDS OF THE FOREST NOW ARE SELFISH AND WILL NOT HELP US.
WISH I WAS HOME...
WHY DO BIG PEOPLE HAVE TO COMPLICATE THINGS?
WHY CAN THEY NOT BE HAPPY WITH WHAT THEY HAVE?
MAYBE I BEEN WITH THEM TOO LONG...
EVEN ME GOT GREEDY... WANTED MORE MAGIC... STRONG MAGIC OF BIG PEOPLE...
YET, HOW CAN I HELP PROTECT NALYN IF I AM WEAK?
MAYBE I TOO SMALL...
TOO SMALL FOR THIS...
TOO LITTLE TO DO ANYTHING...

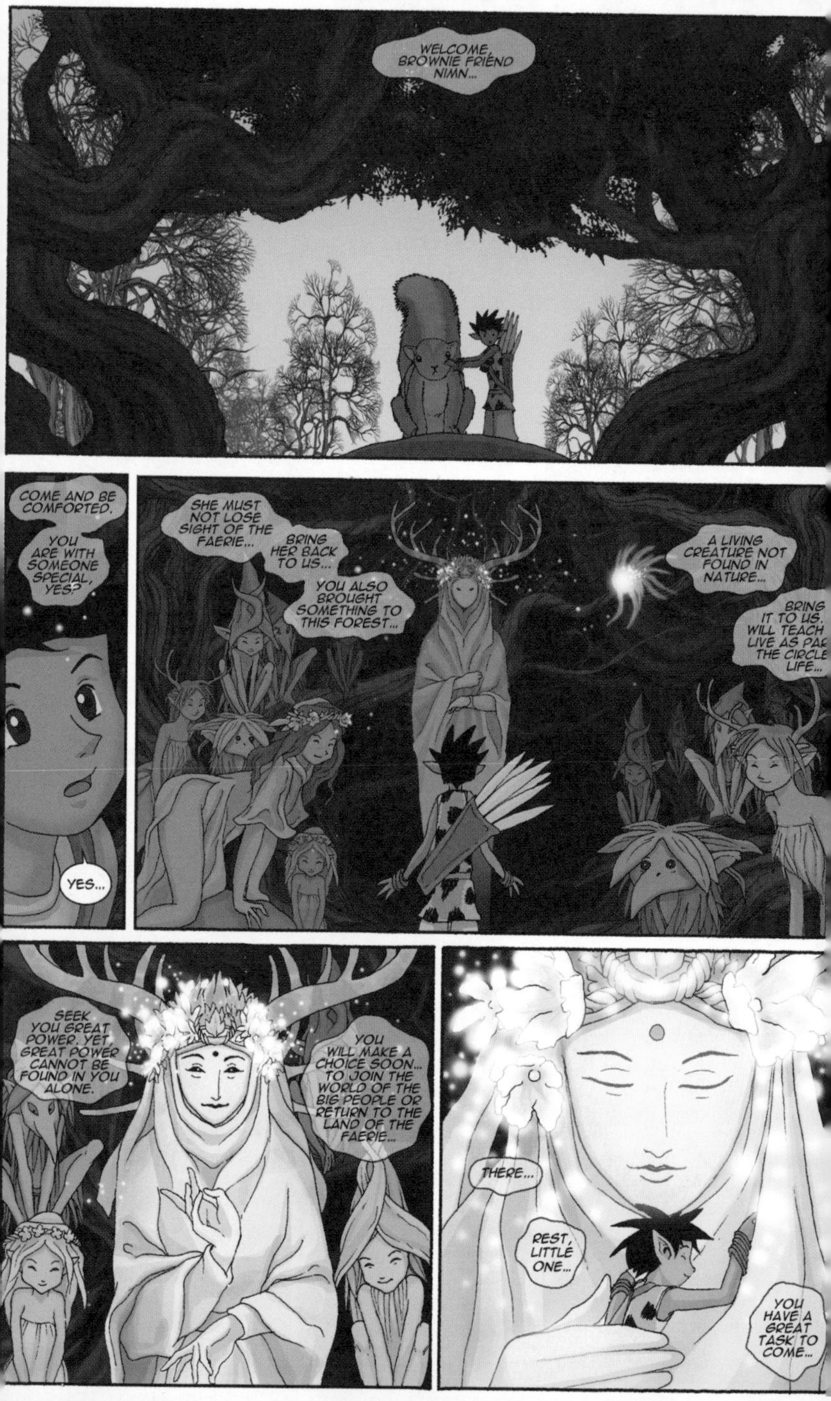
WELCOME, BROWNIE FRIEND NIMN...
COME AND BE COMFORTED.
YOU ARE WITH SOMEONE SPECIAL, YES?
YES...
SHE MUST NOT LOSE SIGHT OF THE FAERIE...
BRING HER BACK TO US...
YOU ALSO BROUGHT SOMETHING TO THIS FOREST...
A LIVING CREATURE NOT FOUND IN NATURE...
SEEK YOU GREAT POWER, YET GREAT POWER CANNOT BE FOUND IN YOU ALONE.
YOU WILL MAKE A CHOICE SOON... TO JOIN THE WORLD OF THE BIG PEOPLE OR RETURN TO THE LAND OF THE FAERIE...
THERE...
REST, LITTLE ONE...
YOU HAVE A GREAT TASK TO COME...

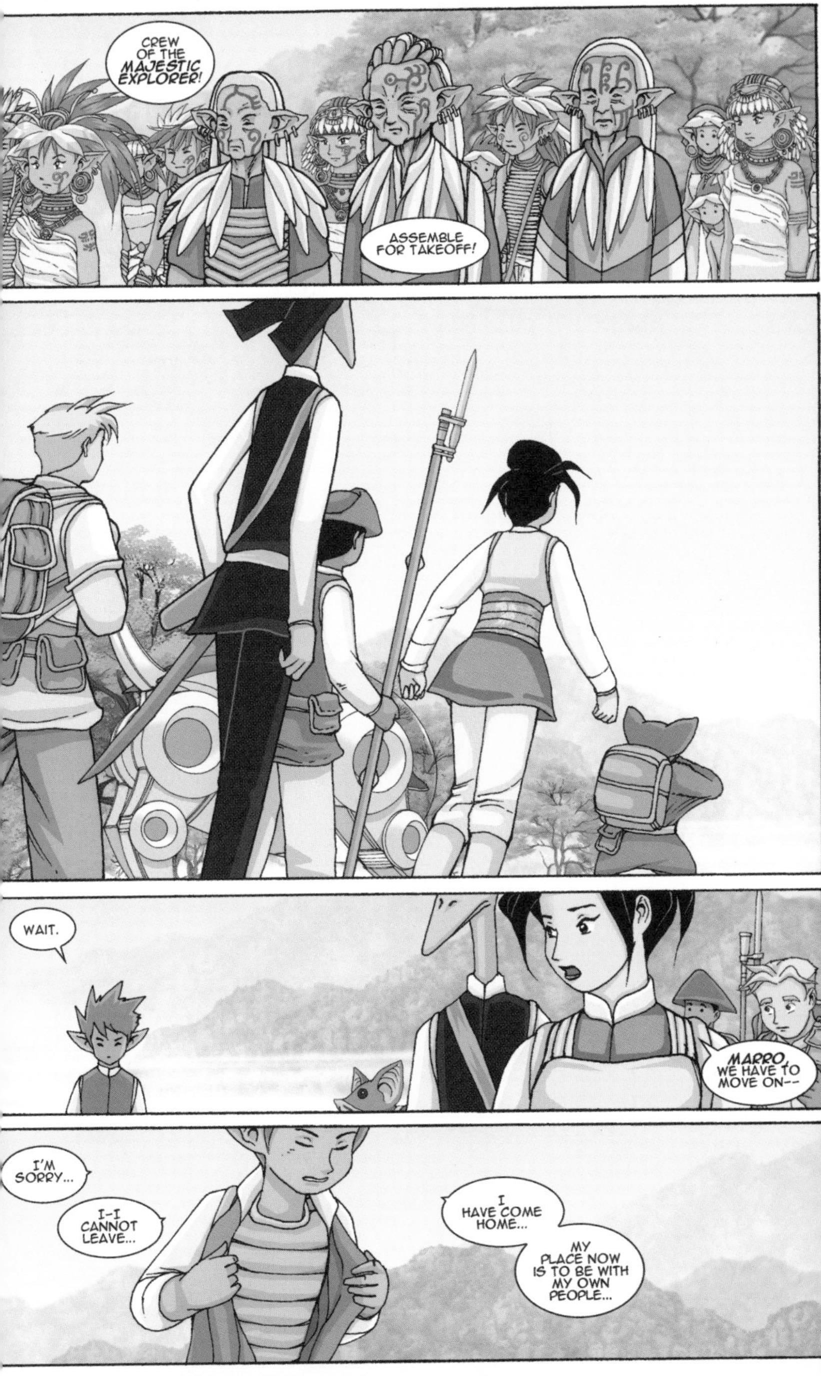
CREW OF THE MAJESTIC EXPLORER!
ASSEMBLE FOR TAKEOFF!
WAIT.
MARRO, WE HAVE TO MOVE ON--
I'M SORRY...
I-I CANNOT LEAVE...
I HAVE COME HOME...
MY PLACE NOW IS TO BE WITH MY OWN PEOPLE...

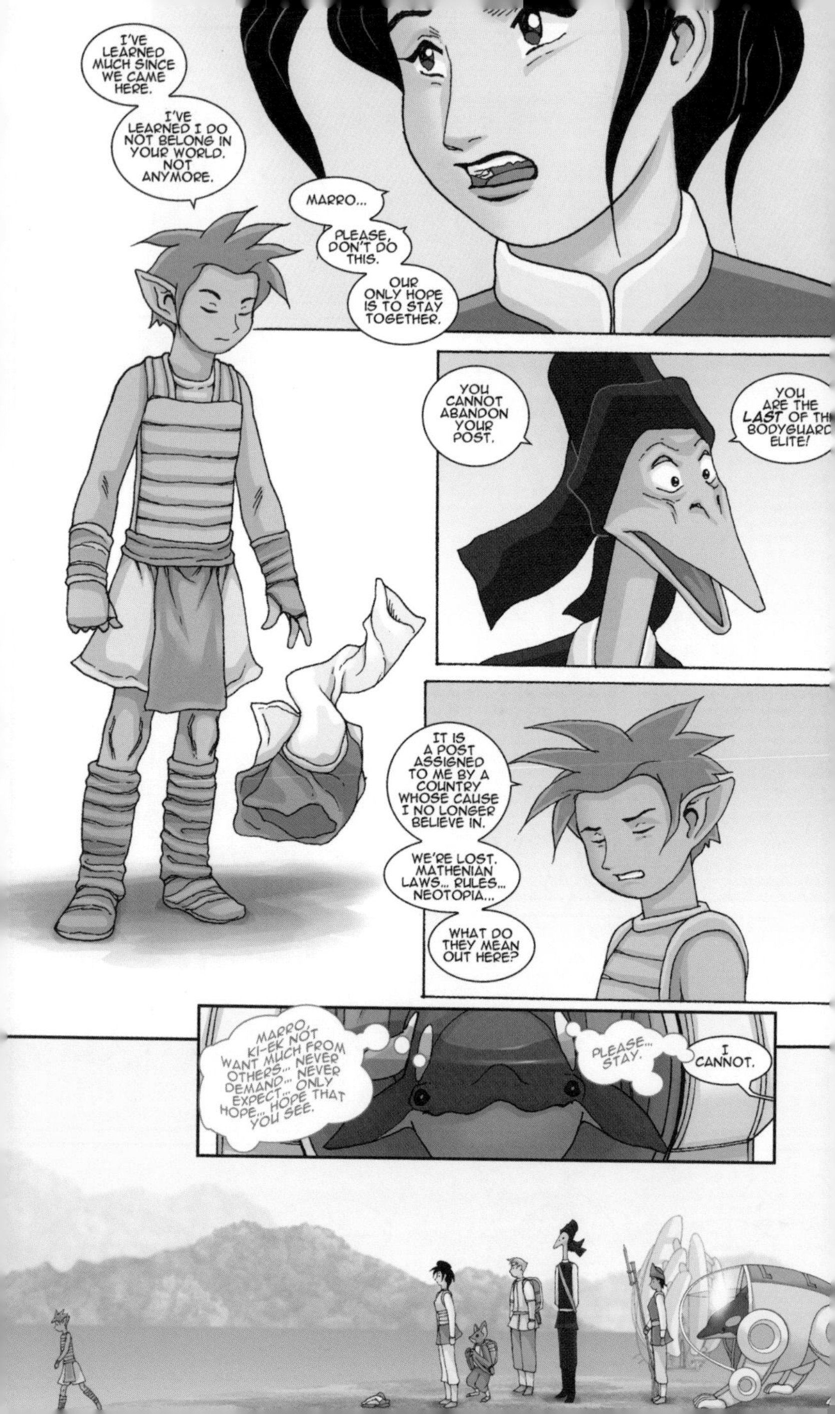
I'VE LEARNED MUCH SINCE WE CAME HERE.
I'VE LEARNED I DO NOT BELONG IN YOUR WORLD. NOT ANYMORE.
MARRO...
PLEASE, DON'T DO THIS.
OUR ONLY HOPE IS TO STAY TOGETHER.
YOU CANNOT ABANDON YOUR POST.
YOU ARE THE *LAST* OF THE BODYGUARD ELITE!
IT IS A POST ASSIGNED TO ME BY A COUNTRY WHOSE CAUSE I NO LONGER BELIEVE IN.
WE'RE LOST. MATHENIAN LAWS... RULES... NEOTOPIA...
WHAT DO THEY MEAN OUT HERE?
MARRO, KI-EK NOT WANT MUCH FROM OTHERS... NEVER DEMAND... NEVER EXPECT... ONLY HOPE... HOPE THAT YOU SEE.
PLEASE... STAY.
I CANNOT.

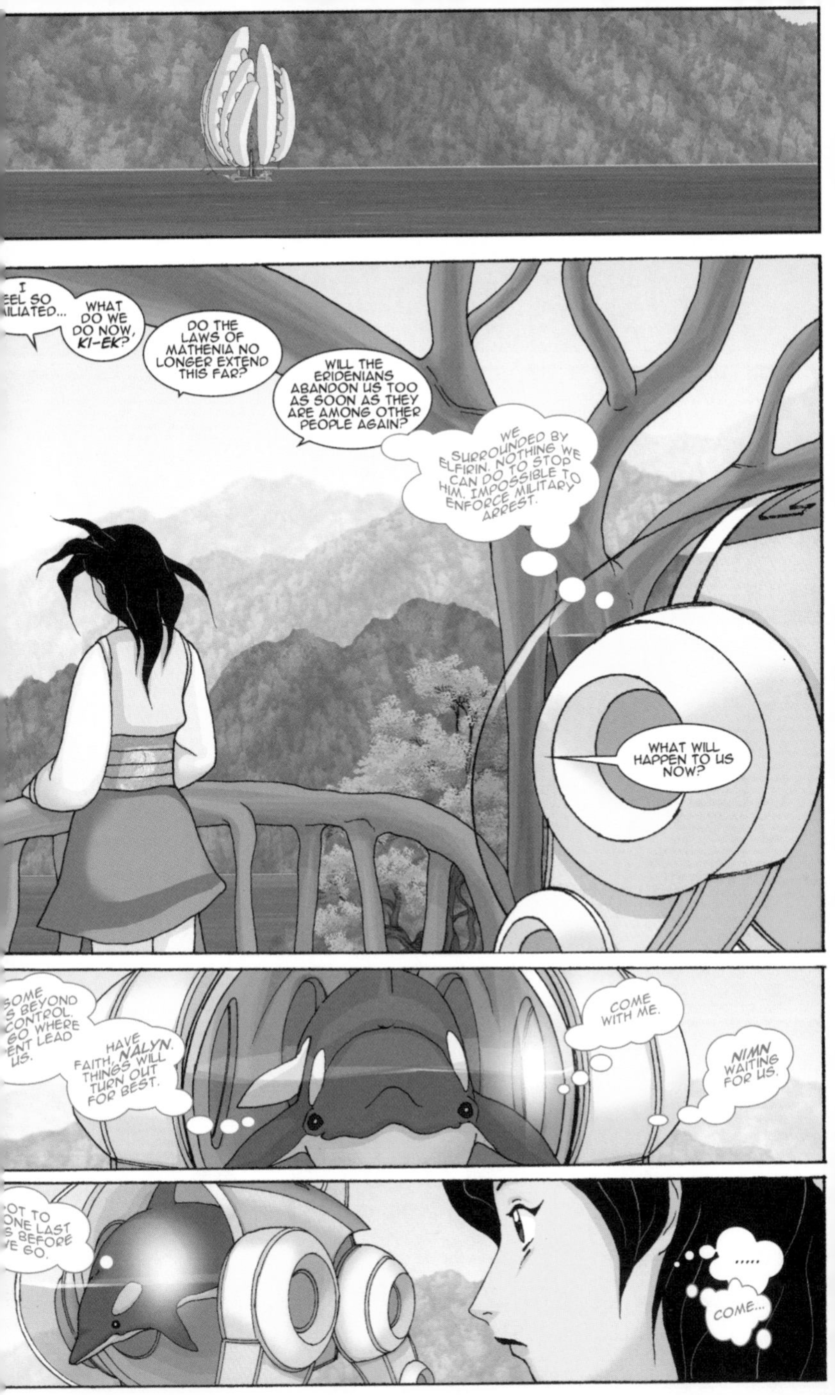
I
EEL SO
IILIATED...
WHAT DO WE DO NOW, KI-EK?
DO THE LAWS OF MATHENIA NO LONGER EXTEND THIS FAR?
WILL THE ERIDENIANS ABANDON US TOO AS SOON AS THEY ARE AMONG OTHER PEOPLE AGAIN?
WE SURROUNDED BY ELFIRIN. NOTHING WE CAN DO TO STOP HIM. IMPOSSIBLE TO ENFORCE MILITARY ARREST.
WHAT WILL HAPPEN TO US NOW?
SOME
S BEYOND
CONTROL.
GO WHERE
ENT LEAD
US.
HAVE FAITH, NALYN. THINGS WILL TURN OUT FOR BEST.
COME WITH ME.
NIMN WAITING FOR US.
OT TO
ONE LAST
S BEFORE
E GO.
......
COME...

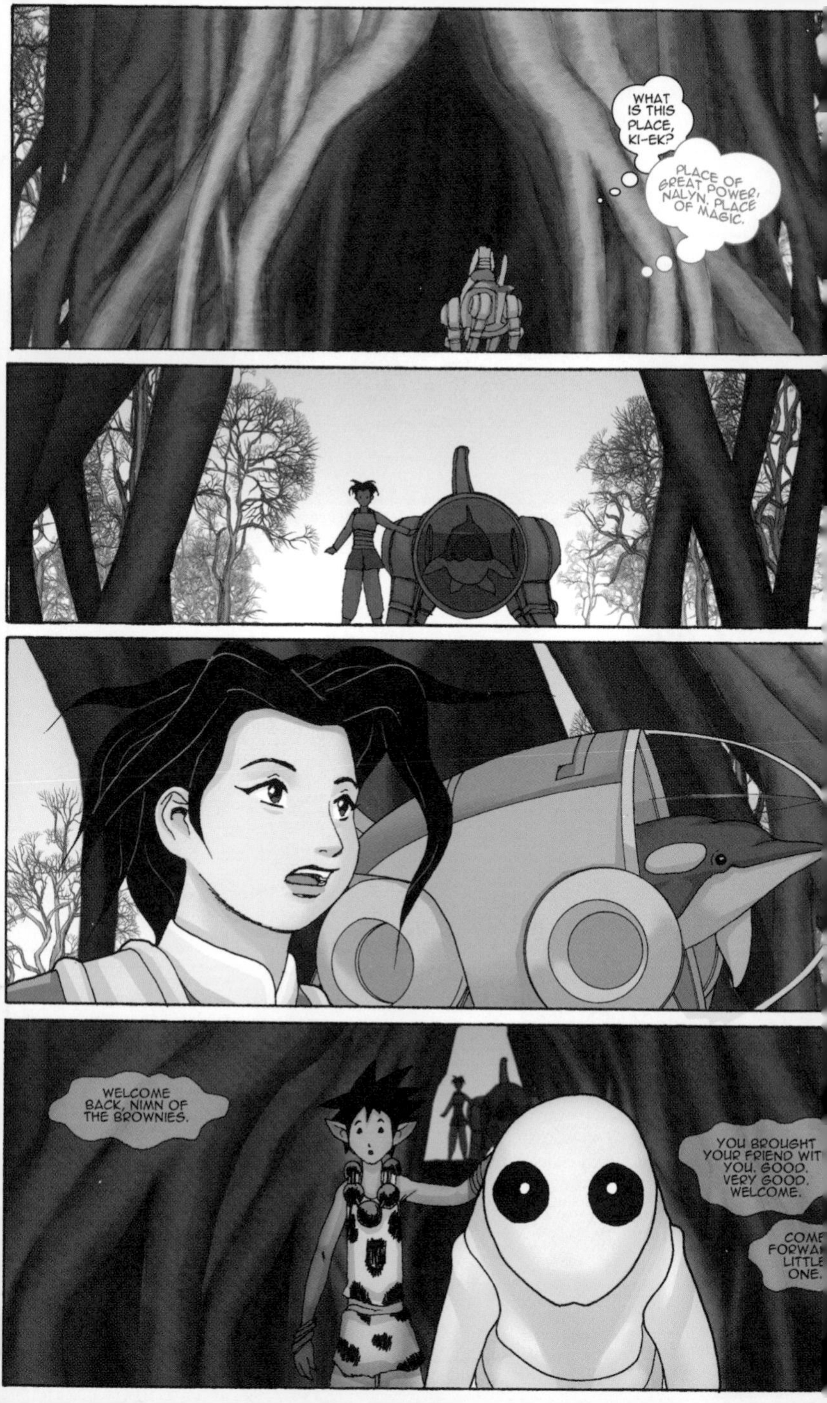
WHAT IS THIS PLACE, KI-EK?
PLACE OF GREAT POWER, NALYN. PLACE OF MAGIC.
WELCOME BACK, NIMN OF THE BROWNIES.
YOU BROUGHT YOUR FRIEND WIT YOU. GOOD. VERY GOOD. WELCOME.
COME FORWA LITTLE ONE.

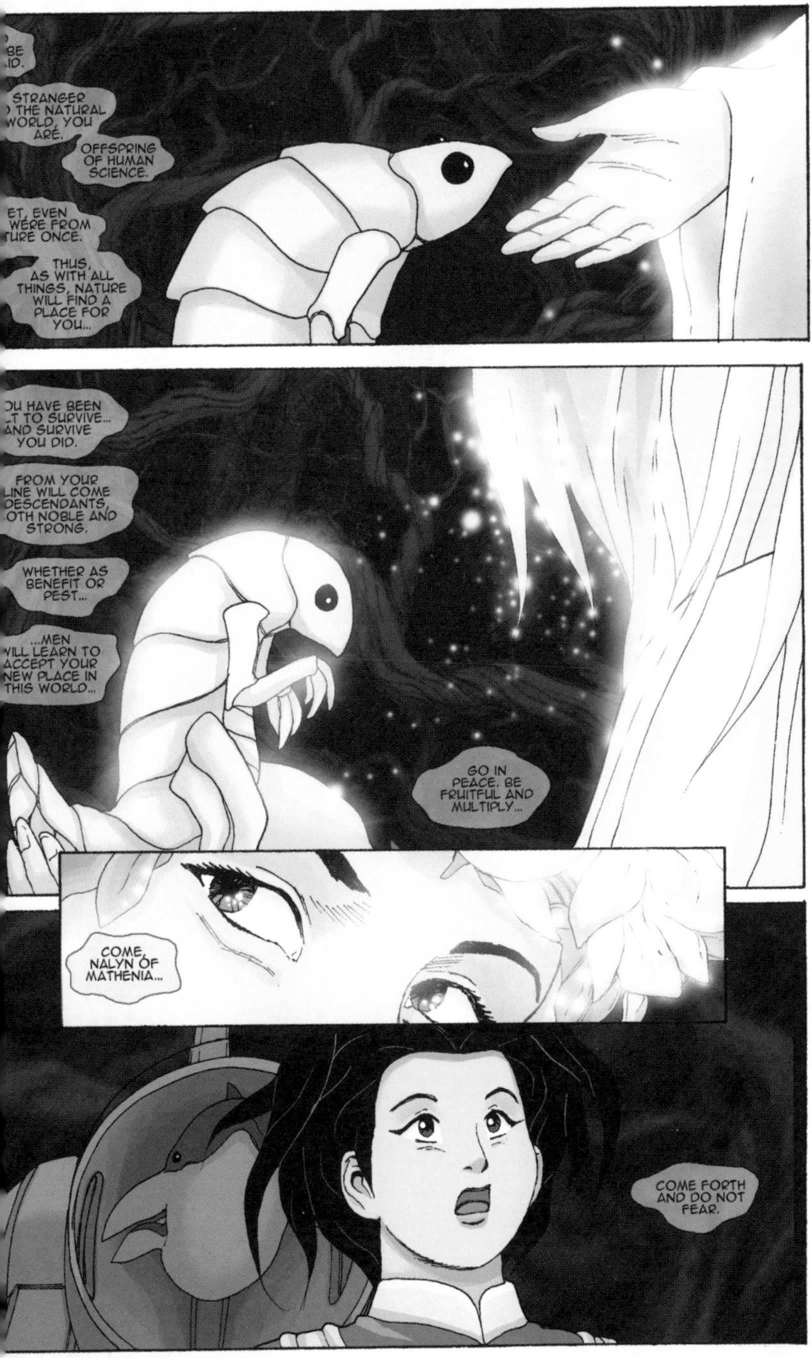
BE
ID.
STRANGER
THE NATURAL
WORLD, YOU
ARE.
OFFSPRING
OF HUMAN
SCIENCE.
ET, EVEN
WERE FROM
TURE ONCE.
THUS,
AS WITH ALL
THINGS, NATURE
WILL FIND A
PLACE FOR
YOU...
OU HAVE BEEN
T TO SURVIVE...
AND SURVIVE
YOU DID.
FROM YOUR
LINE WILL COME
DESCENDANTS,
OTH NOBLE AND
STRONG.
WHETHER AS
BENEFIT OR
PEST...
...MEN
WILL LEARN TO
ACCEPT YOUR
NEW PLACE IN
THIS WORLD...
GO IN
PEACE. BE
FRUITFUL AND
MULTIPLY...
COME,
NALYN OF
MATHENIA...
COME FORTH
AND DO NOT
FEAR.

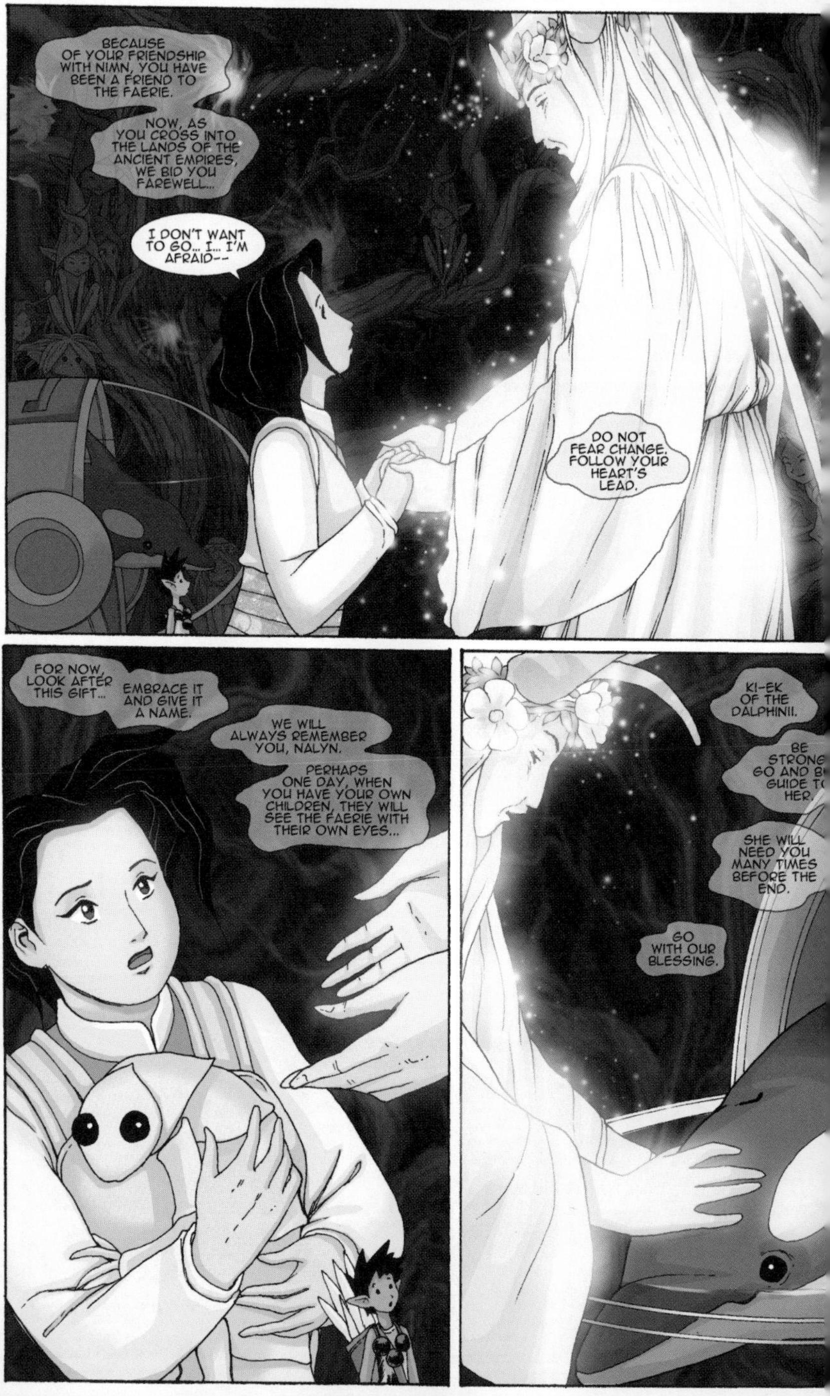
BECAUSE OF YOUR FRIENDSHIP WITH NIMN, YOU HAVE BEEN A FRIEND TO THE FAERIE.
NOW, AS YOU CROSS INTO THE LANDS OF THE ANCIENT EMPIRES, WE BID YOU FAREWELL...
I DON'T WANT TO GO... I... I'M AFRAID--
DO NOT FEAR CHANGE. FOLLOW YOUR HEART'S LEAD.
FOR NOW, LOOK AFTER THIS GIFT...
EMBRACE IT AND GIVE IT A NAME.
WE WILL ALWAYS REMEMBER YOU, NALYN.
PERHAPS ONE DAY, WHEN YOU HAVE YOUR OWN CHILDREN, THEY WILL SEE THE FAERIE WITH THEIR OWN EYES...
KI-EK OF THE DALPHINII.
BE STRONG GO AND B GUIDE T HER.
SHE WILL NEED YOU MANY TIMES BEFORE THE END.
GO WITH OUR BLESSING.

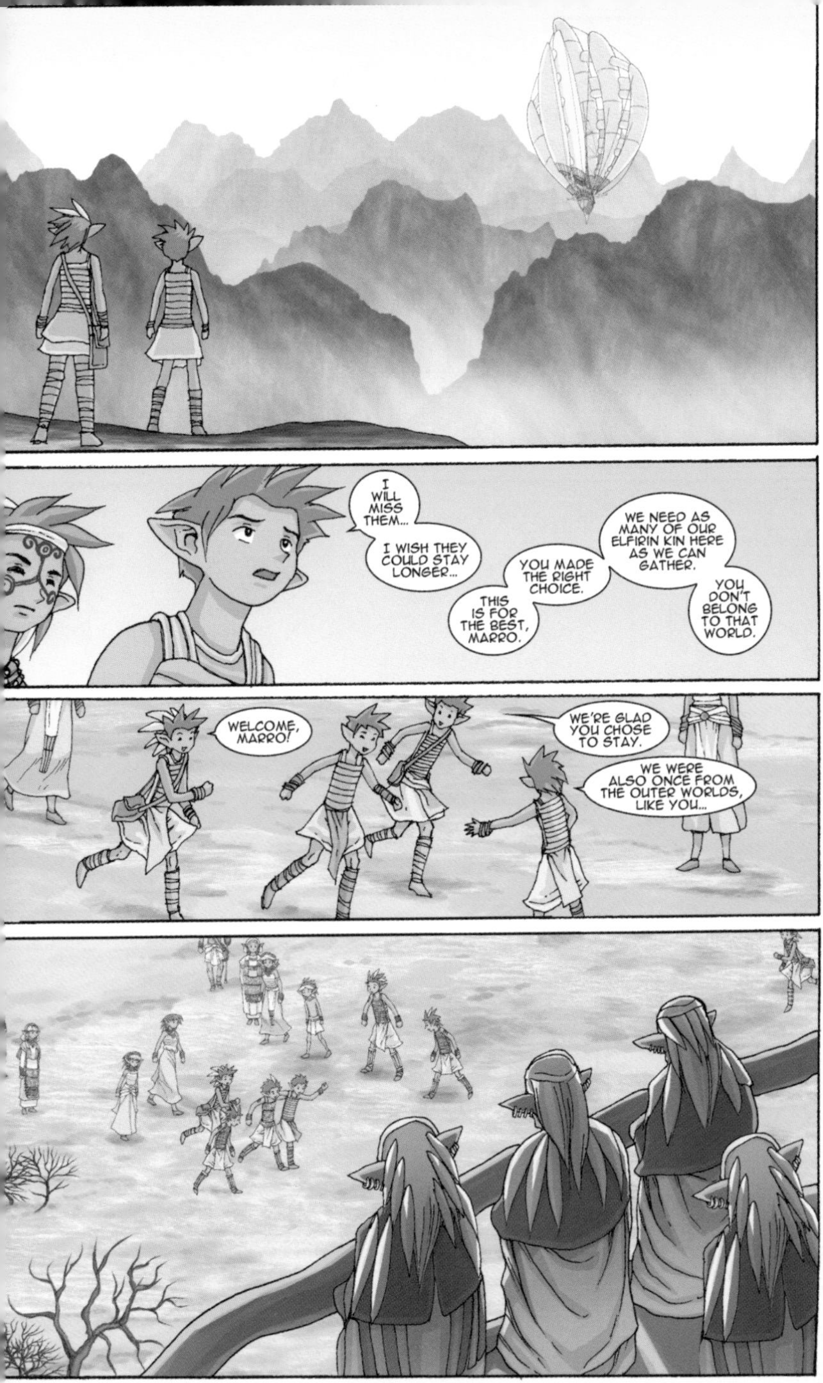
I WILL MISS THEM...
I WISH THEY COULD STAY LONGER...
THIS IS FOR THE BEST, MARRO.
YOU MADE THE RIGHT CHOICE.
WE NEED AS MANY OF OUR ELFIRIN KIN HERE AS WE CAN GATHER.
YOU DON'T BELONG TO THAT WORLD.
WELCOME, MARRO!
WE'RE GLAD YOU CHOSE TO STAY.
WE WERE ALSO ONCE FROM THE OUTER WORLDS, LIKE YOU...

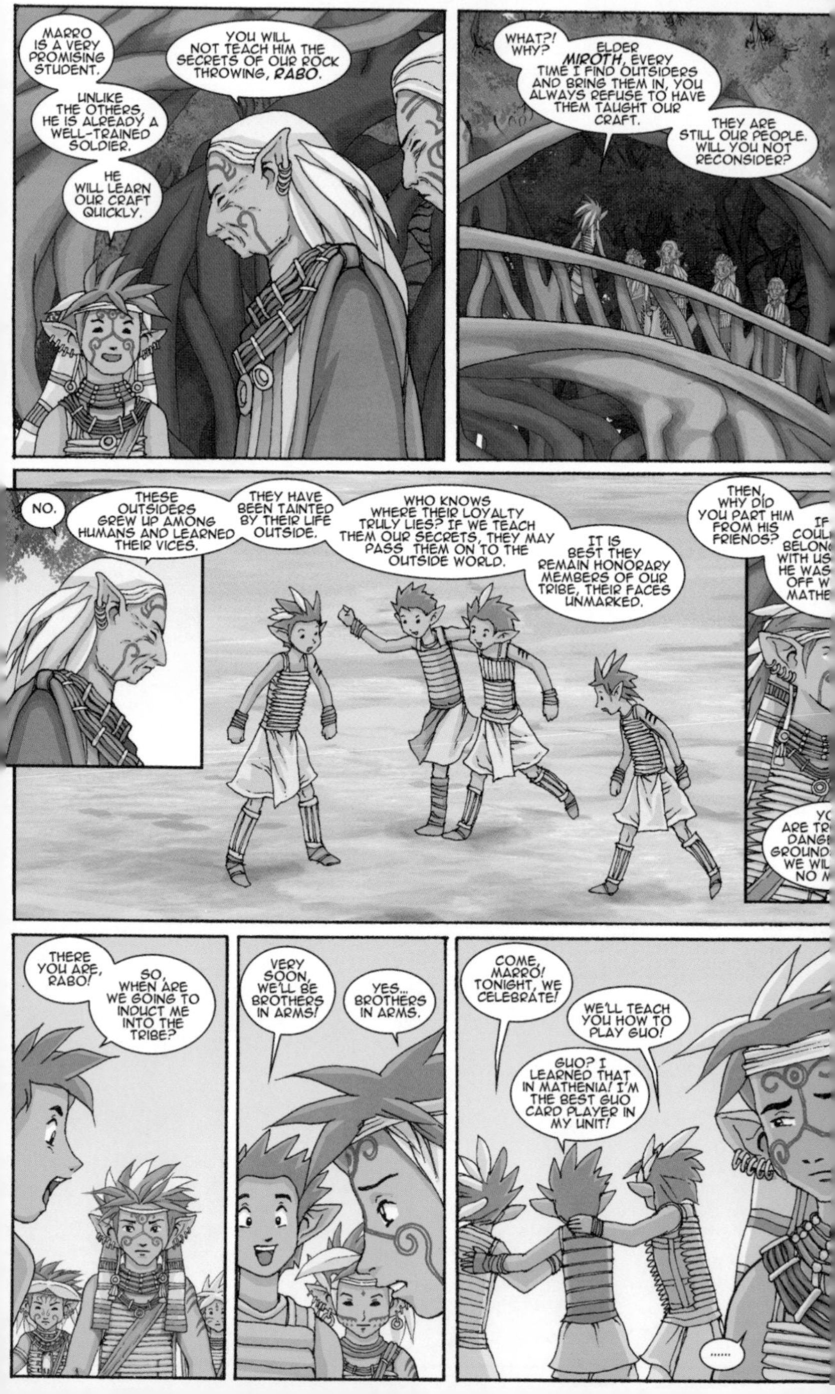
MARRO IS A VERY PROMISING STUDENT.
UNLIKE THE OTHERS, HE IS ALREADY A WELL-TRAINED SOLDIER.
HE WILL LEARN OUR CRAFT QUICKLY.
YOU WILL NOT TEACH HIM THE SECRETS OF OUR ROCK THROWING, RABO.
WHAT?! WHY?
ELDER MIROTH, EVERY TIME I FIND OUTSIDERS AND BRING THEM IN, YOU ALWAYS REFUSE TO HAVE THEM TAUGHT OUR CRAFT.
THEY ARE STILL OUR PEOPLE. WILL YOU NOT RECONSIDER?
NO.
THESE OUTSIDERS GREW UP AMONG HUMANS AND LEARNED THEIR VICES.
THEY HAVE BEEN TAINTED BY THEIR LIFE OUTSIDE.
WHO KNOWS WHERE THEIR LOYALTY TRULY LIES? IF WE TEACH THEM OUR SECRETS, THEY MAY PASS THEM ON TO THE OUTSIDE WORLD.
IT IS BEST THEY REMAIN HONORARY MEMBERS OF OUR TRIBE, THEIR FACES UNMARKED.
THEN, WHY DID YOU PART HIM FROM HIS FRIENDS?
THERE YOU ARE, RABO!
SO, WHEN ARE WE GOING TO INDUCT ME INTO THE TRIBE?
VERY SOON, WE'LL BE BROTHERS IN ARMS!
YES... BROTHERS IN ARMS.
COME, MARRO! TONIGHT, WE CELEBRATE!
WE'LL TEACH YOU HOW TO PLAY GUO!
GUO? I LEARNED THAT IN MATHENIA! I'M THE BEST GUO CARD PLAYER IN MY UNIT!
......

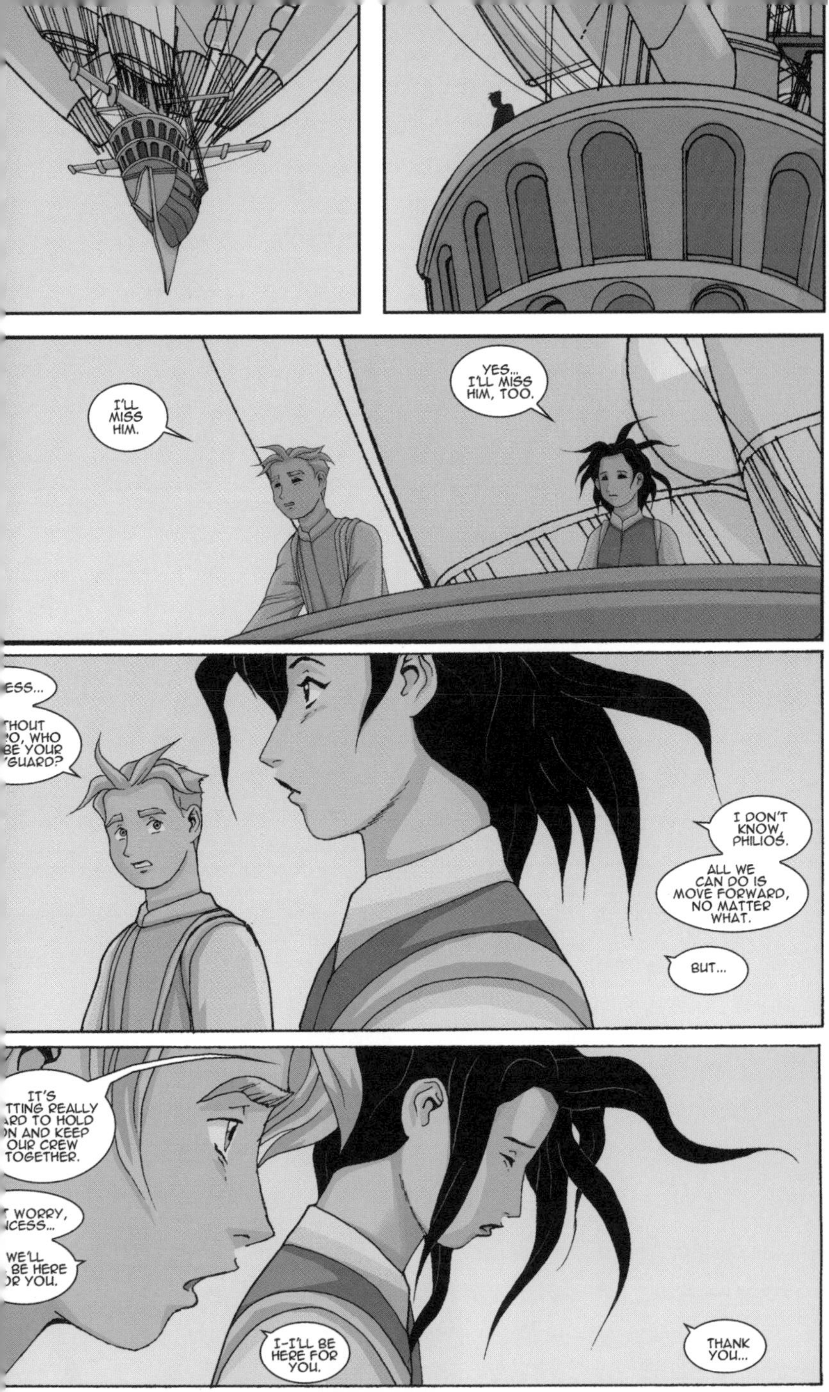
I'LL MISS HIM.
YES... I'LL MISS HIM, TOO.
ESS...
THOUT
O, WHO BE YOUR GUARD?
I DON'T KNOW, PHILIOS.
ALL WE CAN DO IS MOVE FORWARD, NO MATTER WHAT.
BUT...
IT'S TTING REALLY ARD TO HOLD N AND KEEP OUR CREW TOGETHER.
T WORRY, NCESS...
WE'LL BE HERE OR YOU.
I-I'LL BE HERE FOR YOU.
THANK YOU...

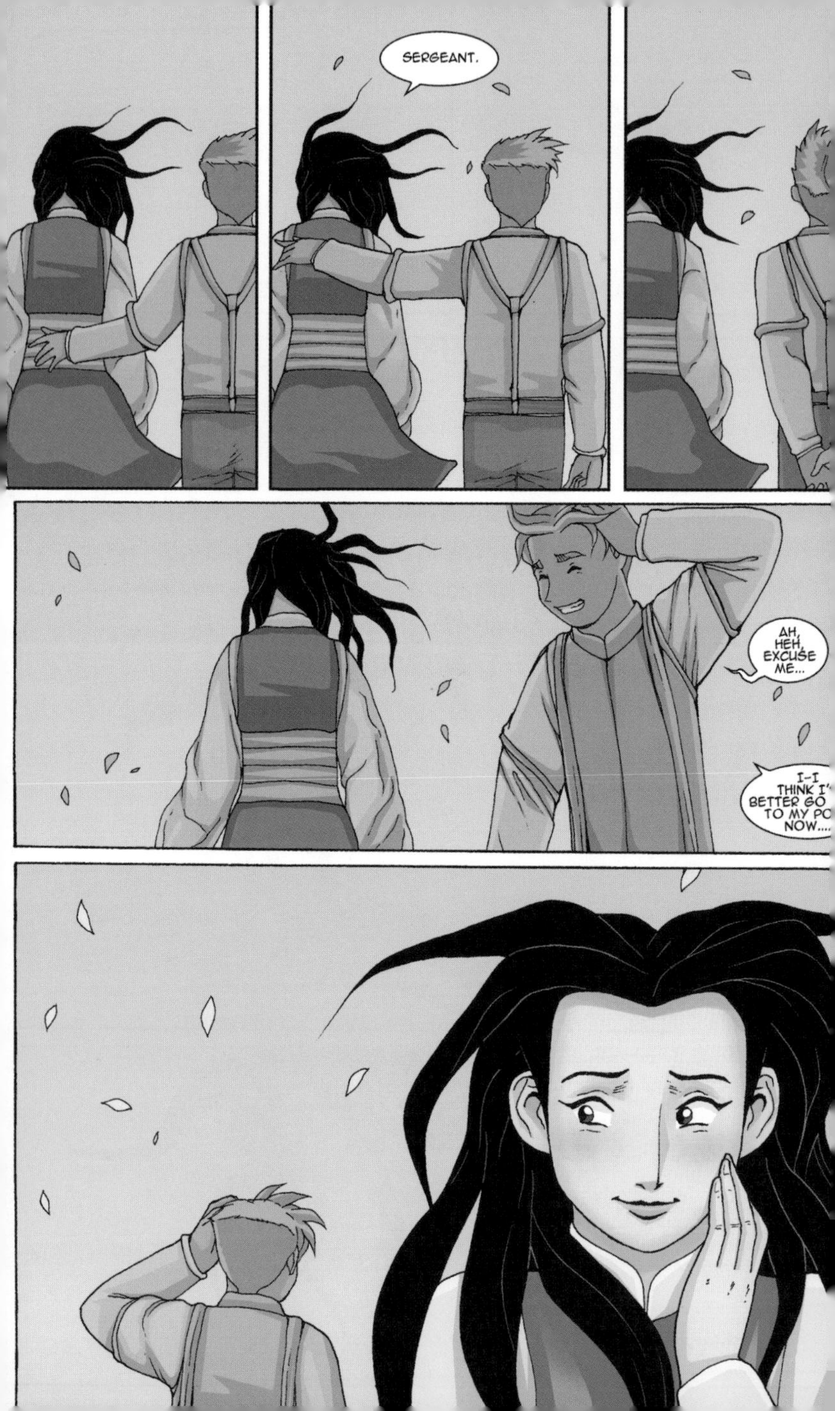
SERGEANT.
AH, HEH, EXCUSE ME...
I-I THINK I'
BETTER GO
TO MY PO
NOW....

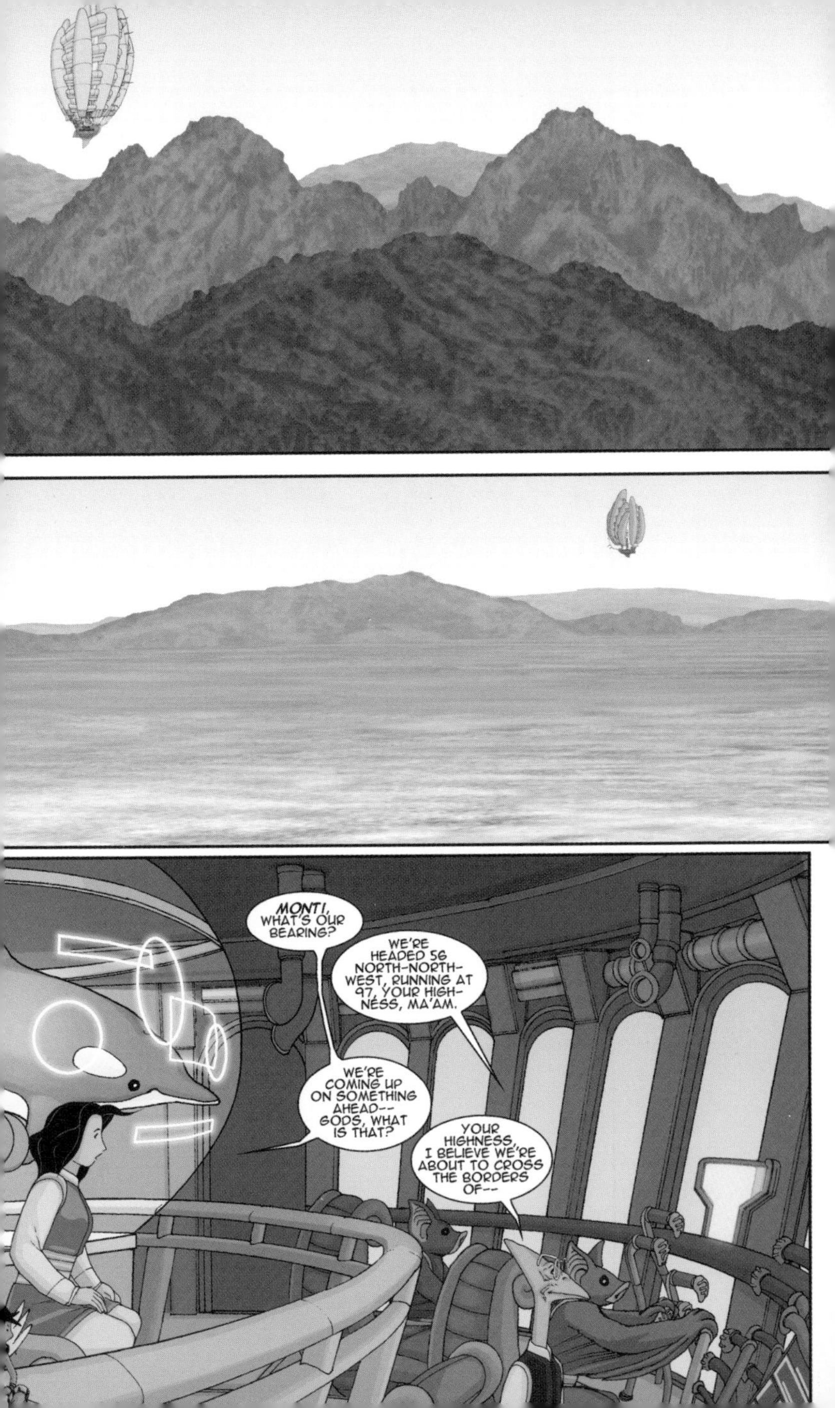
MONTI, WHAT'S OUR BEARING?
WE'RE HEADED 56 NORTH-NORTH-WEST, RUNNING AT 97, YOUR HIGH-NESS, MA'AM.
WE'RE COMING UP ON SOMETHING AHEAD-- GODS, WHAT IS THAT?
YOUR HIGHNESS, I BELIEVE WE'RE ABOUT TO CROSS THE BORDERS OF--

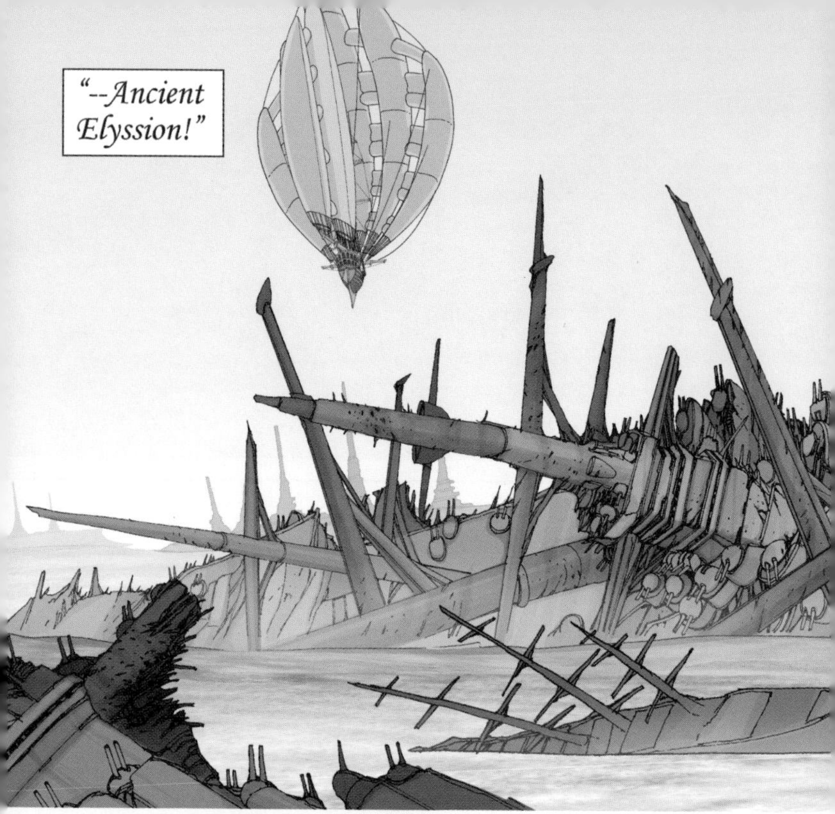
"--Ancient Elyssion!"

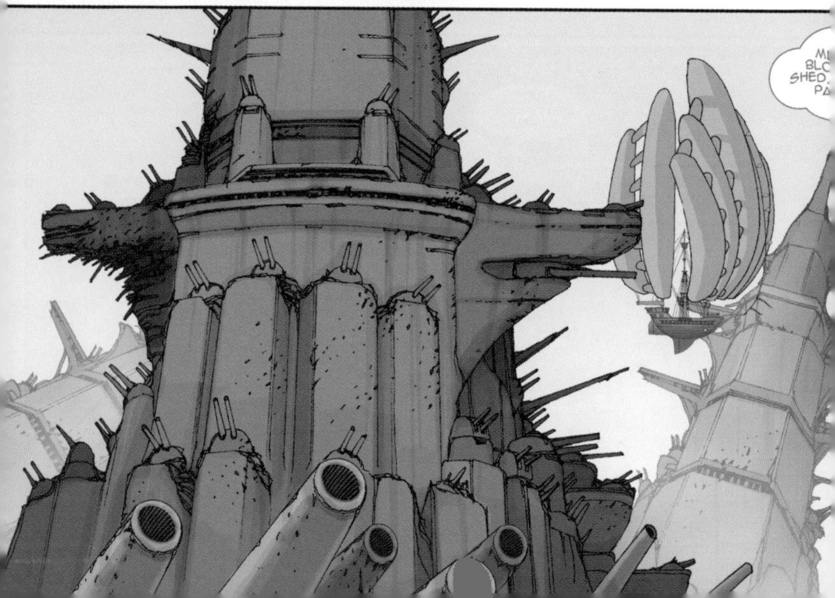

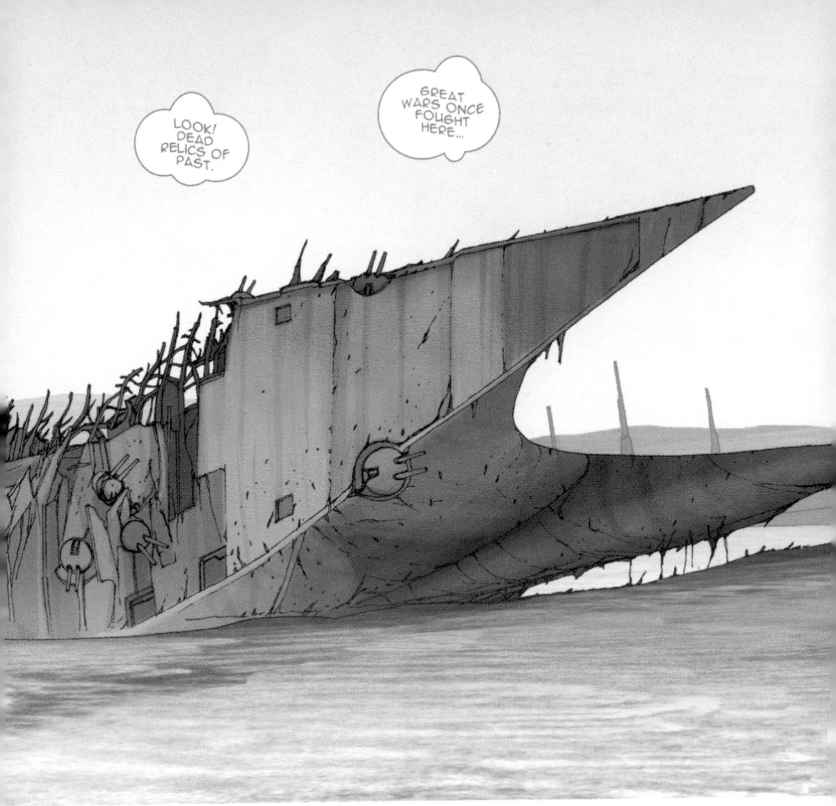
LOOK! DEAD RELICS OF PAST.
GREAT WARS ONCE FOUGHT HERE...

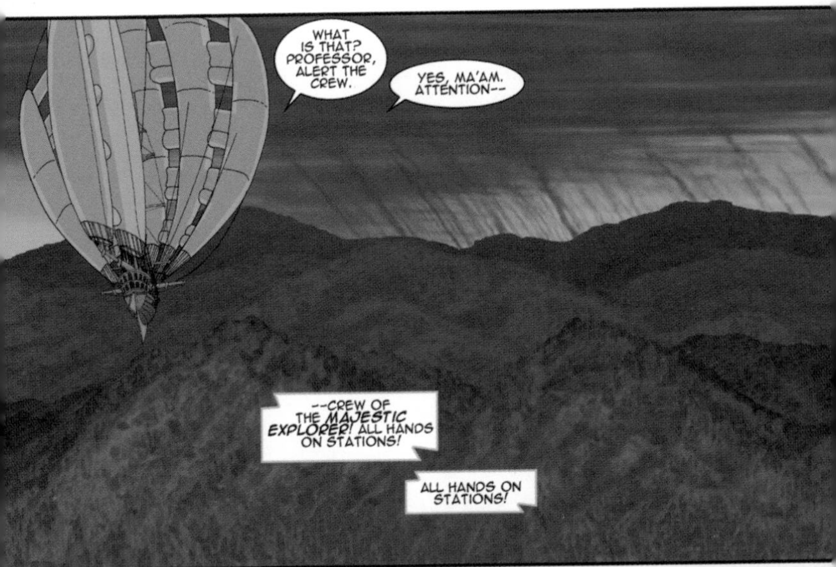
WHAT IS THAT? PROFESSOR, ALERT THE CREW.
YES, MA'AM. ATTENTION--
--CREW OF THE MAJESTIC EXPLORER! ALL HANDS ON STATIONS!
ALL HANDS ON STATIONS!

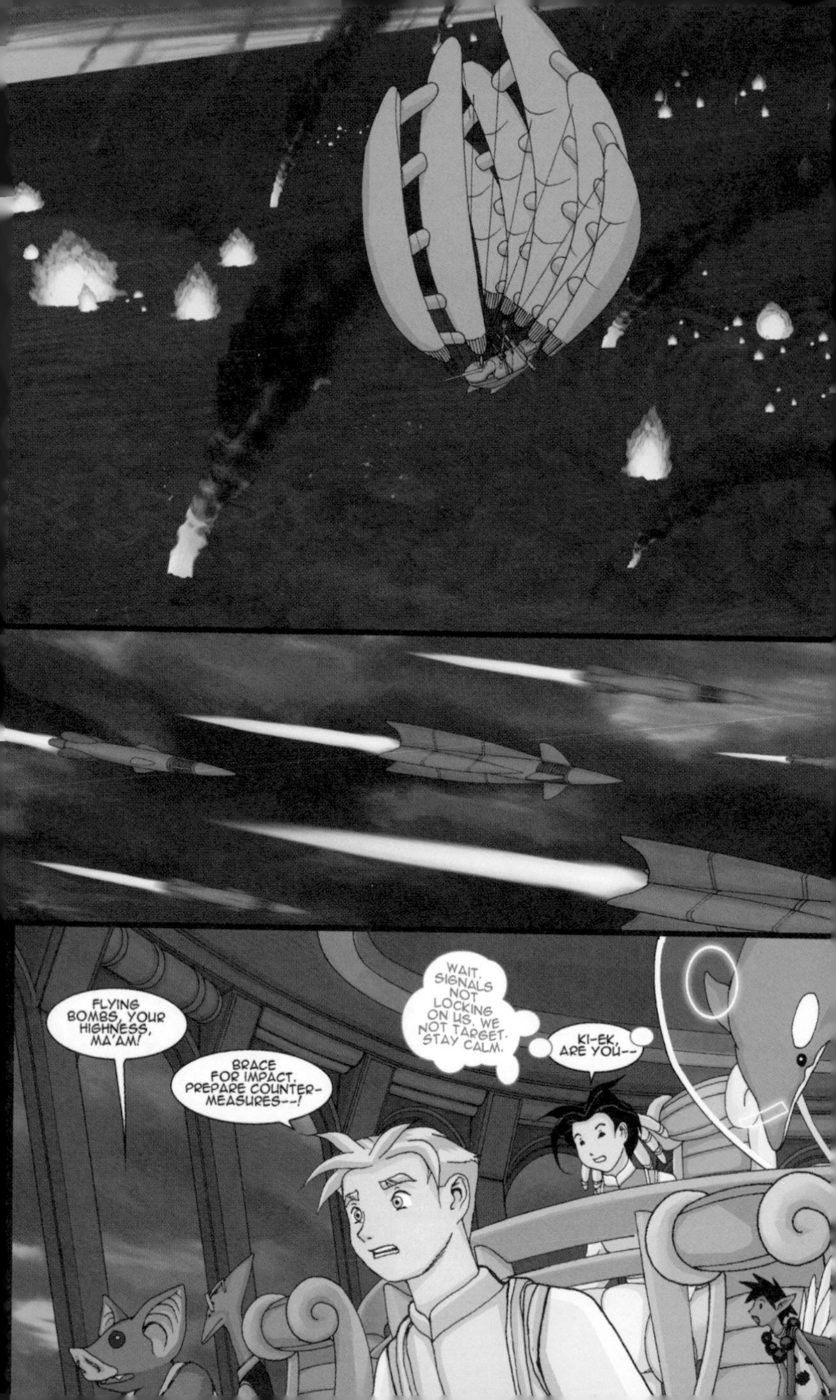
FLYING BOMBS, YOUR HIGHNESS, MA'AM!
BRACE FOR IMPACT. PREPARE COUNTER-MEASURES--!
WAIT. SIGNALS NOT LOCKING ON US. WE NOT TARGET. STAY CALM.
KI-EK, ARE YOU--

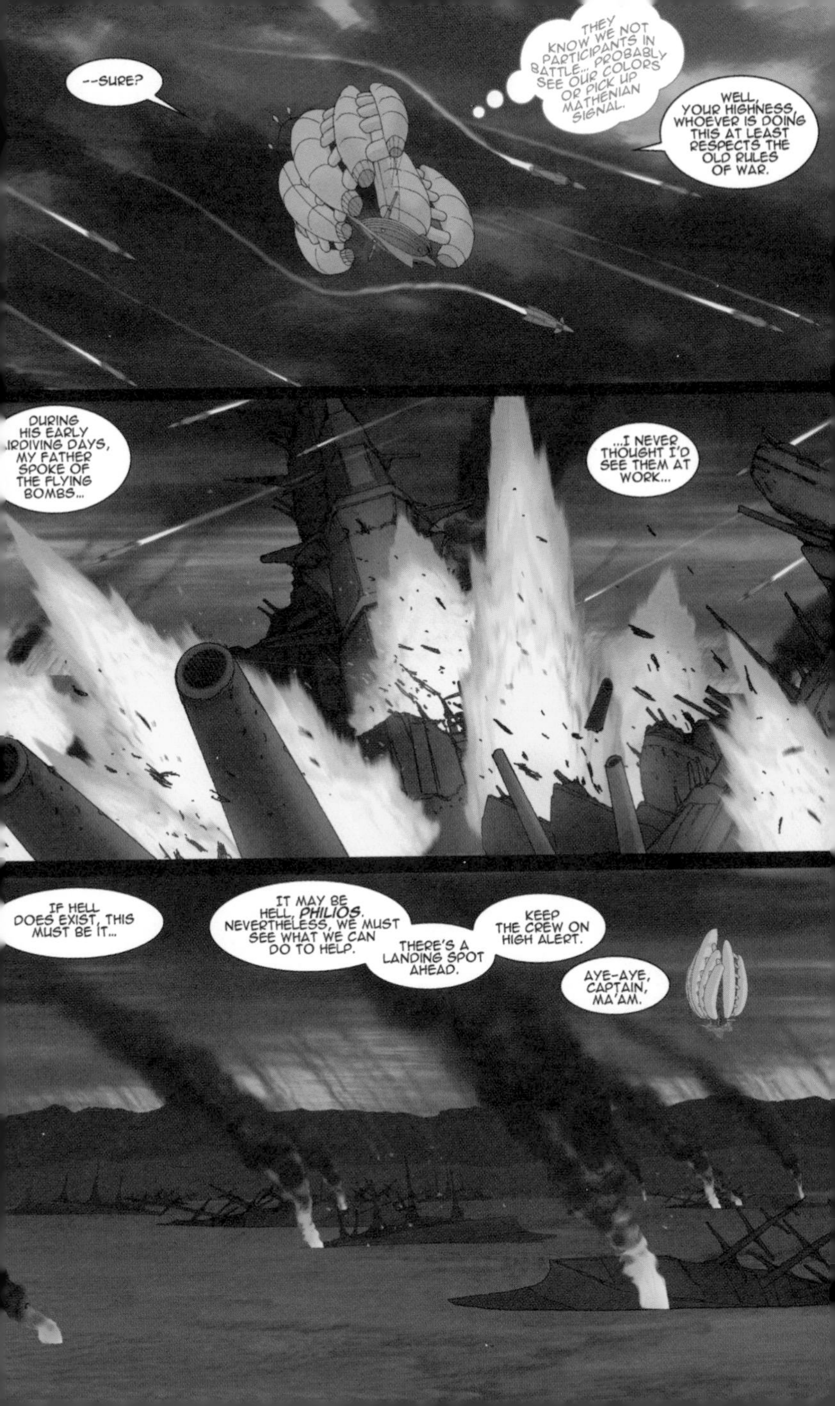
--SURE?
THEY KNOW WE NOT PARTICIPANTS IN BATTLE... PROBABLY SEE OUR COLORS OR PICK UP MATHENIAN SIGNAL.
WELL, YOUR HIGHNESS, WHOEVER IS DOING THIS AT LEAST RESPECTS THE OLD RULES OF WAR.
DURING HIS EARLY AIRDIVING DAYS, MY FATHER SPOKE OF THE FLYING BOMBS...
...I NEVER THOUGHT I'D SEE THEM AT WORK...
IF HELL DOES EXIST, THIS MUST BE IT...
IT MAY BE HELL, *PHILIOS*. NEVERTHELESS, WE MUST SEE WHAT WE CAN DO TO HELP.
THERE'S A LANDING SPOT AHEAD.
KEEP THE CREW ON HIGH ALERT.
AYE-AYE, CAPTAIN, MA'AM.

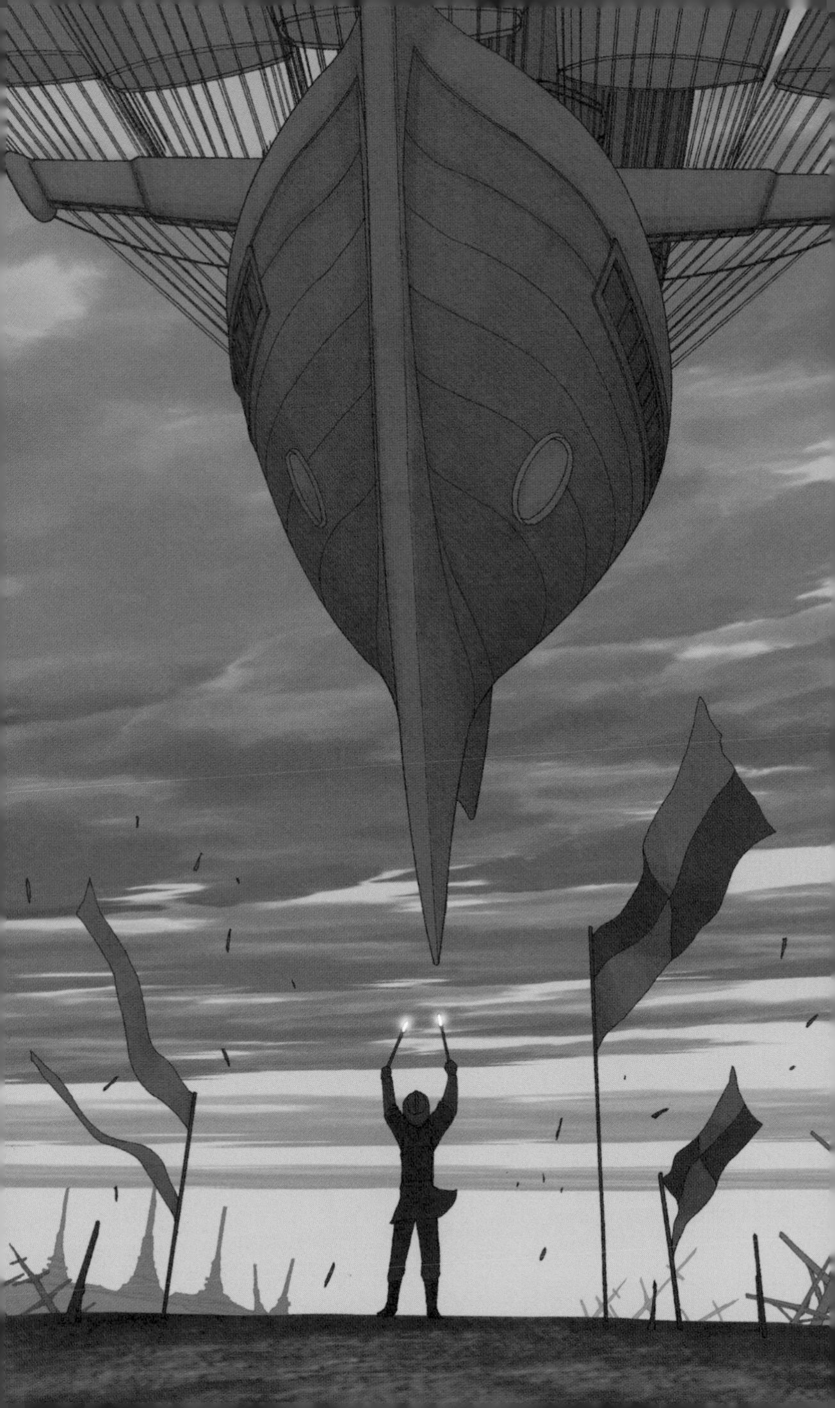

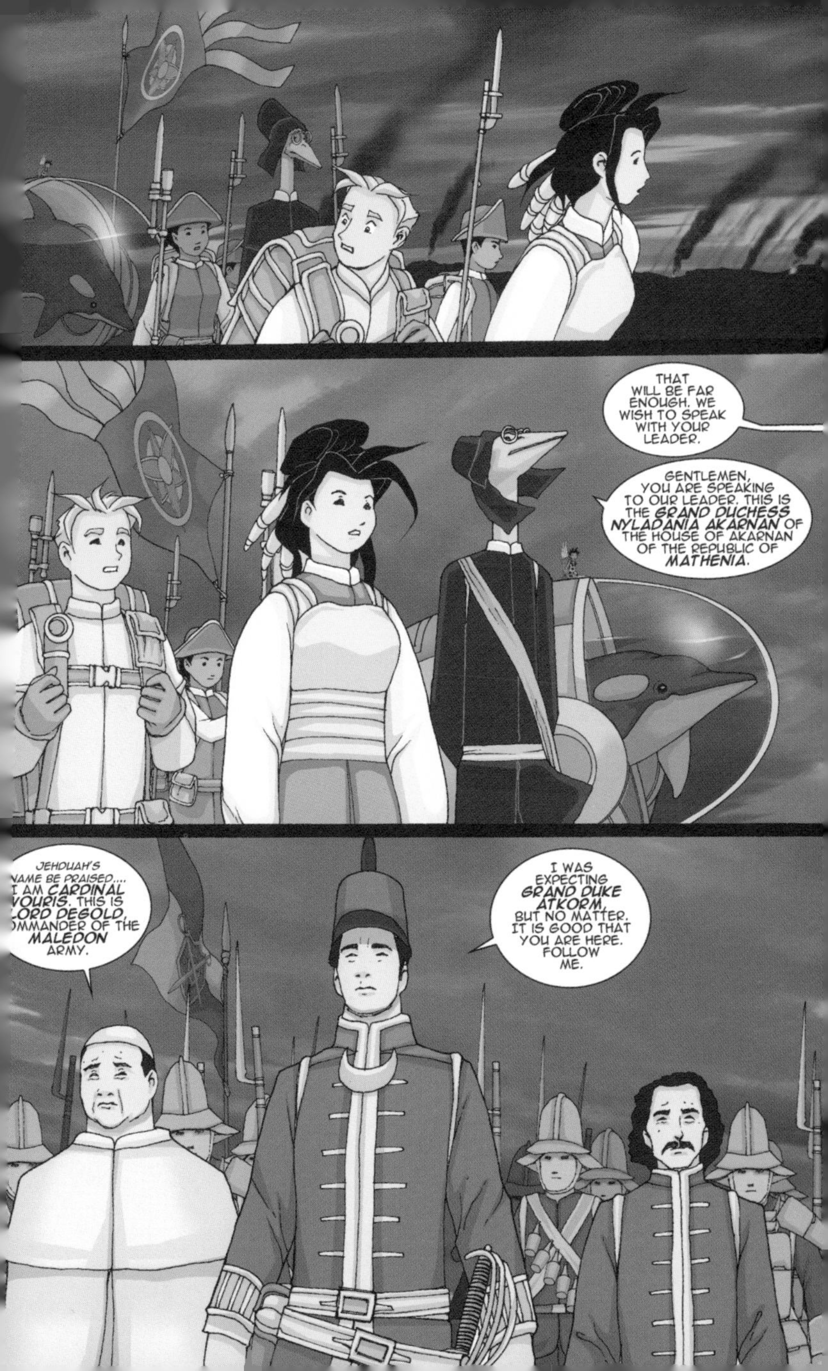
THAT WILL BE FAR ENOUGH. WE WISH TO SPEAK WITH YOUR LEADER.
GENTLEMEN, YOU ARE SPEAKING TO OUR LEADER. THIS IS THE GRAND DUCHESS NYLADANIA AKARNAN OF THE HOUSE OF AKARNAN OF THE REPUBLIC OF MATHENIA.
JEHOUAH'S NAME BE PRAISED.... I AM CARDINAL VOURIS. THIS IS LORD DEGOLD, COMMANDER OF THE MALEDON ARMY.
I WAS EXPECTING GRAND DUKE ATKORM, BUT NO MATTER. IT IS GOOD THAT YOU ARE HERE. FOLLOW ME.

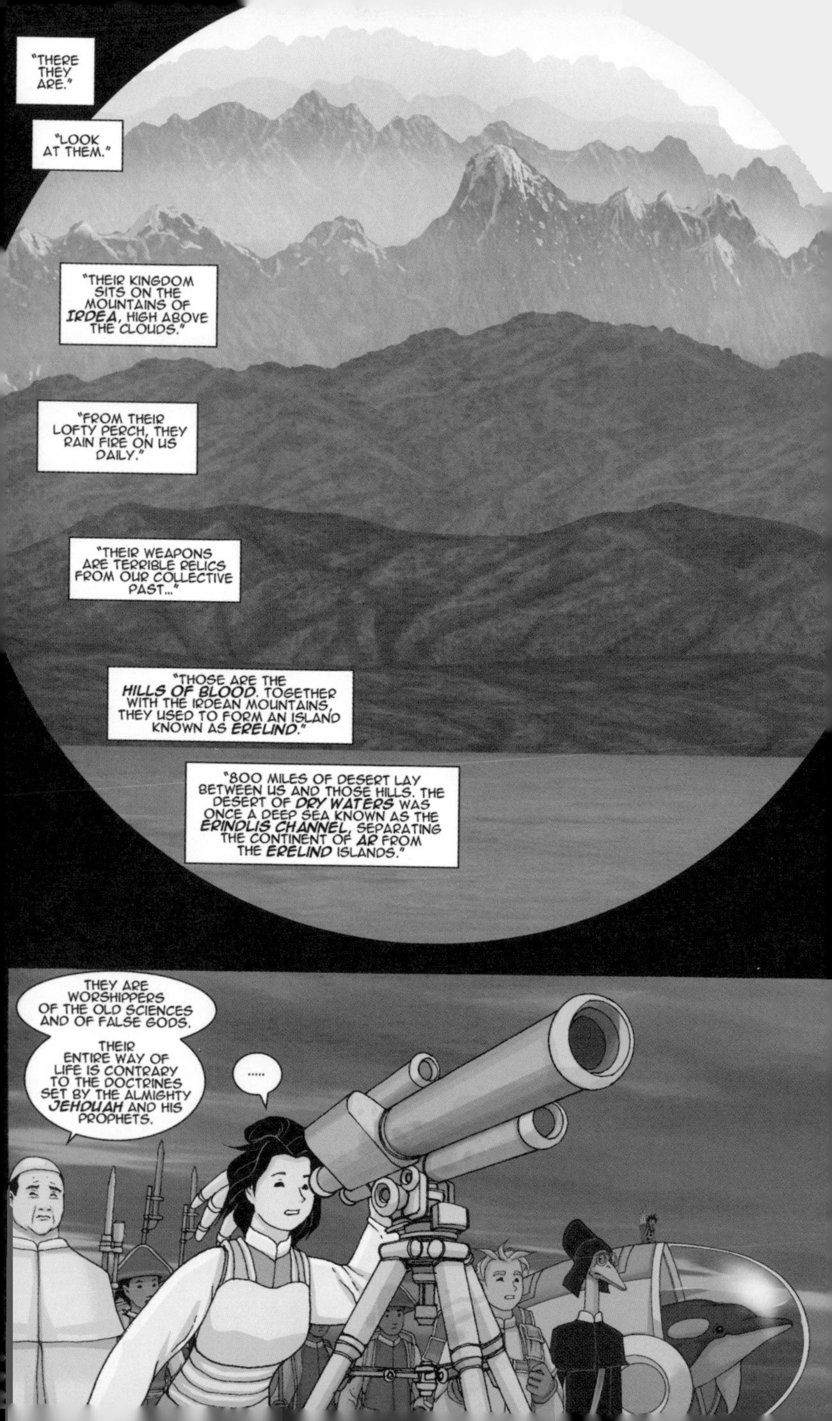

"THERE THEY ARE."
"LOOK AT THEM."
"THEIR KINGDOM SITS ON THE MOUNTAINS OF IRDEA, HIGH ABOVE THE CLOUDS."
"FROM THEIR LOFTY PERCH, THEY RAIN FIRE ON US DAILY."
"THEIR WEAPONS ARE TERRIBLE RELICS FROM OUR COLLECTIVE PAST..."
"THOSE ARE THE HILLS OF BLOOD. TOGETHER WITH THE IRDEAN MOUNTAINS, THEY USED TO FORM AN ISLAND KNOWN AS ERELIND."
"800 MILES OF DESERT LAY BETWEEN US AND THOSE HILLS. THE DESERT OF DRY WATERS WAS ONCE A DEEP SEA KNOWN AS THE ERINDLIS CHANNEL, SEPARATING THE CONTINENT OF AR FROM THE ERELIND ISLANDS."
THEY ARE WORSHIPPERS OF THE OLD SCIENCES AND OF FALSE GODS.
THEIR ENTIRE WAY OF LIFE IS CONTRARY TO THE DOCTRINES SET BY THE ALMIGHTY JEHOUAH AND HIS PROPHETS.
......

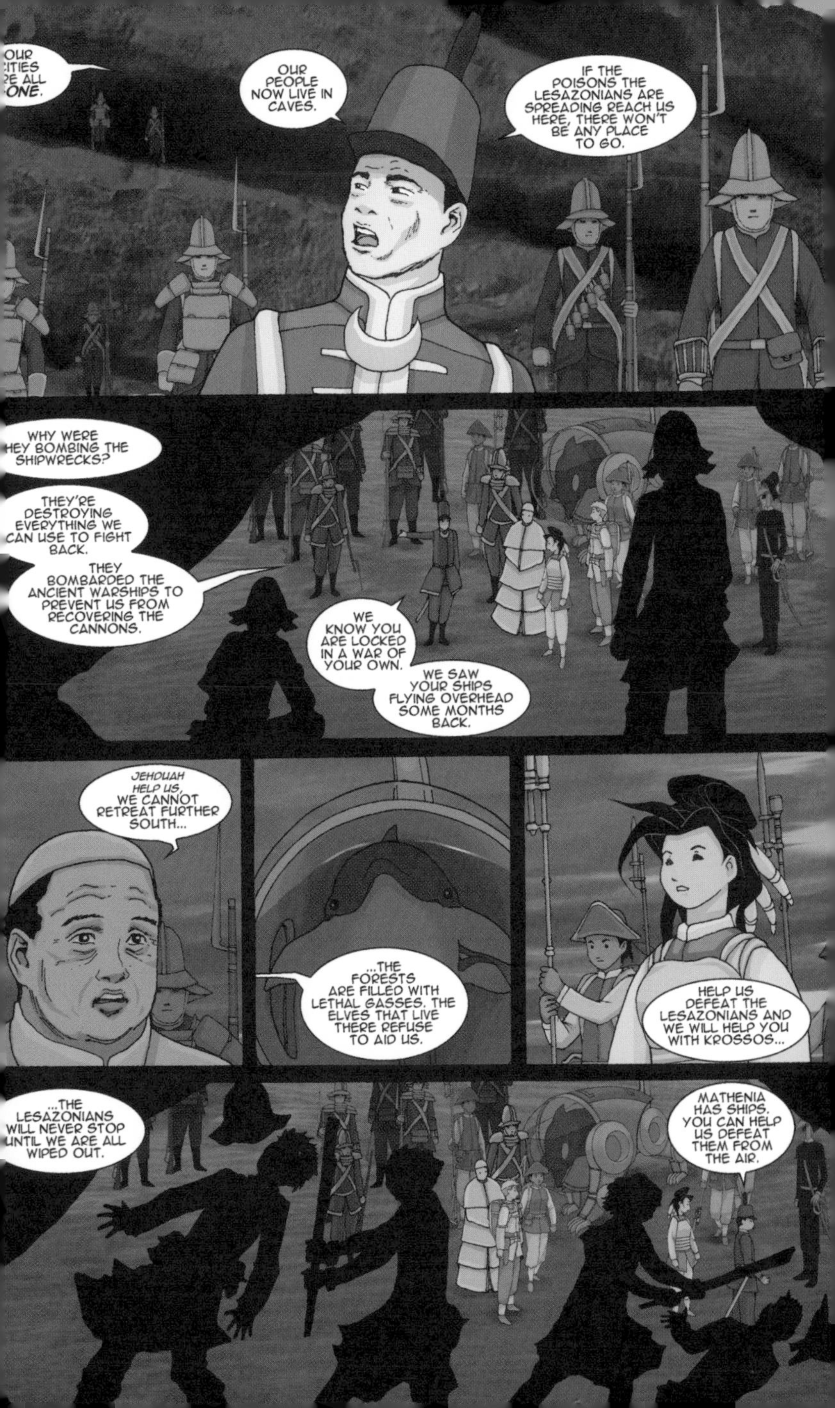
OUR CITIES ARE ALL GONE.
OUR PEOPLE NOW LIVE IN CAVES.
IF THE POISONS THE LESAZONIANS ARE SPREADING REACH US HERE, THERE WON'T BE ANY PLACE TO GO.
WHY WERE THEY BOMBING THE SHIPWRECKS?
THEY'RE DESTROYING EVERYTHING WE CAN USE TO FIGHT BACK.
THEY BOMBARDED THE ANCIENT WARSHIPS TO PREVENT US FROM RECOVERING THE CANNONS.
WE KNOW YOU ARE LOCKED IN A WAR OF YOUR OWN.
WE SAW YOUR SHIPS FLYING OVERHEAD SOME MONTHS BACK.
JEHOUAH HELP US, WE CANNOT RETREAT FURTHER SOUTH...
...THE FORESTS ARE FILLED WITH LETHAL GASSES. THE ELVES THAT LIVE THERE REFUSE TO AID US.
HELP US DEFEAT THE LESAZONIANS AND WE WILL HELP YOU WITH KROSSOS...
...THE LESAZONIANS WILL NEVER STOP UNTIL WE ARE ALL WIPED OUT.
MATHENIA HAS SHIPS. YOU CAN HELP US DEFEAT THEM FROM THE AIR.

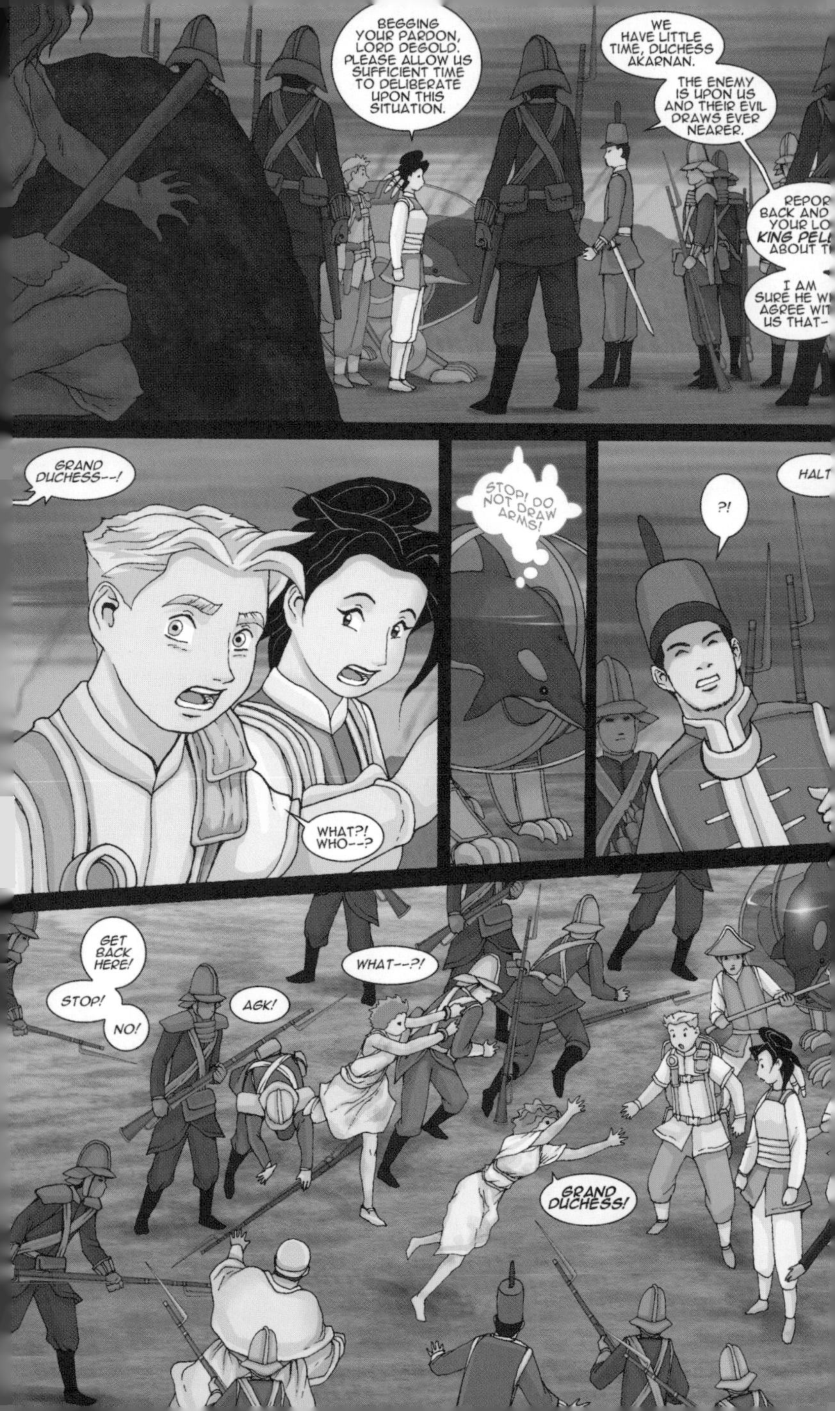
BEGGING YOUR PARDON, LORD DEGOLD. PLEASE ALLOW US SUFFICIENT TIME TO DELIBERATE UPON THIS SITUATION.
WE HAVE LITTLE TIME, DUCHESS AKARNAN.
THE ENEMY IS UPON US AND THEIR EVIL DRAWS EVER NEARER.
REPOR BACK AND YOUR LO KING PEL ABOUT T
I AM SURE HE W AGREE WIT US THAT-
GRAND DUCHESS--!
WHAT?! WHO--?
STOP! DO NOT DRAW ARMS!
?!
HALT
GET BACK HERE!
STOP!
NO!
AGK!
WHAT--?!
GRAND DUCHESS!

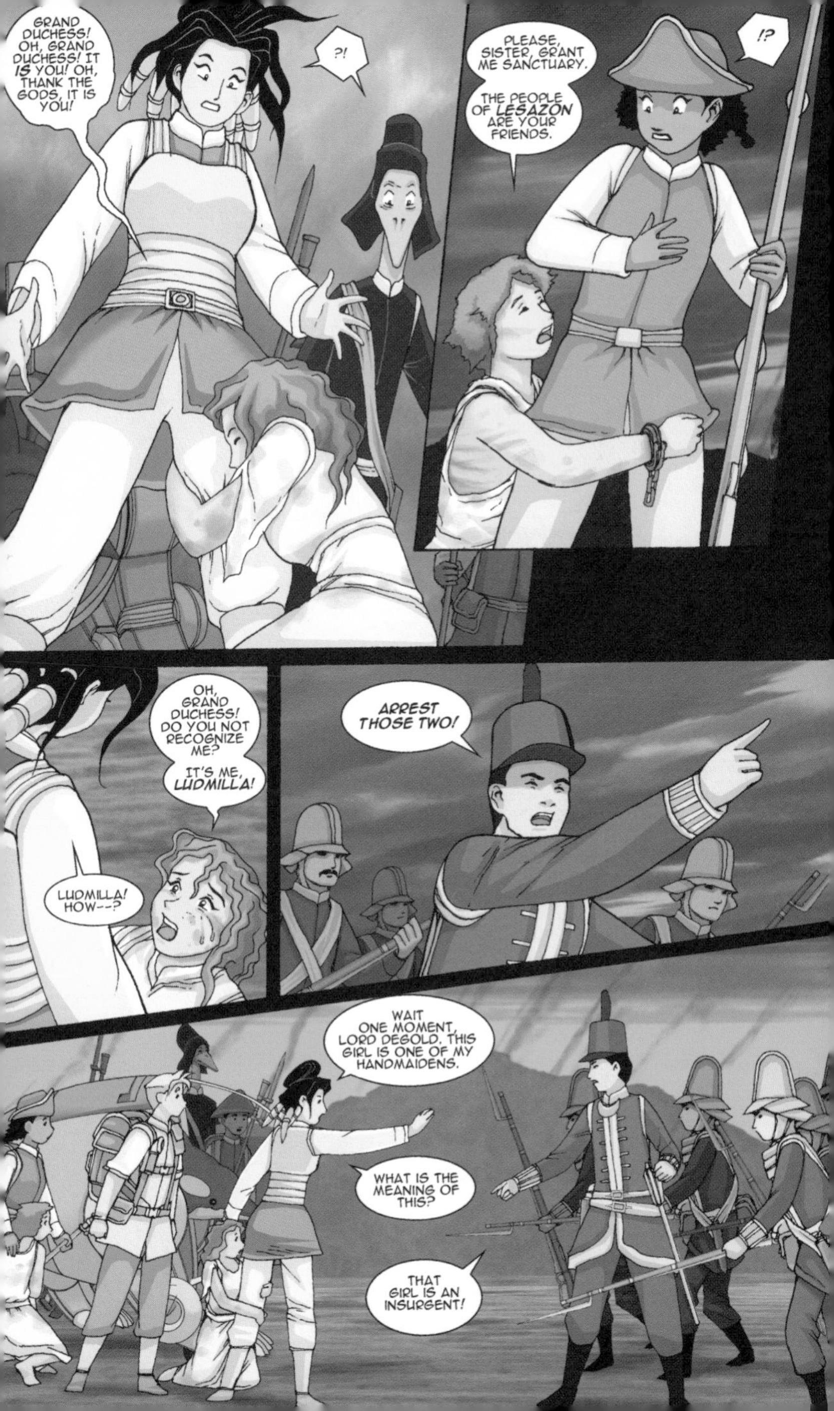
GRAND DUCHESS! OH, GRAND DUCHESS! IT IS YOU! OH, THANK THE GODS, IT IS YOU!
?!
PLEASE, SISTER, GRANT ME SANCTUARY.
THE PEOPLE OF LESAZON ARE YOUR FRIENDS.
!?
OH, GRAND DUCHESS! DO YOU NOT RECOGNIZE ME?
IT'S ME, LUDMILLA!
LUDMILLA! HOW--?
ARREST THOSE TWO!
WAIT ONE MOMENT, LORD DEGOLD. THIS GIRL IS ONE OF MY HANDMAIDENS.
WHAT IS THE MEANING OF THIS?
THAT GIRL IS AN INSURGENT!

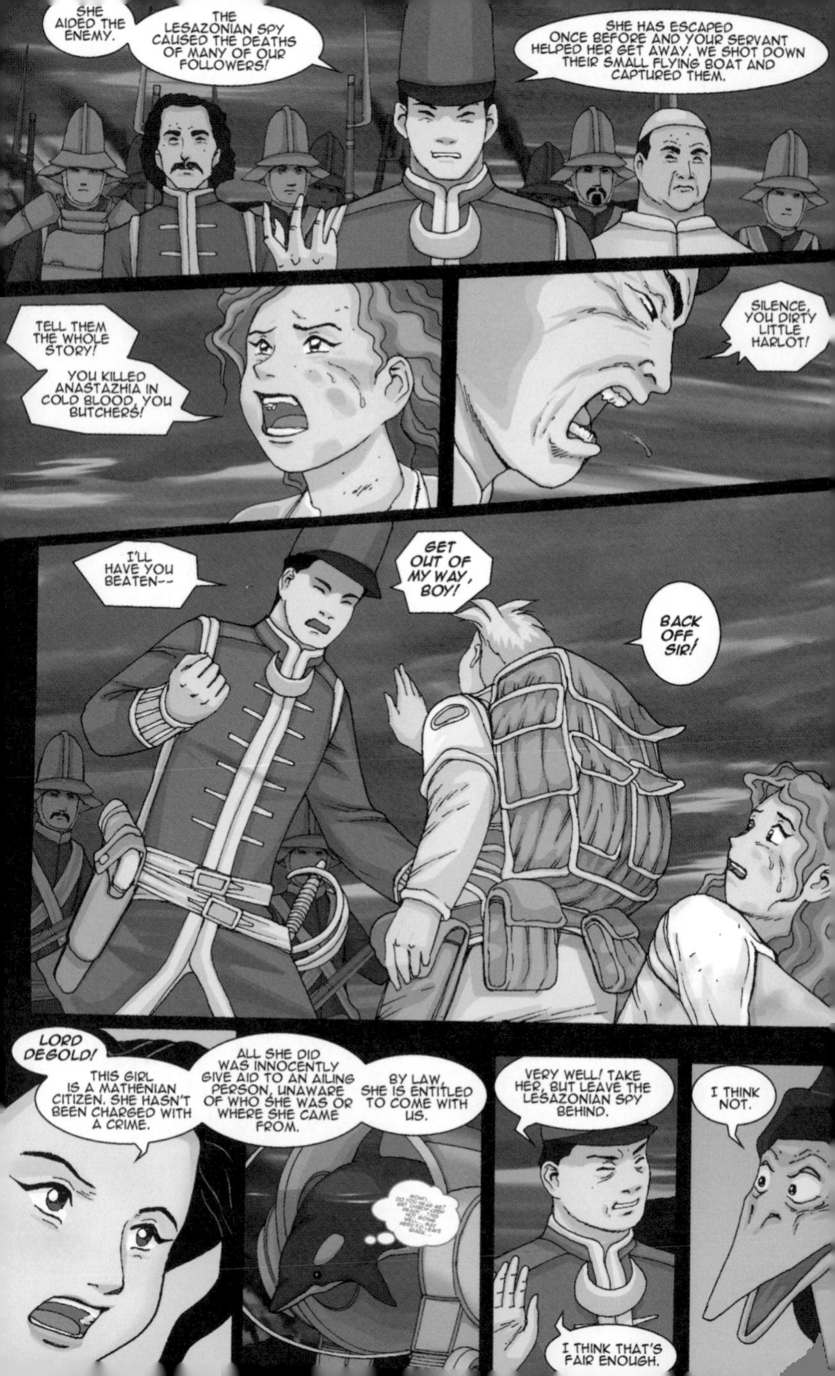

SHE AIDED THE ENEMY.
THE LESAZONIAN SPY CAUSED THE DEATHS OF MANY OF OUR FOLLOWERS!
SHE HAS ESCAPED ONCE BEFORE AND YOUR SERVANT HELPED HER GET AWAY. WE SHOT DOWN THEIR SMALL FLYING BOAT AND CAPTURED THEM.
TELL THEM THE WHOLE STORY!
YOU KILLED ANASTAZHIA IN COLD BLOOD, YOU BUTCHERS!
SILENCE, YOU DIRTY LITTLE HARLOT!
I'LL HAVE YOU BEATEN--
GET OUT OF MY WAY, BOY!
BACK OFF, SIR!
LORD DEGOLD!
THIS GIRL IS A MATHENIAN CITIZEN. SHE HASN'T BEEN CHARGED WITH A CRIME.
ALL SHE DID WAS INNOCENTLY GIVE AID TO AN AILING PERSON, UNAWARE OF WHO SHE WAS OR WHERE SHE CAME FROM.
BY LAW, SHE IS ENTITLED TO COME WITH US.
VERY WELL! TAKE HER, BUT LEAVE THE LESAZONIAN SPY BEHIND.
I THINK NOT.
I THINK THAT'S FAIR ENOUGH.

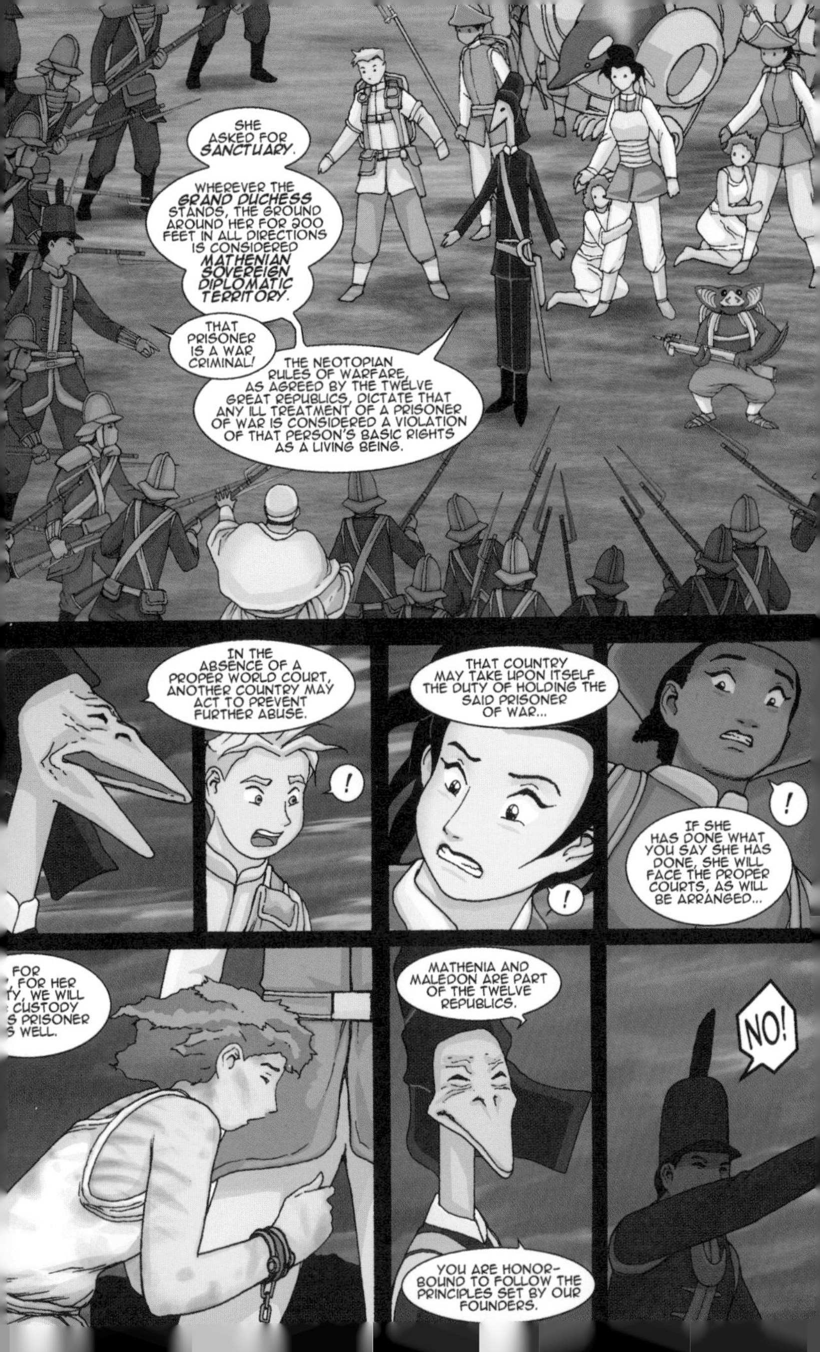
SHE ASKED FOR SANCTUARY.
WHEREVER THE GRAND DUCHESS STANDS, THE GROUND AROUND HER FOR 200 FEET IN ALL DIRECTIONS IS CONSIDERED MATHENIAN SOVEREIGN DIPLOMATIC TERRITORY.
THAT PRISONER IS A WAR CRIMINAL!
THE NEOTOPIAN RULES OF WARFARE, AS AGREED BY THE TWELVE GREAT REPUBLICS, DICTATE THAT ANY ILL TREATMENT OF A PRISONER OF WAR IS CONSIDERED A VIOLATION OF THAT PERSON'S BASIC RIGHTS AS A LIVING BEING.
IN THE ABSENCE OF A PROPER WORLD COURT, ANOTHER COUNTRY MAY ACT TO PREVENT FURTHER ABUSE.
!
THAT COUNTRY MAY TAKE UPON ITSELF THE DUTY OF HOLDING THE SAID PRISONER OF WAR...
!
!
IF SHE HAS DONE WHAT YOU SAY SHE HAS DONE, SHE WILL FACE THE PROPER COURTS, AS WILL BE ARRANGED...
FOR , FOR HER TY, WE WILL CUSTODY S PRISONER S WELL.
MATHENIA AND MALEDON ARE PART OF THE TWELVE REPUBLICS.
YOU ARE HONOR-BOUND TO FOLLOW THE PRINCIPLES SET BY OUR FOUNDERS.
NO!

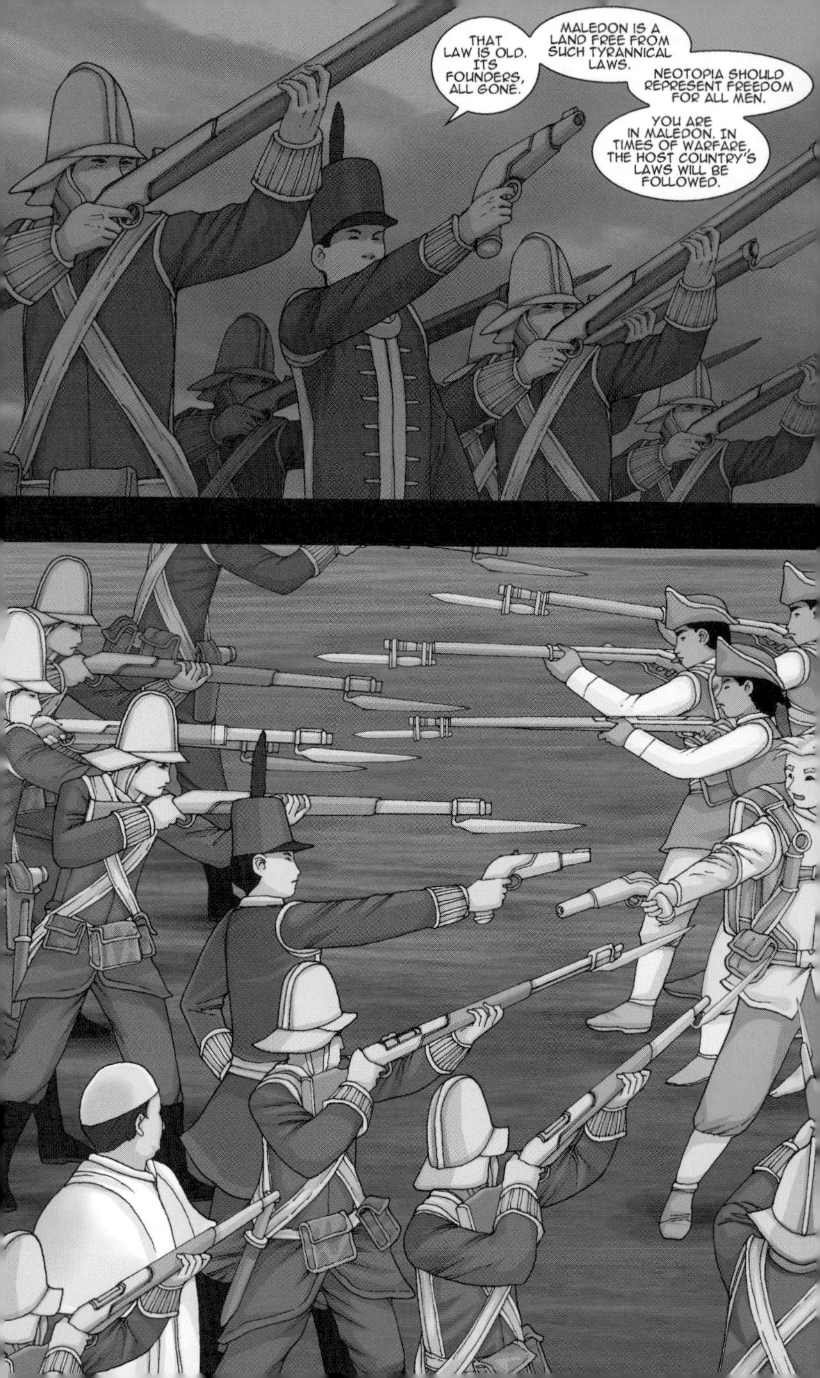
THAT LAW IS OLD. ITS FOUNDERS, ALL GONE.
MALEDON IS A LAND FREE FROM SUCH TYRANNICAL LAWS.
NEOTOPIA SHOULD REPRESENT FREEDOM FOR ALL MEN.
YOU ARE IN MALEDON. IN TIMES OF WARFARE, THE HOST COUNTRY'S LAWS WILL BE FOLLOWED.

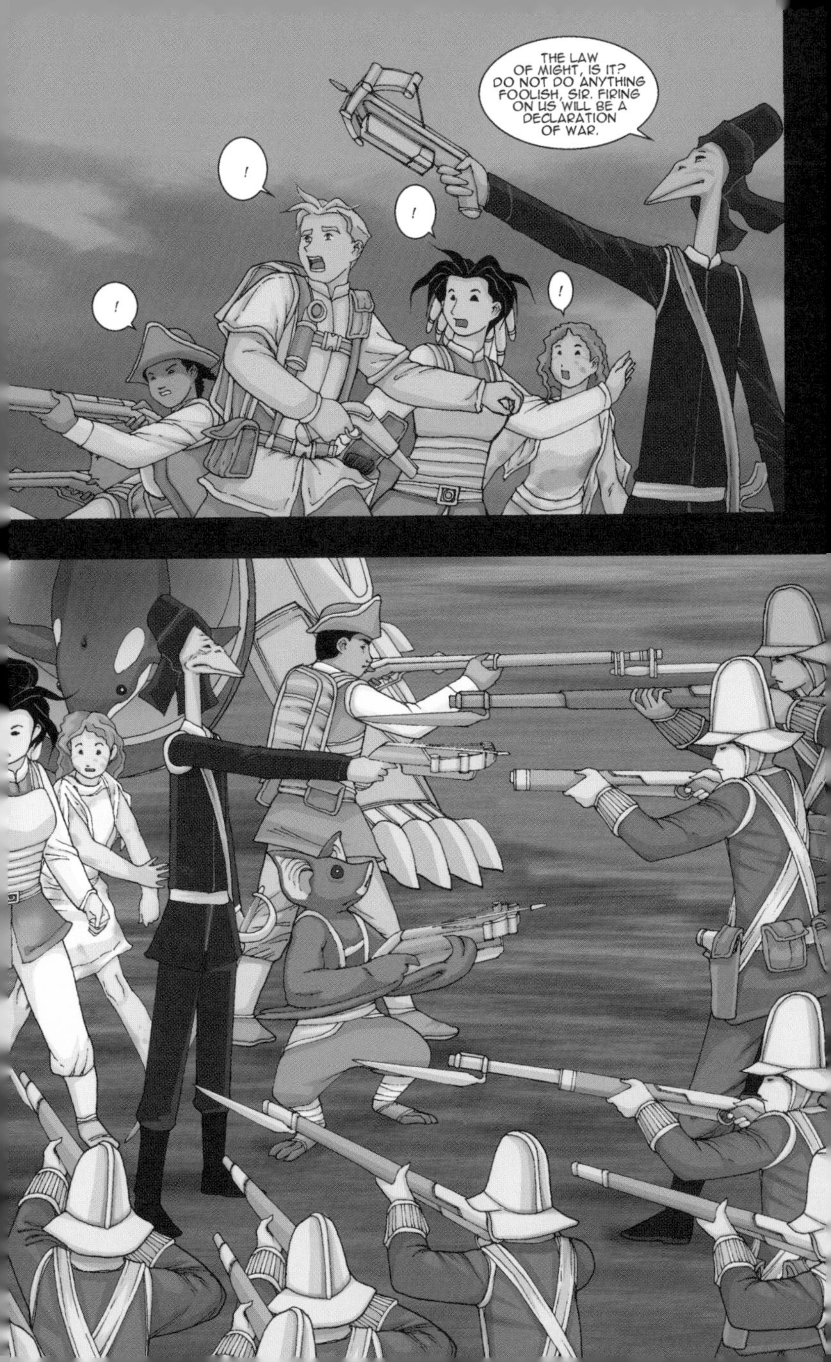
THE LAW OF MIGHT, IS IT? DO NOT DO ANYTHING FOOLISH, SIR. FIRING ON US WILL BE A DECLARATION OF WAR.
!
!
!
!

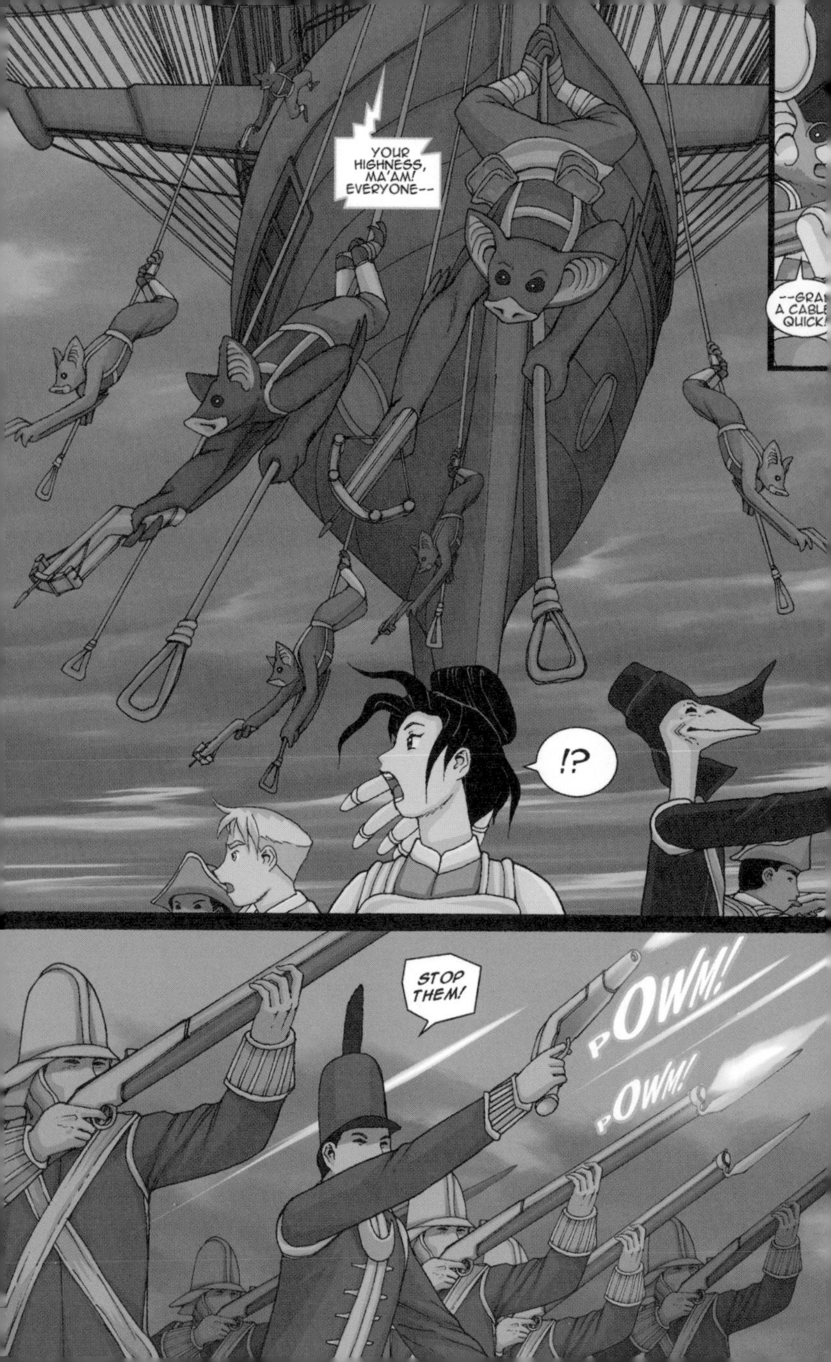
YOUR HIGHNESS, MA'AM! EVERYONE--
--GRA
A CABLE
QUICK!
!?
STOP THEM!
POWM!
POWM!

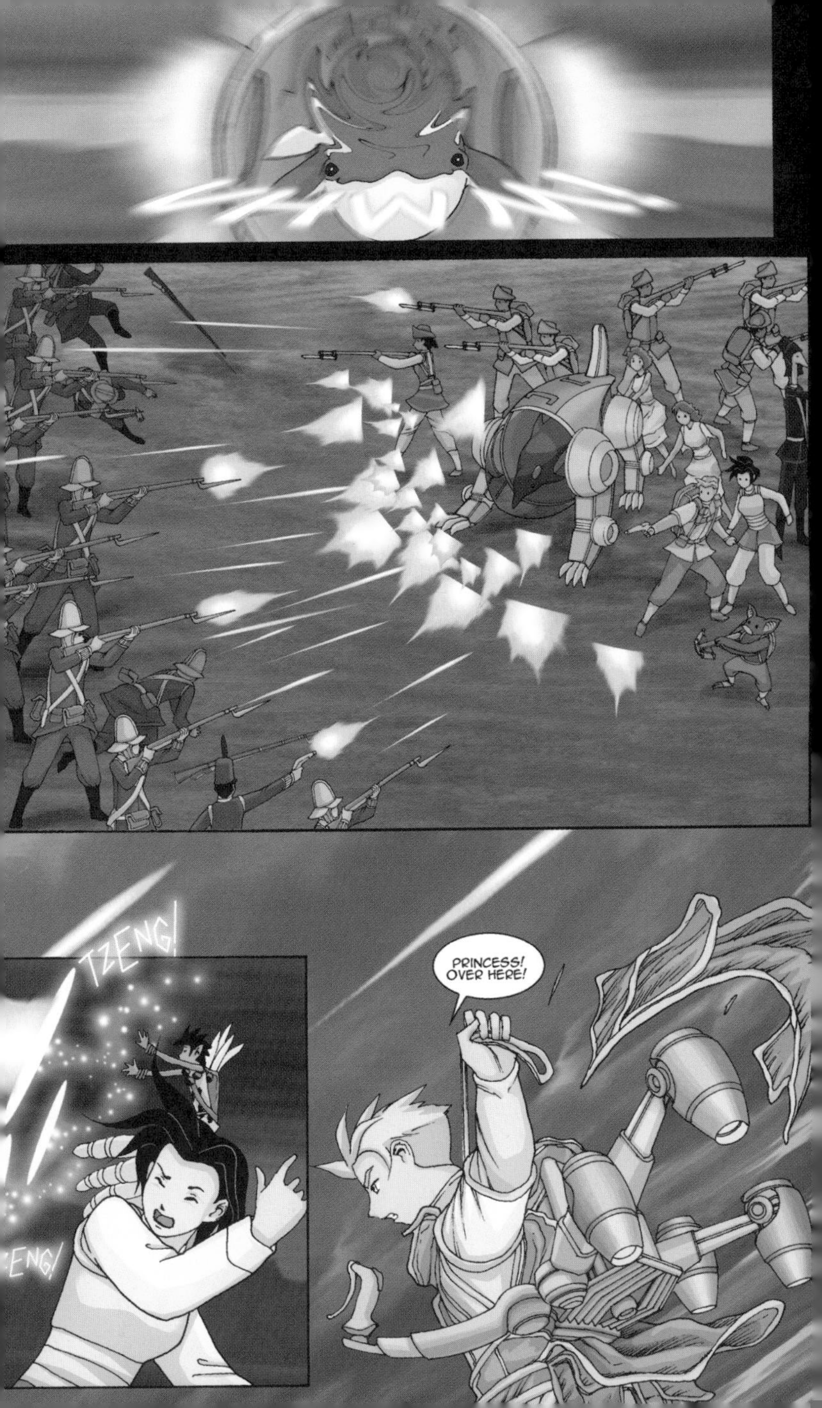
TZENG!
PRINCESS! OVER HERE!
ENG!

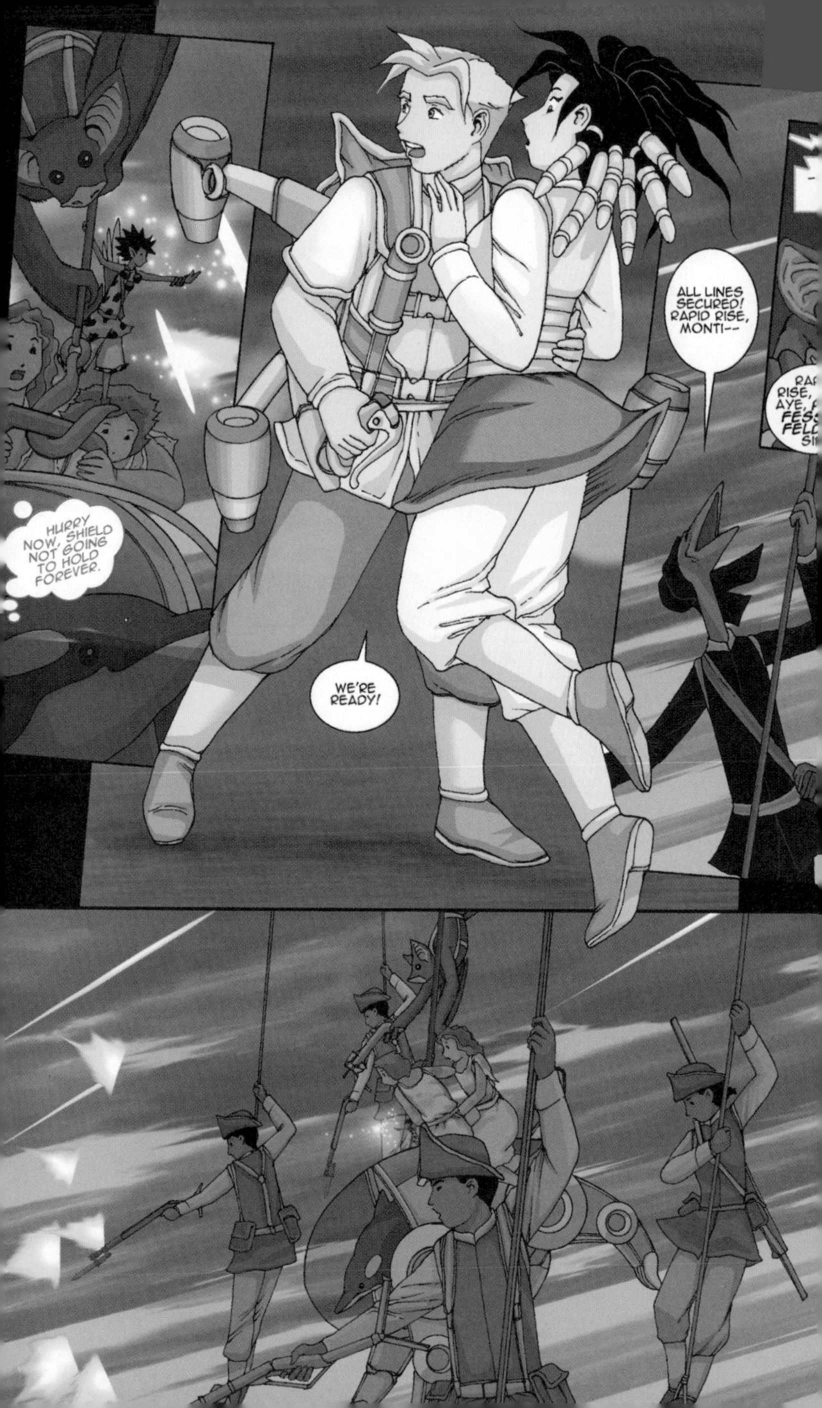
HURRY NOW, SHIELD NOT GOING TO HOLD FOREVER.
WE'RE READY!
ALL LINES SECURED! RAPID RISE, MONTI--

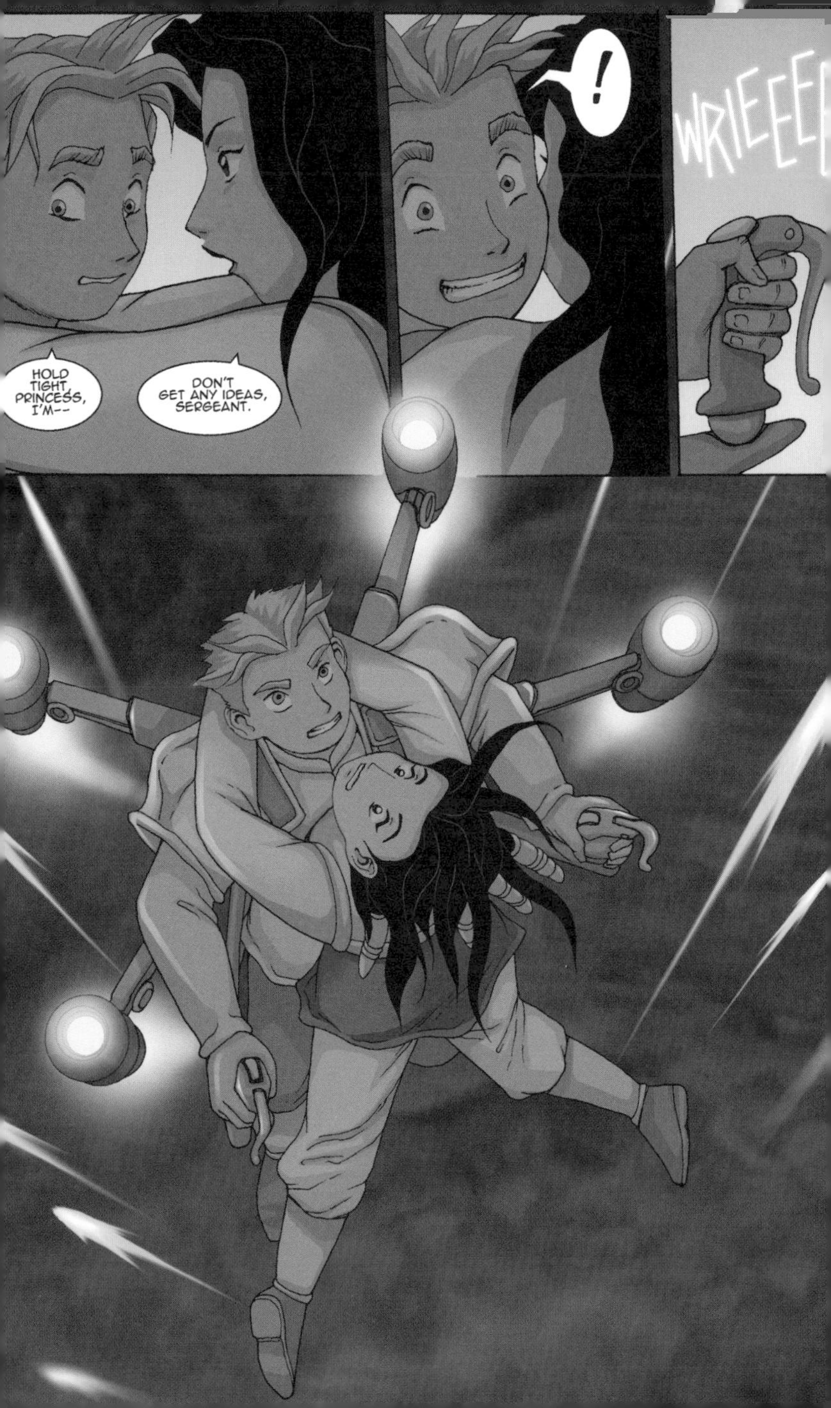
HOLD TIGHT, PRINCESS, I'M--
DON'T GET ANY IDEAS, SERGEANT.
!
WRIEEEE

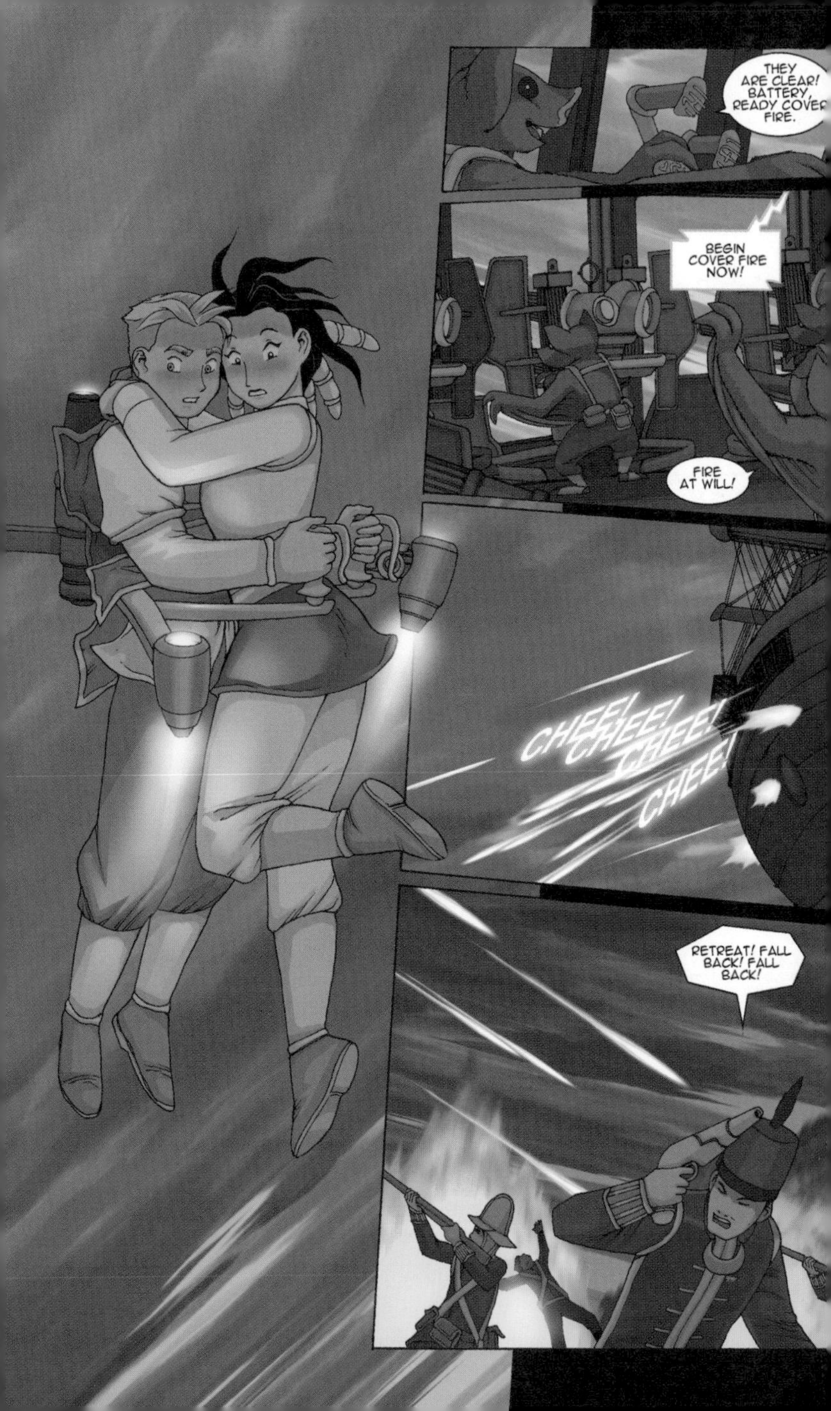
THEY ARE CLEAR! BATTERY, READY COVER FIRE.
BEGIN COVER FIRE NOW!
FIRE AT WILL!
CHEEE! CHEEE! CHEEE! CHEEE!
RETREAT! FALL BACK! FALL BACK!

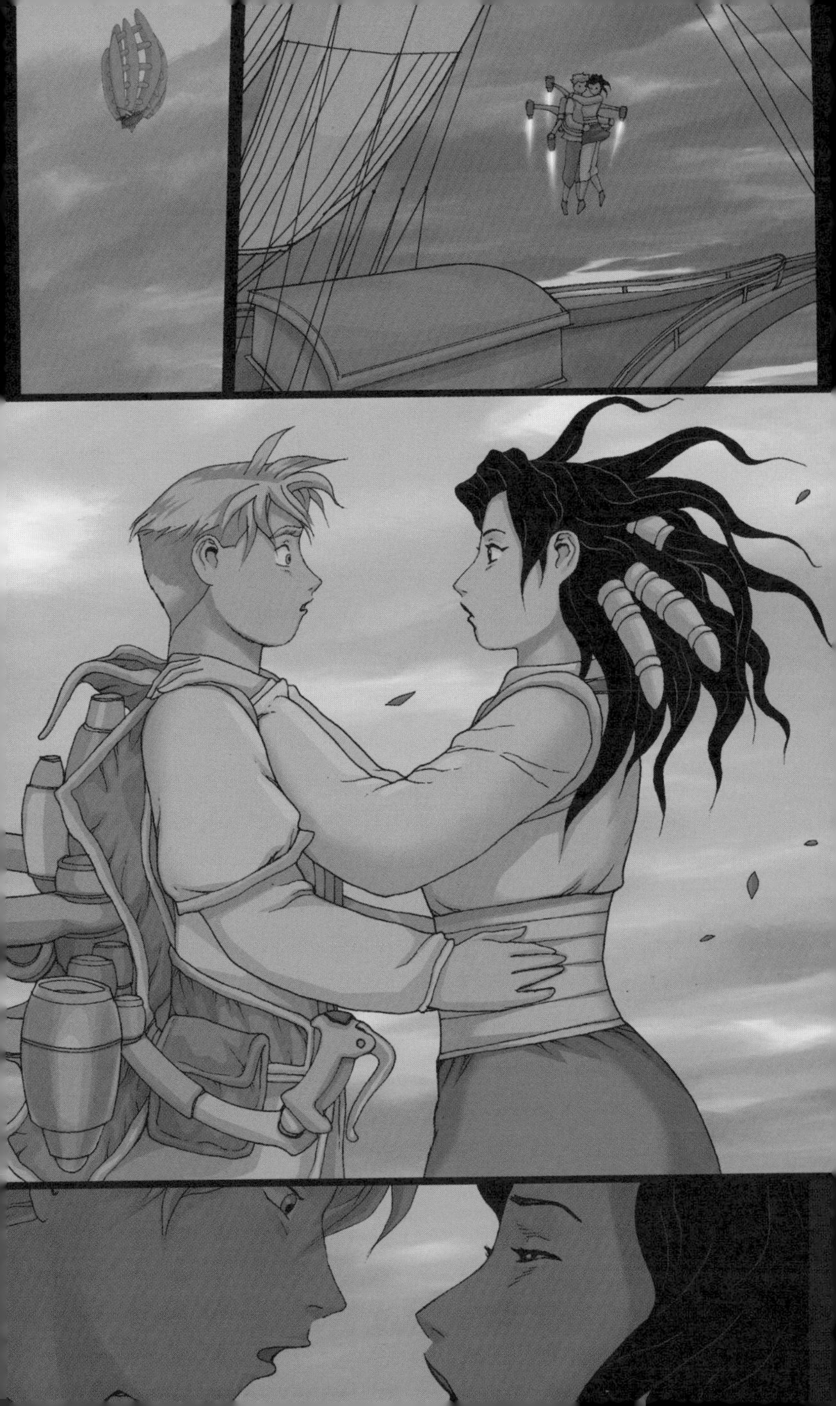

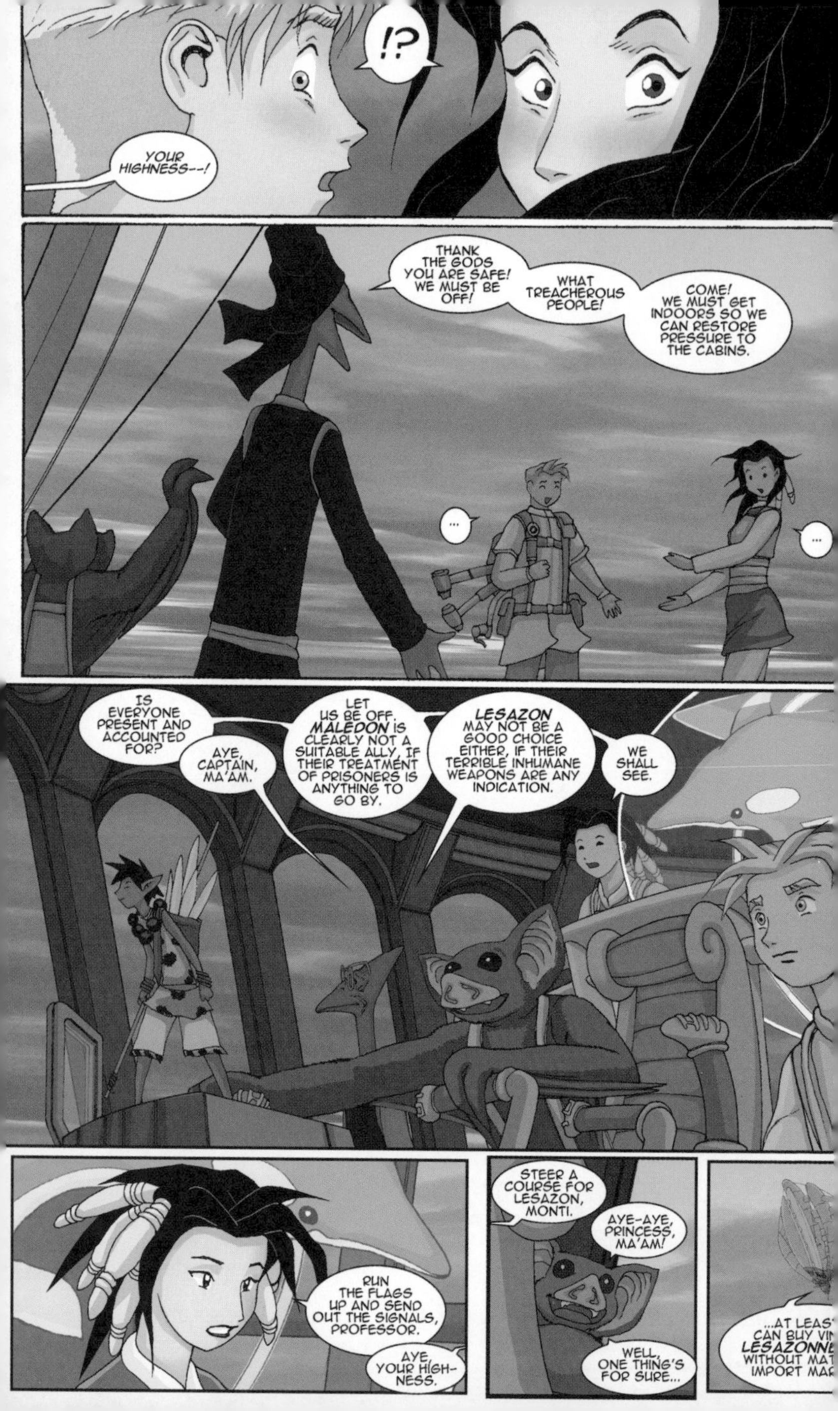
!?
YOUR HIGHNESS--!
THANK THE GODS YOU ARE SAFE! WE MUST BE OFF!
WHAT TREACHEROUS PEOPLE!
COME! WE MUST GET INDOORS SO WE CAN RESTORE PRESSURE TO THE CABINS.
...
...
IS EVERYONE PRESENT AND ACCOUNTED FOR?
AYE, CAPTAIN, MA'AM.
LET US BE OFF. MALEDON IS CLEARLY NOT A SUITABLE ALLY, IF THEIR TREATMENT OF PRISONERS IS ANYTHING TO GO BY.
LESAZON MAY NOT BE A GOOD CHOICE EITHER, IF THEIR TERRIBLE INHUMANE WEAPONS ARE ANY INDICATION.
WE SHALL SEE.
RUN THE FLAGS UP AND SEND OUT THE SIGNALS, PROFESSOR.
AYE, YOUR HIGHNESS.
STEER A COURSE FOR LESAZON, MONTI.
AYE-AYE, PRINCESS, MA'AM!
WELL, ONE THING'S FOR SURE...

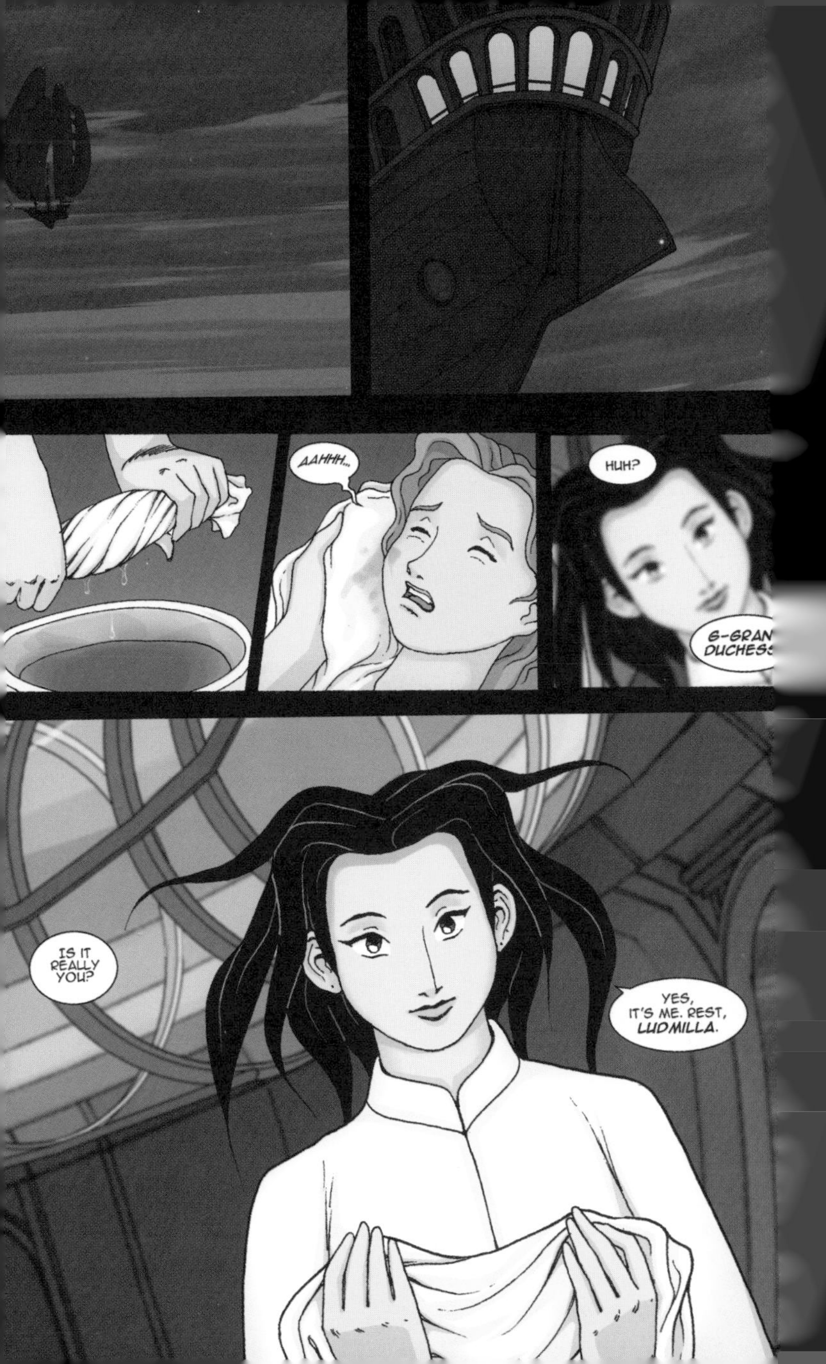
AAHHH...
HUH?
G-GRAND DUCHESS
IS IT REALLY YOU?
YES, IT'S ME. REST, LUDMILLA.

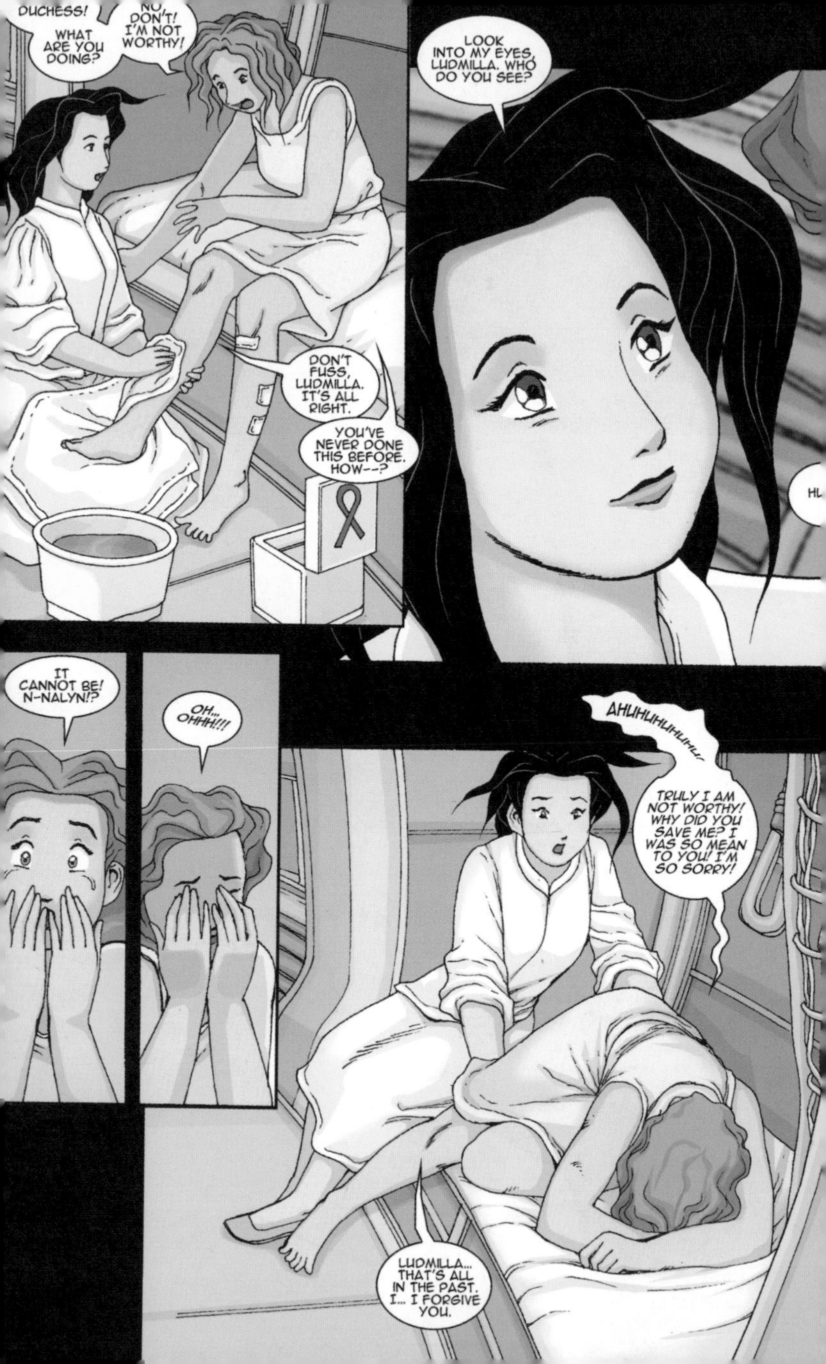
DUCHESS! WHAT ARE YOU DOING?
NO, DON'T! I'M NOT WORTHY!
DON'T FUSS, LUDMILLA. IT'S ALL RIGHT.
YOU'VE NEVER DONE THIS BEFORE. HOW--?
LOOK INTO MY EYES, LUDMILLA. WHO DO YOU SEE?
IT CANNOT BE! N-NALYN!?
OH... OHHH!!!
AHUHUHUHUHU!
TRULY I AM NOT WORTHY! WHY DID YOU SAVE ME? I WAS SO MEAN TO YOU! I'M SO SORRY!
LUDMILLA... THAT'S ALL IN THE PAST. I... I FORGIVE YOU.

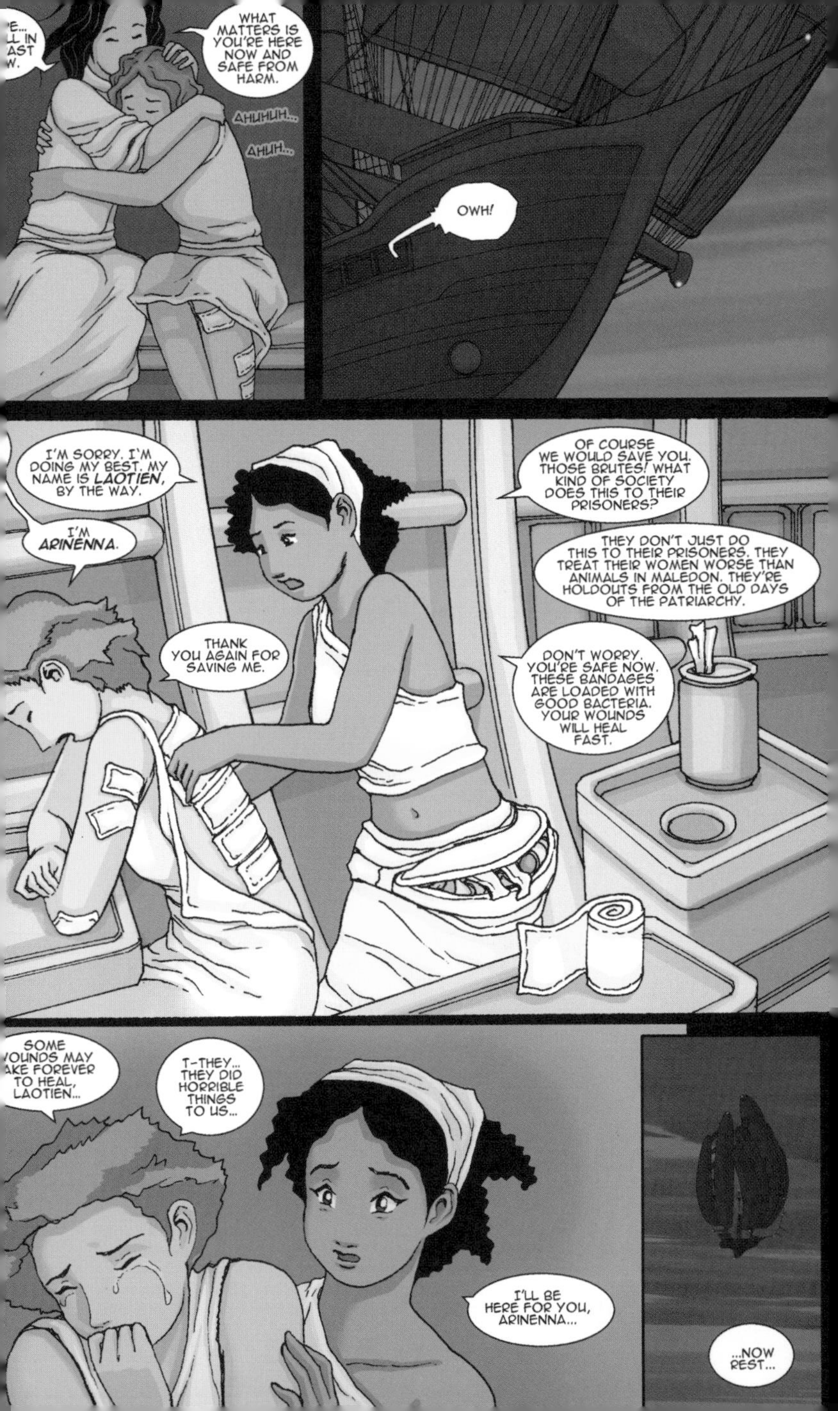

WHAT MATTERS IS YOU'RE HERE NOW AND SAFE FROM HARM.
AHUHUH...
AHUH...
OWH!
I'M SORRY. I'M DOING MY BEST. MY NAME IS *LAOTIEN,* BY THE WAY.
I'M *ARINENNA*.
OF COURSE WE WOULD SAVE YOU. THOSE BRUTES! WHAT KIND OF SOCIETY DOES THIS TO THEIR PRISONERS?
THEY DON'T JUST DO THIS TO THEIR PRISONERS. THEY TREAT THEIR WOMEN WORSE THAN ANIMALS IN MALEDON. THEY'RE HOLDOUTS FROM THE OLD DAYS OF THE PATRIARCHY.
THANK YOU AGAIN FOR SAVING ME.
DON'T WORRY. YOU'RE SAFE NOW. THESE BANDAGES ARE LOADED WITH GOOD BACTERIA. YOUR WOUNDS WILL HEAL FAST.
SOME OUNDS MAY AKE FOREVER TO HEAL, LAOTIEN...
T-THEY... THEY DID HORRIBLE THINGS TO US...
I'LL BE HERE FOR YOU, ARINENNA...
...NOW REST...

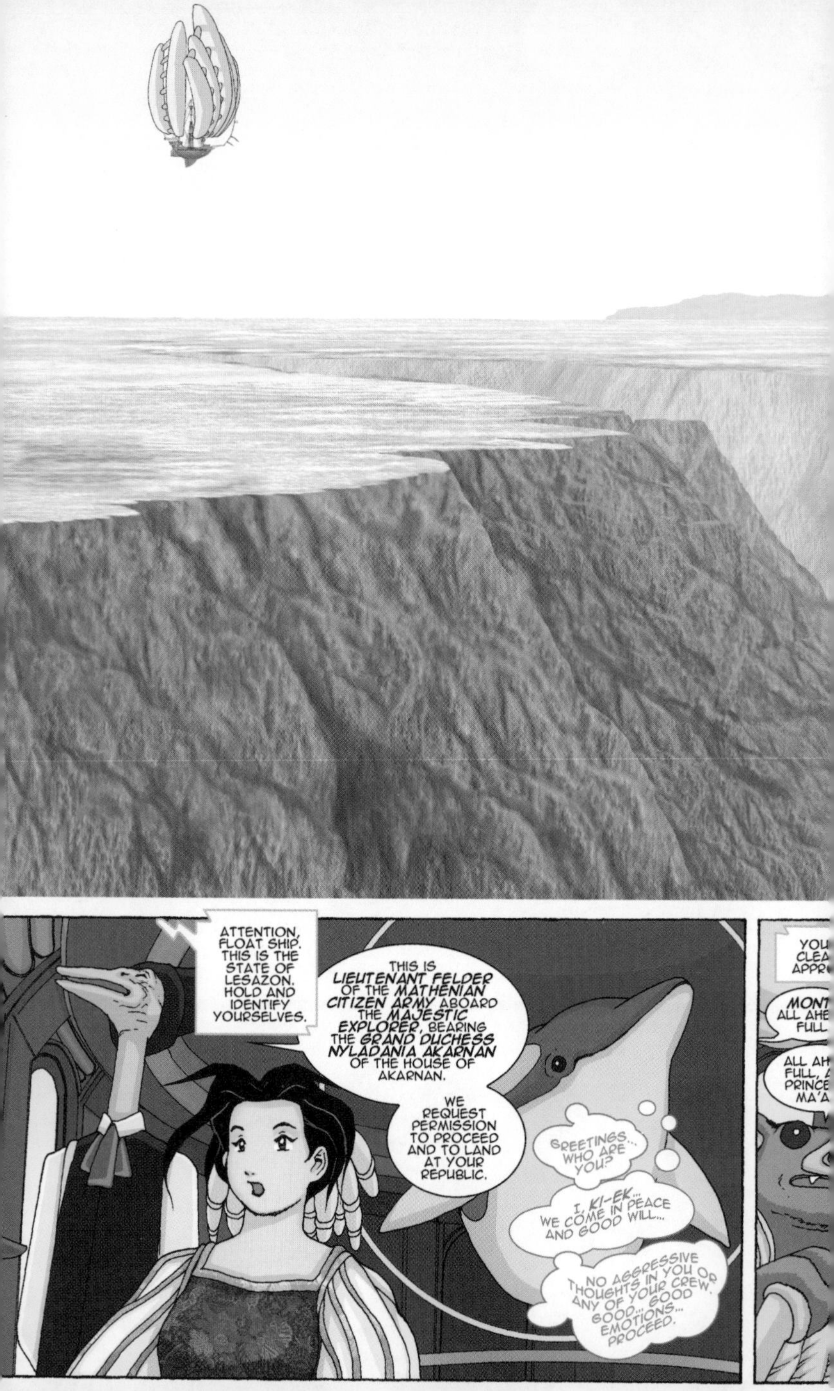

ATTENTION, FLOAT SHIP. THIS IS THE STATE OF LESAZON. HOLD AND IDENTIFY YOURSELVES.
THIS IS LIEUTENANT FELDER OF THE MATHENIAN CITIZEN ARMY ABOARD THE MAJESTIC EXPLORER, BEARING THE GRAND DUCHESS NYLADANIA AKARNAN OF THE HOUSE OF AKARNAN.
WE REQUEST PERMISSION TO PROCEED AND TO LAND AT YOUR REPUBLIC.
GREETINGS... WHO ARE YOU?
I, KI-EK... WE COME IN PEACE AND GOOD WILL...
NO AGGRESSIVE THOUGHTS IN YOU OR ANY OF YOUR CREW. GOOD... GOOD EMOTIONS... PROCEED.

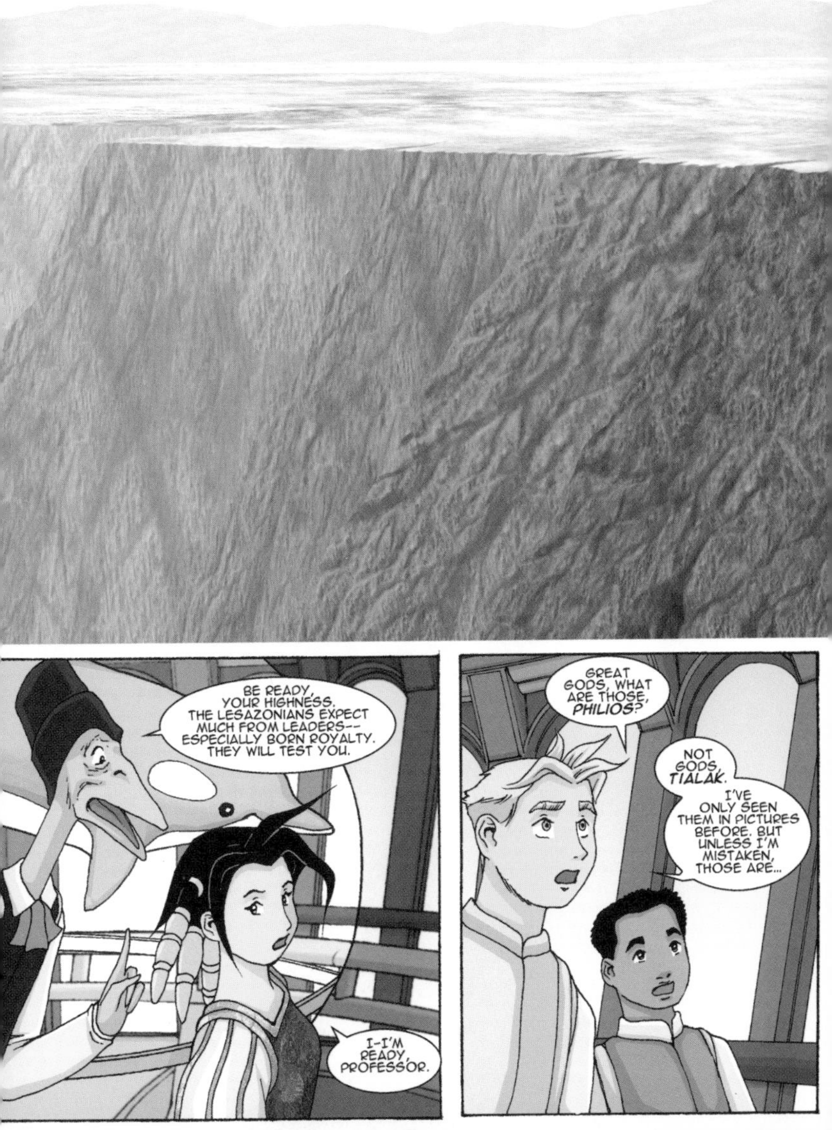
BE READY, YOUR HIGHNESS. THE LESAZONIANS EXPECT MUCH FROM LEADERS-- ESPECIALLY BORN ROYALTY. THEY WILL TEST YOU.
I-I'M READY, PROFESSOR.
GREAT GODS, WHAT ARE THOSE, PHILIOS?
NOT GODS, TIALAK.
I'VE ONLY SEEN THEM IN PICTURES BEFORE. BUT UNLESS I'M MISTAKEN, THOSE ARE...

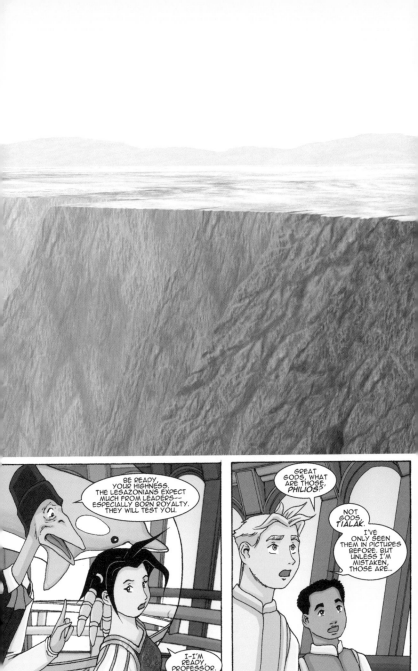

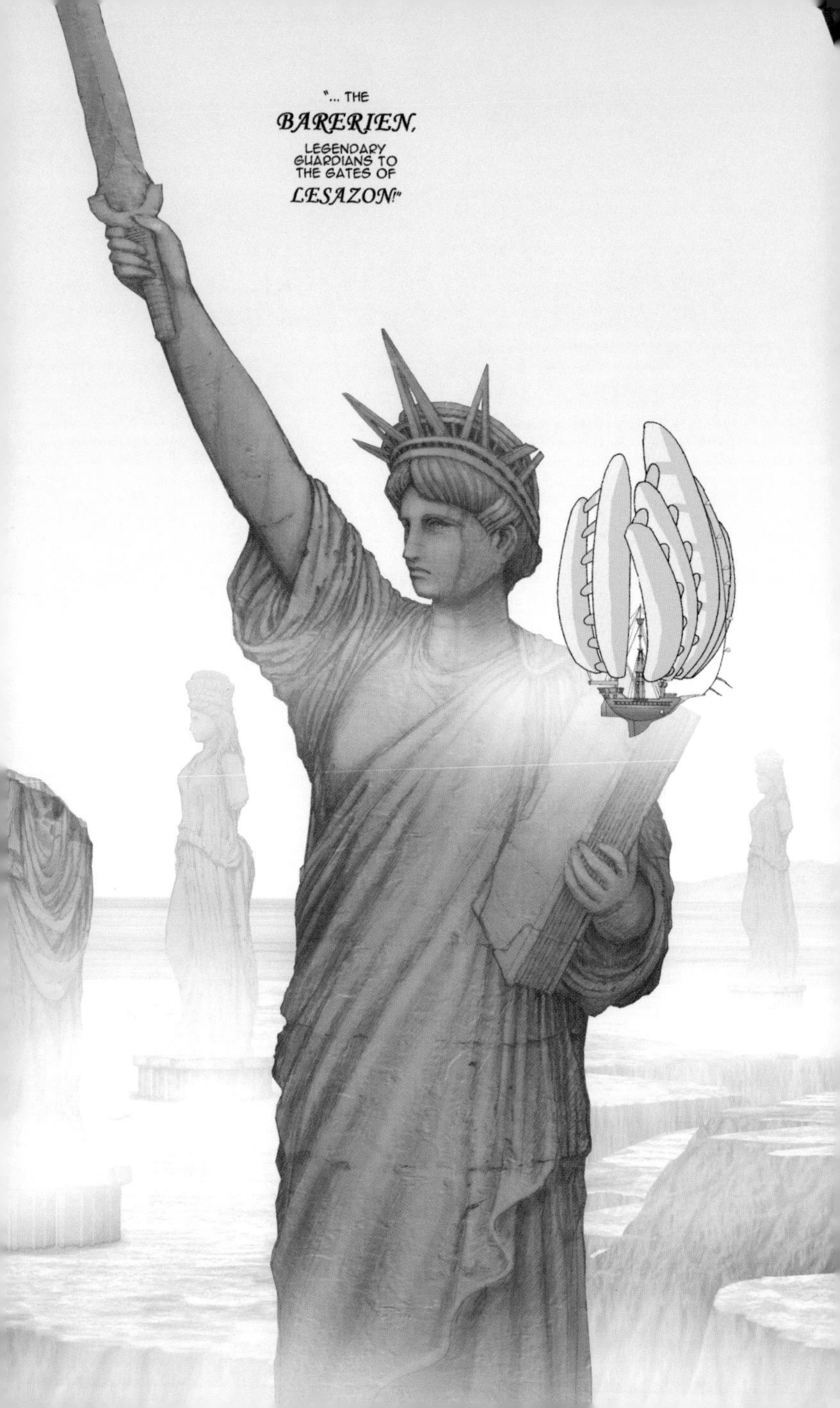
"... THE
BARERIEN,
LEGENDARY GUARDIANS TO THE GATES OF
LESAZON!"

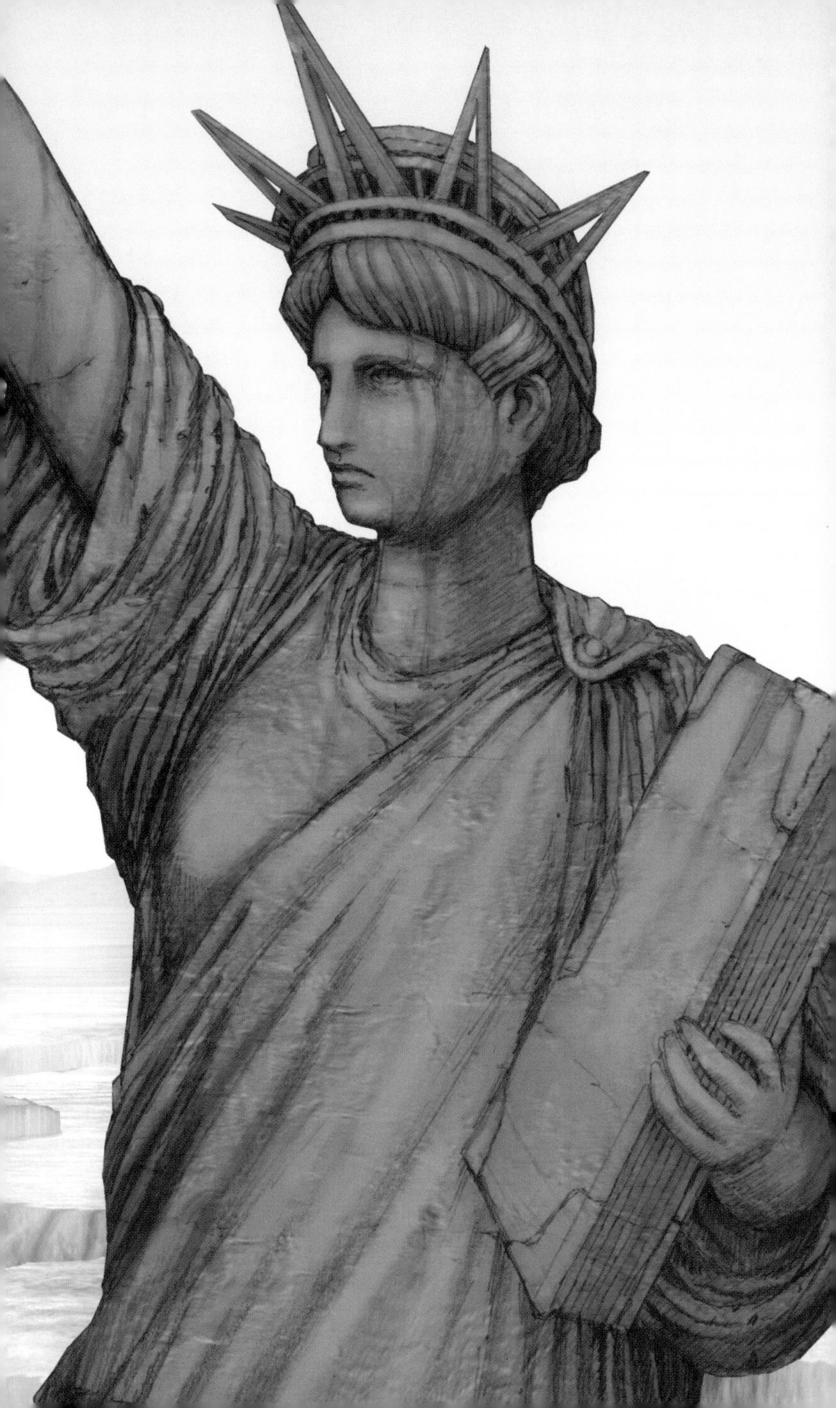

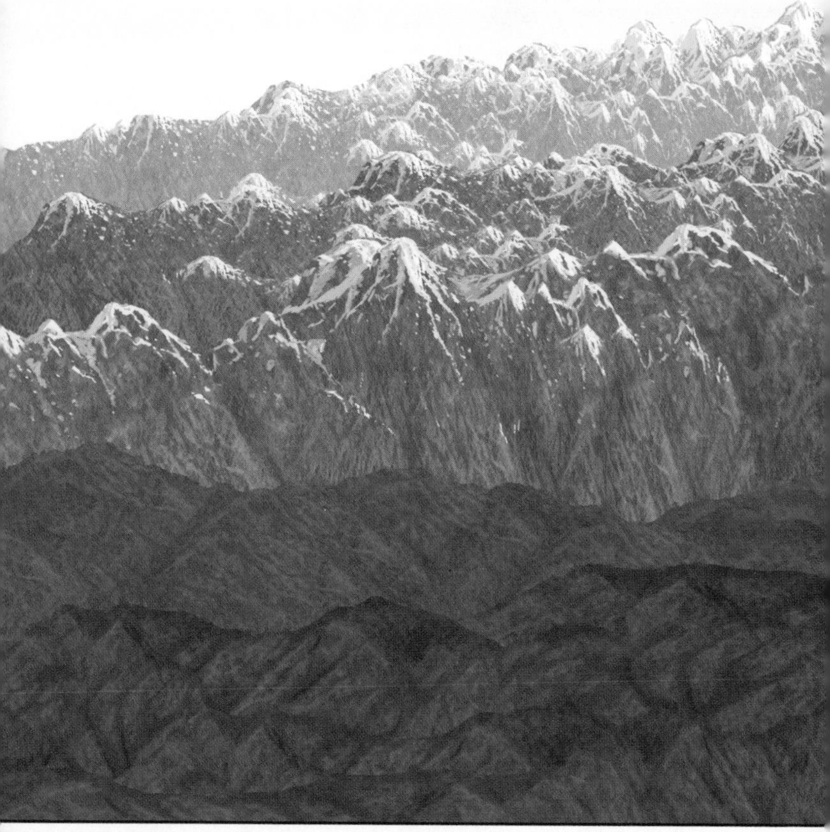

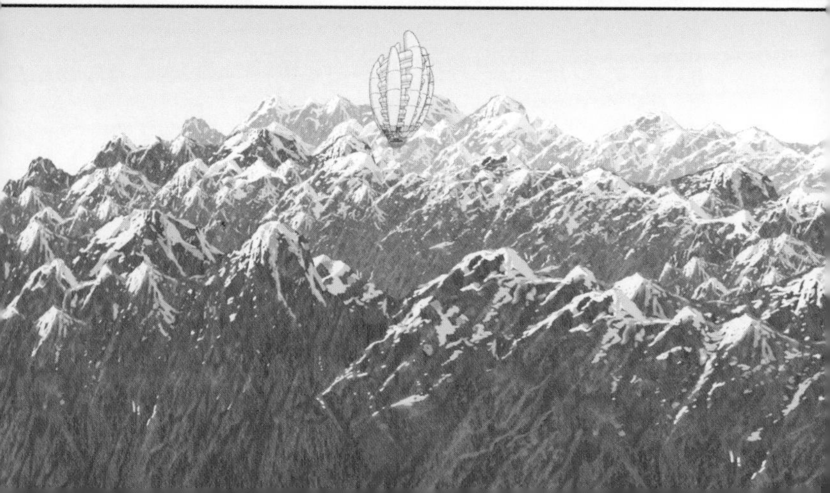

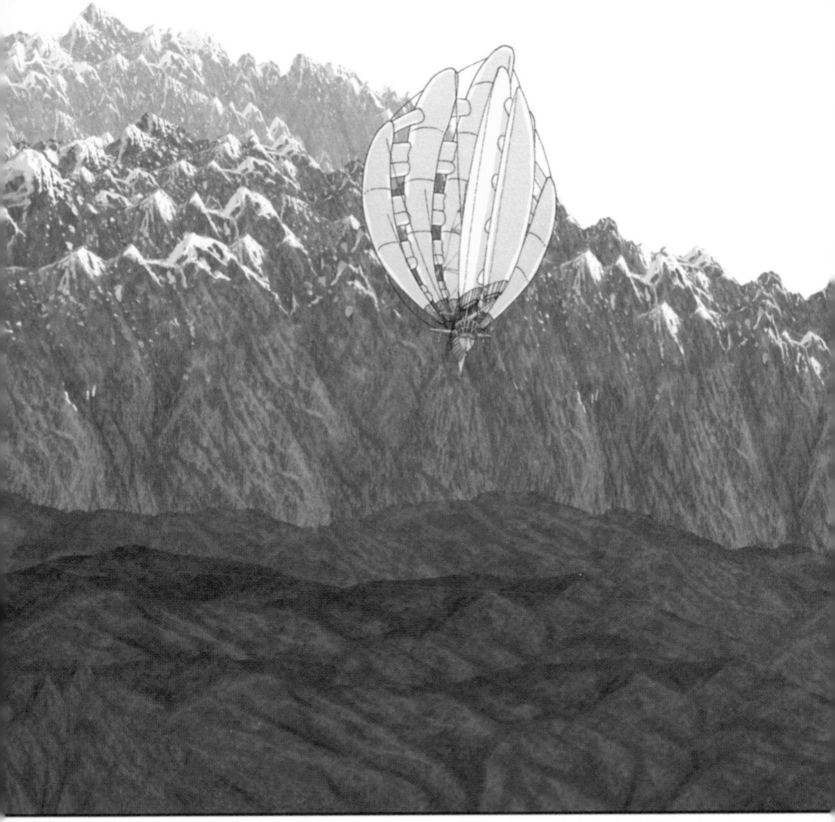

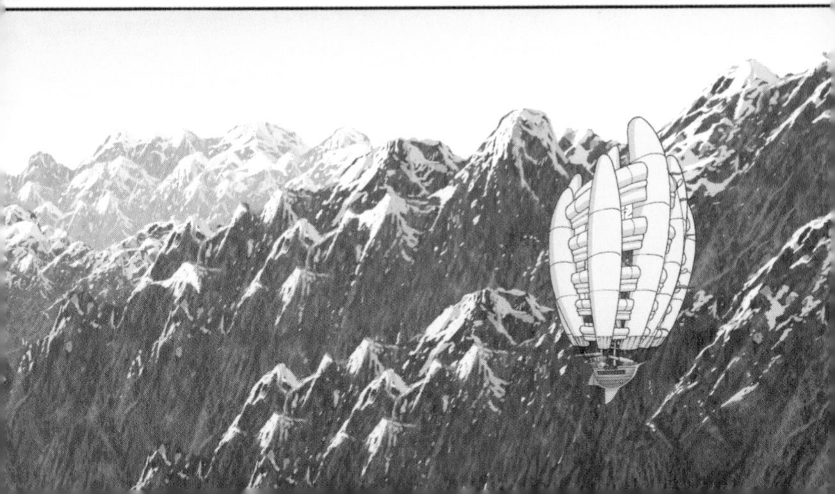

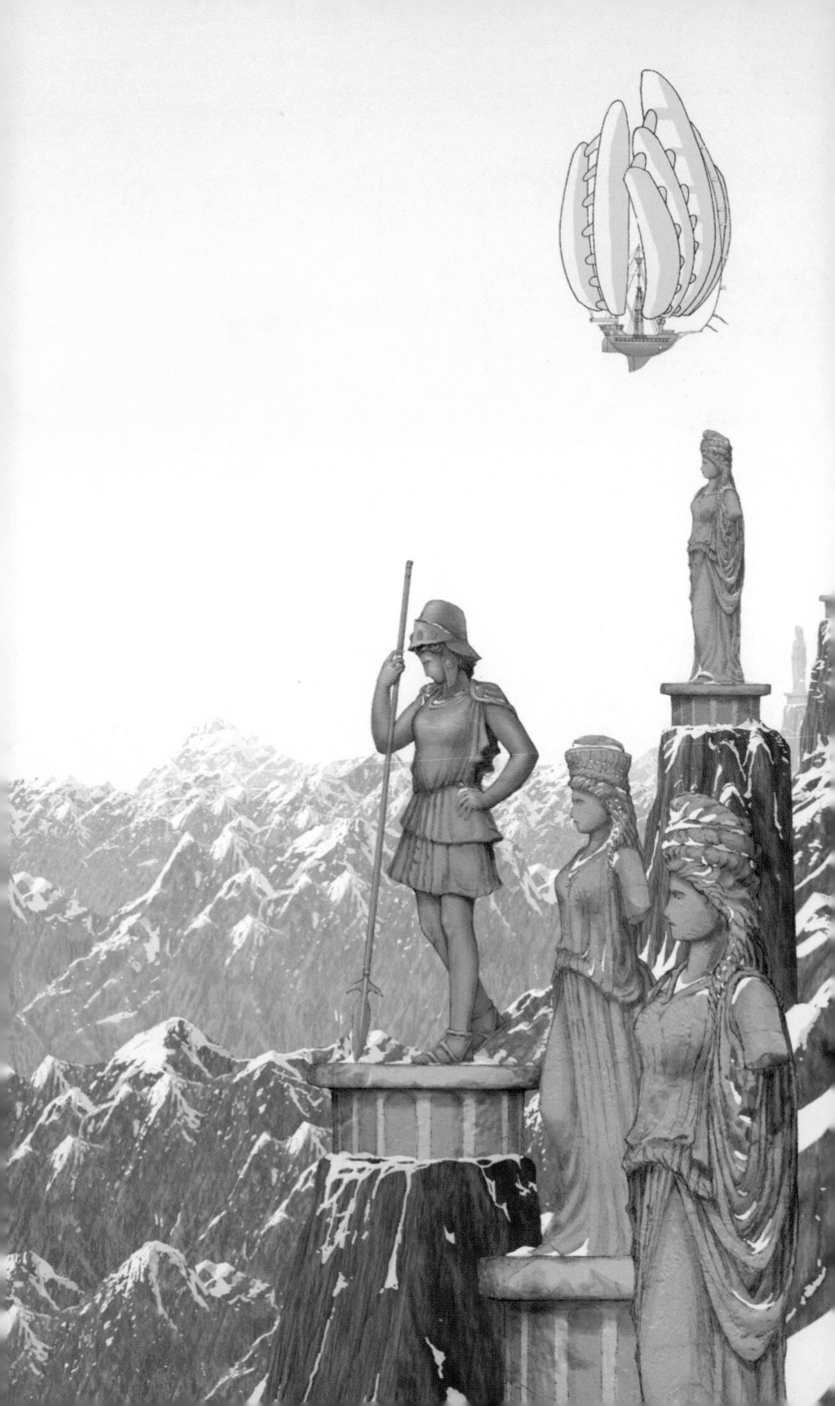

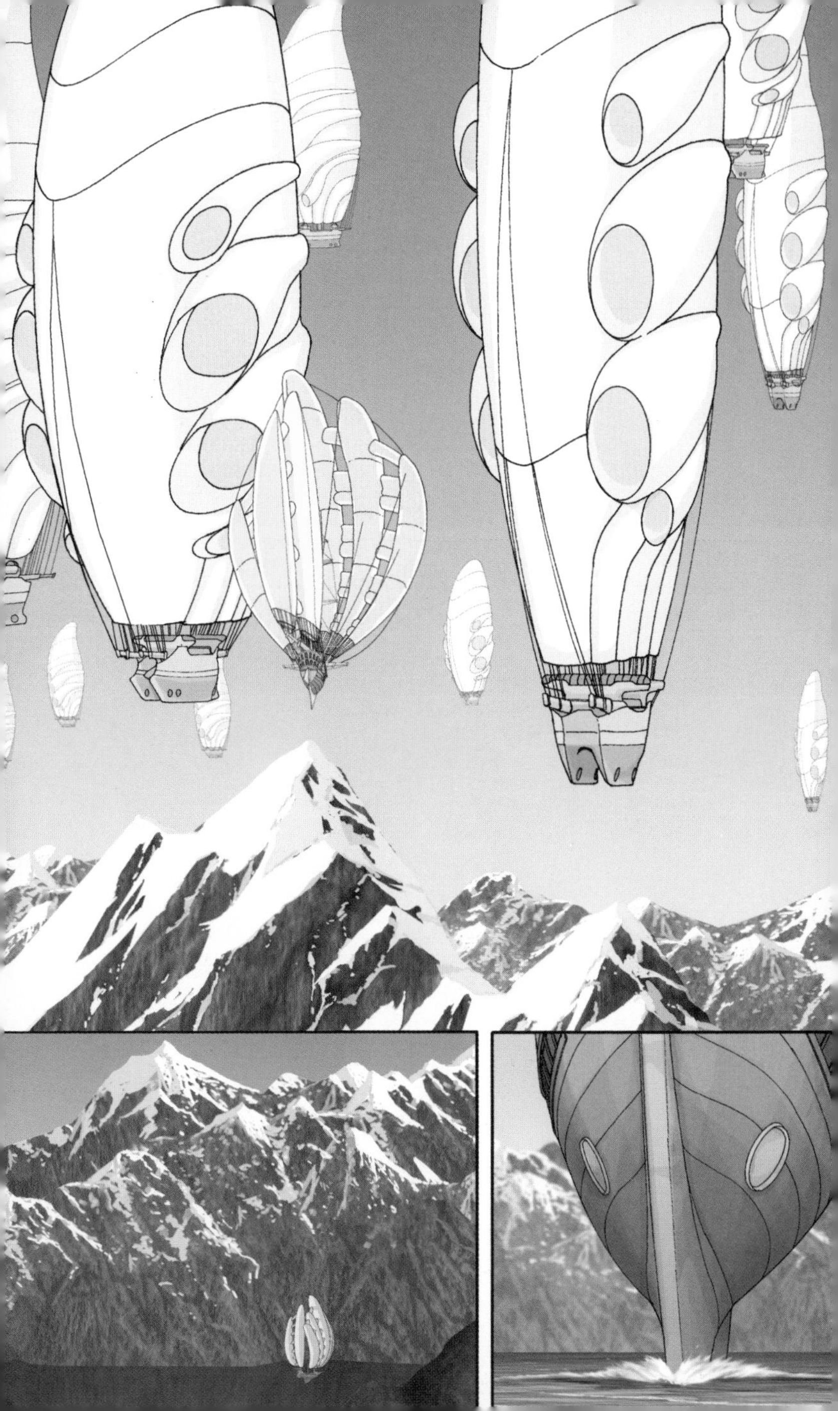

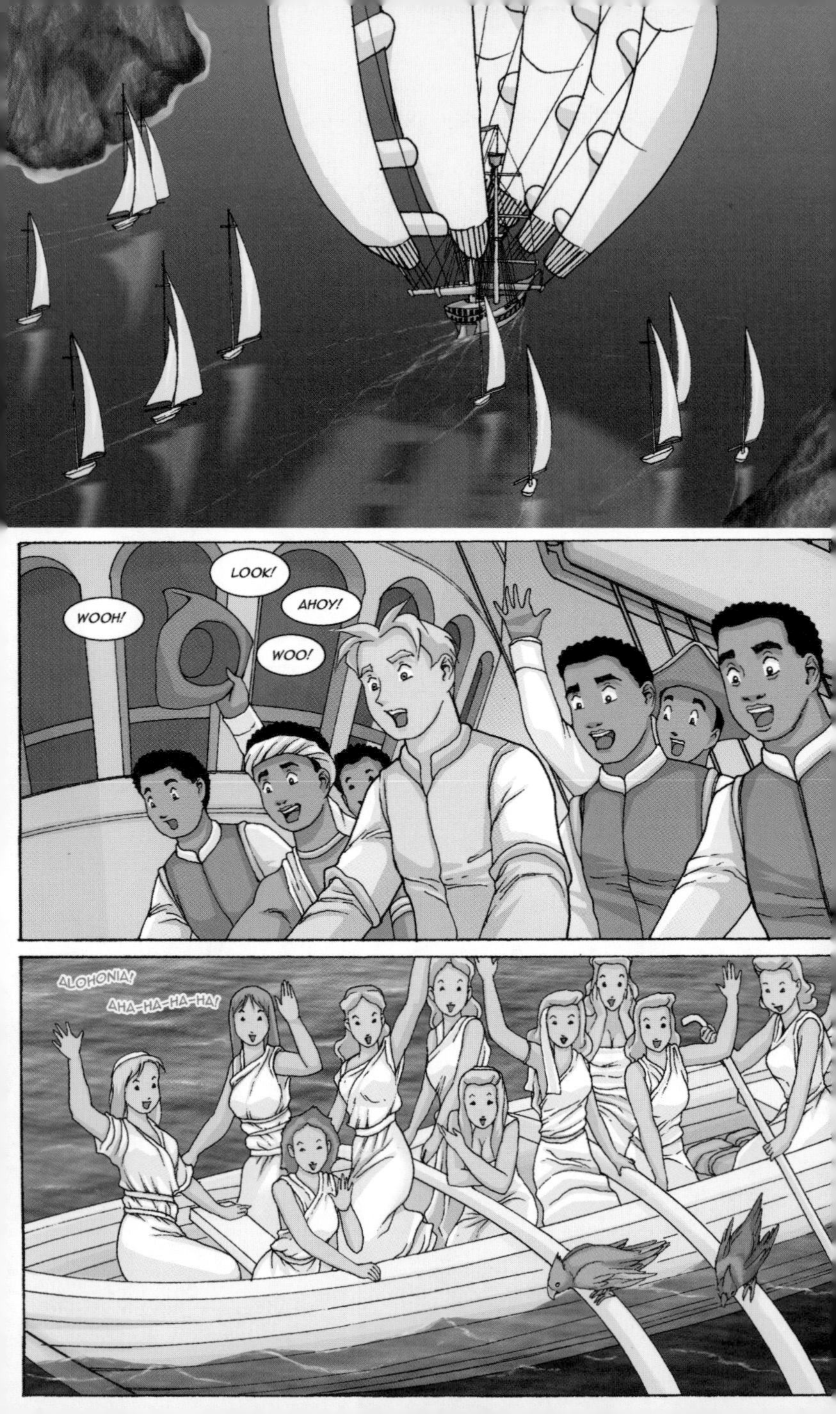
WOOH!
LOOK!
AHOY!
WOO!
ALOHONIA!
AHA-HA-HA-HA!

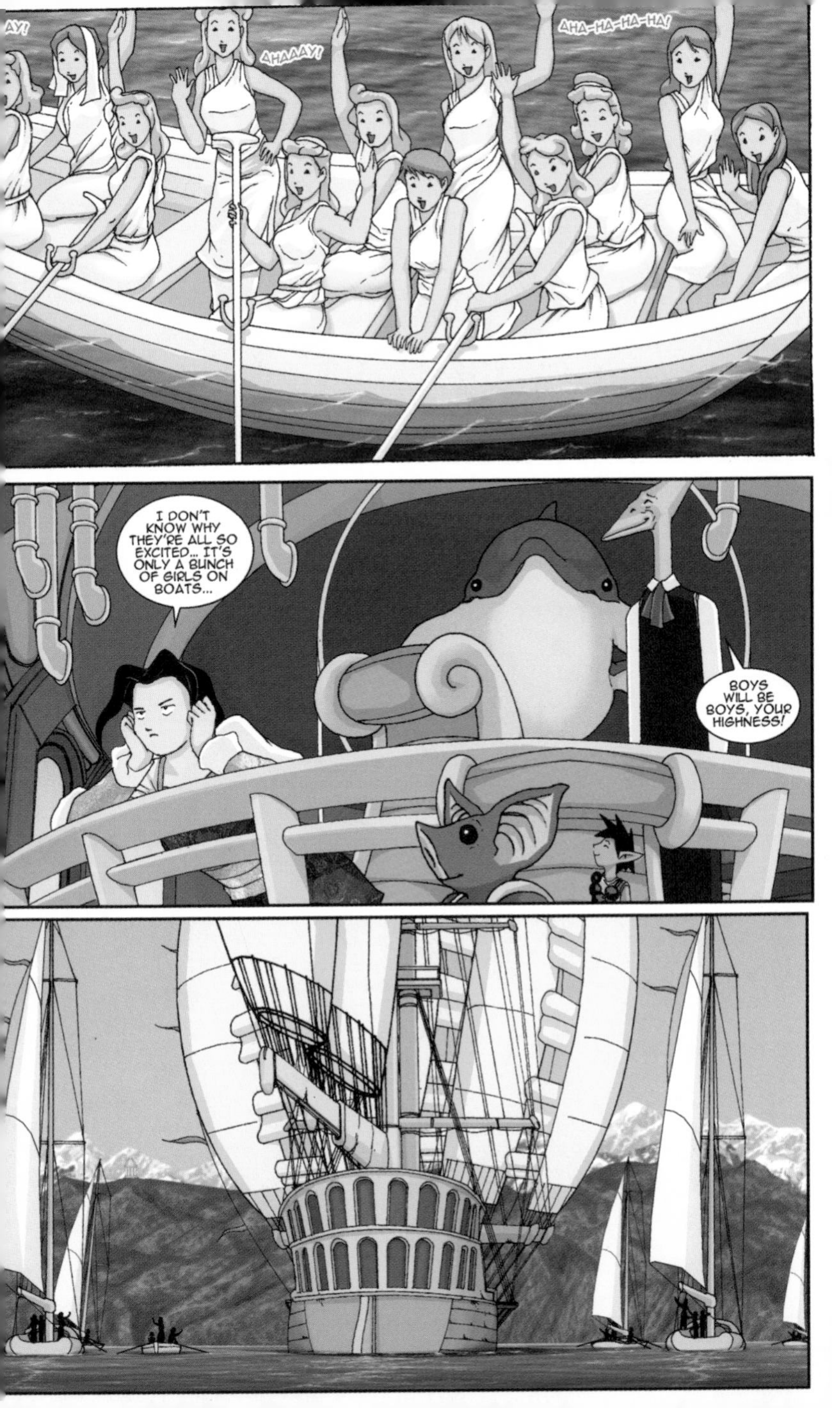
AY!
AHAAAY!
AHA-HA-HA-HA!
I DON'T KNOW WHY THEY'RE ALL SO EXCITED... IT'S ONLY A BUNCH OF GIRLS ON BOATS...
BOYS WILL BE BOYS, YOUR HIGHNESS!

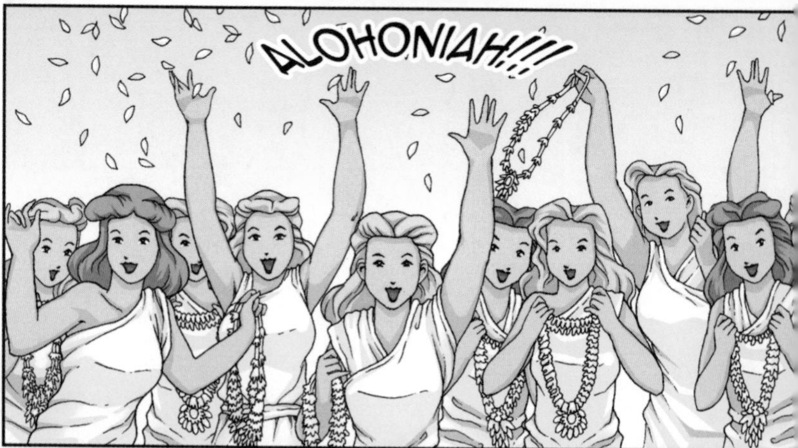
ALOHONIAH!!!!

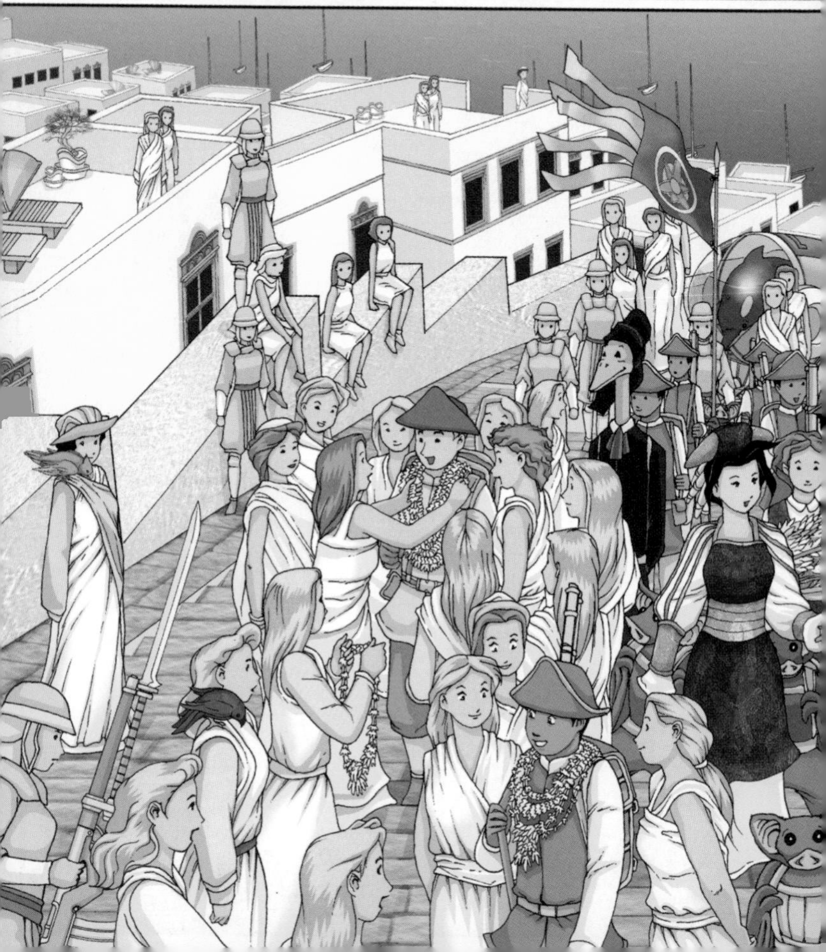

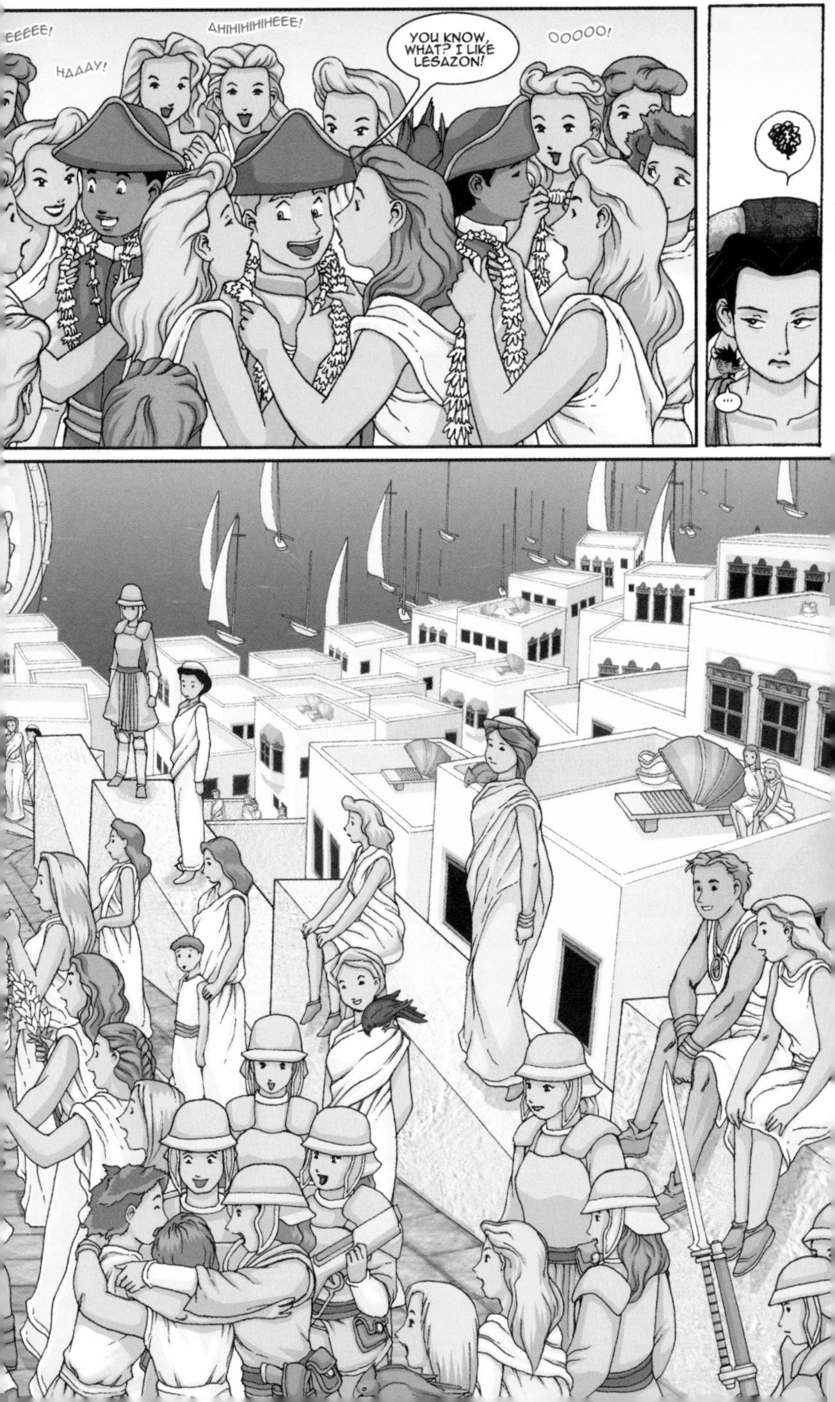
EEEEE!
HAAAY!
AHIHIHIHIHEEE!
YOU KNOW, WHAT? I LIKE LESAZON!
OOOOO!
...

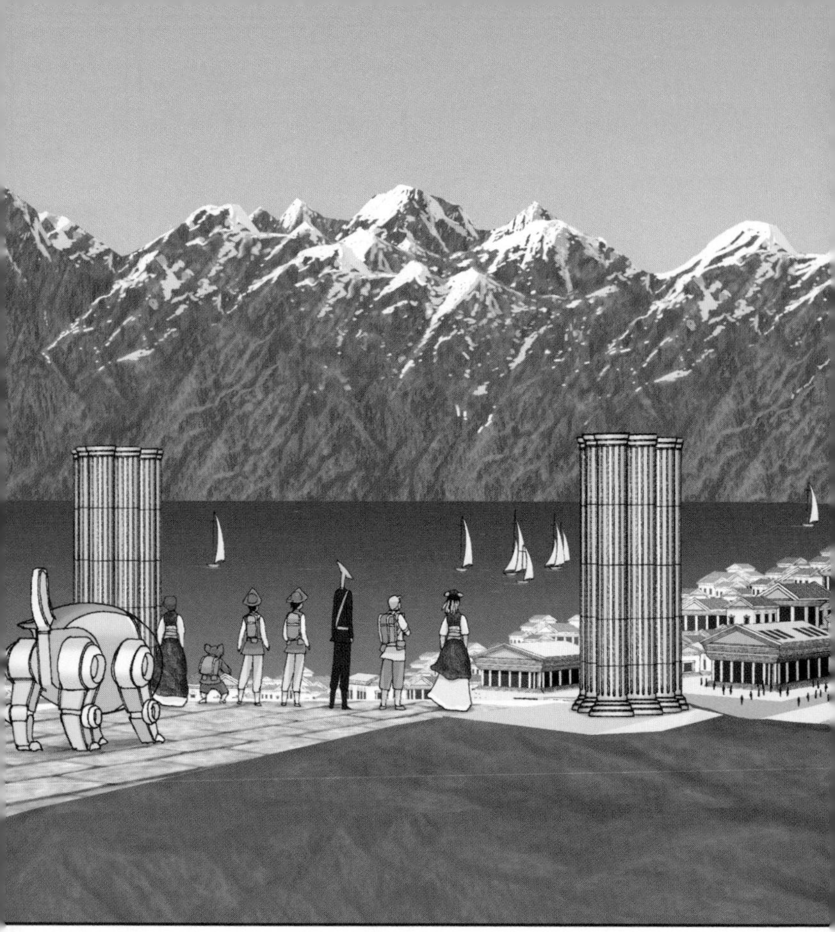

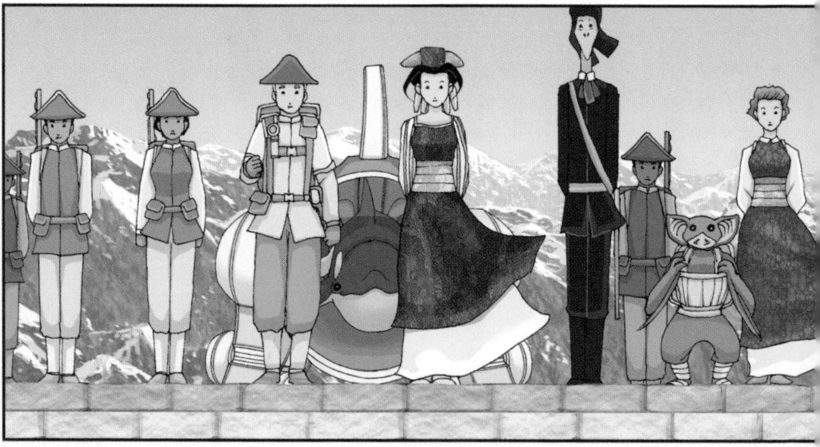

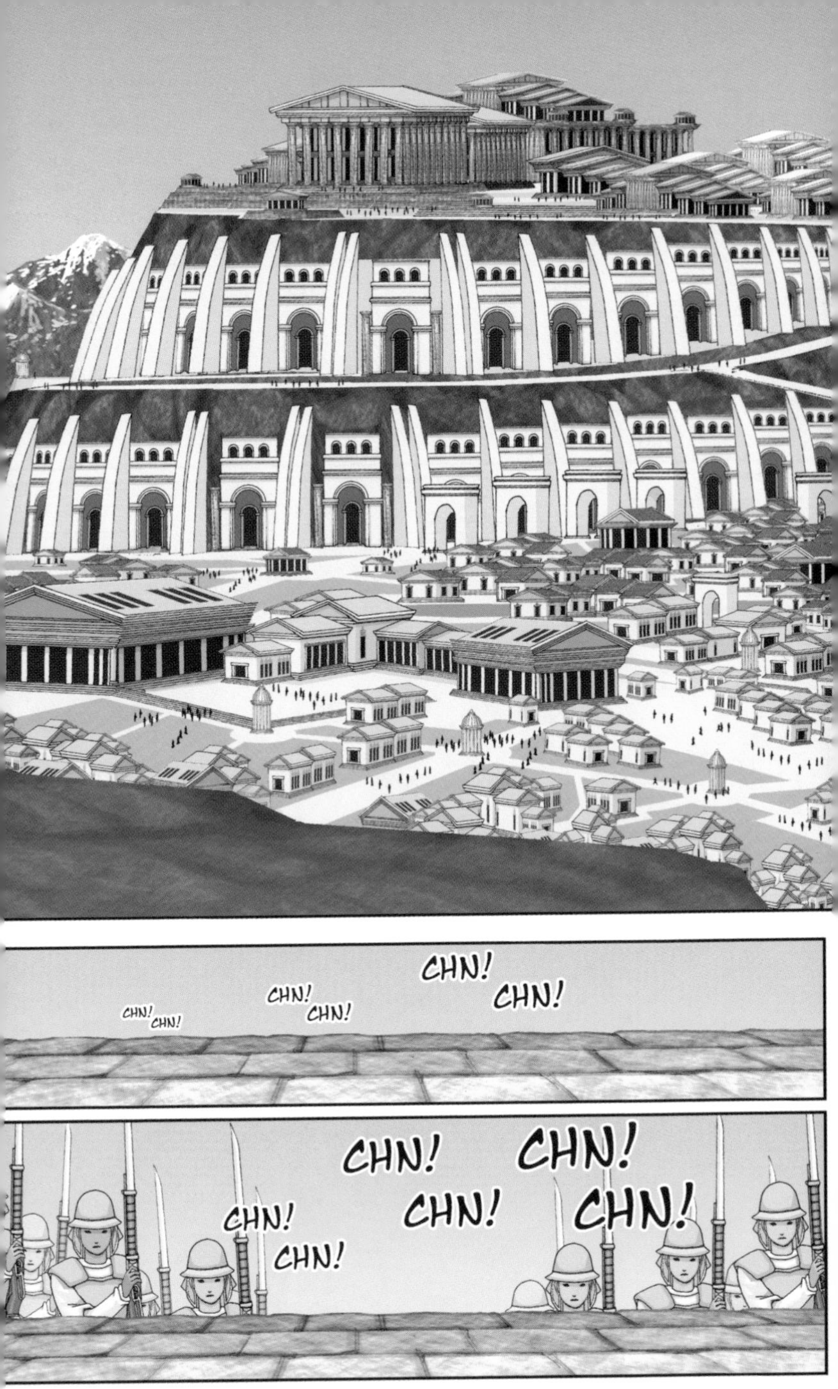

CHN! CHN!
CHN! CHN!
CHN!
CHN!
CHN!
CHN!
CHN!
CHN!
CHN!
CHN!

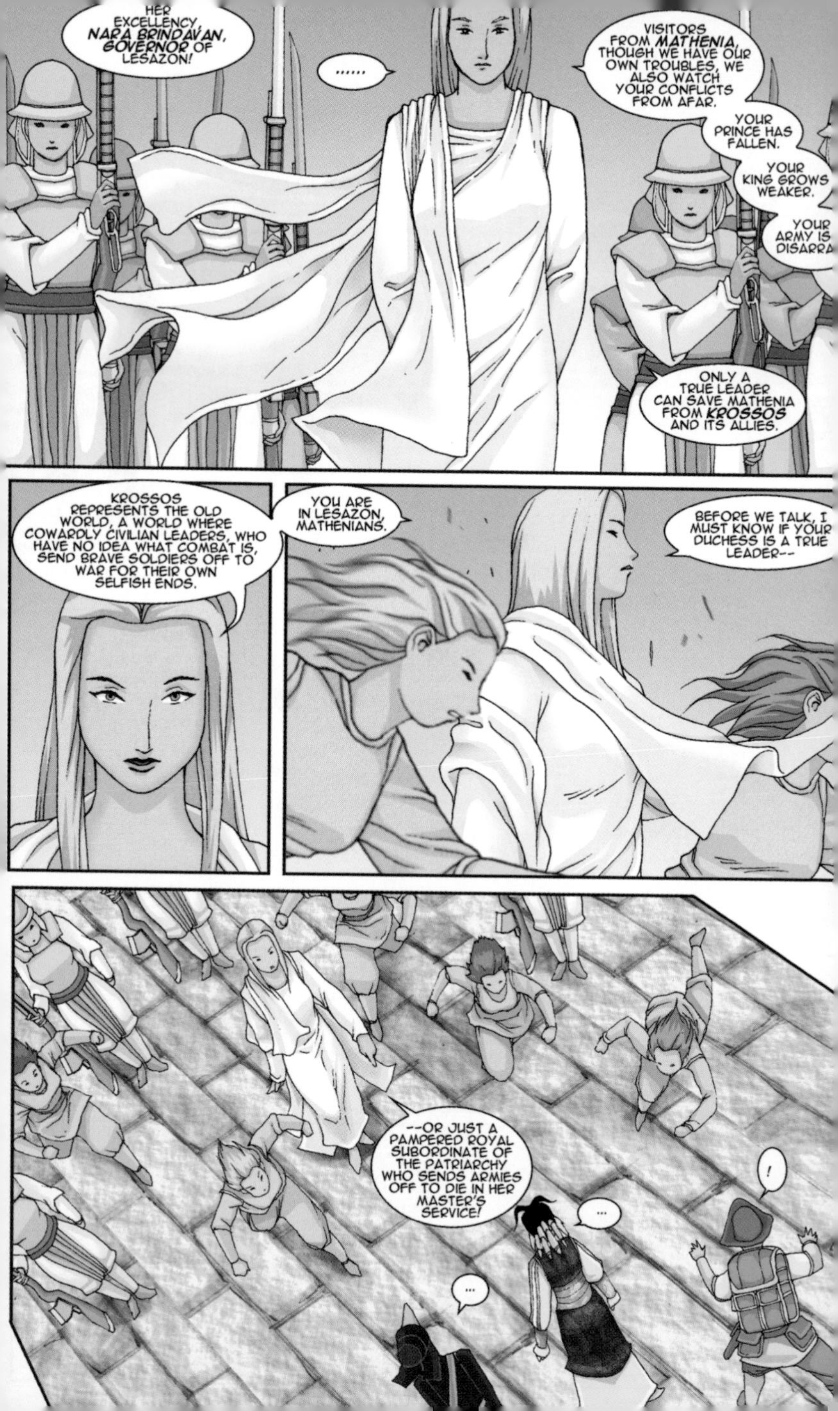
HER EXCELLENCY, NARA BRINDAVAN, GOVERNOR OF LESAZON!
......
VISITORS FROM MATHENIA, THOUGH WE HAVE OUR OWN TROUBLES, WE ALSO WATCH YOUR CONFLICTS FROM AFAR.
YOUR PRINCE HAS FALLEN.
YOUR KING GROWS WEAKER.
YOUR ARMY IS DISARRA
ONLY A TRUE LEADER CAN SAVE MATHENIA FROM KROSSOS AND ITS ALLIES.
KROSSOS REPRESENTS THE OLD WORLD, A WORLD WHERE COWARDLY CIVILIAN LEADERS, WHO HAVE NO IDEA WHAT COMBAT IS, SEND BRAVE SOLDIERS OFF TO WAR FOR THEIR OWN SELFISH ENDS.
YOU ARE IN LESAZON, MATHENIANS.
BEFORE WE TALK, I MUST KNOW IF YOUR DUCHESS IS A TRUE LEADER--
--OR JUST A PAMPERED ROYAL SUBORDINATE OF THE PATRIARCHY WHO SENDS ARMIES OFF TO DIE IN HER MASTER'S SERVICE!
!
...
...

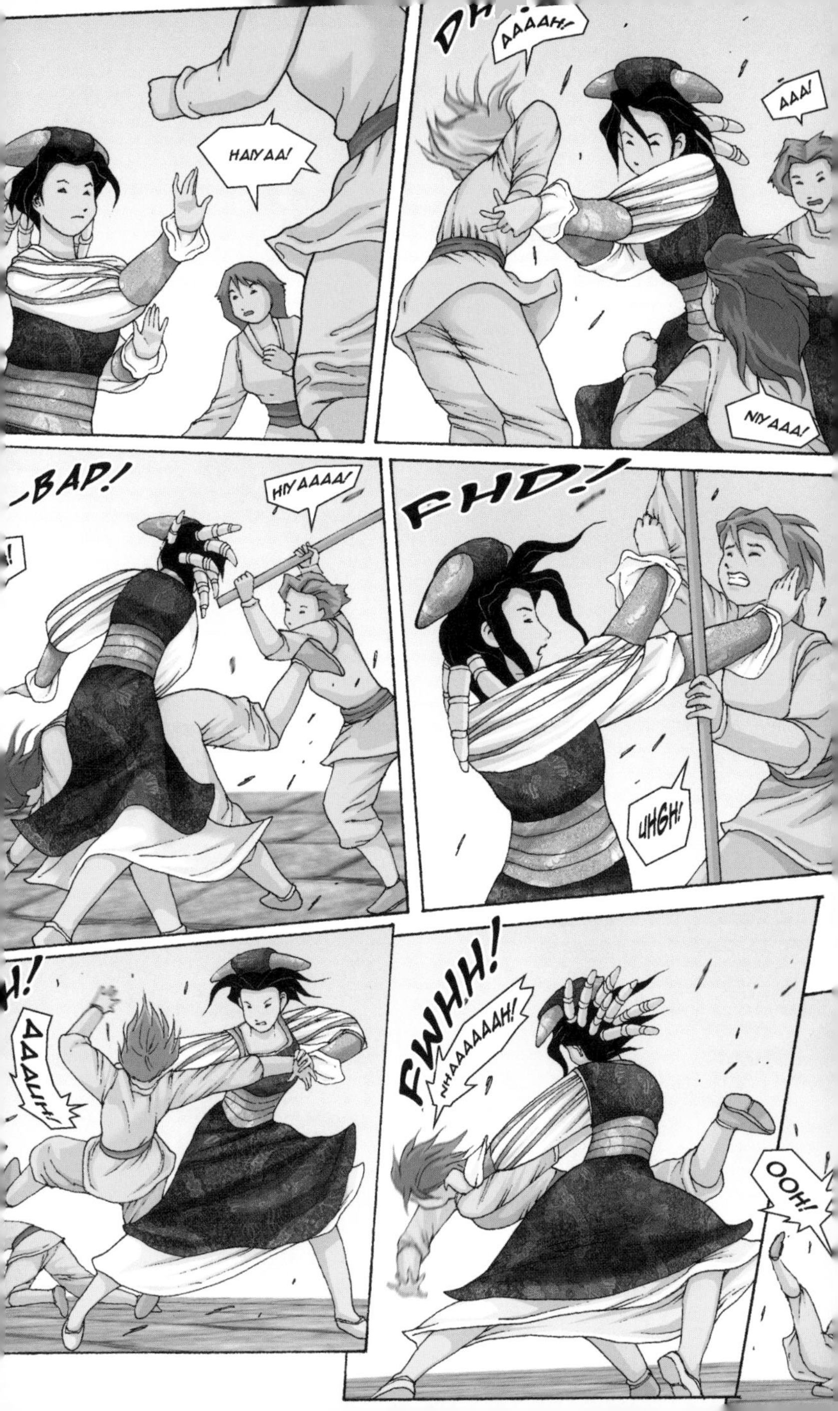
HAIYAA!
AAAAH!
AAA!
NIYAAA!
-BAP!
HIYAAAA!
FHD!
UHGH!
AAAUH!
FWHH!
NHAAAAAAH!
OOH!

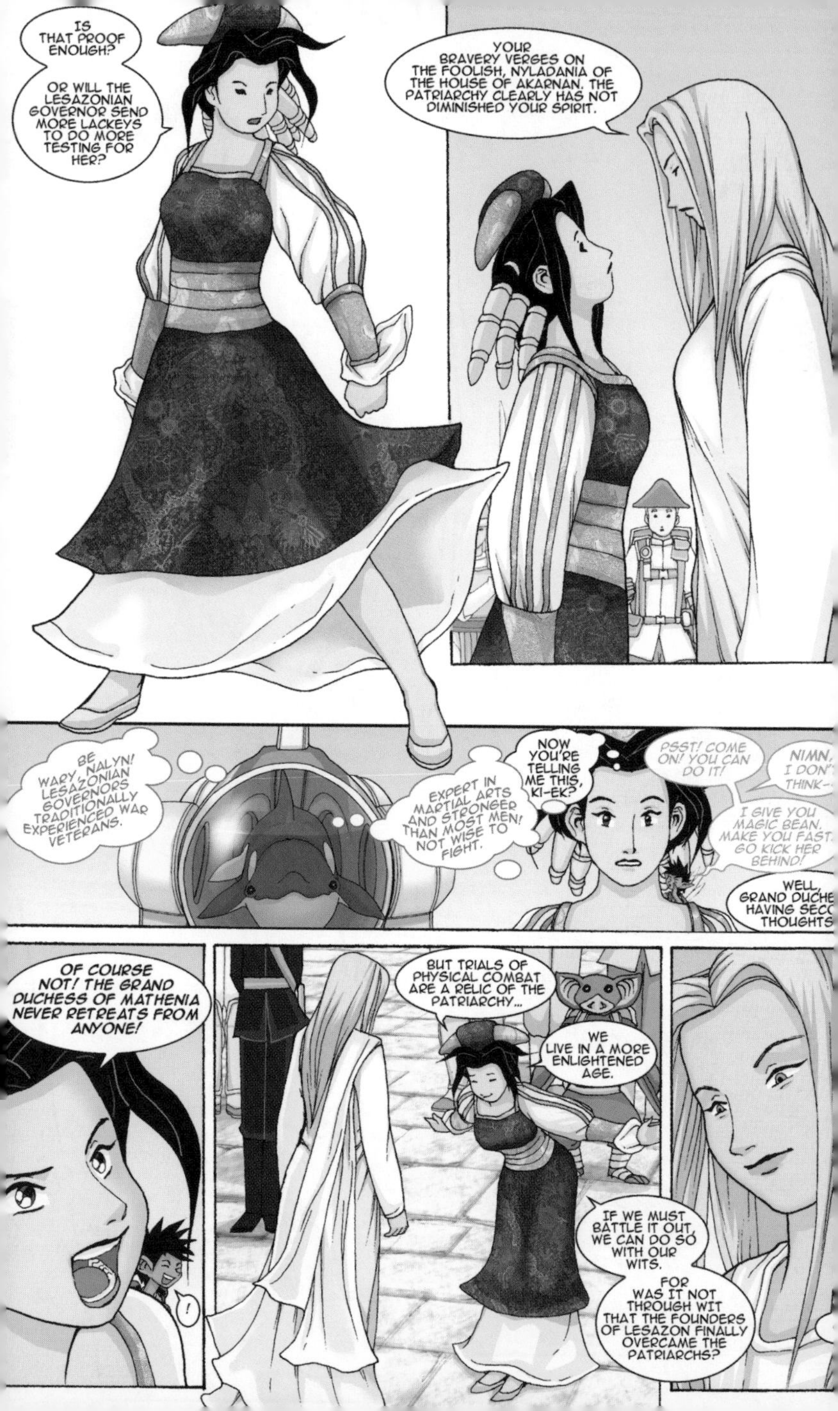
IS THAT PROOF ENOUGH?
OR WILL THE LESAZONIAN GOVERNOR SEND MORE LACKEYS TO DO MORE TESTING FOR HER?
YOUR BRAVERY VERGES ON THE FOOLISH, NYLADANIA OF THE HOUSE OF AKARNAN. THE PATRIARCHY CLEARLY HAS NOT DIMINISHED YOUR SPIRIT.
BE WARY, NALYN! LESAZONIAN GOVERNORS TRADITIONALLY EXPERIENCED WAR VETERANS.
EXPERT IN MARTIAL ARTS AND STRONGER THAN MOST MEN! NOT WISE TO FIGHT.
NOW YOU'RE TELLING ME THIS, KI-EK?
PSST! COME ON! YOU CAN DO IT!
I GIVE YOU MAGIC BEAN. MAKE YOU FAST. GO KICK HER BEHIND!
OF COURSE NOT! THE GRAND DUCHESS OF MATHENIA NEVER RETREATS FROM ANYONE!
!
BUT TRIALS OF PHYSICAL COMBAT ARE A RELIC OF THE PATRIARCHY...
WE LIVE IN A MORE ENLIGHTENED AGE.
IF WE MUST BATTLE IT OUT, WE CAN DO SO WITH OUR WITS.
FOR WAS IT NOT THROUGH WIT THAT THE FOUNDERS OF LESAZON FINALLY OVERCAME THE PATRIARCHS?

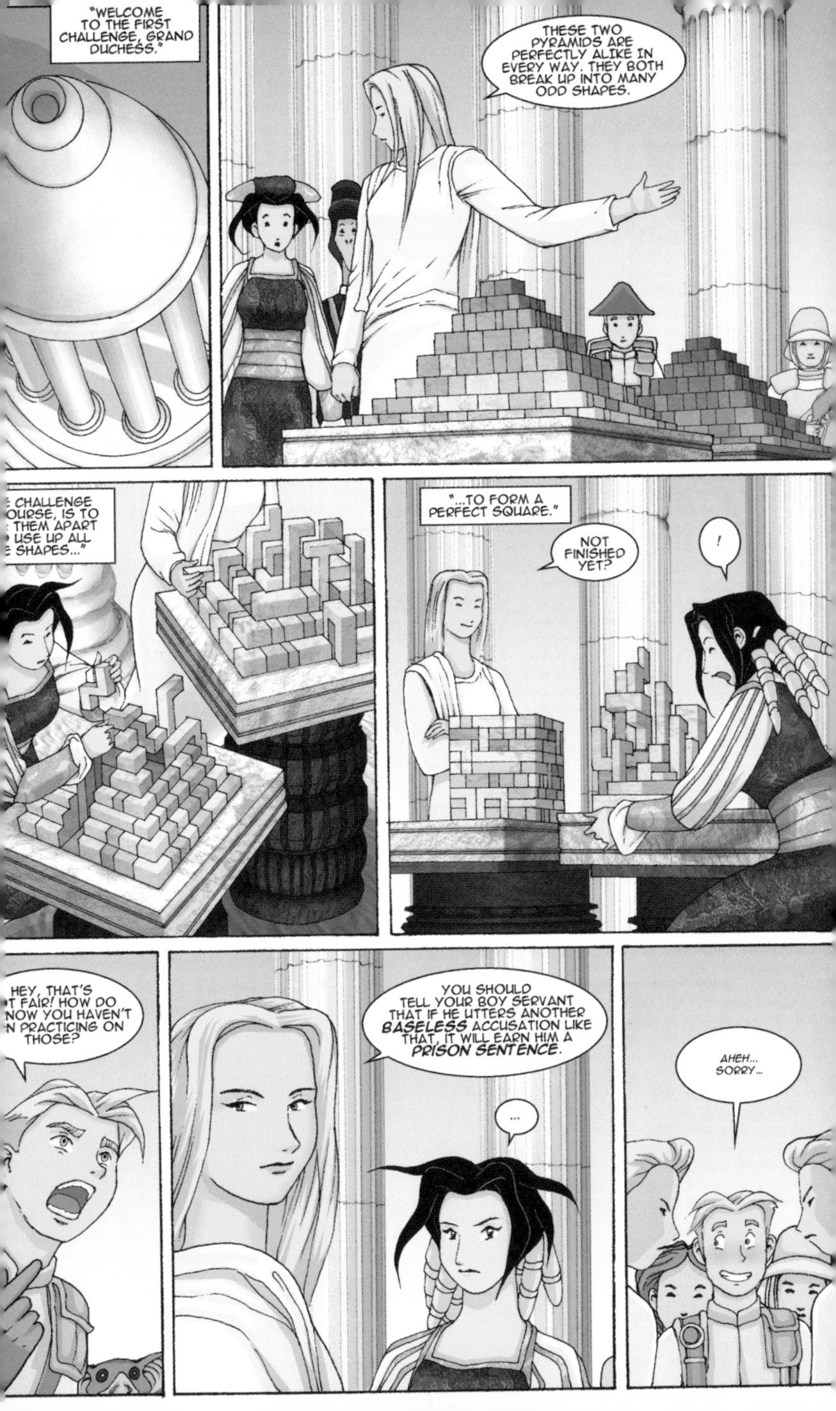
"WELCOME TO THE FIRST CHALLENGE, GRAND DUCHESS."
THESE TWO PYRAMIDS ARE PERFECTLY ALIKE IN EVERY WAY. THEY BOTH BREAK UP INTO MANY ODD SHAPES.
E CHALLENGE OURSE, IS TO E THEM APART USE UP ALL E SHAPES..."
"...TO FORM A PERFECT SQUARE."
NOT FINISHED YET?
!
HEY, THAT'S T FAIR! HOW DO NOW YOU HAVEN'T N PRACTICING ON THOSE?
YOU SHOULD TELL YOUR BOY SERVANT THAT IF HE UTTERS ANOTHER BASELESS ACCUSATION LIKE THAT, IT WILL EARN HIM A PRISON SENTENCE.
...
AHEH... SORRY...

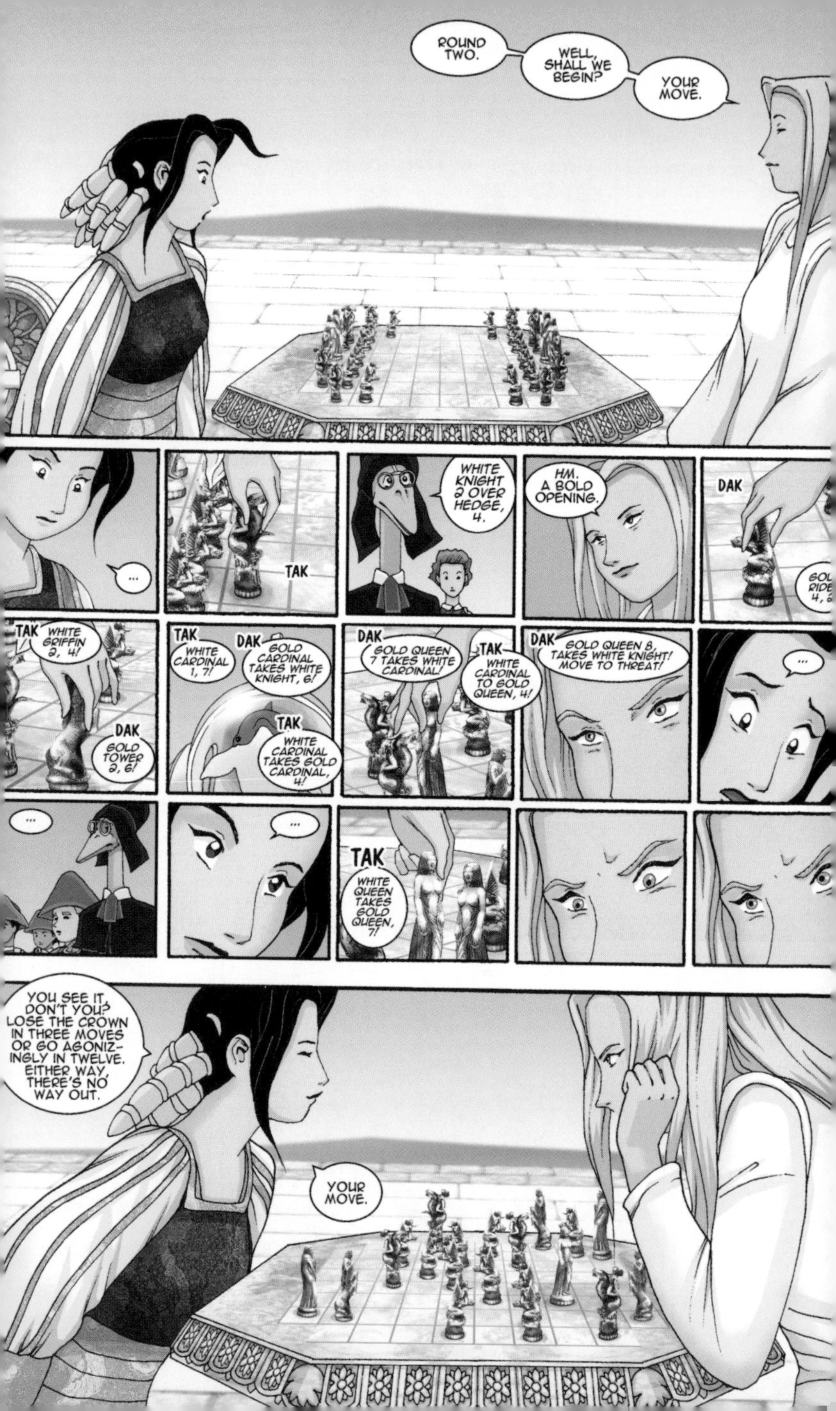
ROUND TWO.
WELL, SHALL WE BEGIN?
YOUR MOVE.
...
TAK
WHITE KNIGHT 2 OVER HEDGE, 4.
HM. A BOLD OPENING.
DAK
TAK
WHITE GRIFFIN 2, 4!
DAK
GOLD TOWER 2, 6!
TAK
WHITE CARDINAL 1, 7!
DAK
GOLD CARDINAL TAKES WHITE KNIGHT, 6!
TAK
WHITE CARDINAL TAKES GOLD CARDINAL, 4!
DAK
GOLD QUEEN 7 TAKES WHITE CARDINAL!
TAK
WHITE CARDINAL TO GOLD QUEEN, 4!
DAK
GOLD QUEEN 8, TAKES WHITE KNIGHT! MOVE TO THREAT!
...
...
...
TAK
WHITE QUEEN TAKES GOLD QUEEN, 7!
YOU SEE IT, DON'T YOU? LOSE THE CROWN IN THREE MOVES OR GO AGONIZINGLY IN TWELVE. EITHER WAY, THERE'S NO WAY OUT.
YOUR MOVE.

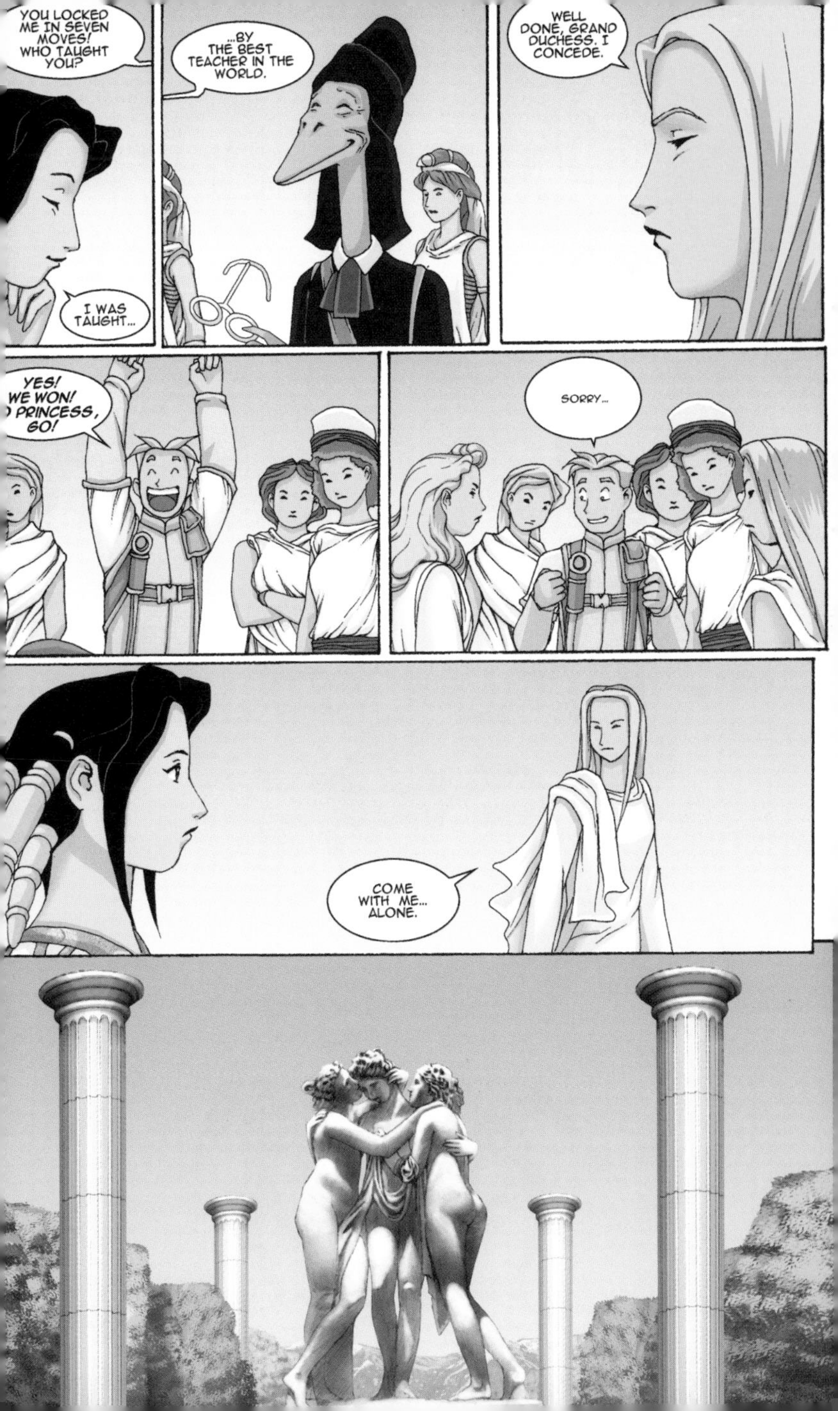
YOU LOCKED ME IN SEVEN MOVES! WHO TAUGHT YOU?
I WAS TAUGHT...
...BY THE BEST TEACHER IN THE WORLD.
WELL DONE, GRAND DUCHESS. I CONCEDE.
YES! WE WON! PRINCESS, GO!
SORRY...
COME WITH ME... ALONE.

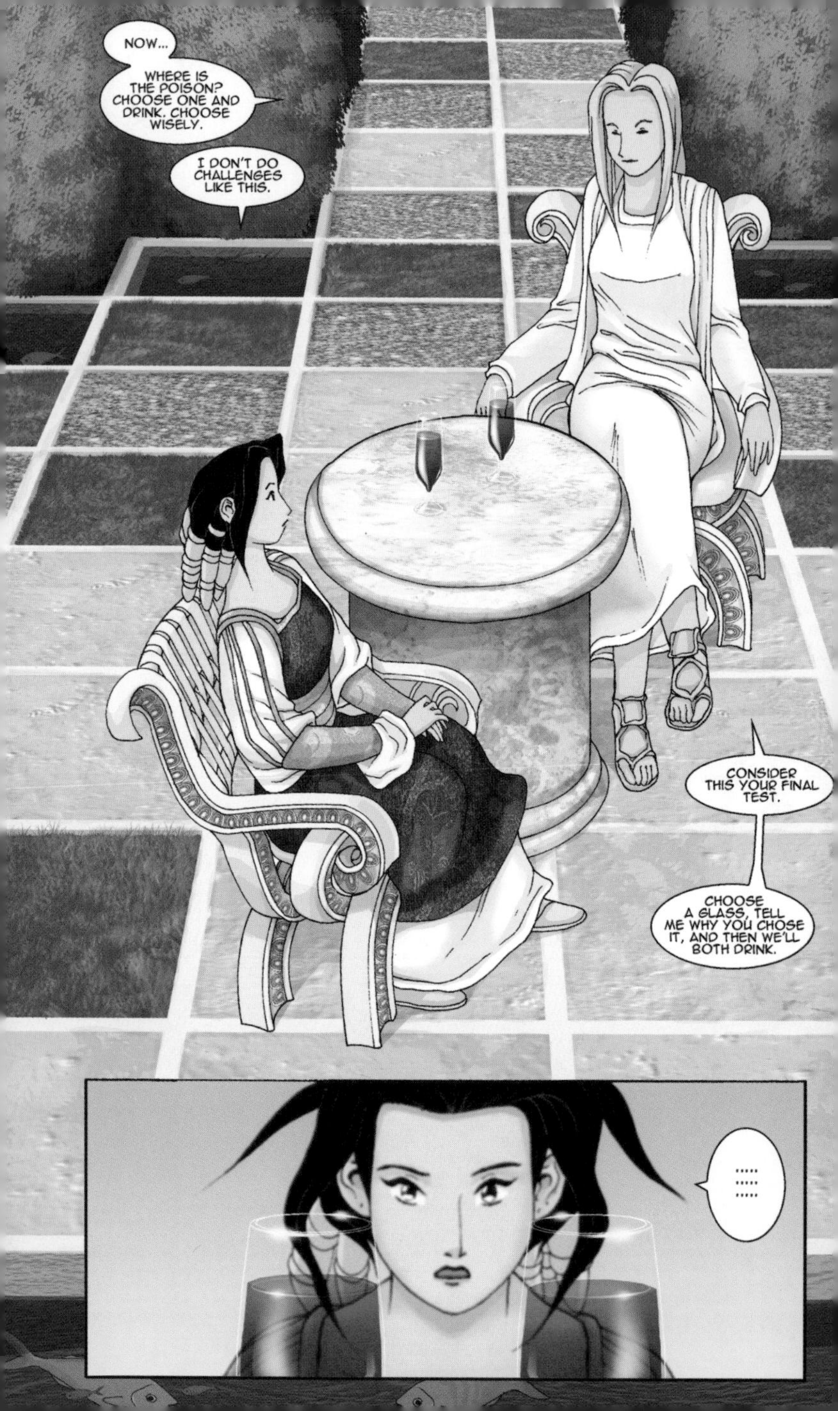
NOW...
WHERE IS THE POISON? CHOOSE ONE AND DRINK. CHOOSE WISELY.
I DON'T DO CHALLENGES LIKE THIS.
CONSIDER THIS YOUR FINAL TEST.
CHOOSE A GLASS, TELL ME WHY YOU CHOSE IT, AND THEN WE'LL BOTH DRINK.
.....
.....
.....

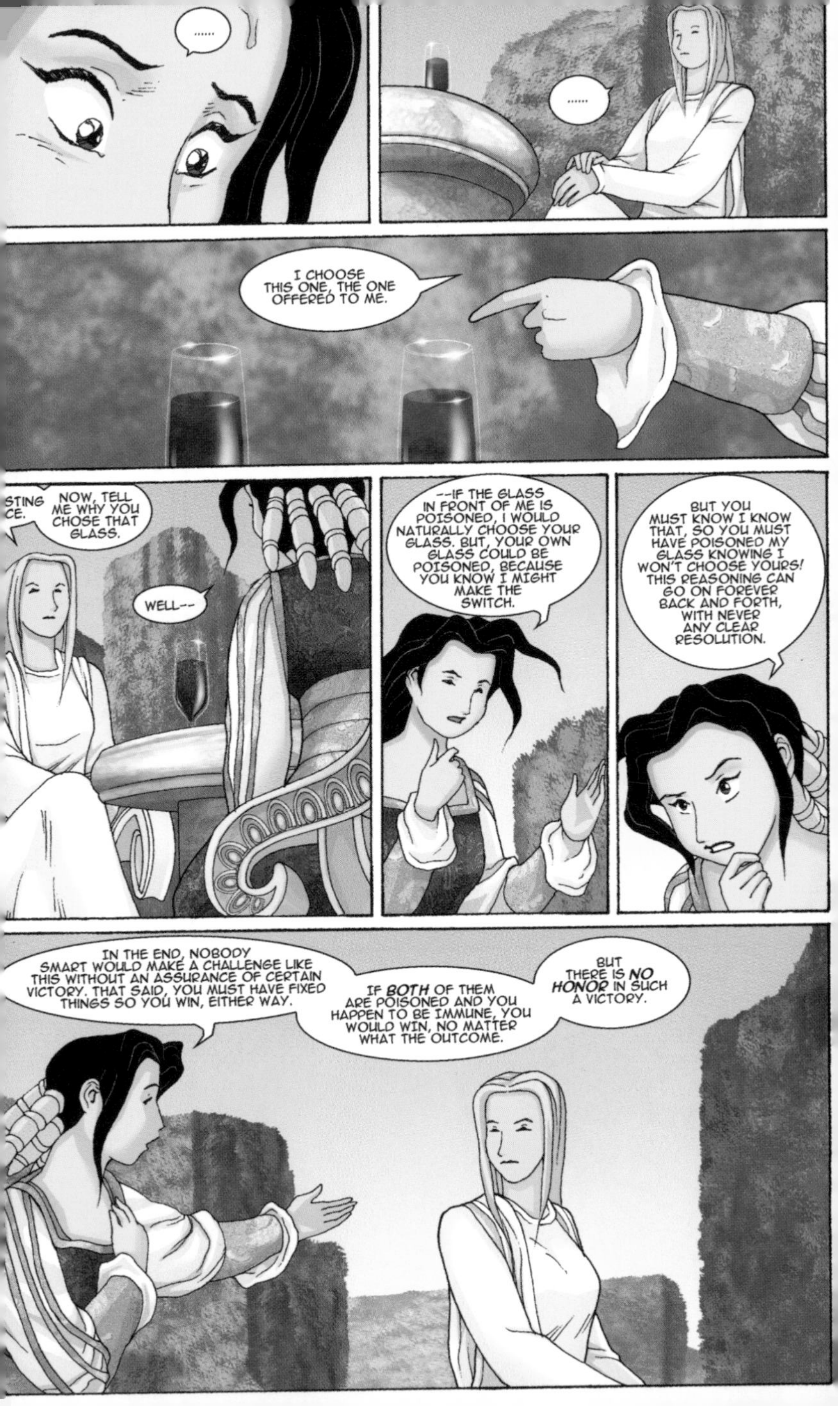
......
......
I CHOOSE THIS ONE, THE ONE OFFERED TO ME.
STING CE.
NOW, TELL ME WHY YOU CHOSE THAT GLASS.
WELL--
--IF THE GLASS IN FRONT OF ME IS POISONED, I WOULD NATURALLY CHOOSE YOUR GLASS. BUT, YOUR OWN GLASS COULD BE POISONED, BECAUSE YOU KNOW I MIGHT MAKE THE SWITCH.
BUT YOU MUST KNOW I KNOW THAT, SO YOU MUST HAVE POISONED MY GLASS KNOWING I WON'T CHOOSE YOURS! THIS REASONING CAN GO ON FOREVER BACK AND FORTH, WITH NEVER ANY CLEAR RESOLUTION.
IN THE END, NOBODY SMART WOULD MAKE A CHALLENGE LIKE THIS WITHOUT AN ASSURANCE OF CERTAIN VICTORY. THAT SAID, YOU MUST HAVE FIXED THINGS SO YOU WIN, EITHER WAY.
IF *BOTH* OF THEM ARE POISONED AND YOU HAPPEN TO BE IMMUNE, YOU WOULD WIN, NO MATTER WHAT THE OUTCOME.
BUT THERE IS *NO HONOR* IN SUCH A VICTORY.

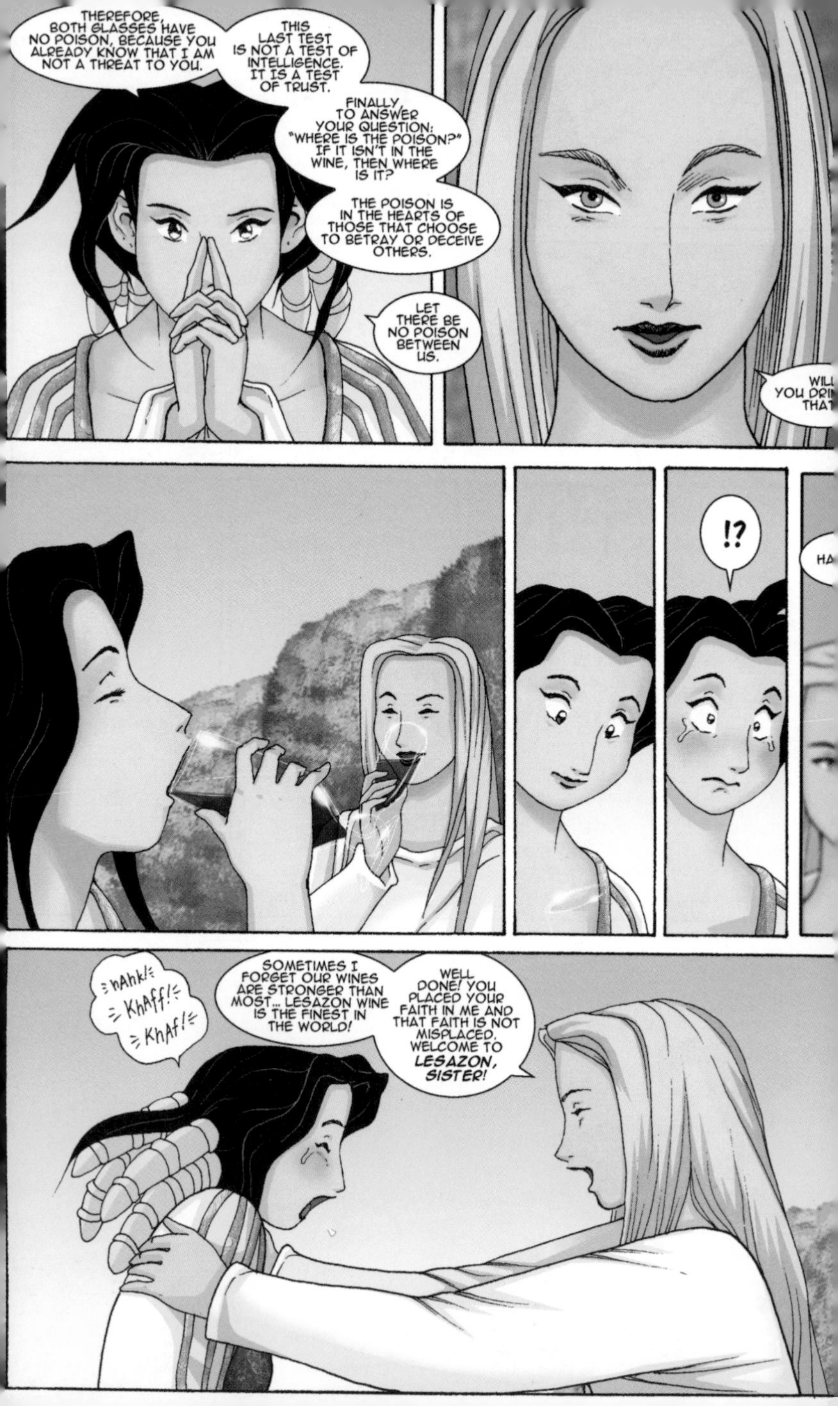

THEREFORE, BOTH GLASSES HAVE NO POISON, BECAUSE YOU ALREADY KNOW THAT I AM NOT A THREAT TO YOU.
THIS LAST TEST IS NOT A TEST OF INTELLIGENCE. IT IS A TEST OF TRUST.
FINALLY, TO ANSWER YOUR QUESTION: "WHERE IS THE POISON?" IF IT ISN'T IN THE WINE, THEN WHERE IS IT?
THE POISON IS IN THE HEARTS OF THOSE THAT CHOOSE TO BETRAY OR DECEIVE OTHERS.
LET THERE BE NO POISON BETWEEN US.
WILL YOU DRIN THAT
!?
HA
hAhk! KhAff! KhAf!
SOMETIMES I FORGET OUR WINES ARE STRONGER THAN MOST... LESAZON WINE IS THE FINEST IN THE WORLD!
WELL DONE! YOU PLACED YOUR FAITH IN ME AND THAT FAITH IS NOT MISPLACED. WELCOME TO *LESAZON, SISTER!*

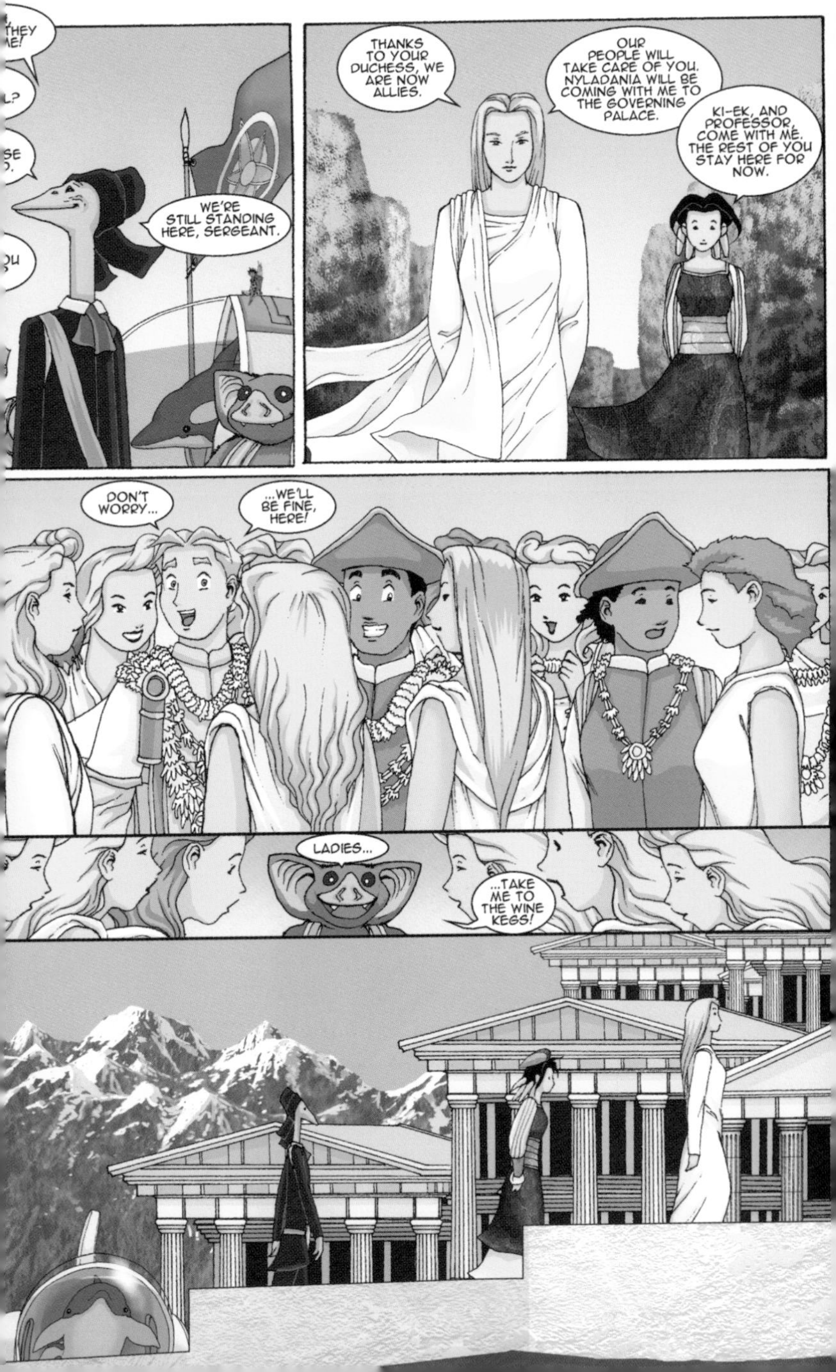
WE'RE STILL STANDING HERE, SERGEANT.
THANKS TO YOUR DUCHESS, WE ARE NOW ALLIES.
OUR PEOPLE WILL TAKE CARE OF YOU. NYLADANIA WILL BE COMING WITH ME TO THE GOVERNING PALACE.
KI-EK, AND PROFESSOR, COME WITH ME. THE REST OF YOU STAY HERE FOR NOW.
DON'T WORRY...
...WE'LL BE FINE, HERE!
LADIES...
...TAKE ME TO THE WINE KEGS!

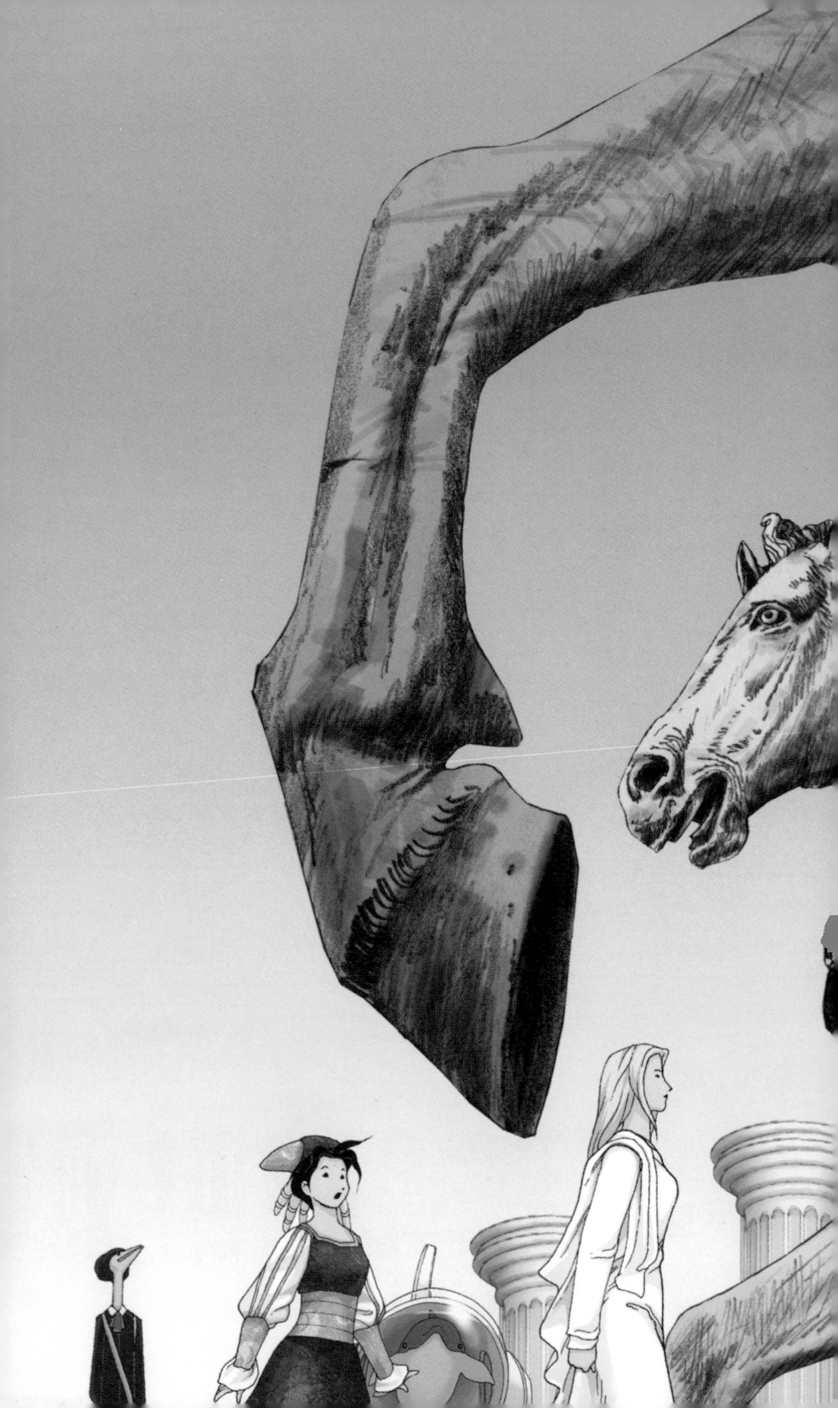

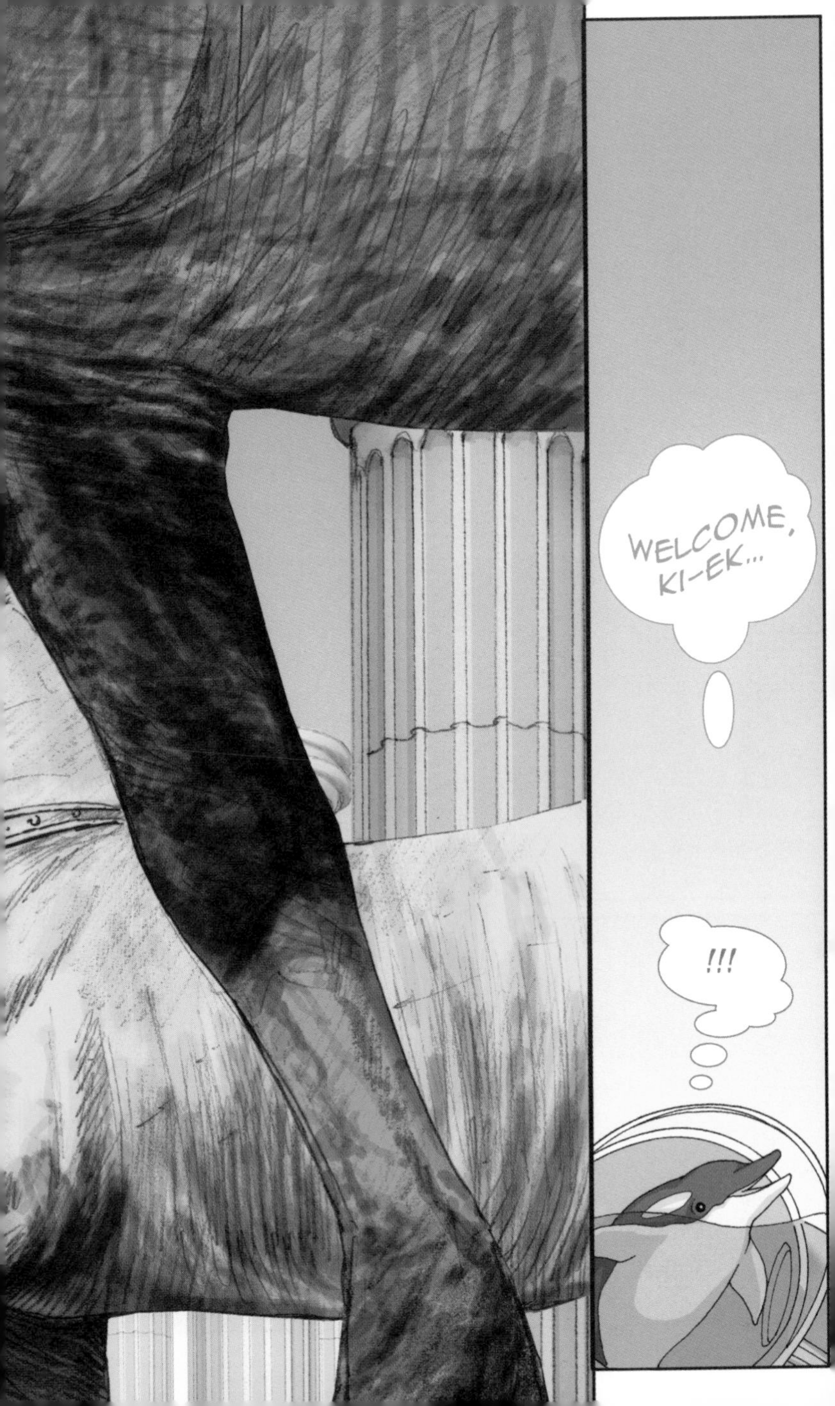
WELCOME, KI-EK...
!!!

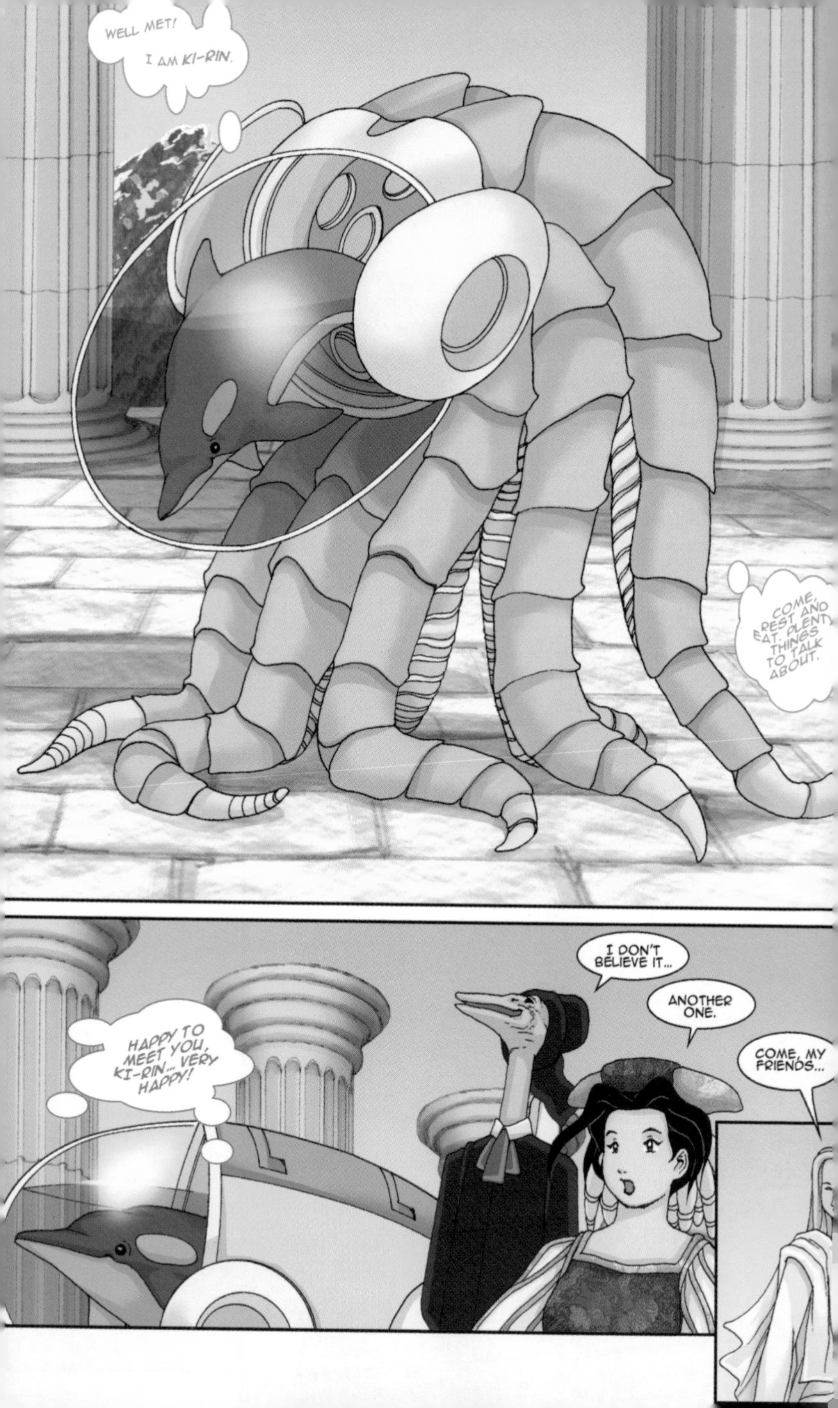
WELL MET!
I AM KI-RIN.
COME, REST AND EAT. PLENTY THINGS TO TALK ABOUT.
I DON'T BELIEVE IT...
ANOTHER ONE.
HAPPY TO MEET YOU, KI-RIN... VERY HAPPY!
COME, MY FRIENDS...

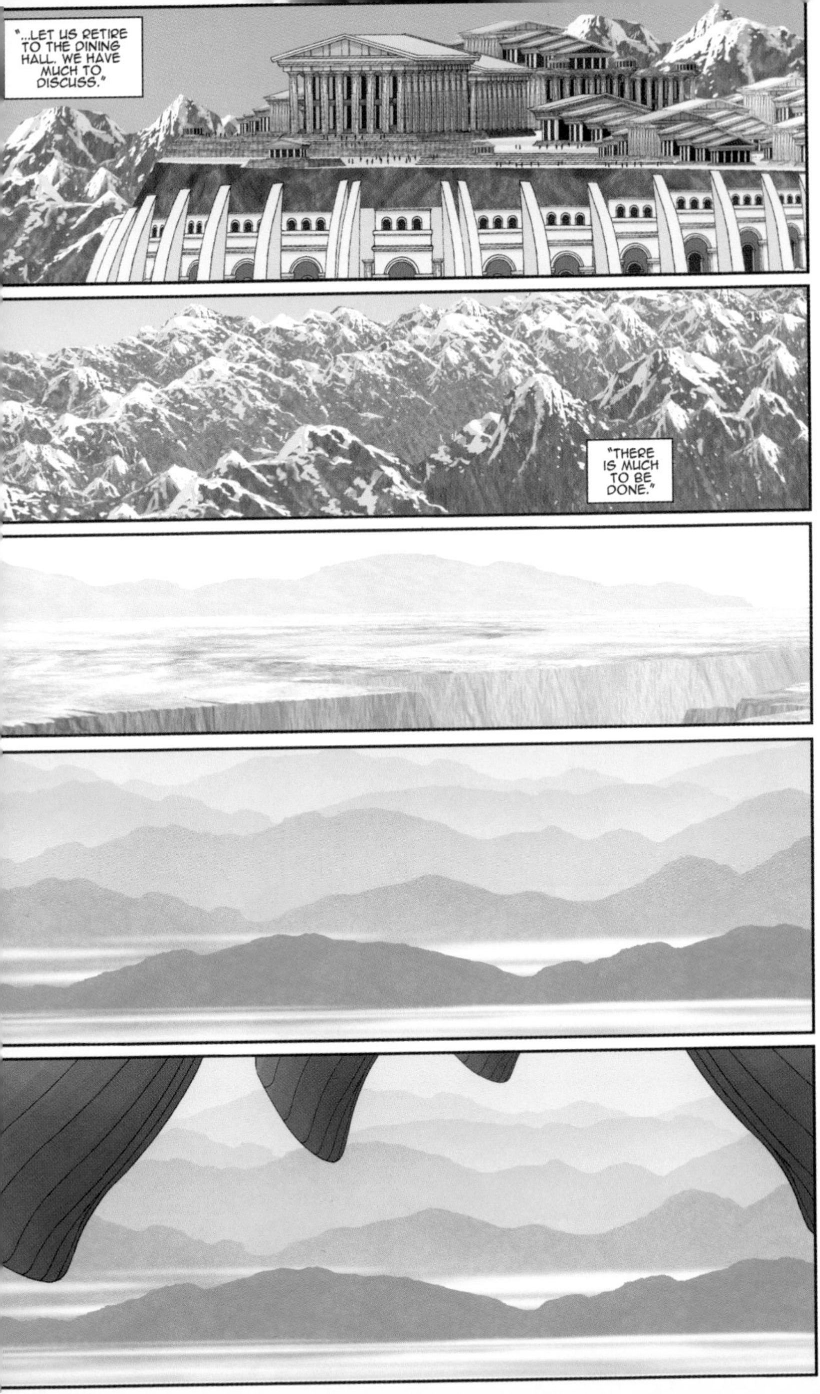
"...LET US RETIRE TO THE DINING HALL. WE HAVE MUCH TO DISCUSS."
"THERE IS MUCH TO BE DONE."

GREAT GENERAL KAIZLER, WE HAVE REACHED THE CONTINENT OF AR.

EXCELLENT.

PROCEED.

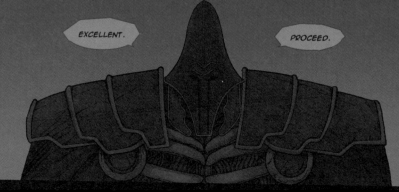

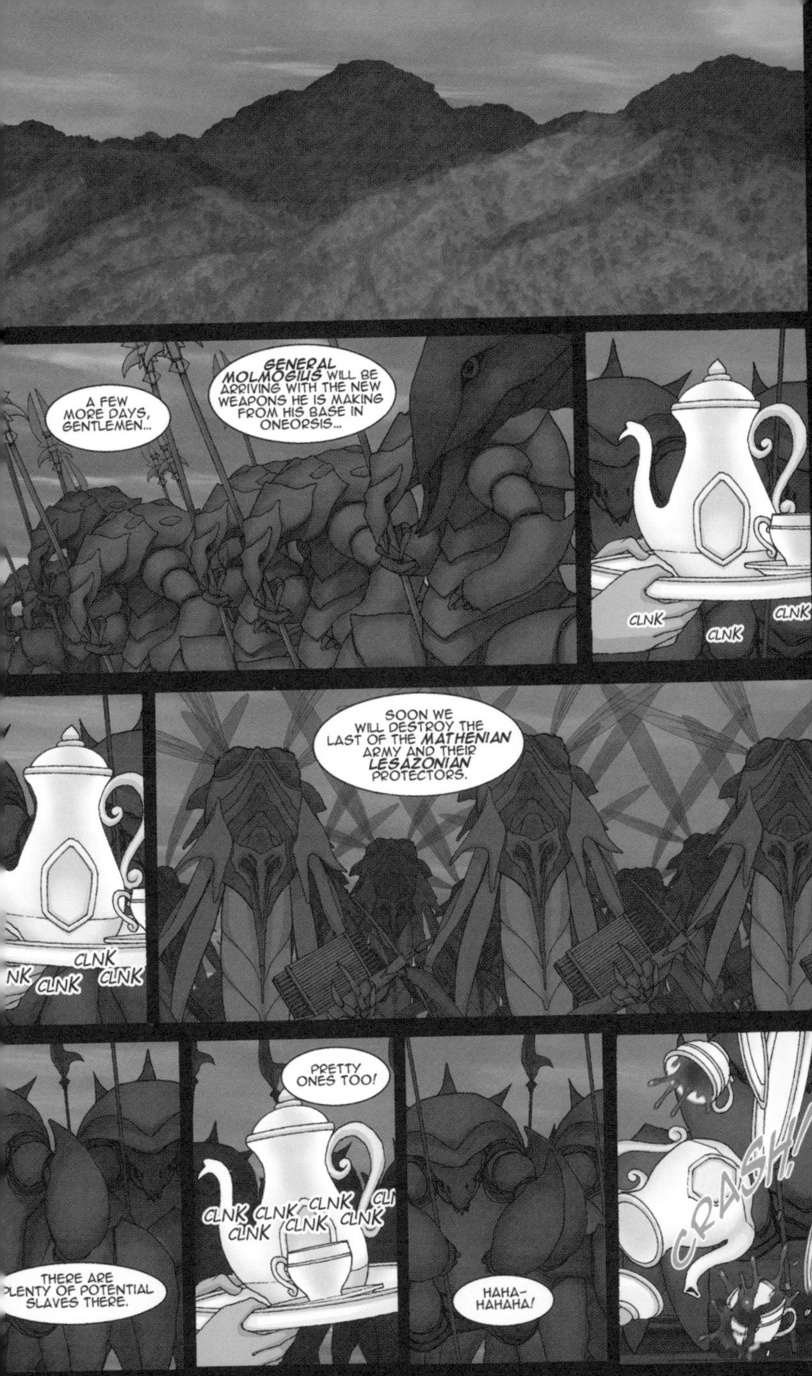
A FEW MORE DAYS, GENTLEMEN...
GENERAL MOLMOGIUS WILL BE ARRIVING WITH THE NEW WEAPONS HE IS MAKING FROM HIS BASE IN ONEORSIS...
CLNK
CLNK
CLNK
SOON WE WILL DESTROY THE LAST OF THE MATHENIAN ARMY AND THEIR LESAZONIAN PROTECTORS.
CLNK
CLNK
CLNK
THERE ARE PLENTY OF POTENTIAL SLAVES THERE.
PRETTY ONES TOO!
CLNK CLNK CLNK CLNK CLNK CLNK
HAHA-HAHAHA!
CRASH!!

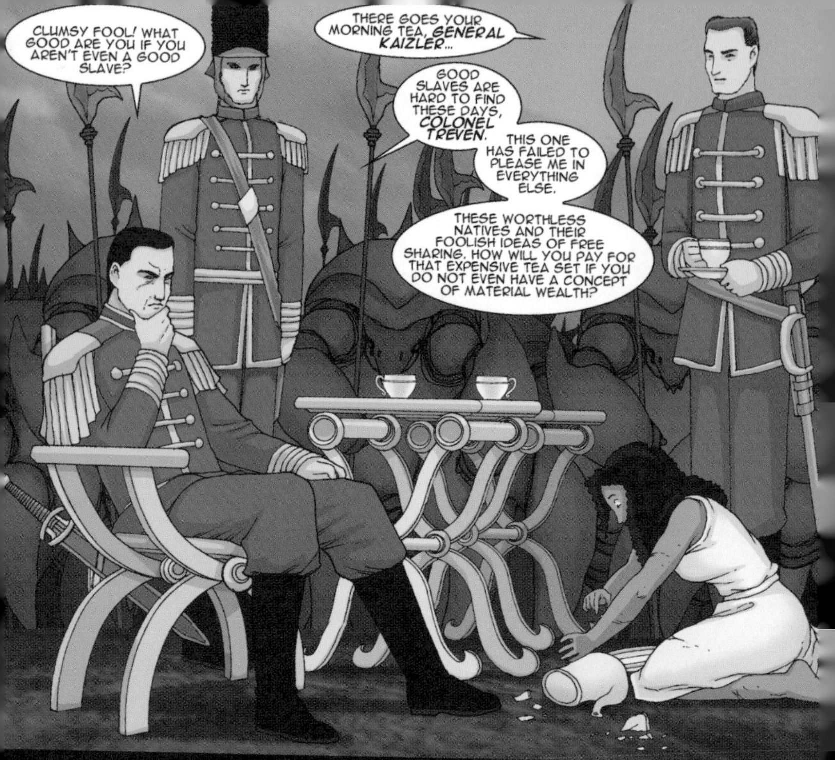
CLUMSY FOOL! WHAT GOOD ARE YOU IF YOU AREN'T EVEN A GOOD SLAVE?
THERE GOES YOUR MORNING TEA, GENERAL KAIZLER...
GOOD SLAVES ARE HARD TO FIND THESE DAYS, COLONEL TREVEN.
THIS ONE HAS FAILED TO PLEASE ME IN EVERYTHING ELSE.
THESE WORTHLESS NATIVES AND THEIR FOOLISH IDEAS OF FREE SHARING. HOW WILL YOU PAY FOR THAT EXPENSIVE TEA SET IF YOU DO NOT EVEN HAVE A CONCEPT OF MATERIAL WEALTH?

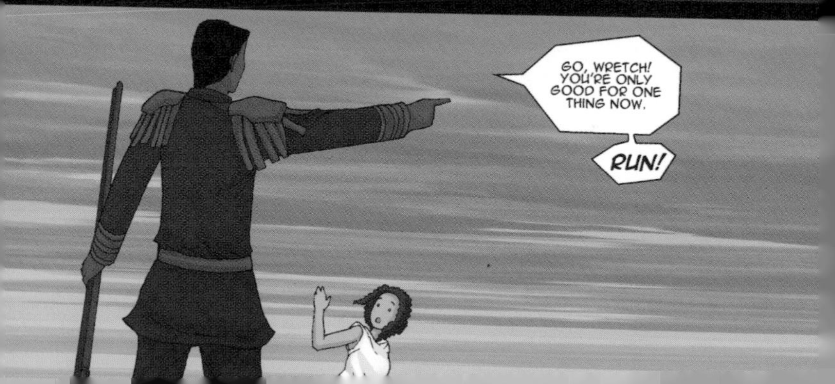
GO, WRETCH! YOU'RE ONLY GOOD FOR ONE THING NOW.
RUN!

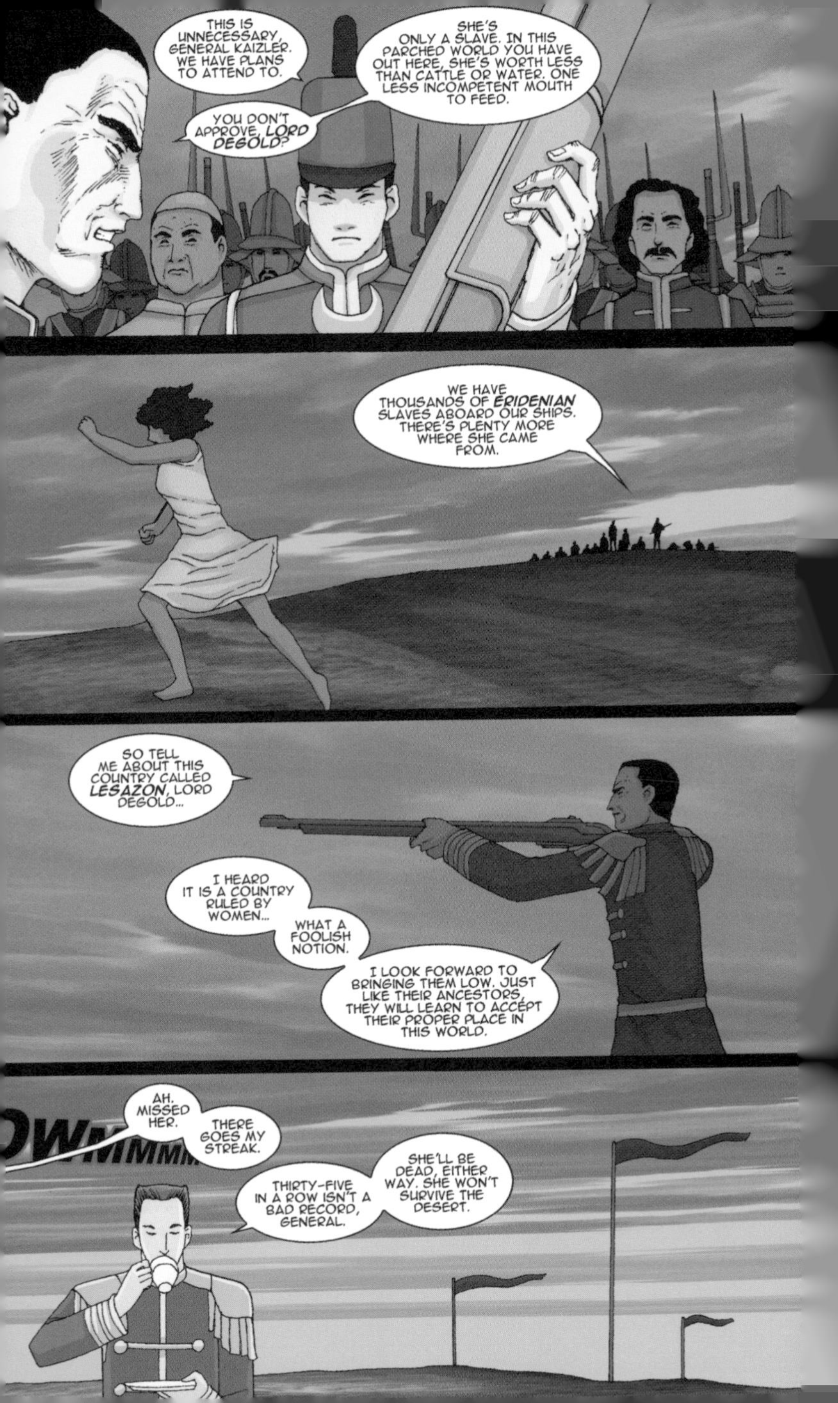

THIS IS UNNECESSARY, GENERAL KAIZLER. WE HAVE PLANS TO ATTEND TO.
YOU DON'T APPROVE, LORD DEGOLD?
SHE'S ONLY A SLAVE. IN THIS PARCHED WORLD YOU HAVE OUT HERE, SHE'S WORTH LESS THAN CATTLE OR WATER. ONE LESS INCOMPETENT MOUTH TO FEED.
WE HAVE THOUSANDS OF ERIDENIAN SLAVES ABOARD OUR SHIPS. THERE'S PLENTY MORE WHERE SHE CAME FROM.
SO TELL ME ABOUT THIS COUNTRY CALLED LESAZON, LORD DEGOLD...
I HEARD IT IS A COUNTRY RULED BY WOMEN...
WHAT A FOOLISH NOTION.
I LOOK FORWARD TO BRINGING THEM LOW. JUST LIKE THEIR ANCESTORS, THEY WILL LEARN TO ACCEPT THEIR PROPER PLACE IN THIS WORLD.
OWMMM
AH. MISSED HER.
THERE GOES MY STREAK.
THIRTY-FIVE IN A ROW ISN'T A BAD RECORD, GENERAL.
SHE'LL BE DEAD, EITHER WAY. SHE WON'T SURVIVE THE DESERT.

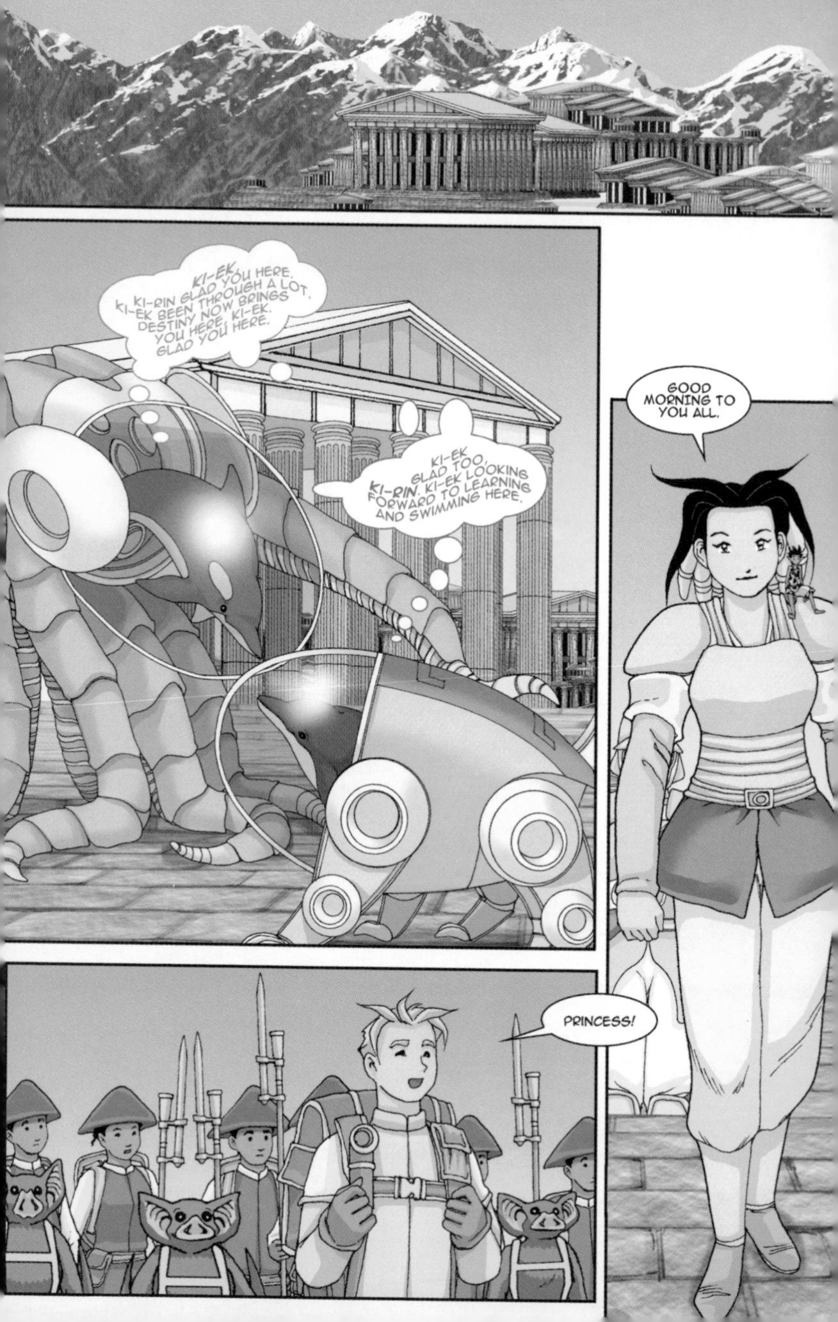

KI-EK, KI-RIN GLAD YOU HERE. KI-EK BEEN THROUGH A LOT. DESTINY NOW BRINGS YOU HERE, KI-EK. GLAD YOU HERE.
KI-EK GLAD TOO, KI-RIN. KI-EK LOOKING FORWARD TO LEARNING AND SWIMMING HERE.
GOOD MORNING TO YOU ALL.
PRINCESS!

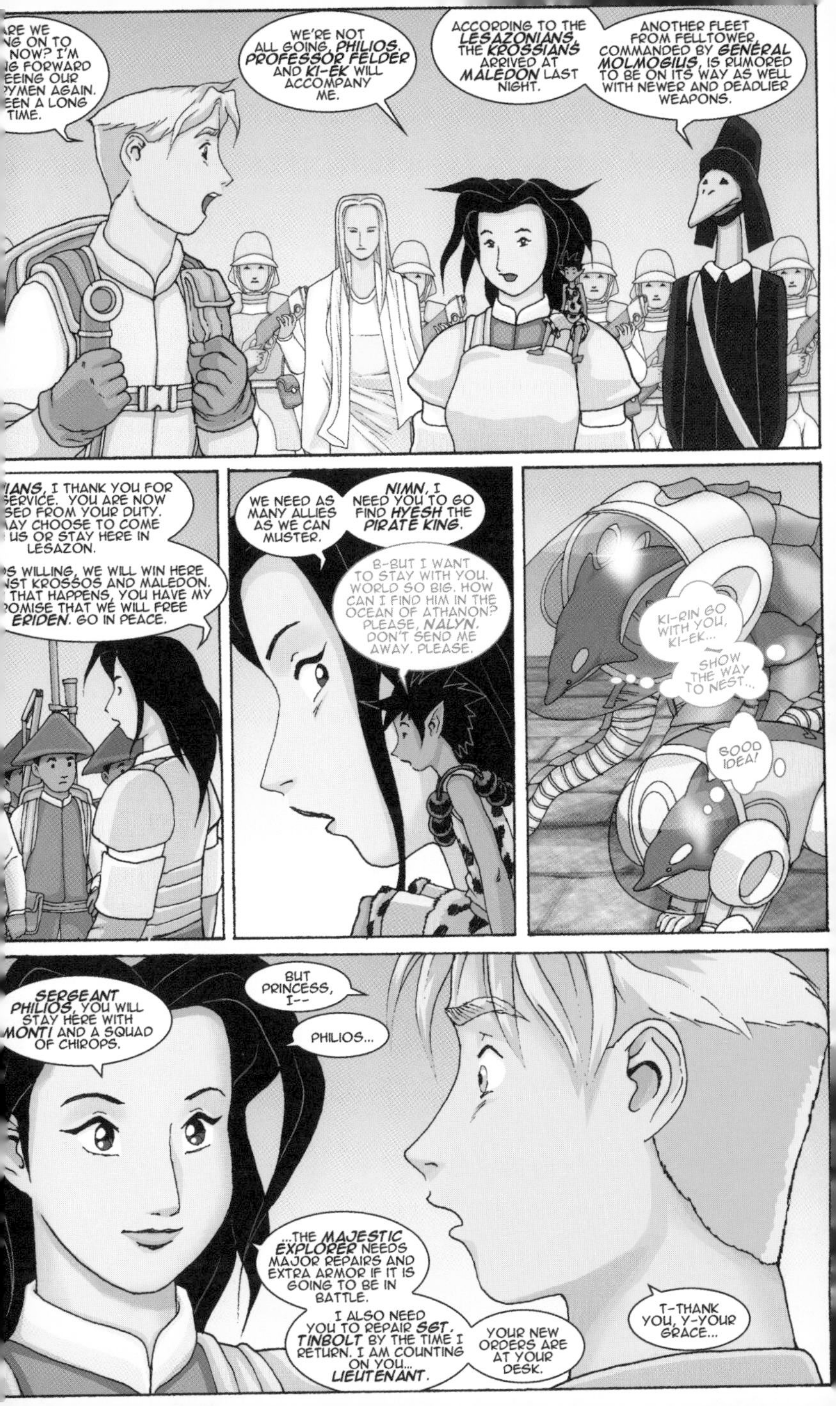

ARE WE
NG ON TO
NOW? I'M
NG FORWARD
EEING OUR
PYMEN AGAIN.
EEN A LONG
TIME.
WE'RE NOT ALL GOING, PHILIOS. PROFESSOR FELDER AND KI-EK WILL ACCOMPANY ME.
ACCORDING TO THE LESAZONIANS, THE KROSSIANS ARRIVED AT MALEDON LAST NIGHT.
ANOTHER FLEET FROM FELLTOWER, COMMANDED BY GENERAL MOLMOGIUS, IS RUMORED TO BE ON ITS WAY AS WELL WITH NEWER AND DEADLIER WEAPONS.
IANS, I THANK YOU FOR
SERVICE. YOU ARE NOW
SED FROM YOUR DUTY.
AY CHOOSE TO COME
US OR STAY HERE IN
LESAZON.
OS WILLING, WE WILL WIN HERE
NST KROSSOS AND MALEDON.
THAT HAPPENS, YOU HAVE MY
ROMISE THAT WE WILL FREE
ERIDEN. GO IN PEACE.
WE NEED AS MANY ALLIES AS WE CAN MUSTER.
NIMN, I NEED YOU TO GO FIND HYESH THE PIRATE KING.
B-BUT I WANT TO STAY WITH YOU. WORLD SO BIG. HOW CAN I FIND HIM IN THE OCEAN OF ATHANON? PLEASE, NALYN. DON'T SEND ME AWAY. PLEASE.
KI-RIN GO WITH YOU, KI-EK...
SHOW THE WAY TO NEST...
GOOD IDEA!
SERGEANT PHILIOS, YOU WILL STAY HERE WITH MONTI AND A SQUAD OF CHIROPS.
BUT PRINCESS, I--
PHILIOS...
...THE MAJESTIC EXPLORER NEEDS MAJOR REPAIRS AND EXTRA ARMOR IF IT IS GOING TO BE IN BATTLE.
I ALSO NEED YOU TO REPAIR SGT. TINBOLT BY THE TIME I RETURN. I AM COUNTING ON YOU... LIEUTENANT.
YOUR NEW ORDERS ARE AT YOUR DESK.
T-THANK YOU, Y-YOUR GRACE...

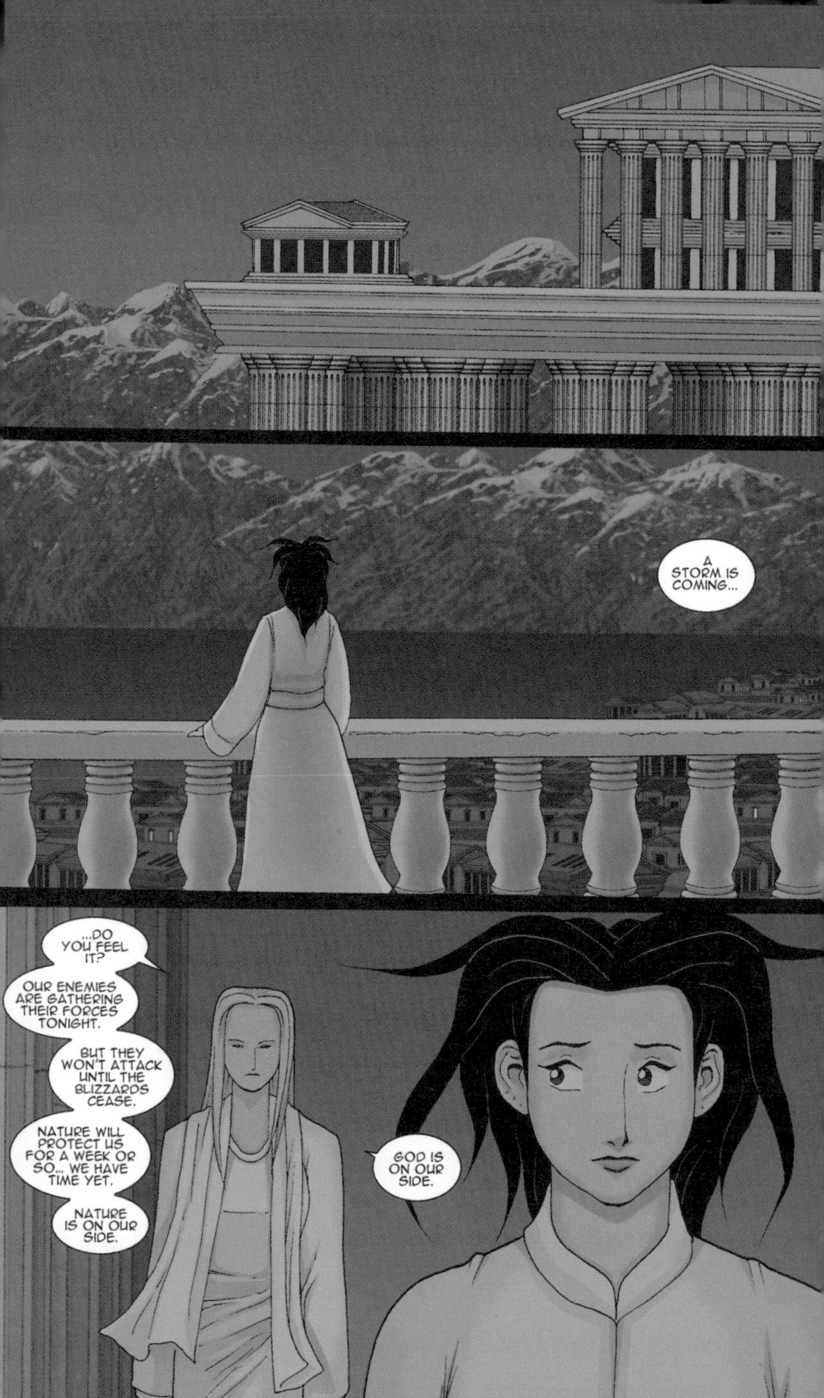
A STORM IS COMING...
...DO YOU FEEL IT?
OUR ENEMIES ARE GATHERING THEIR FORCES TONIGHT.
BUT THEY WON'T ATTACK UNTIL THE BLIZZARDS CEASE.
NATURE WILL PROTECT US FOR A WEEK OR SO... WE HAVE TIME YET.
NATURE IS ON OUR SIDE.
GOD IS ON OUR SIDE.

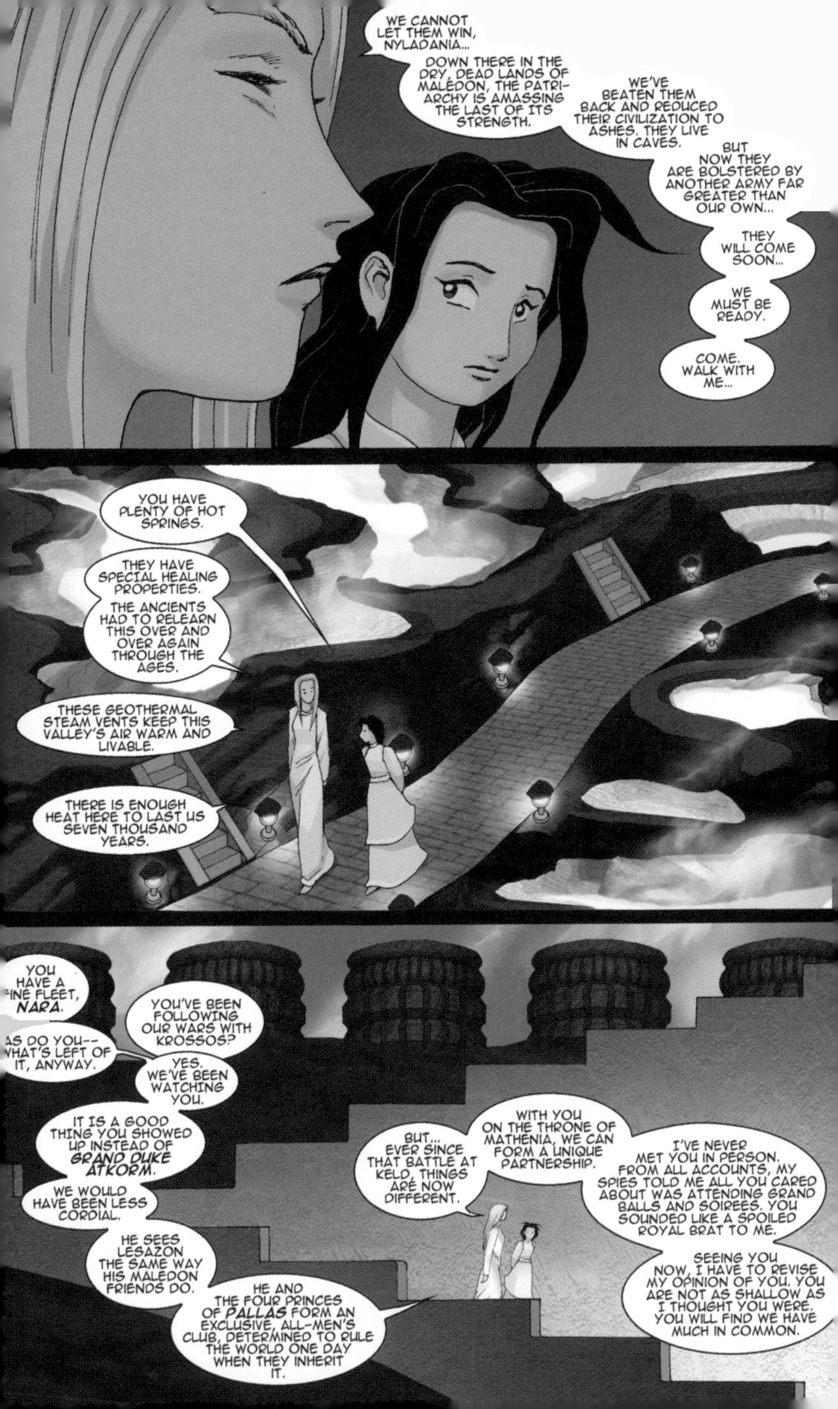

WE CANNOT LET THEM WIN, NYLADANIA...
DOWN THERE IN THE DRY, DEAD LANDS OF MALÉDON, THE PATRIARCHY IS AMASSING THE LAST OF ITS STRENGTH.
WE'VE BEATEN THEM BACK AND REDUCED THEIR CIVILIZATION TO ASHES. THEY LIVE IN CAVES.
BUT NOW THEY ARE BOLSTERED BY ANOTHER ARMY FAR GREATER THAN OUR OWN...
THEY WILL COME SOON...
WE MUST BE READY.
COME. WALK WITH ME...
YOU HAVE PLENTY OF HOT SPRINGS.
THEY HAVE SPECIAL HEALING PROPERTIES.
THE ANCIENTS HAD TO RELEARN THIS OVER AND OVER AGAIN THROUGH THE AGES.
THESE GEOTHERMAL STEAM VENTS KEEP THIS VALLEY'S AIR WARM AND LIVABLE.
THERE IS ENOUGH HEAT HERE TO LAST US SEVEN THOUSAND YEARS.
YOU HAVE A FINE FLEET, NARA.
AS DO YOU-- WHAT'S LEFT OF IT, ANYWAY.
YOU'VE BEEN FOLLOWING OUR WARS WITH KROSSOS?
YES. WE'VE BEEN WATCHING YOU.
IT IS A GOOD THING YOU SHOWED UP INSTEAD OF GRAND DUKE ATKORM.
WE WOULD HAVE BEEN LESS CORDIAL.
HE SEES LESAZON THE SAME WAY HIS MALEDON FRIENDS DO.
HE AND THE FOUR PRINCES OF PALLAS FORM AN EXCLUSIVE, ALL-MEN'S CLUB, DETERMINED TO RULE THE WORLD ONE DAY WHEN THEY INHERIT IT.
I'VE NEVER MET YOU IN PERSON. FROM ALL ACCOUNTS, MY SPIES TOLD ME ALL YOU CARED ABOUT WAS ATTENDING GRAND BALLS AND SOIREES. YOU SOUNDED LIKE A SPOILED ROYAL BRAT TO ME.
SEEING YOU NOW, I HAVE TO REVISE MY OPINION OF YOU. YOU ARE NOT AS SHALLOW AS I THOUGHT YOU WERE. YOU WILL FIND WE HAVE MUCH IN COMMON.
BUT... EVER SINCE THAT BATTLE AT KELD, THINGS ARE NOW DIFFERENT.
WITH YOU ON THE THRONE OF MATHENIA, WE CAN FORM A UNIQUE PARTNERSHIP.

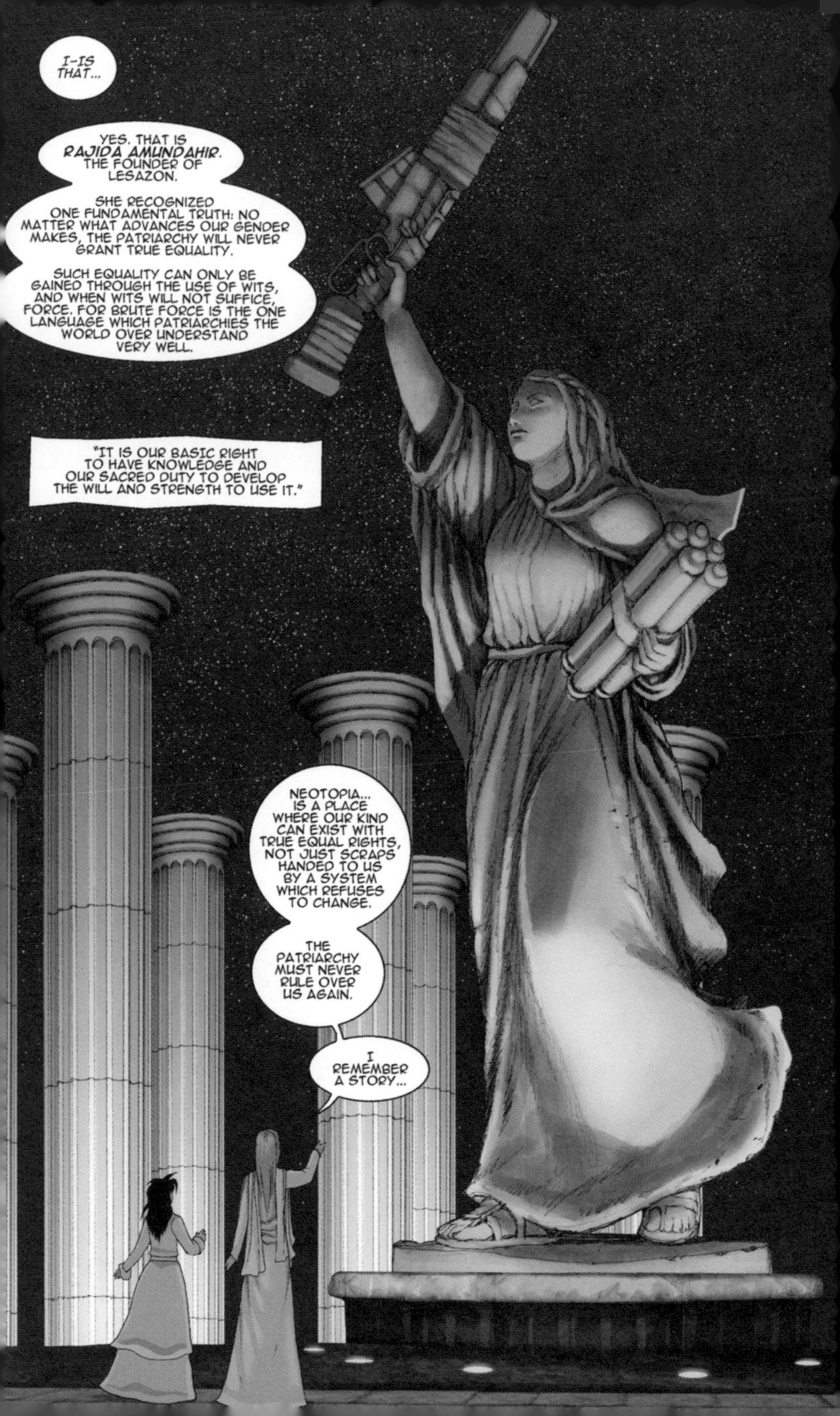
I-IS THAT...
YES. THAT IS *RAJIDA AMUNDAHIR*. THE FOUNDER OF LESAZON.
SHE RECOGNIZED ONE FUNDAMENTAL TRUTH: NO MATTER WHAT ADVANCES OUR GENDER MAKES, THE PATRIARCHY WILL NEVER GRANT TRUE EQUALITY.
SUCH EQUALITY CAN ONLY BE GAINED THROUGH THE USE OF WITS, AND WHEN WITS WILL NOT SUFFICE, FORCE. FOR BRUTE FORCE IS THE ONE LANGUAGE WHICH PATRIARCHIES THE WORLD OVER UNDERSTAND VERY WELL.
"IT IS OUR BASIC RIGHT TO HAVE KNOWLEDGE AND OUR SACRED DUTY TO DEVELOP THE WILL AND STRENGTH TO USE IT."
NEOTOPIA... IS A PLACE WHERE OUR KIND CAN EXIST WITH TRUE EQUAL RIGHTS, NOT JUST SCRAPS HANDED TO US BY A SYSTEM WHICH REFUSES TO CHANGE.
THE PATRIARCHY MUST NEVER RULE OVER US AGAIN.
I REMEMBER A STORY...

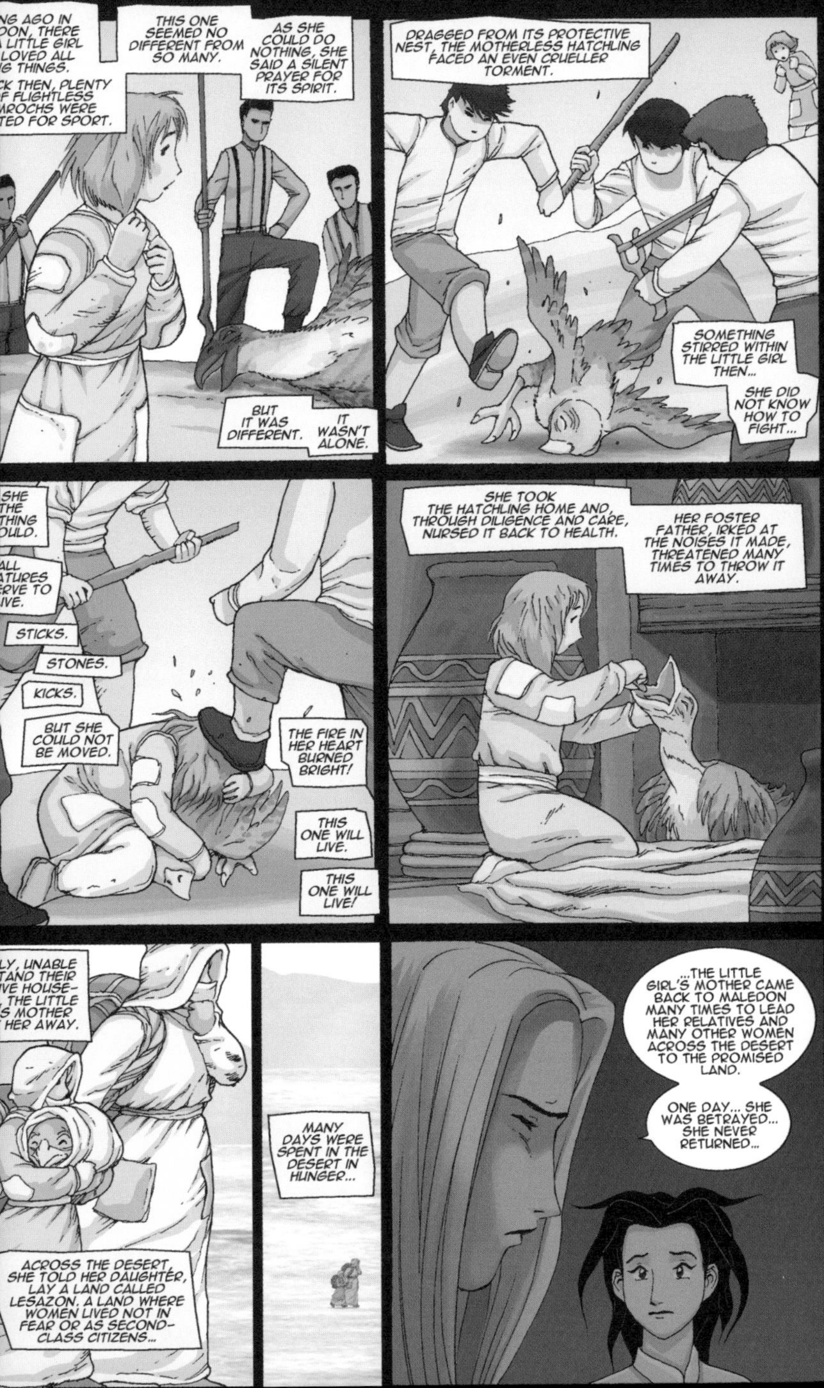
NG AGO IN
DON, THERE
A LITTLE GIRL
LOVED ALL
G THINGS.
CK THEN, PLENTY
F FLIGHTLESS
MAROCHS WERE
TED FOR SPORT.
THIS ONE SEEMED NO DIFFERENT FROM SO MANY.
AS SHE COULD DO NOTHING, SHE SAID A SILENT PRAYER FOR ITS SPIRIT.
BUT IT WAS DIFFERENT.
IT WASN'T ALONE.
DRAGGED FROM ITS PROTECTIVE NEST, THE MOTHERLESS HATCHLING FACED AN EVEN CRUELLER TORMENT.
SOMETHING STIRRED WITHIN THE LITTLE GIRL THEN...
SHE DID NOT KNOW HOW TO FIGHT...
SHE
THE
THING
OULD.
ALL
ATURES
ERVE TO
IVE.
STICKS.
STONES.
KICKS.
BUT SHE COULD NOT BE MOVED.
THE FIRE IN HER HEART BURNED BRIGHT!
THIS ONE WILL LIVE.
THIS ONE WILL LIVE!
SHE TOOK THE HATCHLING HOME AND, THROUGH DILIGENCE AND CARE, NURSED IT BACK TO HEALTH.
HER FOSTER FATHER, IRKED AT THE NOISES IT MADE, THREATENED MANY TIMES TO THROW IT AWAY.
LY, UNABLE
TAND THEIR
IVE HOUSE-
, THE LITTLE
'S MOTHER
HER AWAY.
ACROSS THE DESERT, SHE TOLD HER DAUGHTER, LAY A LAND CALLED LESAZON. A LAND WHERE WOMEN LIVED NOT IN FEAR OR AS SECOND-CLASS CITIZENS...
MANY DAYS WERE SPENT IN THE DESERT IN HUNGER...
...THE LITTLE GIRL'S MOTHER CAME BACK TO MALEDON MANY TIMES TO LEAD HER RELATIVES AND MANY OTHER WOMEN ACROSS THE DESERT TO THE PROMISED LAND.
ONE DAY... SHE WAS BETRAYED... SHE NEVER RETURNED...

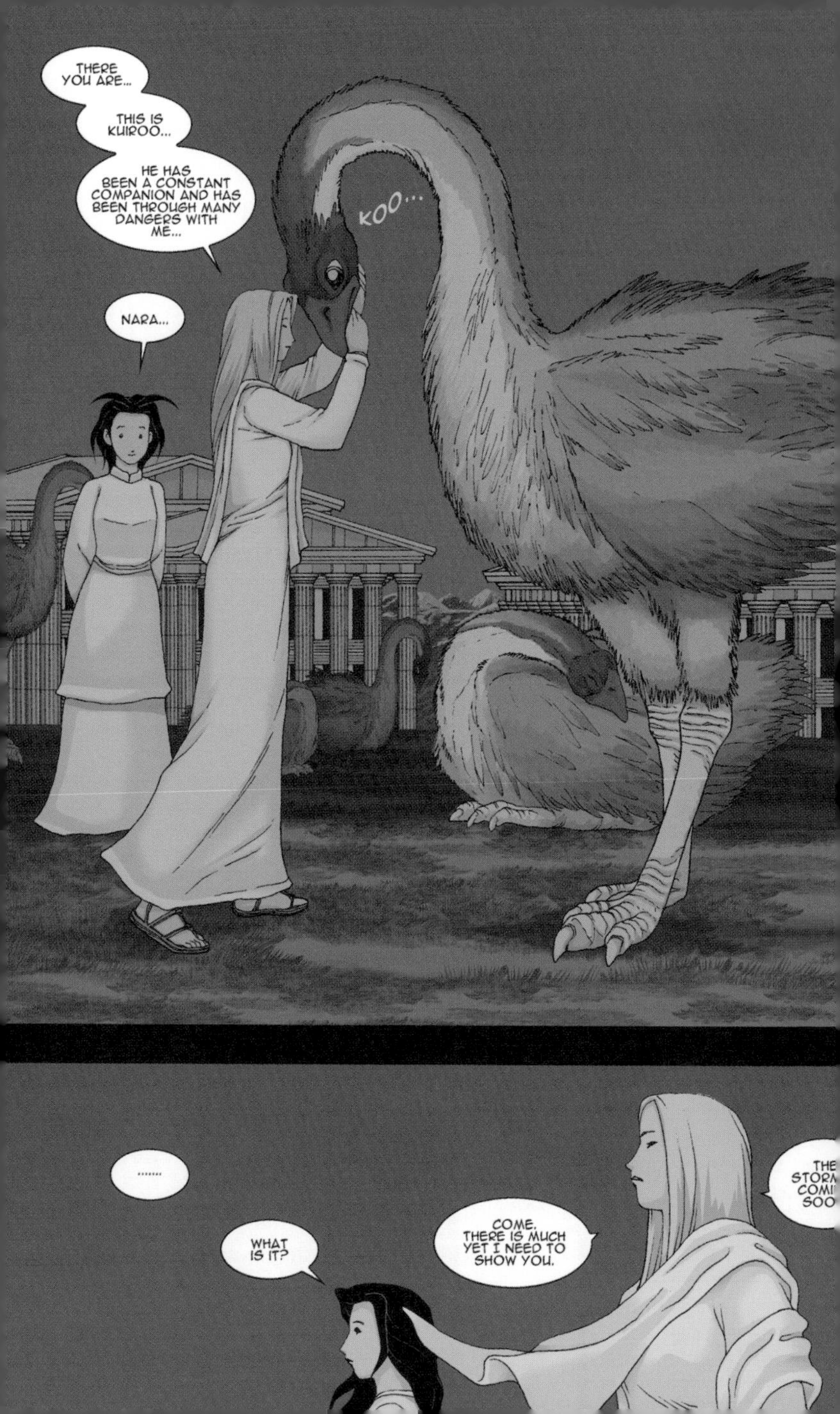
THERE YOU ARE...
THIS IS KUIROO...
HE HAS BEEN A CONSTANT COMPANION AND HAS BEEN THROUGH MANY DANGERS WITH ME...
KOO...
NARA...
......
WHAT IS IT?
COME. THERE IS MUCH YET I NEED TO SHOW YOU.
THE STORM COMI SOO

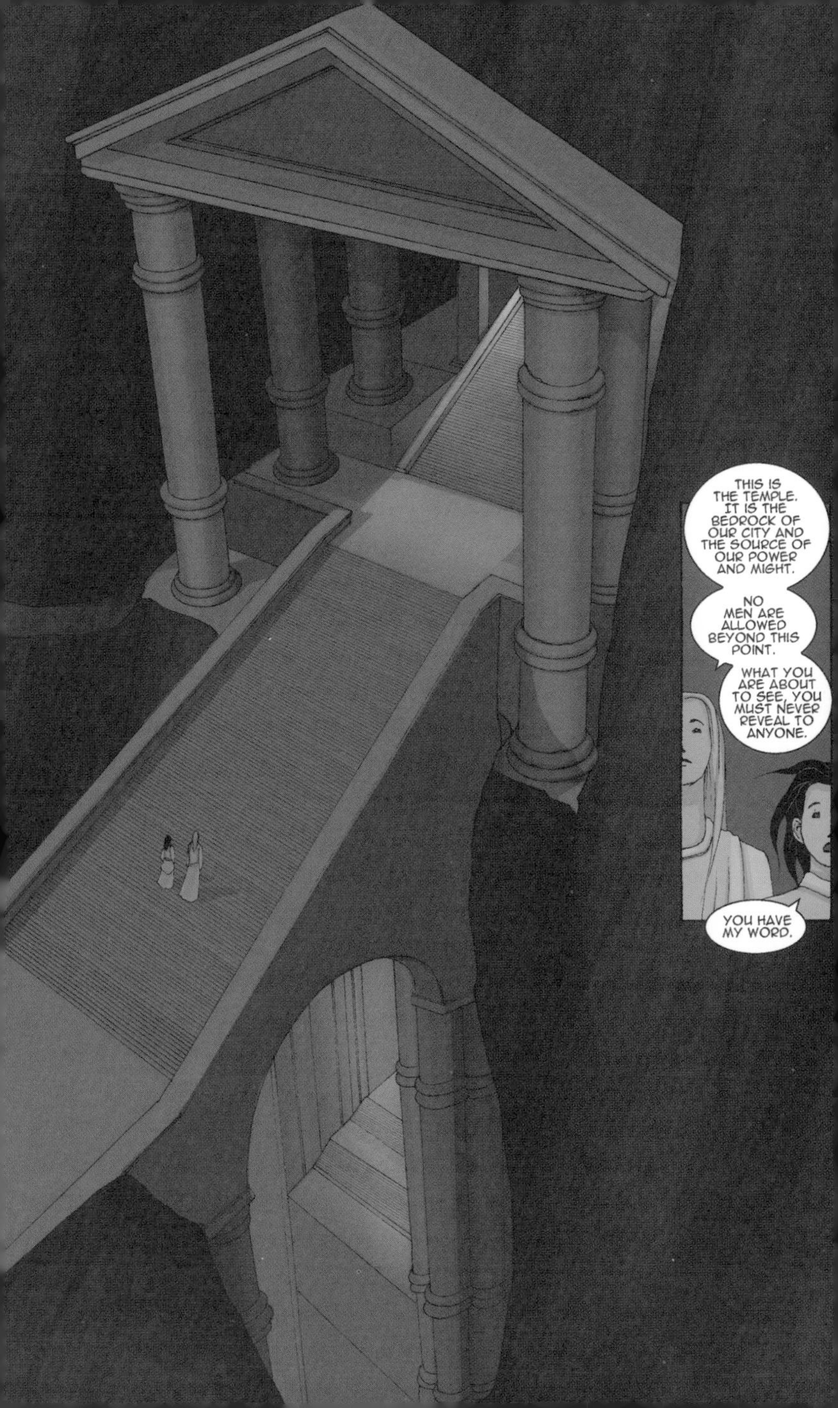
THIS IS THE TEMPLE. IT IS THE BEDROCK OF OUR CITY AND THE SOURCE OF OUR POWER AND MIGHT.
NO MEN ARE ALLOWED BEYOND THIS POINT.
WHAT YOU ARE ABOUT TO SEE, YOU MUST NEVER REVEAL TO ANYONE.
YOU HAVE MY WORD.

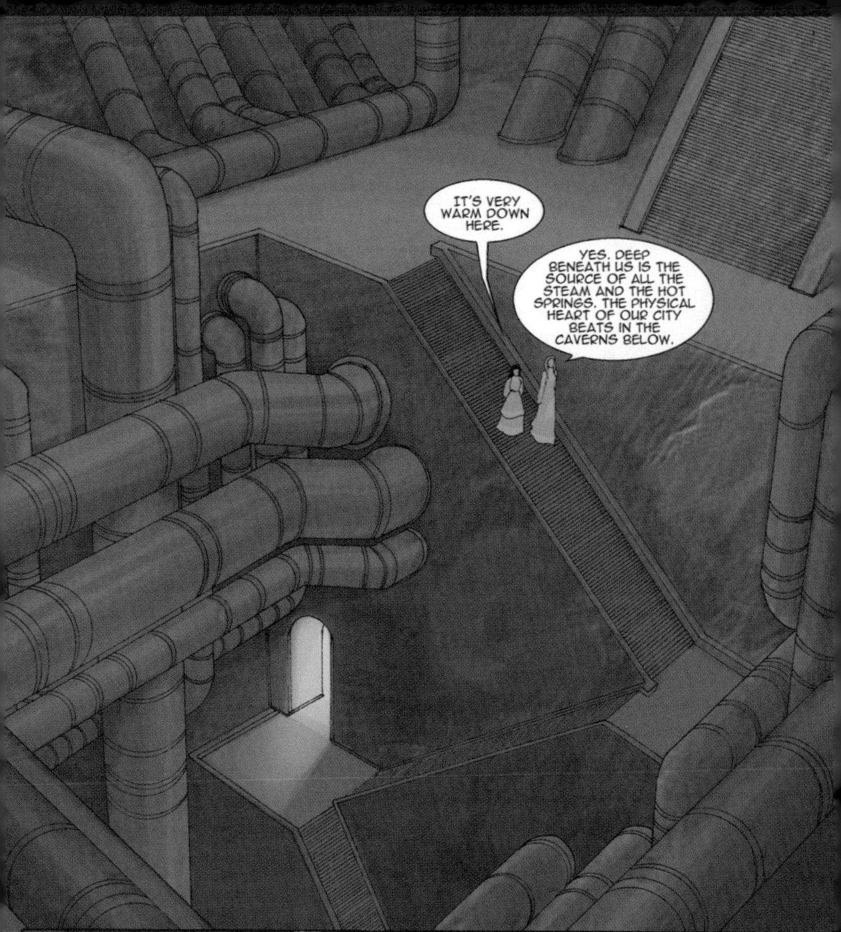
IT'S VERY WARM DOWN HERE.
YES. DEEP BENEATH US IS THE SOURCE OF ALL THE STEAM AND THE HOT SPRINGS. THE PHYSICAL HEART OF OUR CITY BEATS IN THE CAVERNS BELOW.
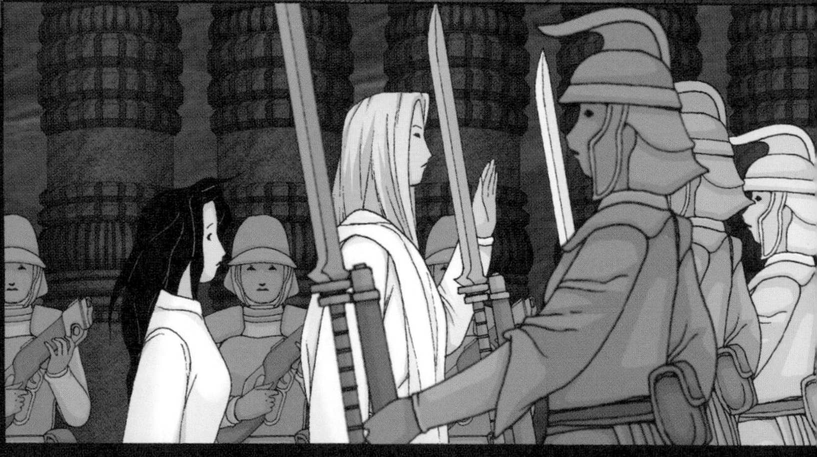

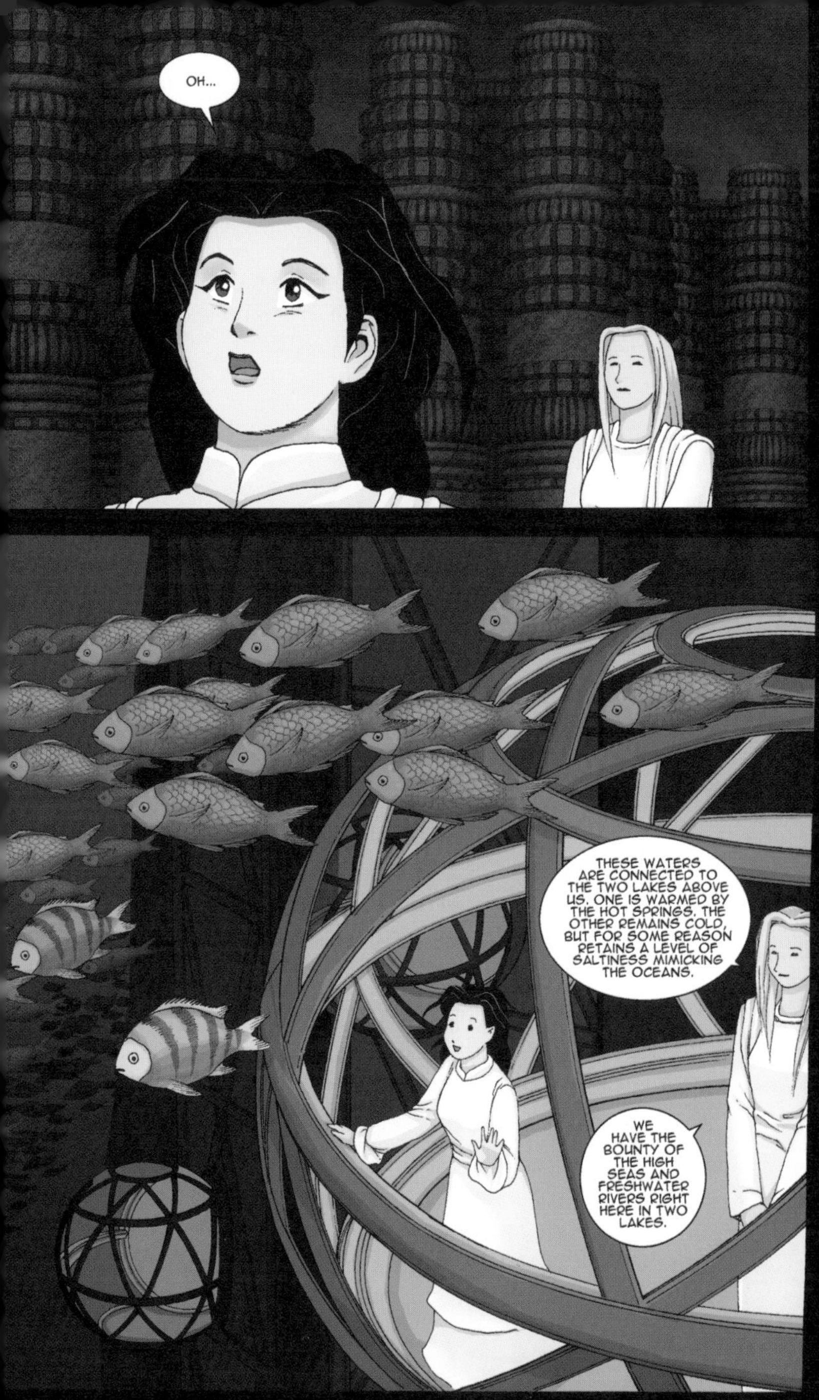
OH...
THESE WATERS ARE CONNECTED TO THE TWO LAKES ABOVE US. ONE IS WARMED BY THE HOT SPRINGS. THE OTHER REMAINS COLD, BUT FOR SOME REASON RETAINS A LEVEL OF SALTINESS MIMICKING THE OCEANS.
WE HAVE THE BOUNTY OF THE HIGH SEAS AND FRESHWATER RIVERS RIGHT HERE IN TWO LAKES.

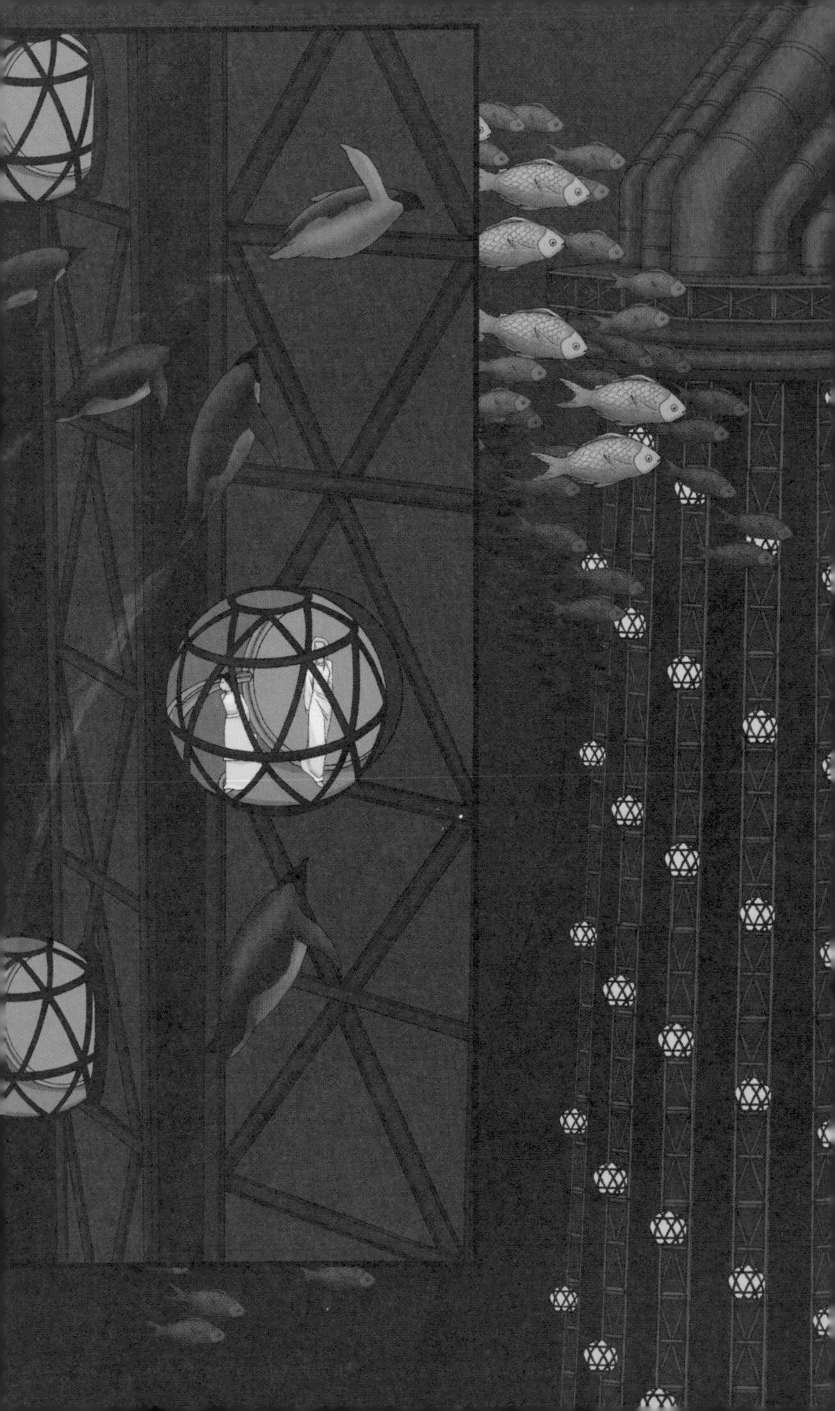

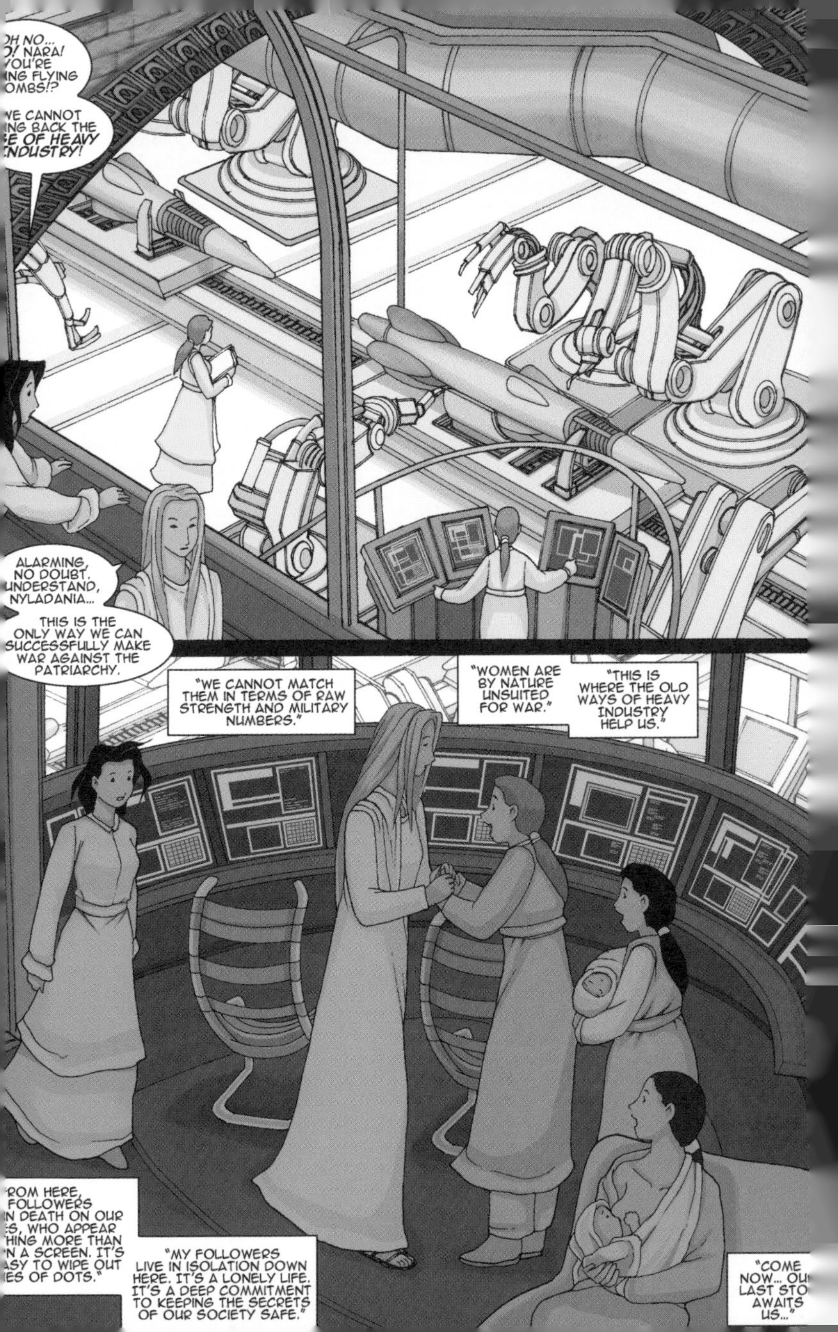

OH NO... O! NARA! YOU'RE ING FLYING OMBS!?
WE CANNOT ING BACK THE E OF HEAVY INDUSTRY!
ALARMING, NO DOUBT. UNDERSTAND, NYLADANIA...
THIS IS THE ONLY WAY WE CAN SUCCESSFULLY MAKE WAR AGAINST THE PATRIARCHY.
"WE CANNOT MATCH THEM IN TERMS OF RAW STRENGTH AND MILITARY NUMBERS."
"WOMEN ARE BY NATURE UNSUITED FOR WAR."
"THIS IS WHERE THE OLD WAYS OF HEAVY INDUSTRY HELP US."
ROM HERE, FOLLOWERS N DEATH ON OUR S, WHO APPEAR HING MORE THAN N A SCREEN. IT'S ASY TO WIPE OUT ES OF DOTS."
"MY FOLLOWERS LIVE IN ISOLATION DOWN HERE. IT'S A LONELY LIFE. IT'S A DEEP COMMITMENT TO KEEPING THE SECRETS OF OUR SOCIETY SAFE."
"COME NOW... OU LAST STO AWAITS US..."

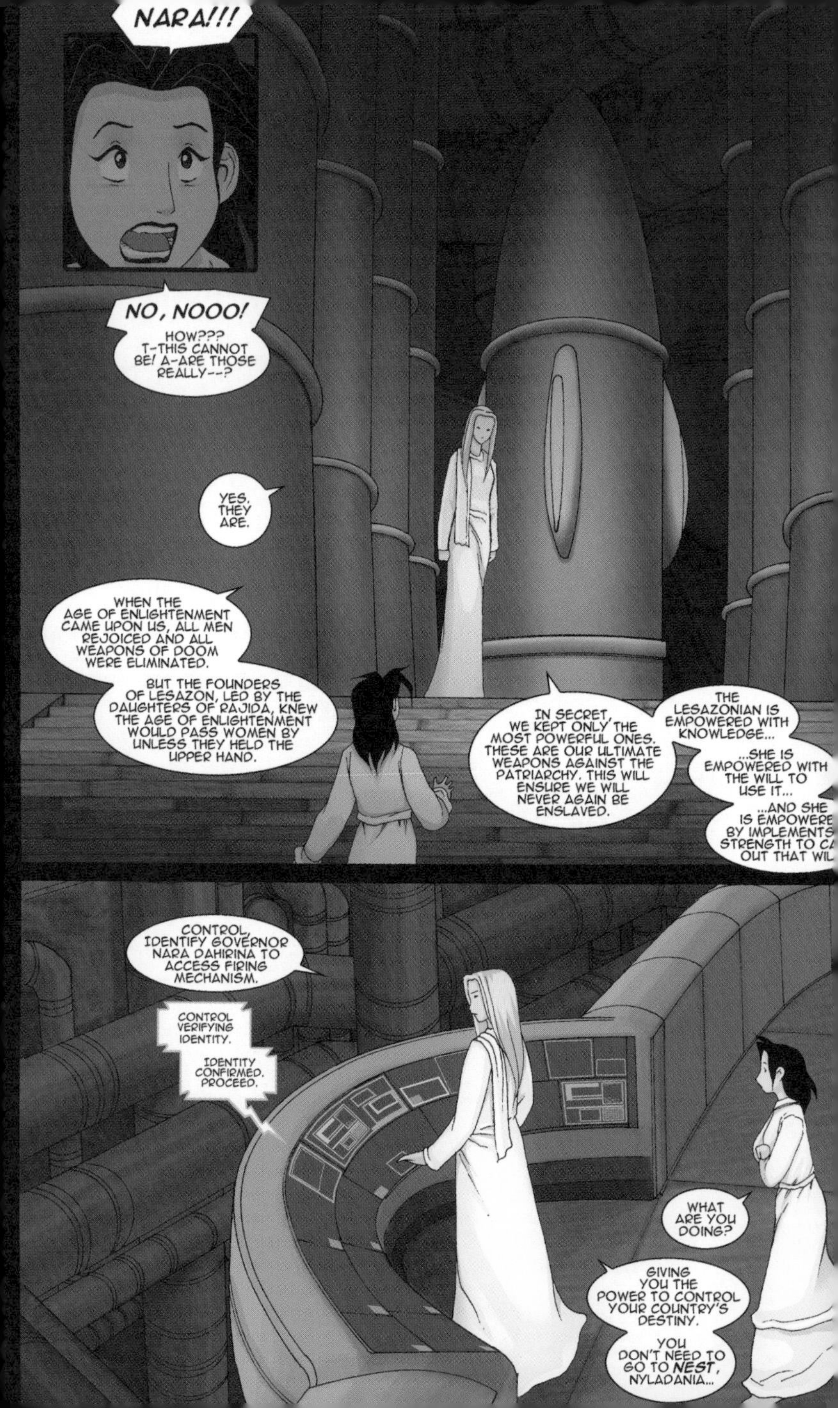
NARA!!!
NO, NOOO!
HOW??? T-THIS CANNOT BE! A-ARE THOSE REALLY--?
YES, THEY ARE.
WHEN THE AGE OF ENLIGHTENMENT CAME UPON US, ALL MEN REJOICED AND ALL WEAPONS OF DOOM WERE ELIMINATED.
BUT THE FOUNDERS OF LESAZON, LED BY THE DAUGHTERS OF RAJIDA, KNEW THE AGE OF ENLIGHTENMENT WOULD PASS WOMEN BY UNLESS THEY HELD THE UPPER HAND.
IN SECRET, WE KEPT ONLY THE MOST POWERFUL ONES. THESE ARE OUR ULTIMATE WEAPONS AGAINST THE PATRIARCHY. THIS WILL ENSURE WE WILL NEVER AGAIN BE ENSLAVED.
THE LESAZONIAN IS EMPOWERED WITH KNOWLEDGE...
...SHE IS EMPOWERED WITH THE WILL TO USE IT...
CONTROL, IDENTIFY GOVERNOR NARA DAHIRINA TO ACCESS FIRING MECHANISM.
CONTROL VERIFYING IDENTITY.
IDENTITY CONFIRMED. PROCEED.
WHAT ARE YOU DOING?
GIVING YOU THE POWER TO CONTROL YOUR COUNTRY'S DESTINY.
YOU DON'T NEED TO GO TO NEST, NYLADANIA...

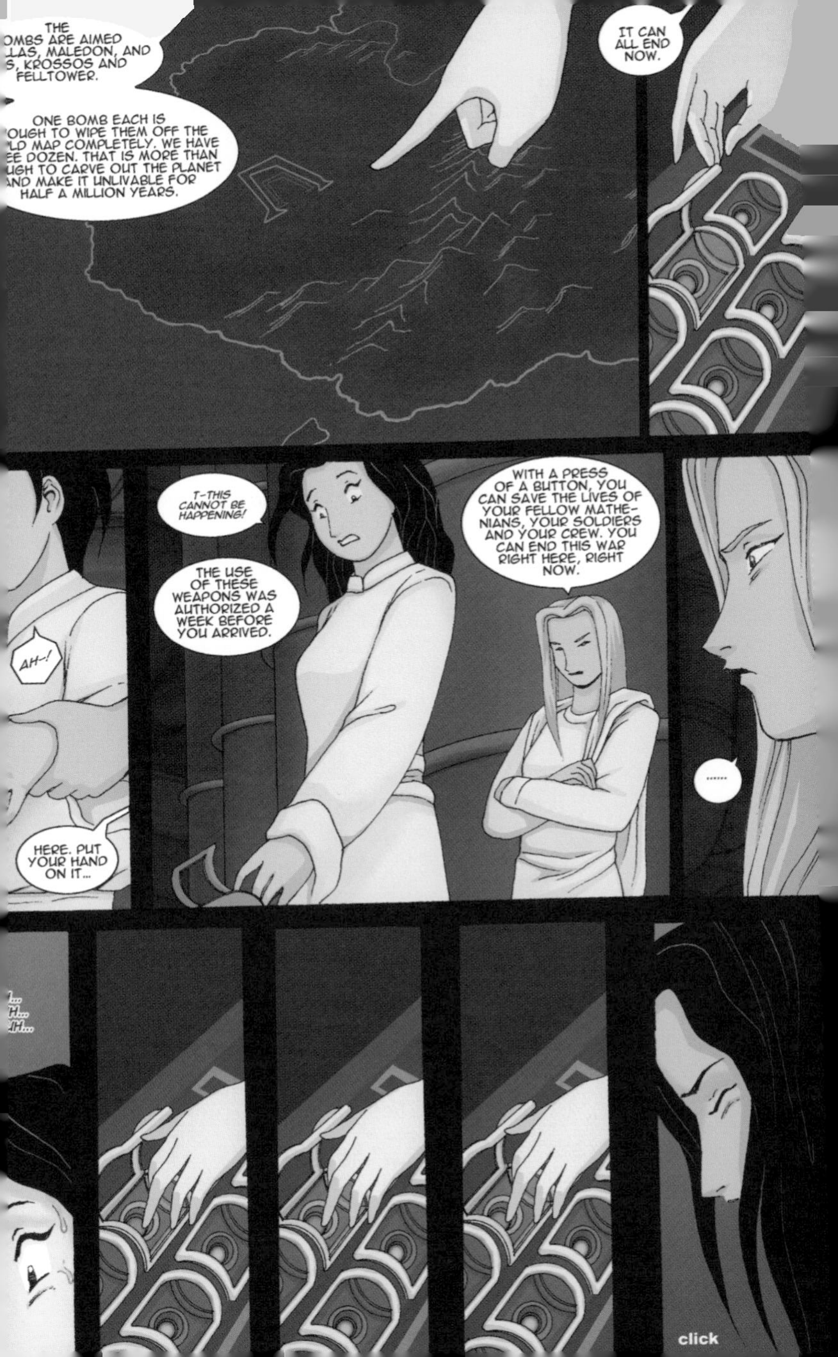
THE
OMBS ARE AIMED
LLAS, MALEDON, AND
S, KROSSOS AND
FELLTOWER.
ONE BOMB EACH IS
OUGH TO WIPE THEM OFF THE
LD MAP COMPLETELY. WE HAVE
EE DOZEN. THAT IS MORE THAN
UGH TO CARVE OUT THE PLANET
AND MAKE IT UNLIVABLE FOR
HALF A MILLION YEARS.
IT CAN ALL END NOW.
T-THIS CANNOT BE HAPPENING!
THE USE OF THESE WEAPONS WAS AUTHORIZED A WEEK BEFORE YOU ARRIVED.
WITH A PRESS OF A BUTTON, YOU CAN SAVE THE LIVES OF YOUR FELLOW MATHE-NIANS, YOUR SOLDIERS AND YOUR CREW. YOU CAN END THIS WAR RIGHT HERE, RIGHT NOW.
AH-!
......
HERE. PUT YOUR HAND ON IT...
click

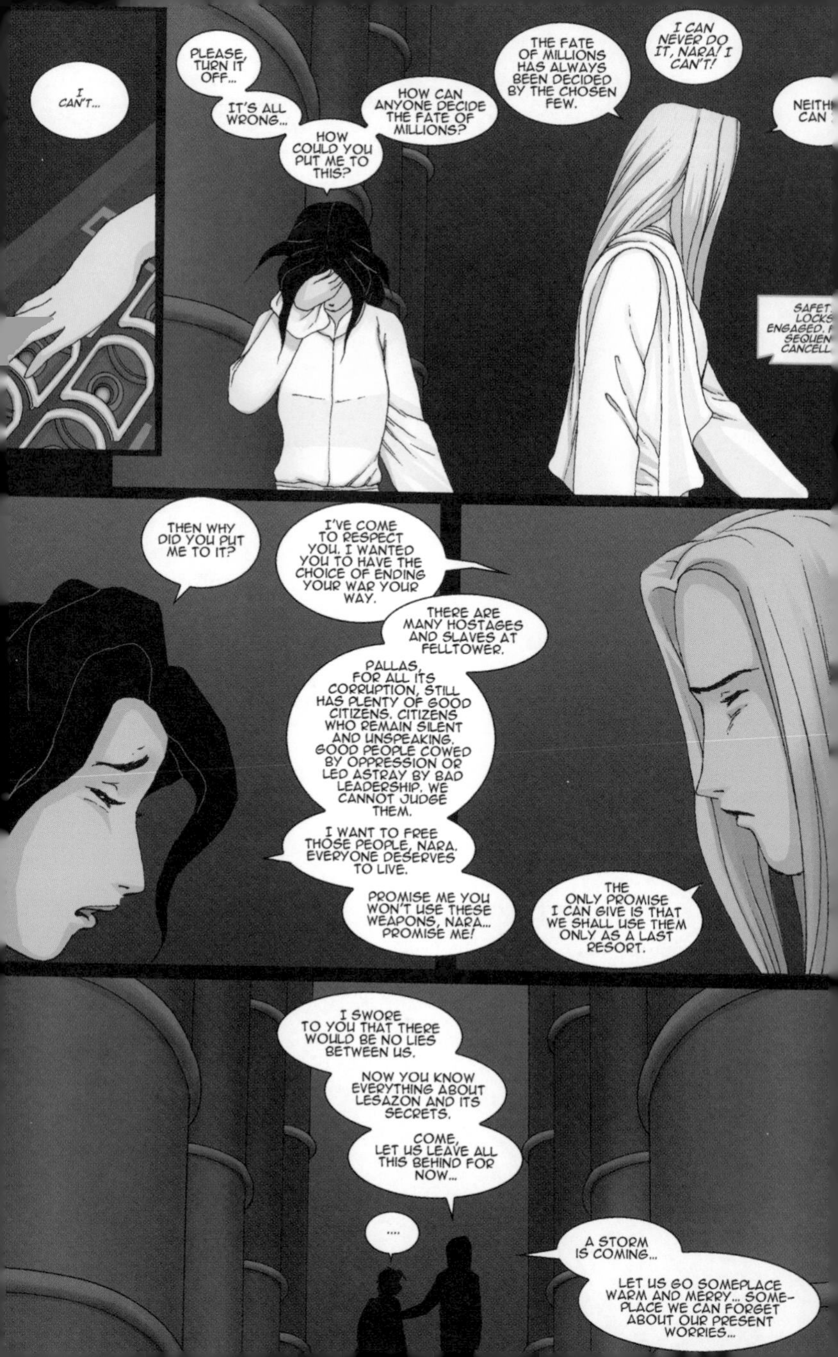
I CAN'T...
PLEASE, TURN IT OFF...
IT'S ALL WRONG...
HOW COULD YOU PUT ME TO THIS?
HOW CAN ANYONE DECIDE THE FATE OF MILLIONS?
THE FATE OF MILLIONS HAS ALWAYS BEEN DECIDED BY THE CHOSEN FEW.
I CAN NEVER DO IT, NARA! I CAN'T!
THEN WHY DID YOU PUT ME TO IT?
I'VE COME TO RESPECT YOU. I WANTED YOU TO HAVE THE CHOICE OF ENDING YOUR WAR YOUR WAY.
THERE ARE MANY HOSTAGES AND SLAVES AT FELLTOWER.
PALLAS, FOR ALL ITS CORRUPTION, STILL HAS PLENTY OF GOOD CITIZENS. CITIZENS WHO REMAIN SILENT AND UNSPEAKING. GOOD PEOPLE COWED BY OPPRESSION OR LED ASTRAY BY BAD LEADERSHIP. WE CANNOT JUDGE THEM.
I WANT TO FREE THOSE PEOPLE, NARA. EVERYONE DESERVES TO LIVE.
PROMISE ME YOU WON'T USE THESE WEAPONS, NARA... PROMISE ME!
THE ONLY PROMISE I CAN GIVE IS THAT WE SHALL USE THEM ONLY AS A LAST RESORT.
I SWORE TO YOU THAT THERE WOULD BE NO LIES BETWEEN US.
NOW YOU KNOW EVERYTHING ABOUT LESAZON AND ITS SECRETS.
COME, LET US LEAVE ALL THIS BEHIND FOR NOW...
....
A STORM IS COMING...
LET US GO SOMEPLACE WARM AND MERRY... SOME-PLACE WE CAN FORGET ABOUT OUR PRESENT WORRIES...

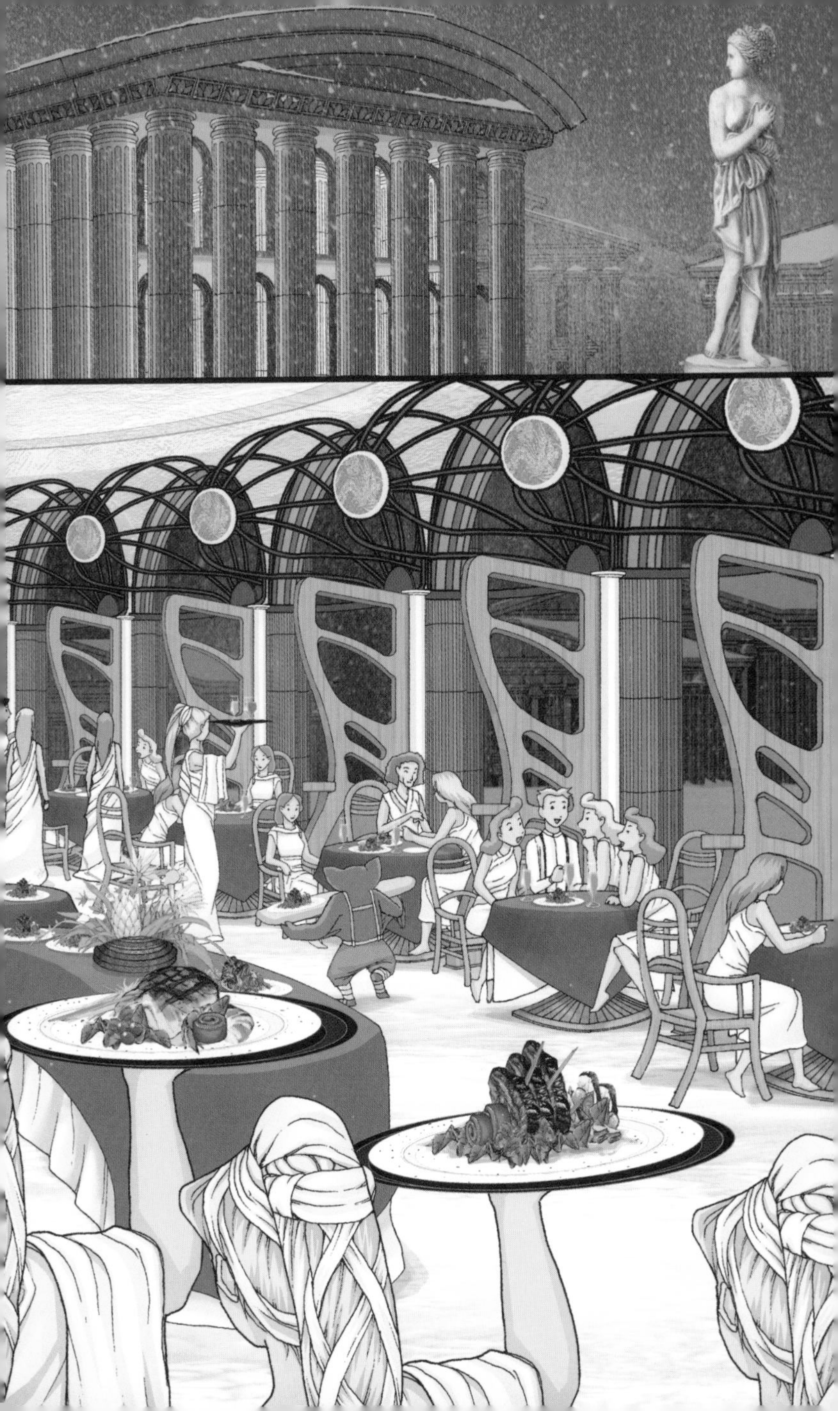

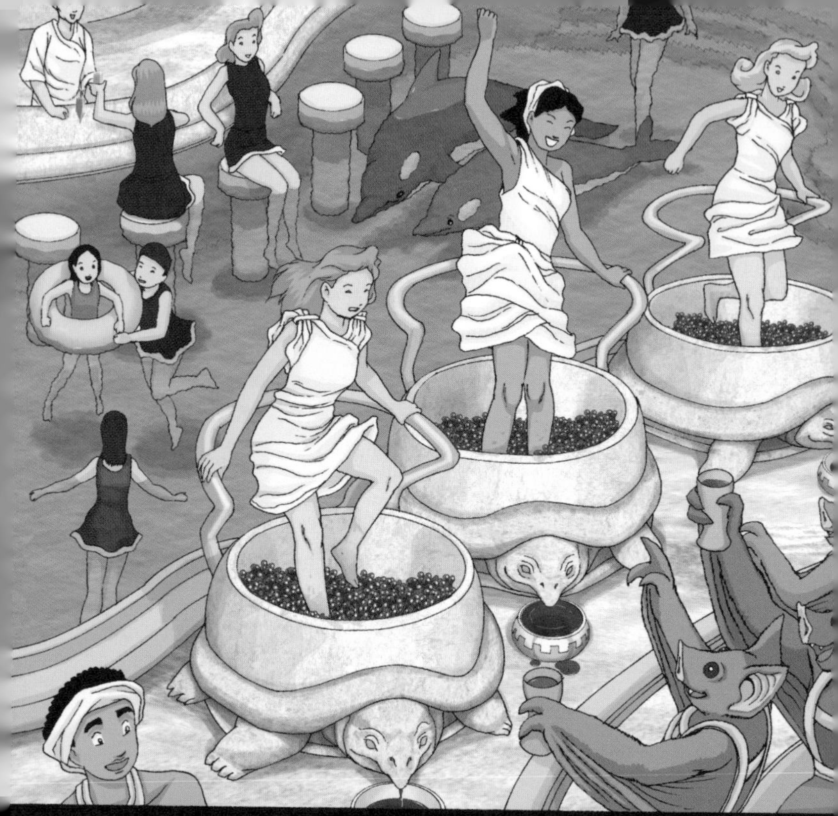
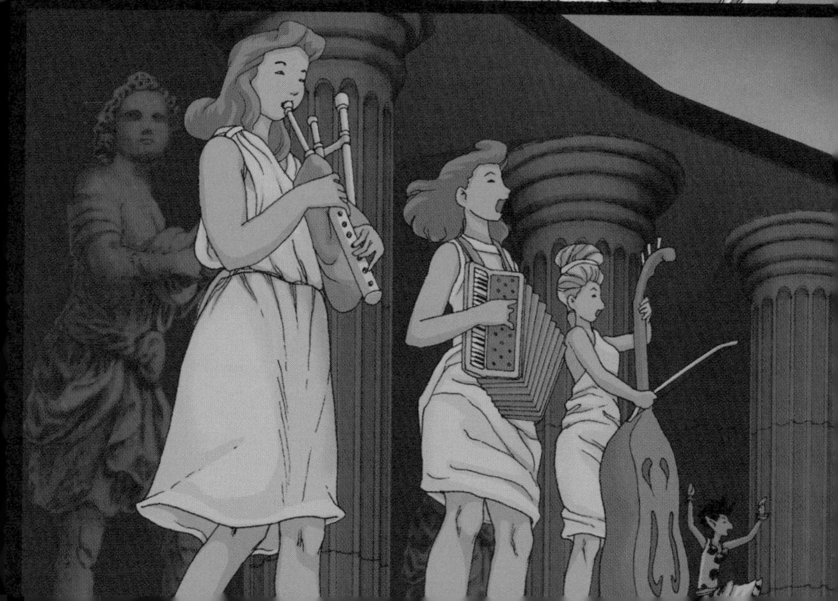

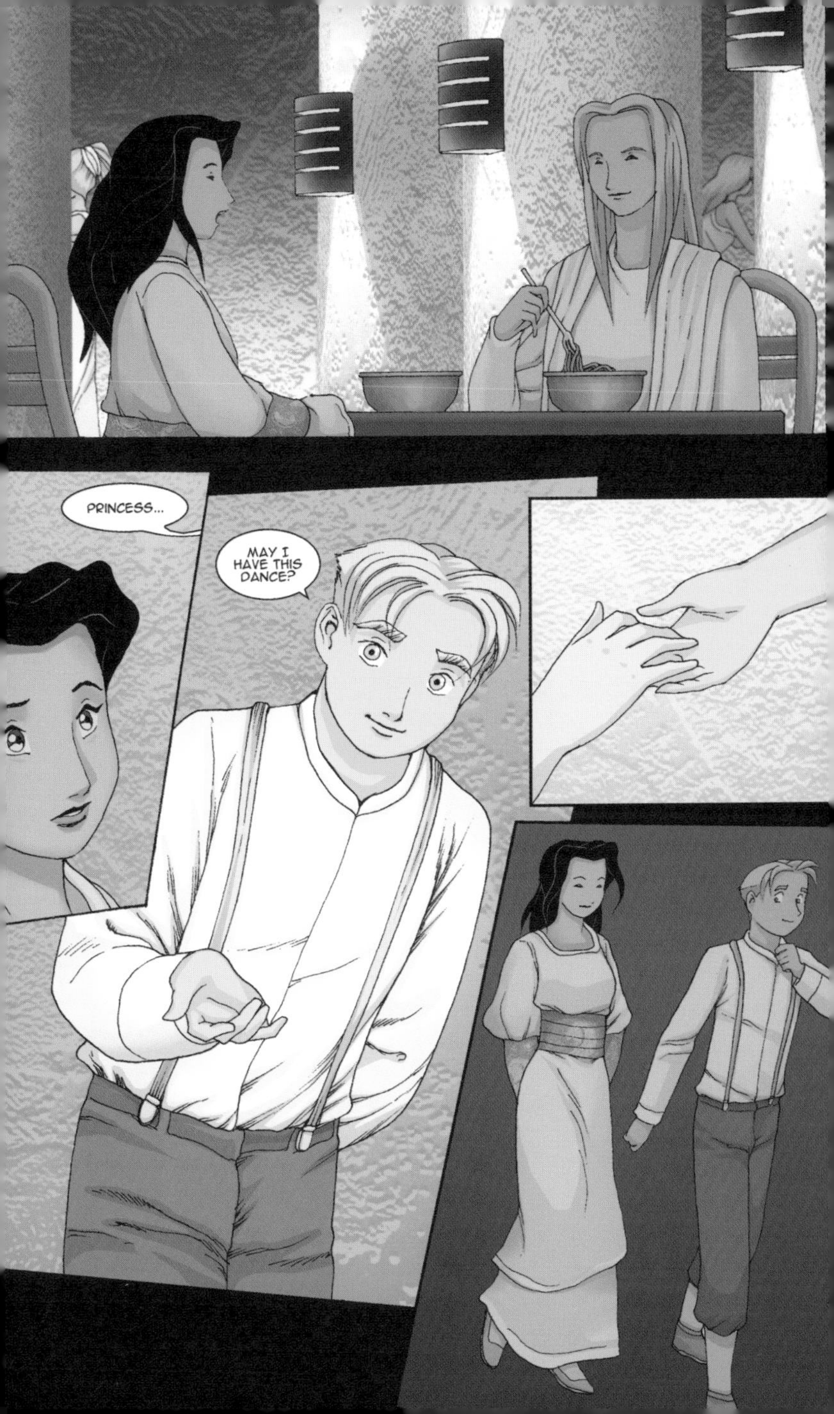
PRINCESS...
MAY I HAVE THIS DANCE?

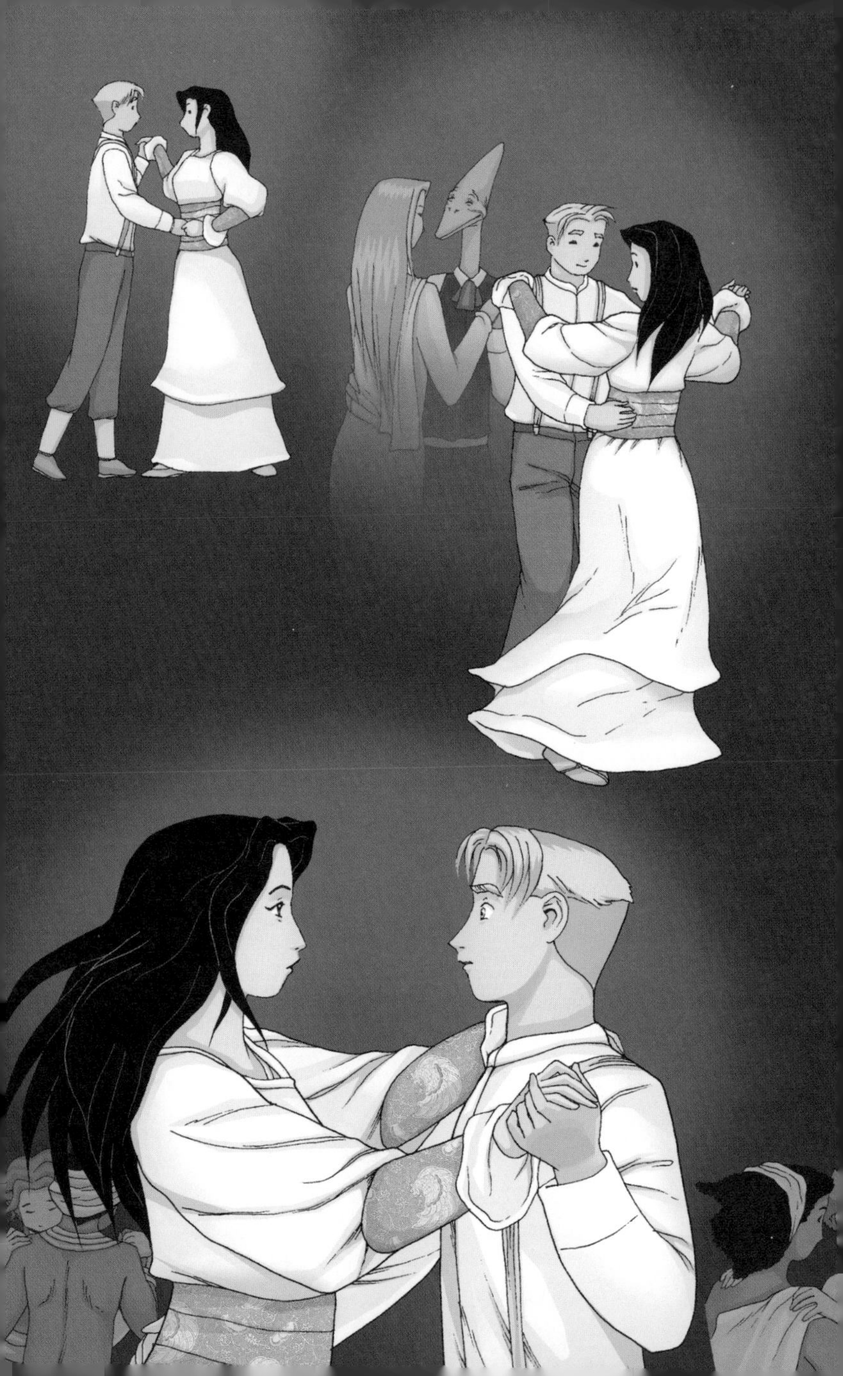

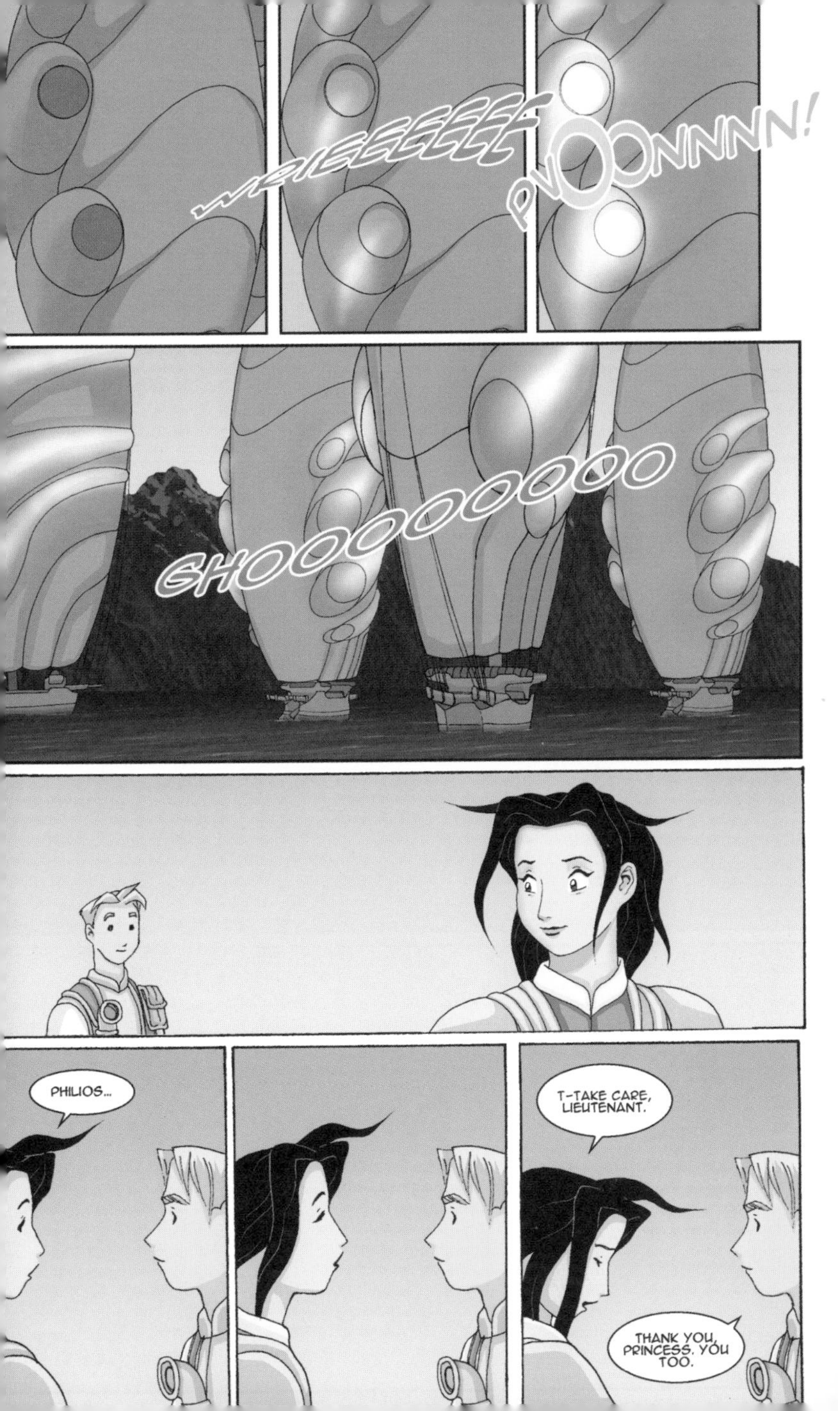
WHEEEEEEEE
PVOONNNNN!
GHOOOOOOOOOO
PHILIOS...
T-TAKE CARE, LIEUTENANT.
THANK YOU, PRINCESS. YOU TOO.

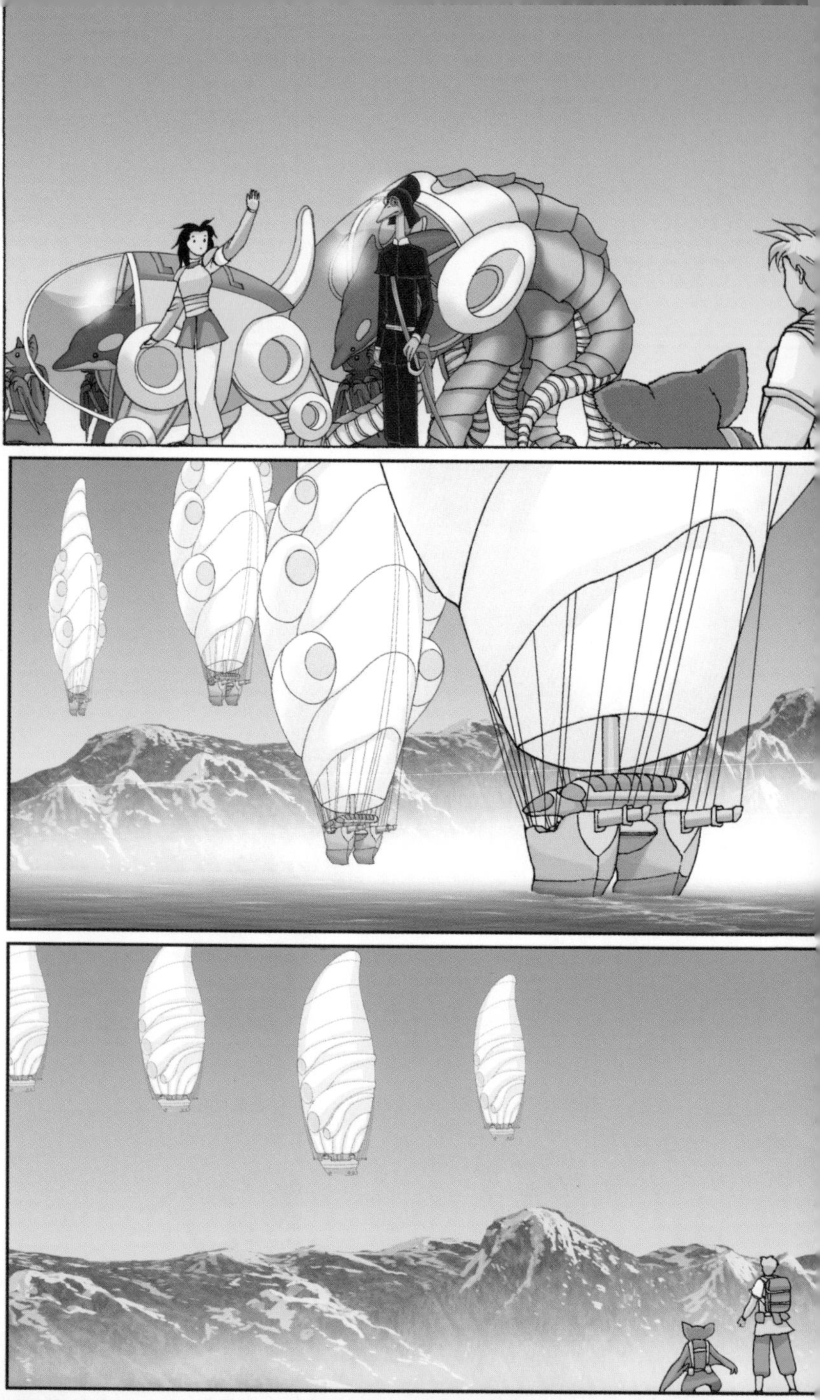

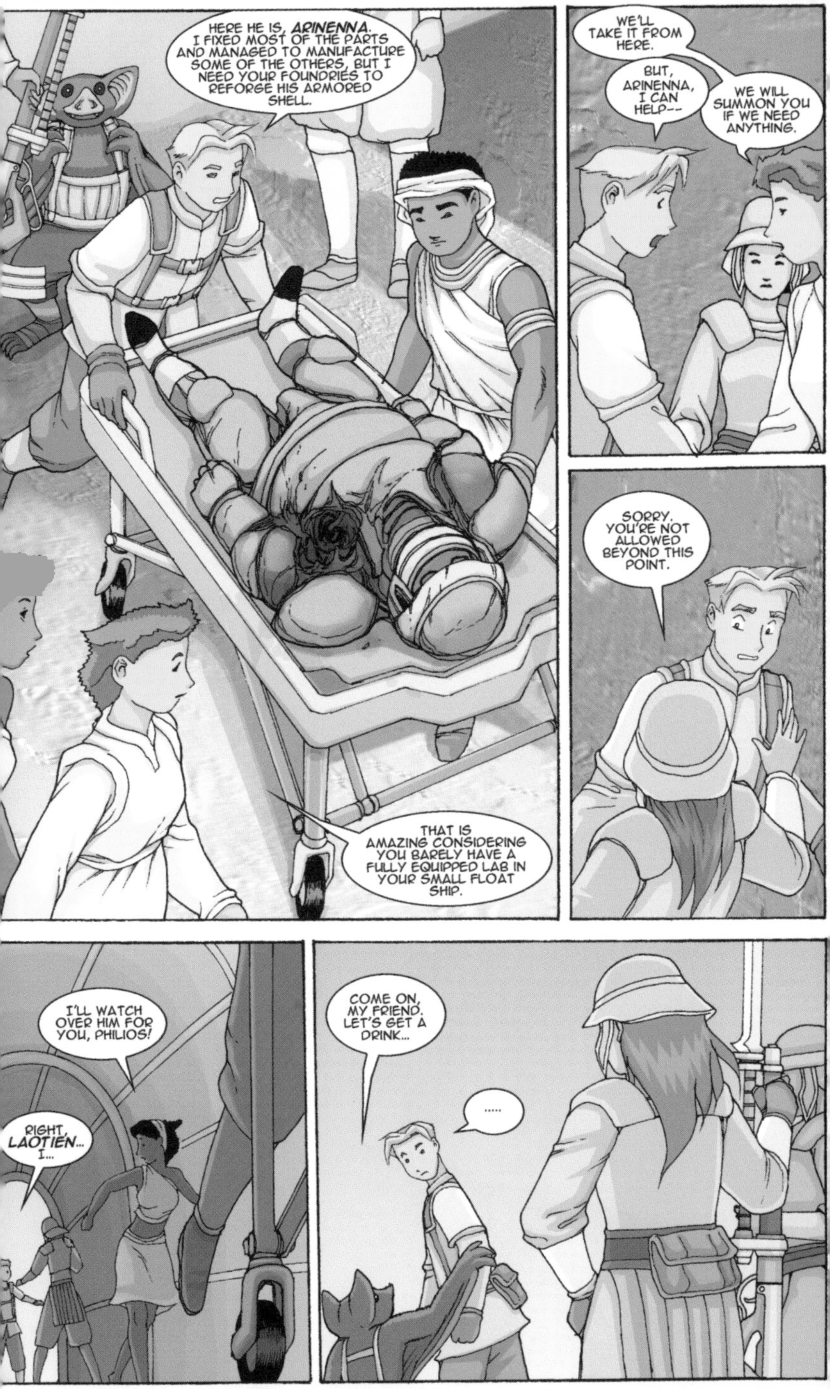
HERE HE IS, ARINENNA. I FIXED MOST OF THE PARTS AND MANAGED TO MANUFACTURE SOME OF THE OTHERS, BUT I NEED YOUR FOUNDRIES TO REFORGE HIS ARMORED SHELL.
THAT IS AMAZING CONSIDERING YOU BARELY HAVE A FULLY EQUIPPED LAB IN YOUR SMALL FLOAT SHIP.
WE'LL TAKE IT FROM HERE.
BUT, ARINENNA, I CAN HELP--
WE WILL SUMMON YOU IF WE NEED ANYTHING.
SORRY. YOU'RE NOT ALLOWED BEYOND THIS POINT.
I'LL WATCH OVER HIM FOR YOU, PHILIOS!
RIGHT, LAOTIEN... I...
COME ON, MY FRIEND. LET'S GET A DRINK...
.....

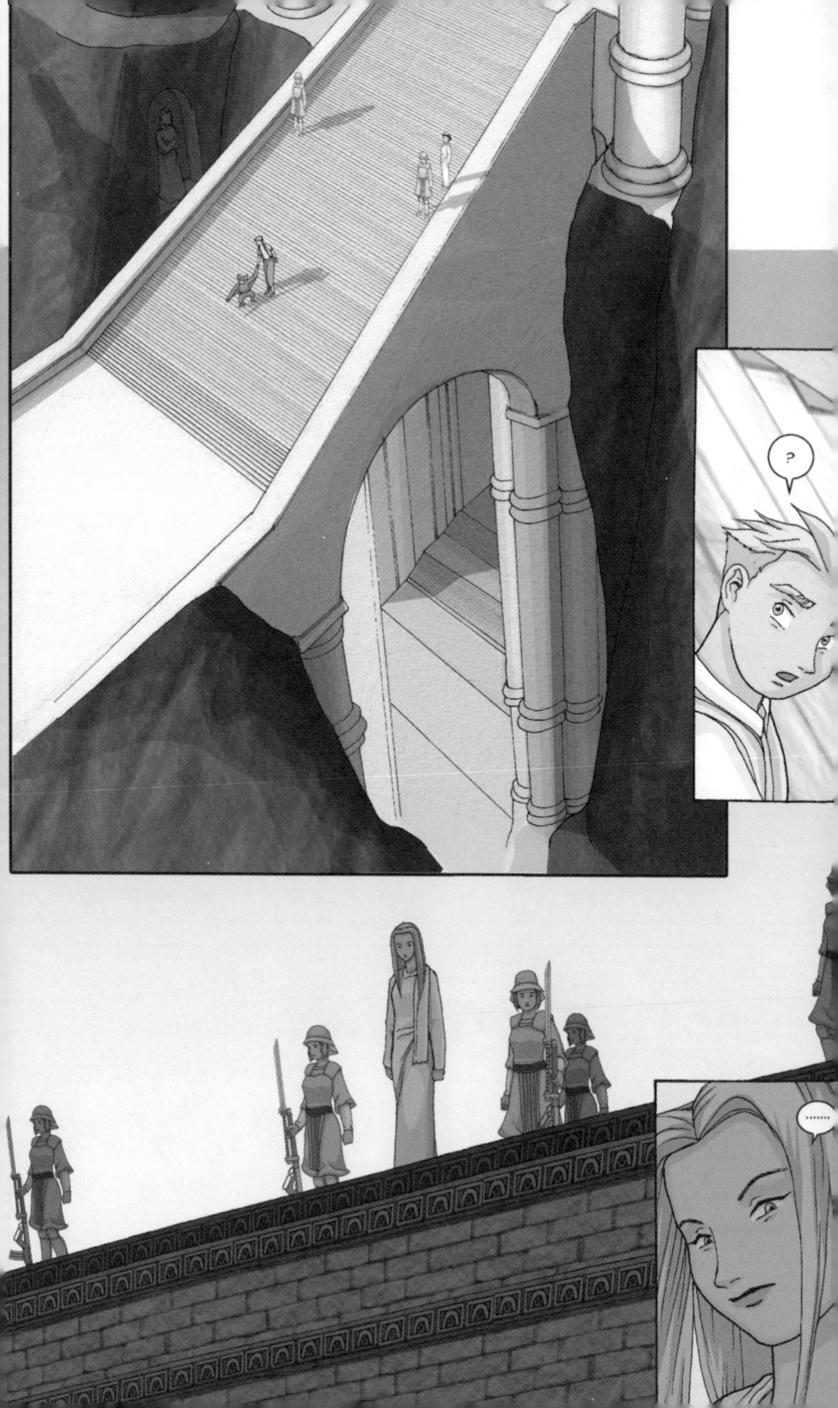
?
......

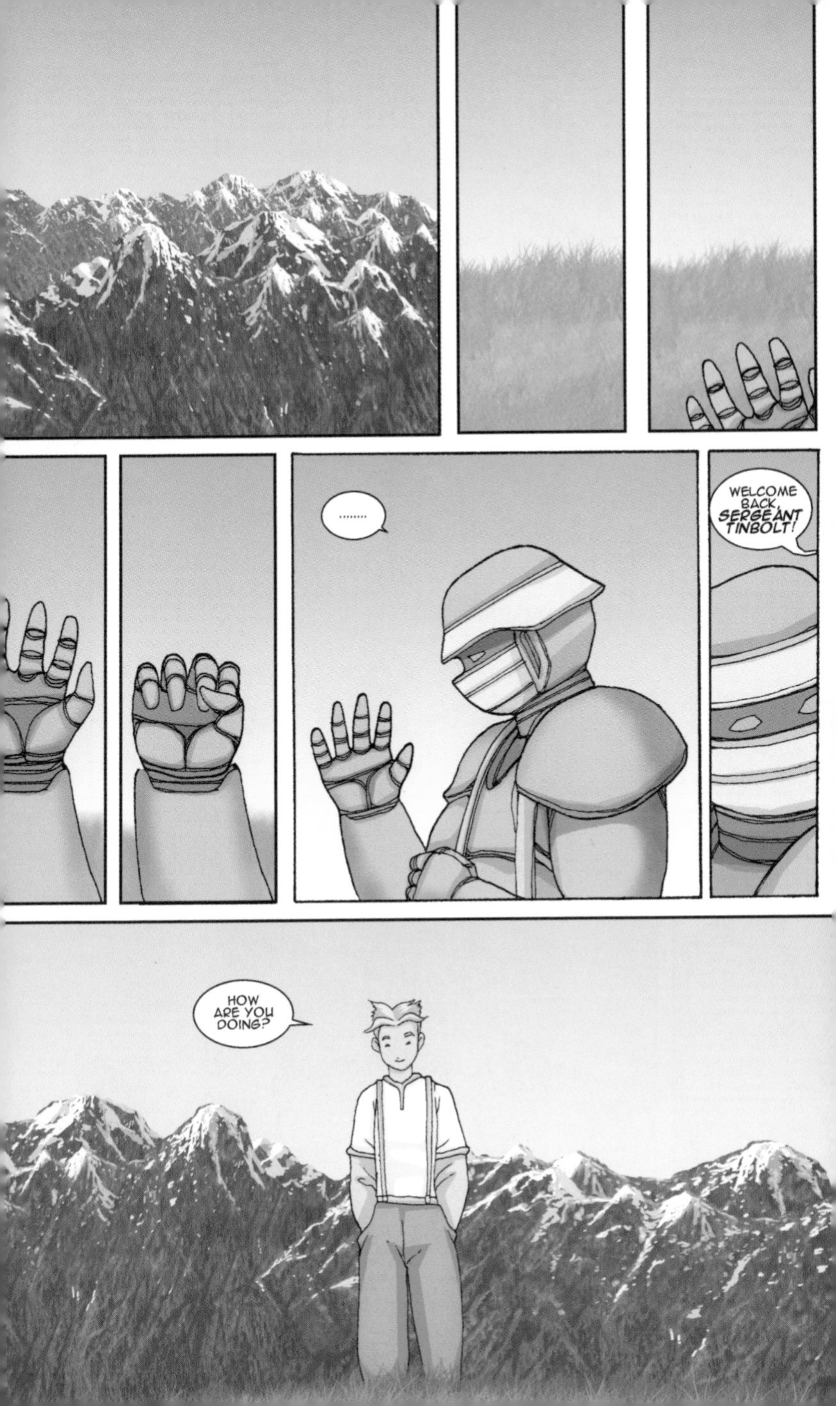
....
WELCOME BACK, SERGEANT TINBOLT!
HOW ARE YOU DOING?

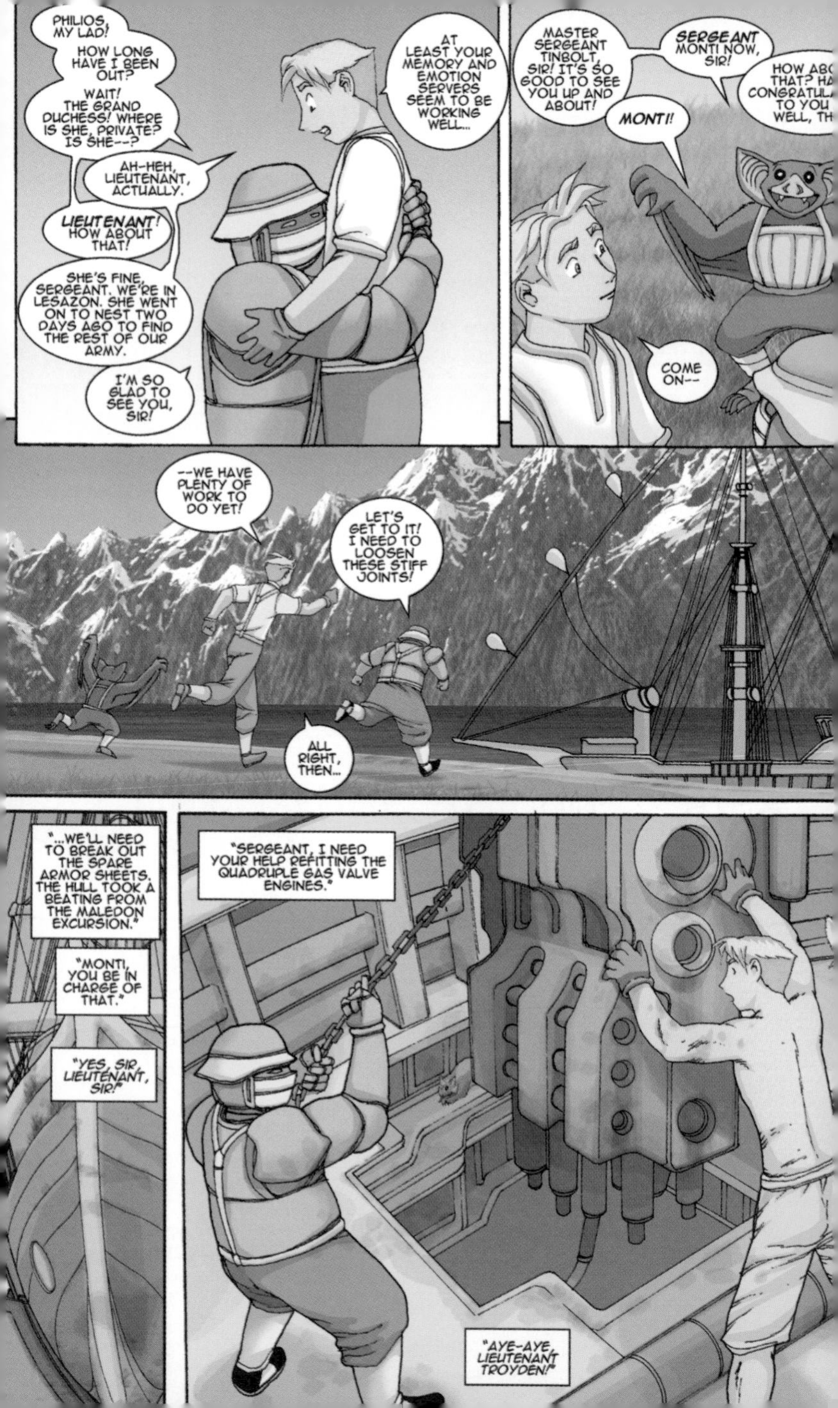
PHILIOS, MY LAD!
HOW LONG HAVE I BEEN OUT?
WAIT! THE GRAND DUCHESS! WHERE IS SHE, PRIVATE? IS SHE--?
AT LEAST YOUR MEMORY AND EMOTION SERVERS SEEM TO BE WORKING WELL...
AH-HEH, LIEUTENANT, ACTUALLY.
LIEUTENANT! HOW ABOUT THAT!
SHE'S FINE, SERGEANT. WE'RE IN LESAZON. SHE WENT ON TO NEST TWO DAYS AGO TO FIND THE REST OF OUR ARMY.
I'M SO GLAD TO SEE YOU, SIR!
MASTER SERGEANT TINBOLT, SIR! IT'S SO GOOD TO SEE YOU UP AND ABOUT!
SERGEANT MONTI NOW, SIR!
MONTI!
COME ON--
--WE HAVE PLENTY OF WORK TO DO YET!
LET'S GET TO IT! I NEED TO LOOSEN THESE STIFF JOINTS!
ALL RIGHT, THEN...
"...WE'LL NEED TO BREAK OUT THE SPARE ARMOR SHEETS. THE HULL TOOK A BEATING FROM THE MALEDON EXCURSION."
"MONTI, YOU BE IN CHARGE OF THAT."
"YES, SIR, LIEUTENANT, SIR!"
"SERGEANT, I NEED YOUR HELP REFITTING THE QUADRUPLE GAS VALVE ENGINES."
"AYE-AYE, LIEUTENANT TROYDEN!"

HELLO, PHILIOS!

LAOTIEN!

LIEUTENANT, WHERE DO YOU WANT THIS?

THE BOTTOM DECK, *TIALAK*, AT THE HYDROCAULDRON CHAMBER.

TIALAK...

THANK YOU.

"WE'RE MAKING GOOD TIME."

"THE REPAIRS AND REFITTING WILL BE DONE IN THIRTY MORE HOURS."

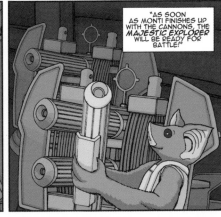

"AS SOON AS MONTI FINISHES UP WITH THE CANNONS, THE *MAJESTIC EXPLORER* WILL BE READY FOR BATTLE!"

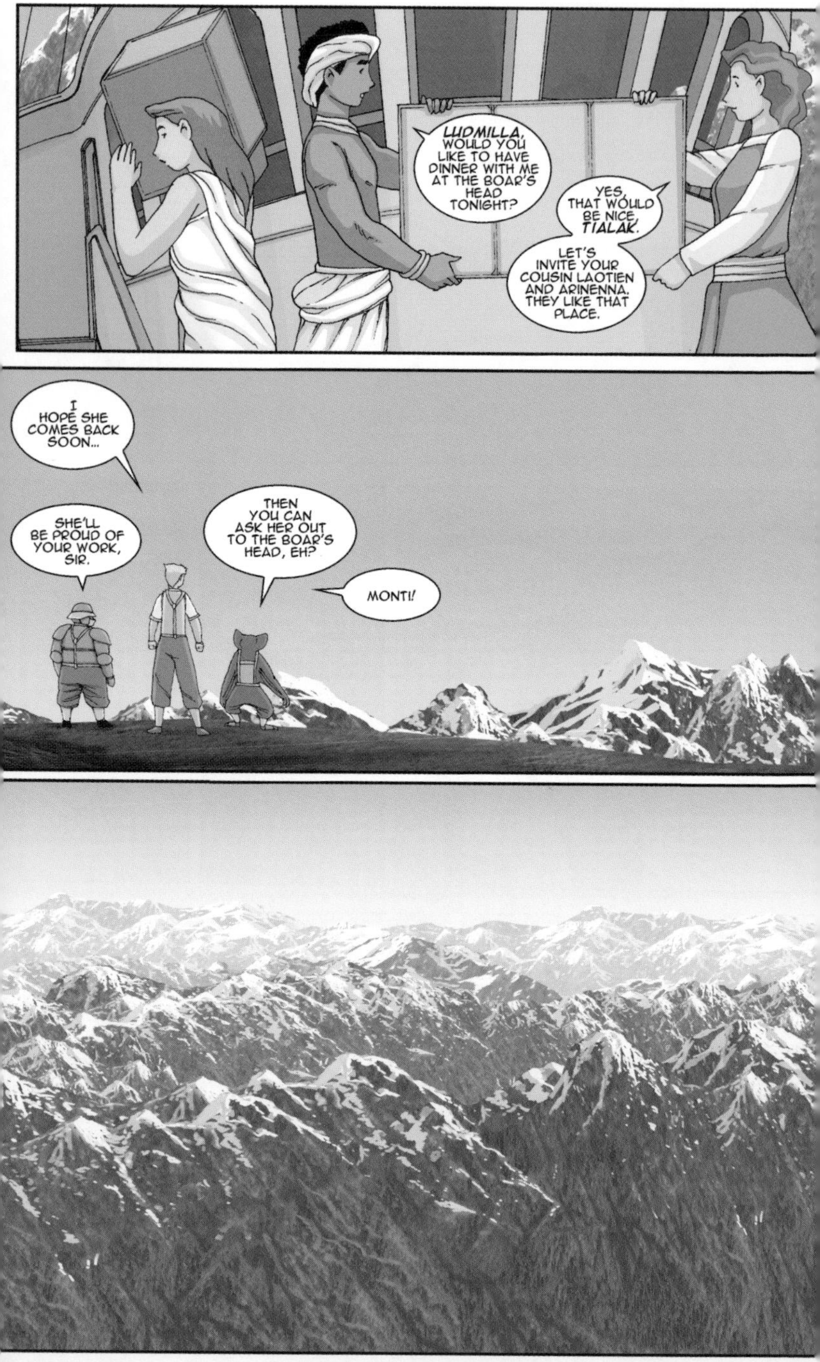
LUDMILLA, WOULD YOU LIKE TO HAVE DINNER WITH ME AT THE BOAR'S HEAD TONIGHT?
YES, THAT WOULD BE NICE, TIALAK.
LET'S INVITE YOUR COUSIN LAOTIEN AND ARINENNA. THEY LIKE THAT PLACE.
I HOPE SHE COMES BACK SOON...
SHE'LL BE PROUD OF YOUR WORK, SIR.
THEN YOU CAN ASK HER OUT TO THE BOAR'S HEAD, EH?
MONTI!

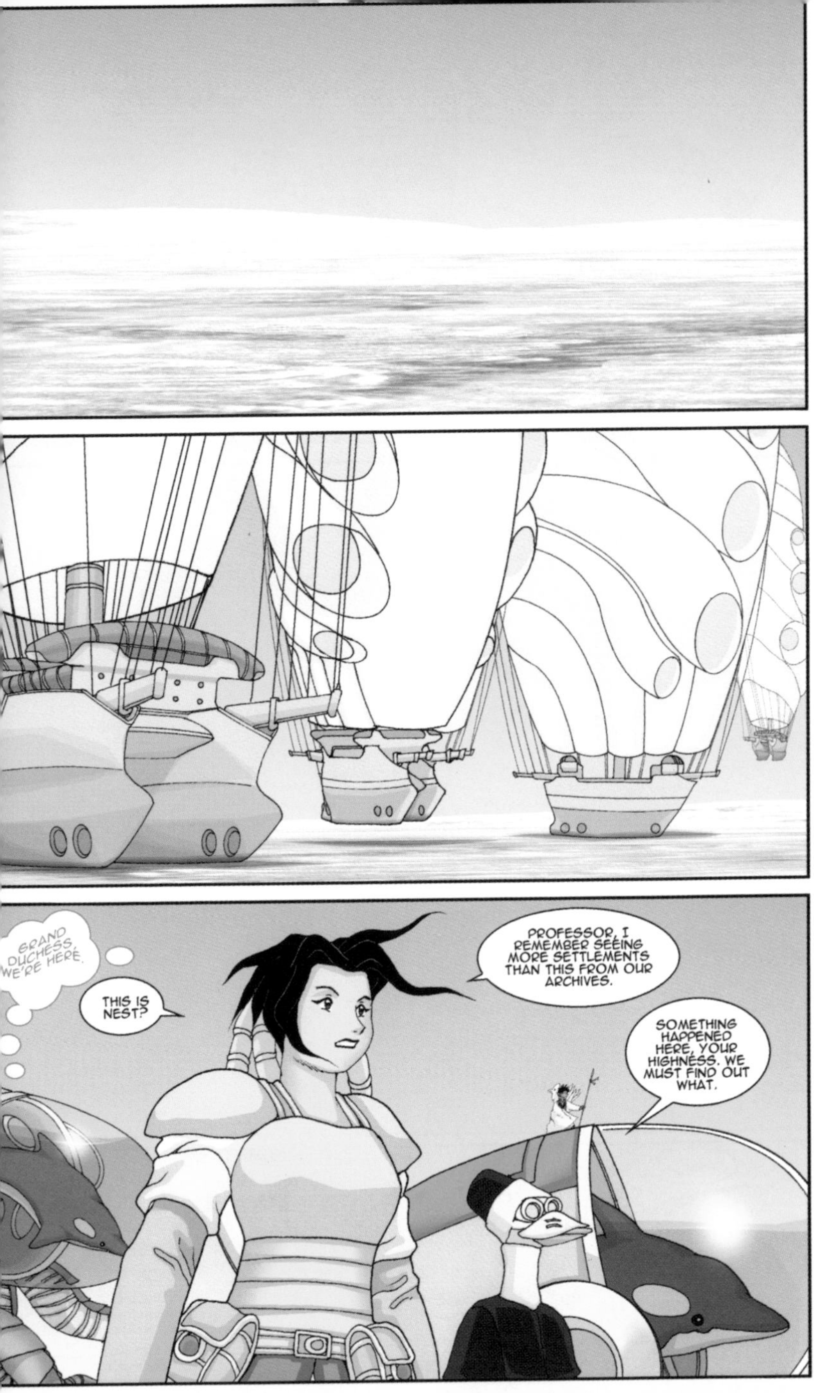
GRAND DUCHESS, WE'RE HERE.
THIS IS NEST?
PROFESSOR, I REMEMBER SEEING MORE SETTLEMENTS THAN THIS FROM OUR ARCHIVES.
SOMETHING HAPPENED HERE, YOUR HIGHNESS. WE MUST FIND OUT WHAT.

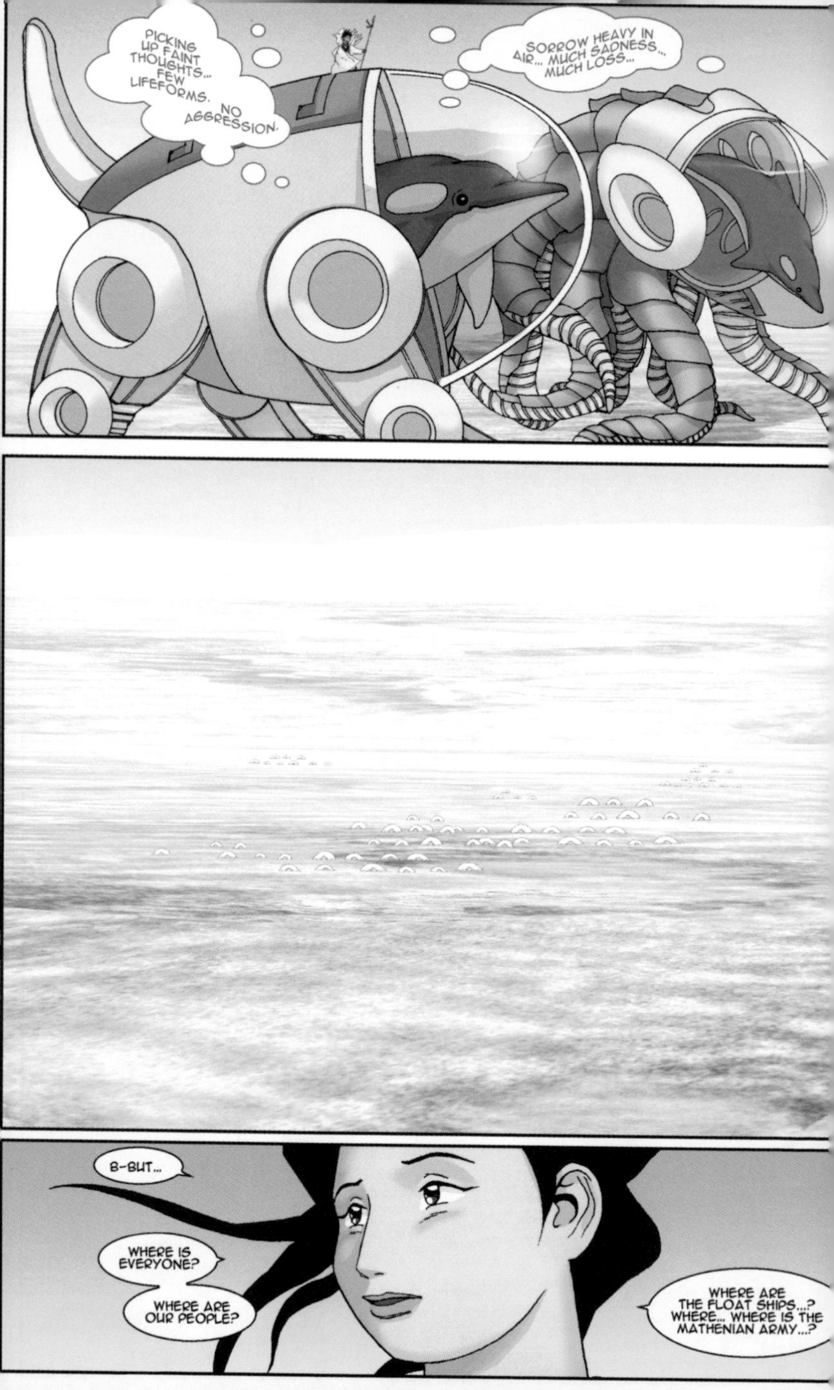
PICKING UP FAINT THOUGHTS... FEW LIFEFORMS. NO AGGRESSION.
SORROW HEAVY IN AIR... MUCH SADNESS... MUCH LOSS...
B-BUT...
WHERE IS EVERYONE?
WHERE ARE OUR PEOPLE?
WHERE ARE THE FLOAT SHIPS...? WHERE... WHERE IS THE MATHENIAN ARMY...?

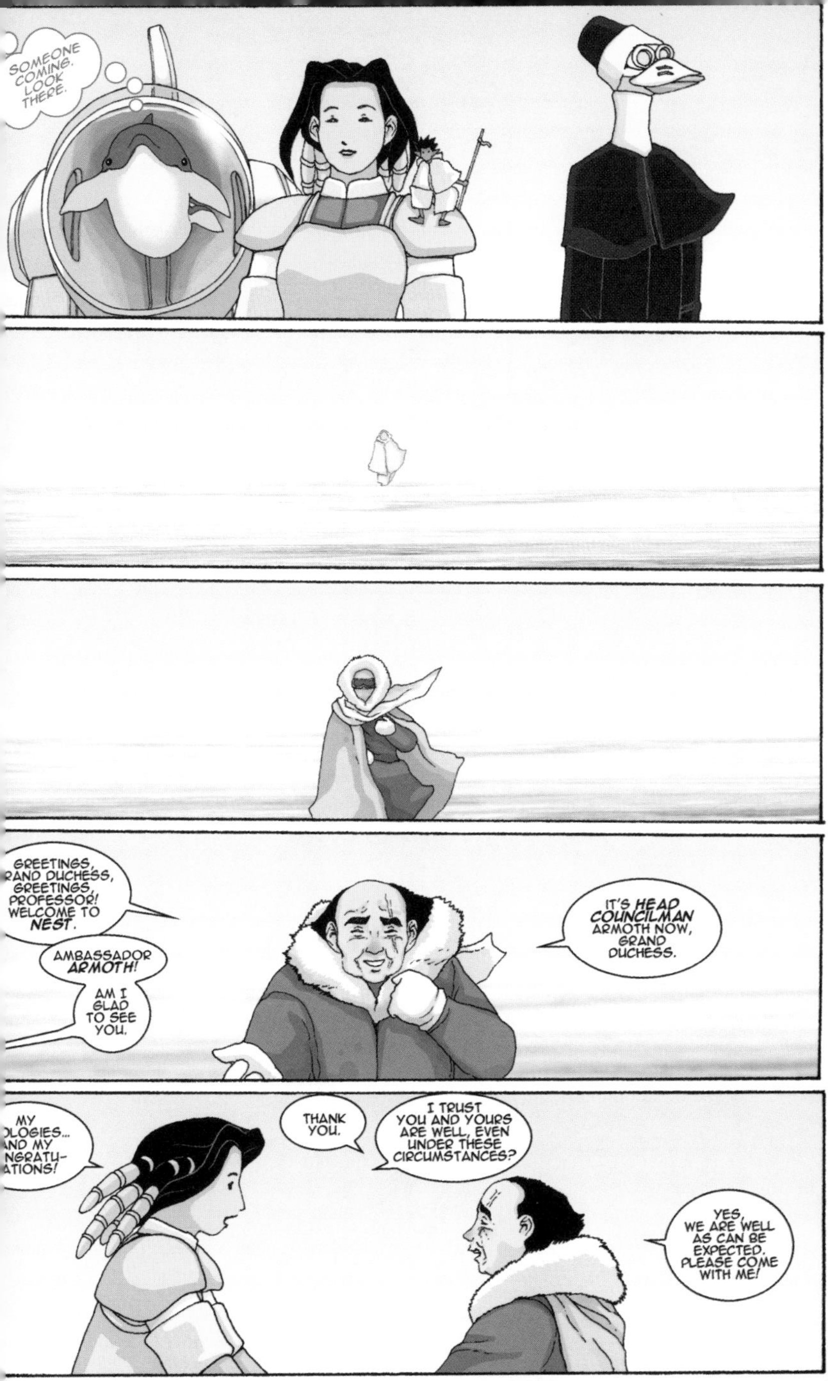
SOMEONE COMING. LOOK THERE.
GREETINGS, RAND DUCHESS, GREETINGS, PROFESSOR! WELCOME TO NEST.
AMBASSADOR ARMOTH!
AM I GLAD TO SEE YOU.
IT'S HEAD COUNCILMAN ARMOTH NOW, GRAND DUCHESS.
MY LOGIES... AND MY NGRATU-ATIONS!
THANK YOU.
I TRUST YOU AND YOURS ARE WELL, EVEN UNDER THESE CIRCUMSTANCES?
YES, WE ARE WELL AS CAN BE EXPECTED. PLEASE COME WITH ME!

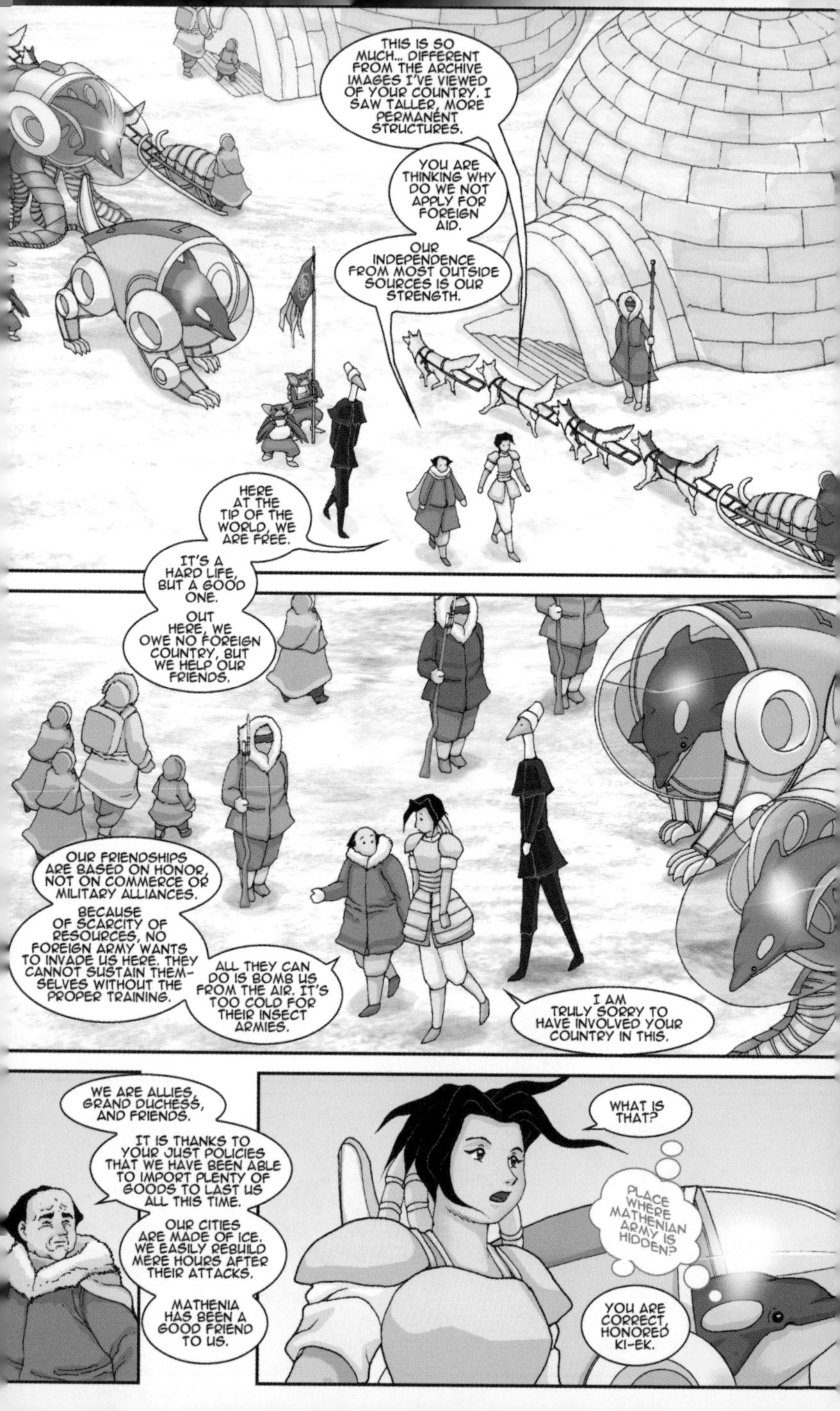

THIS IS SO MUCH... DIFFERENT FROM THE ARCHIVE IMAGES I'VE VIEWED OF YOUR COUNTRY. I SAW TALLER, MORE PERMANENT STRUCTURES.
YOU ARE THINKING WHY DO WE NOT APPLY FOR FOREIGN AID.
OUR INDEPENDENCE FROM MOST OUTSIDE SOURCES IS OUR STRENGTH.
HERE AT THE TIP OF THE WORLD, WE ARE FREE.
IT'S A HARD LIFE, BUT A GOOD ONE.
OUT HERE, WE OWE NO FOREIGN COUNTRY, BUT WE HELP OUR FRIENDS.
OUR FRIENDSHIPS ARE BASED ON HONOR, NOT ON COMMERCE OR MILITARY ALLIANCES.
BECAUSE OF SCARCITY OF RESOURCES, NO FOREIGN ARMY WANTS TO INVADE US HERE. THEY CANNOT SUSTAIN THEM-SELVES WITHOUT THE PROPER TRAINING.
ALL THEY CAN DO IS BOMB US FROM THE AIR. IT'S TOO COLD FOR THEIR INSECT ARMIES.
I AM TRULY SORRY TO HAVE INVOLVED YOUR COUNTRY IN THIS.
WE ARE ALLIES, GRAND DUCHESS, AND FRIENDS.
IT IS THANKS TO YOUR JUST POLICIES THAT WE HAVE BEEN ABLE TO IMPORT PLENTY OF GOODS TO LAST US ALL THIS TIME.
OUR CITIES ARE MADE OF ICE. WE EASILY REBUILD MERE HOURS AFTER THEIR ATTACKS.
MATHENIA HAS BEEN A GOOD FRIEND TO US.
WHAT IS THAT?
PLACE WHERE MATHENIAN ARMY IS HIDDEN?
YOU ARE CORRECT, HONORED KI-EK.

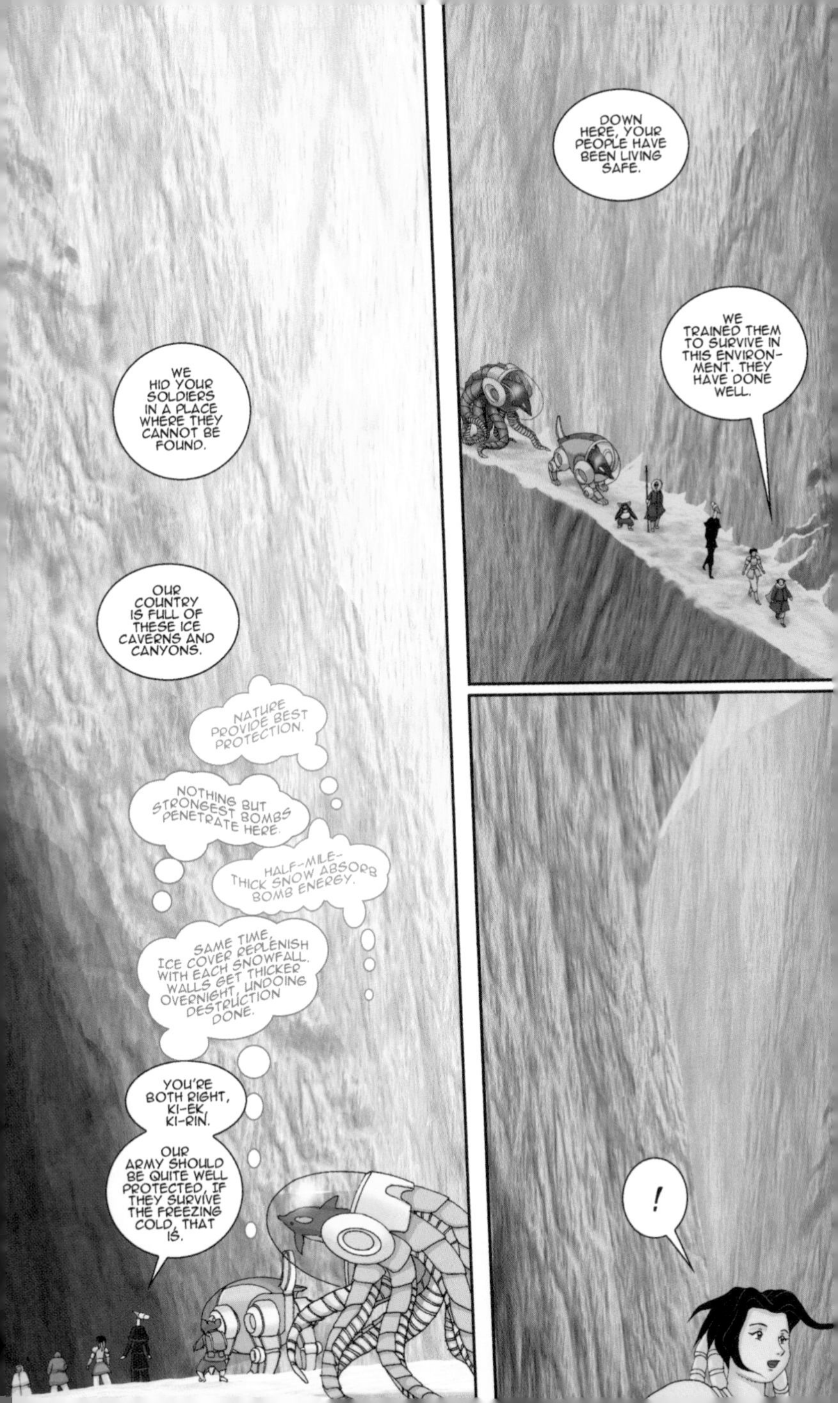
WE HID YOUR SOLDIERS IN A PLACE WHERE THEY CANNOT BE FOUND.
OUR COUNTRY IS FULL OF THESE ICE CAVERNS AND CANYONS.
NATURE PROVIDE BEST PROTECTION.
NOTHING BUT STRONGEST BOMBS PENETRATE HERE.
HALF-MILE-THICK SNOW ABSORB BOMB ENERGY.
SAME TIME, ICE COVER REPLENISH WITH EACH SNOWFALL. WALLS GET THICKER OVERNIGHT, UNDOING DESTRUCTION DONE.
YOU'RE BOTH RIGHT, KI-EK, KI-RIN.
OUR ARMY SHOULD BE QUITE WELL PROTECTED, IF THEY SURVIVE THE FREEZING COLD, THAT IS.
DOWN HERE, YOUR PEOPLE HAVE BEEN LIVING SAFE.
WE TRAINED THEM TO SURVIVE IN THIS ENVIRON-MENT. THEY HAVE DONE WELL.
!

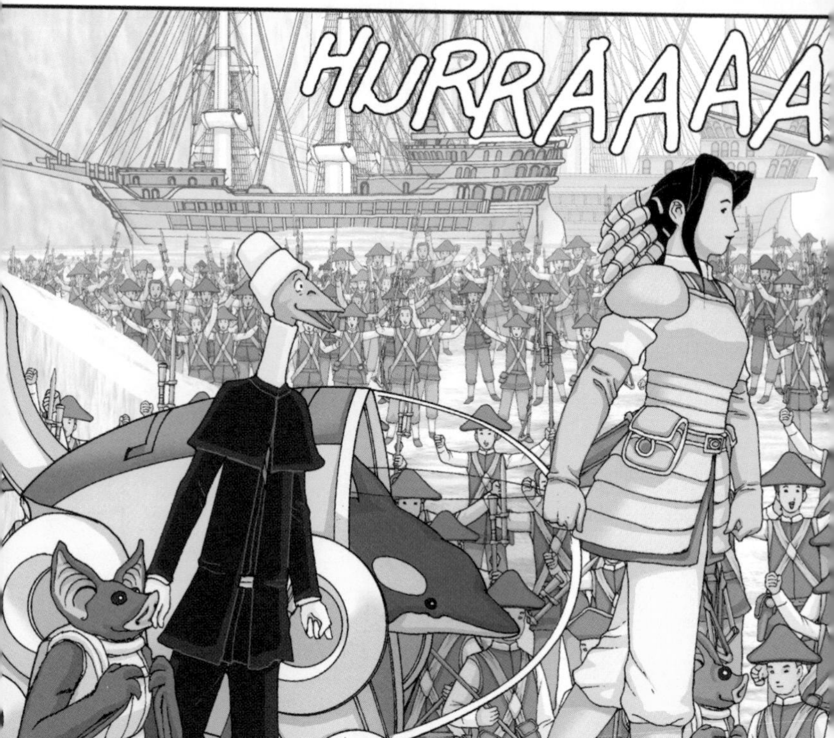
HURRAAAAA

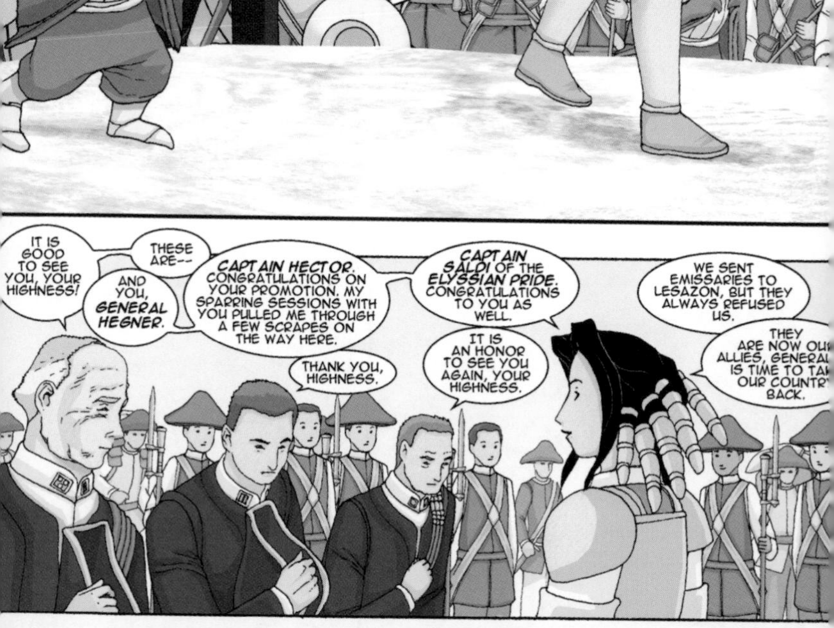
IT IS GOOD TO SEE YOU, YOUR HIGHNESS!
THESE ARE--
AND YOU, GENERAL HEGNER.
CAPTAIN HECTOR. CONGRATULATIONS ON YOUR PROMOTION. MY SPARRING SESSIONS WITH YOU PULLED ME THROUGH A FEW SCRAPES ON THE WAY HERE.
THANK YOU, HIGHNESS.
CAPTAIN SALDI OF THE ELYSSIAN PRIDE. CONGRATULATIONS TO YOU AS WELL.
IT IS AN HONOR TO SEE YOU AGAIN, YOUR HIGHNESS.
WE SENT EMISSARIES TO LESAZON, BUT THEY ALWAYS REFUSED US.

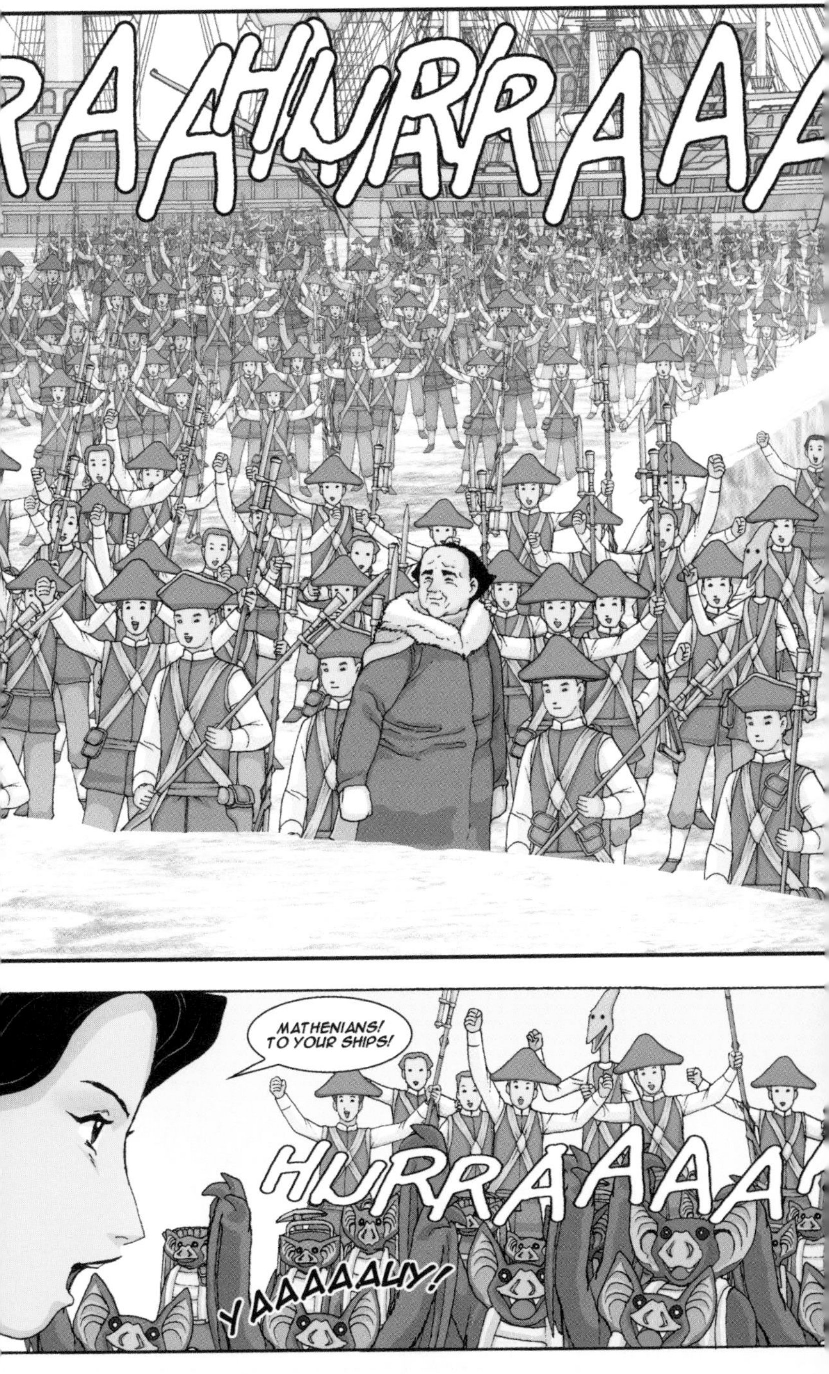
RAAHURRAAAA
MATHENIANS! TO YOUR SHIPS!
HURRAAAA
YAAAAALLY!

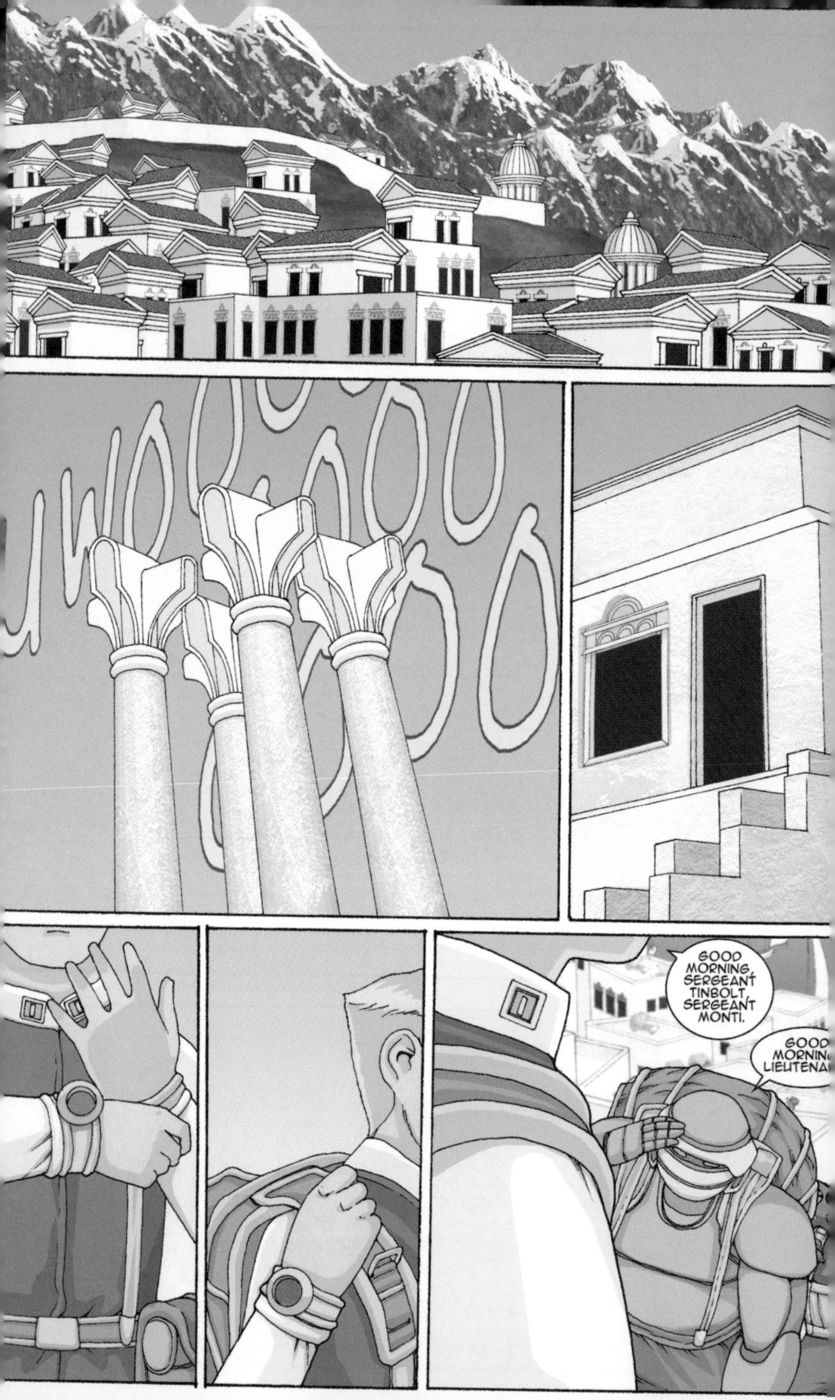
GOOD MORNING, SERGEANT TINBOLT, SERGEANT MONTI.
GOOD MORNING LIEUTENA

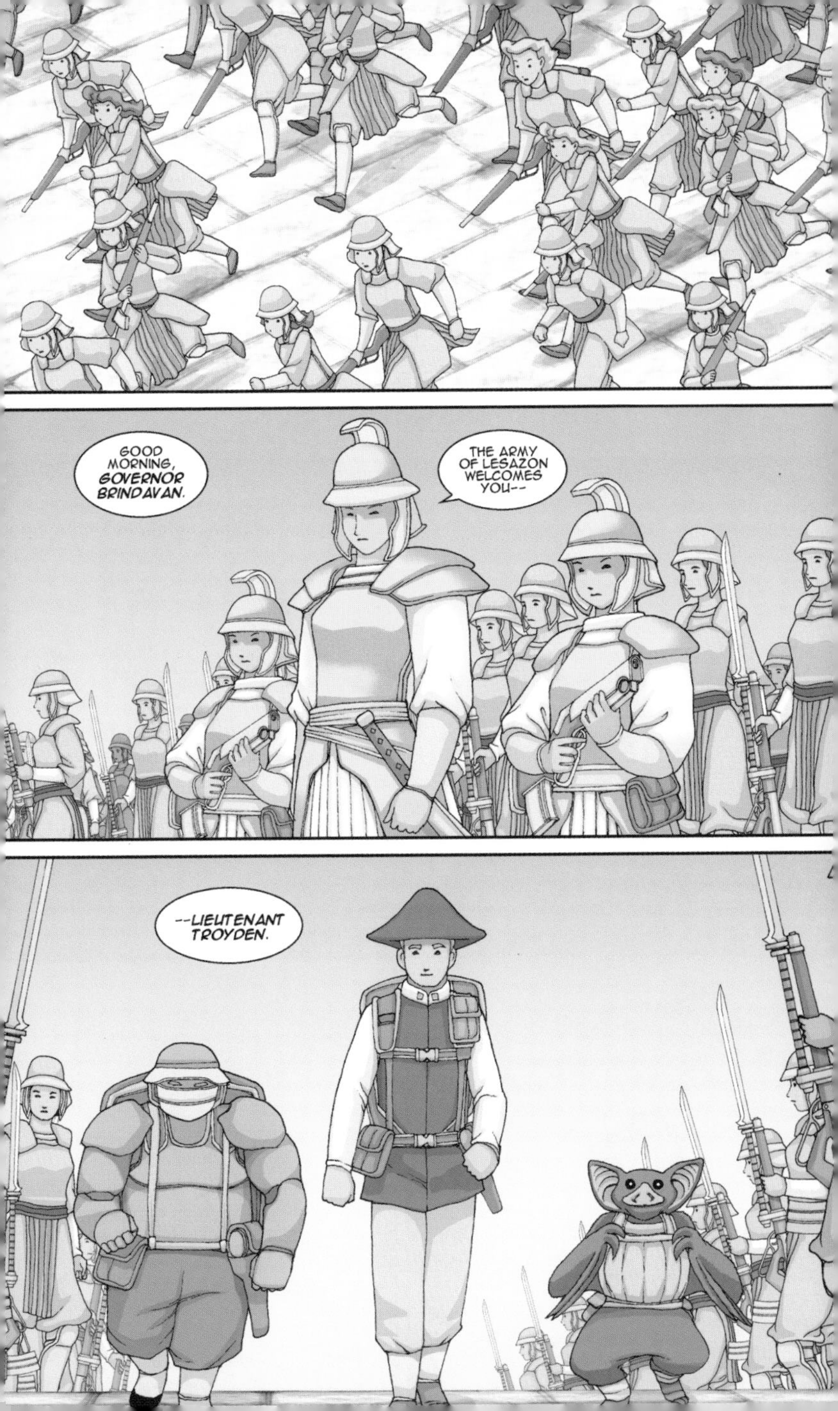
GOOD MORNING, GOVERNOR BRINDAVAN.
THE ARMY OF LESAZON WELCOMES YOU--
--LIEUTENANT TROYDEN.

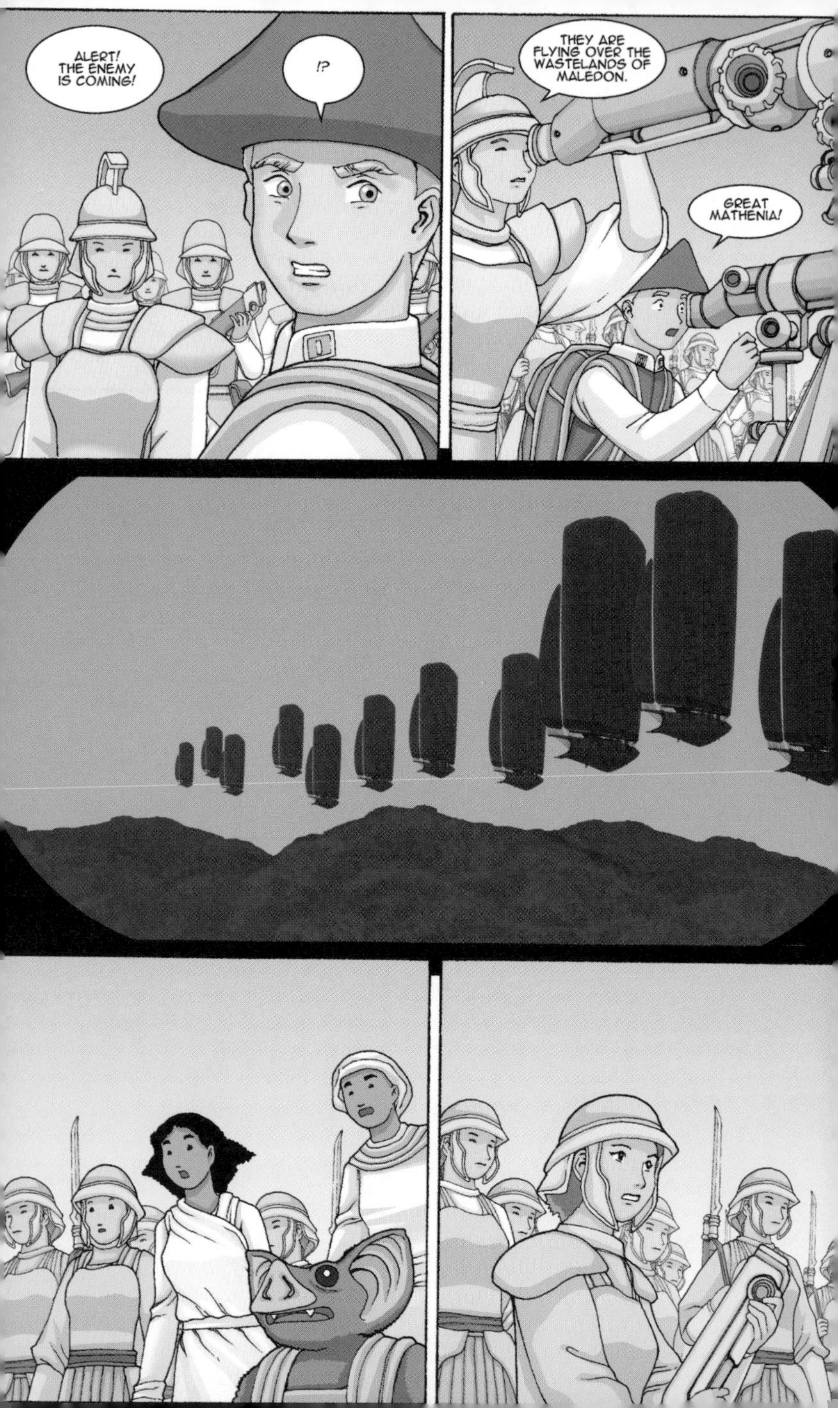
ALERT! THE ENEMY IS COMING!
!?
THEY ARE FLYING OVER THE WASTELANDS OF MALEDON.
GREAT MATHENIA!

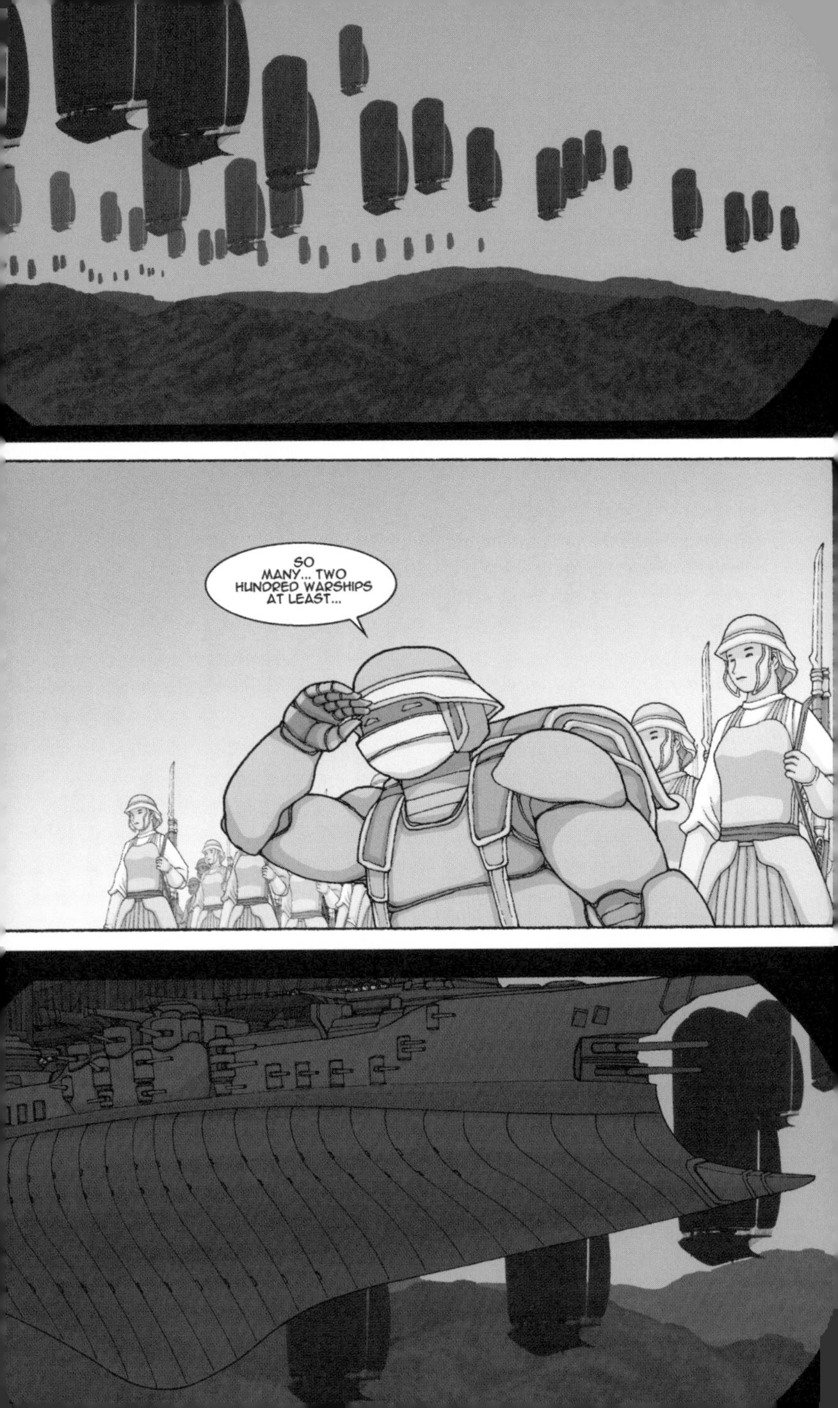
SO MANY... TWO HUNDRED WARSHIPS AT LEAST...

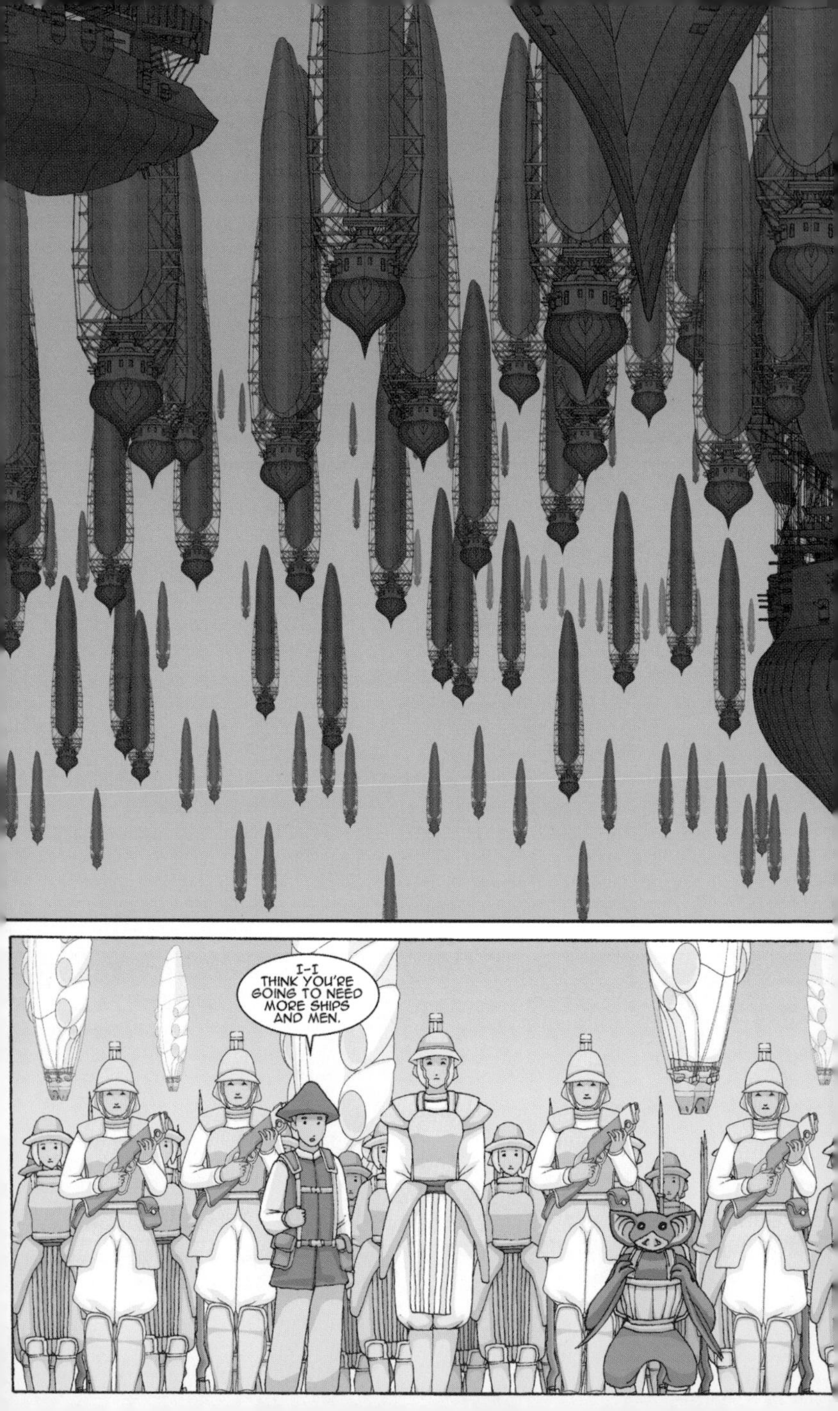
I-I THINK YOU'RE GOING TO NEED MORE SHIPS AND MEN.

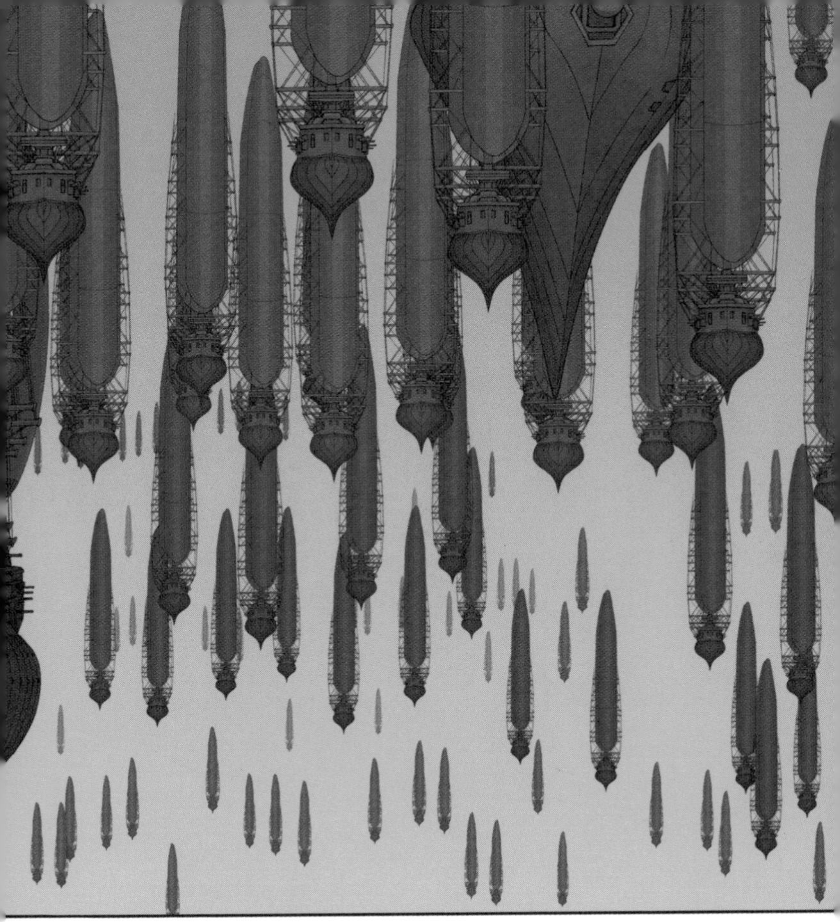

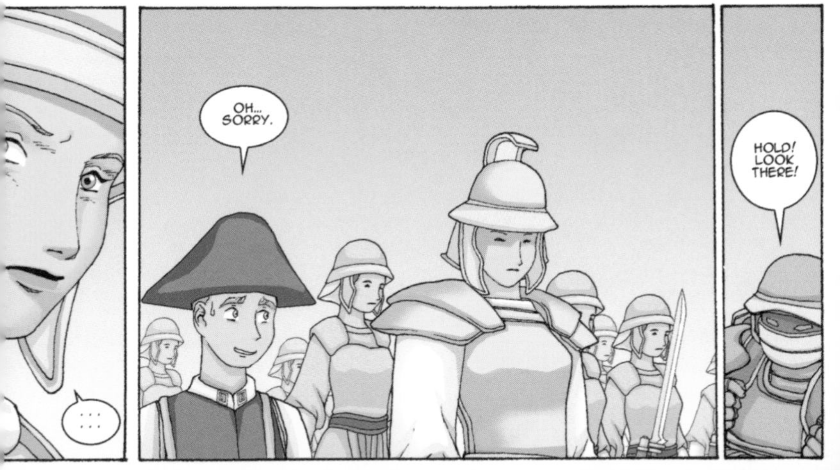
...
OH... SORRY.
HOLD! LOOK THERE!

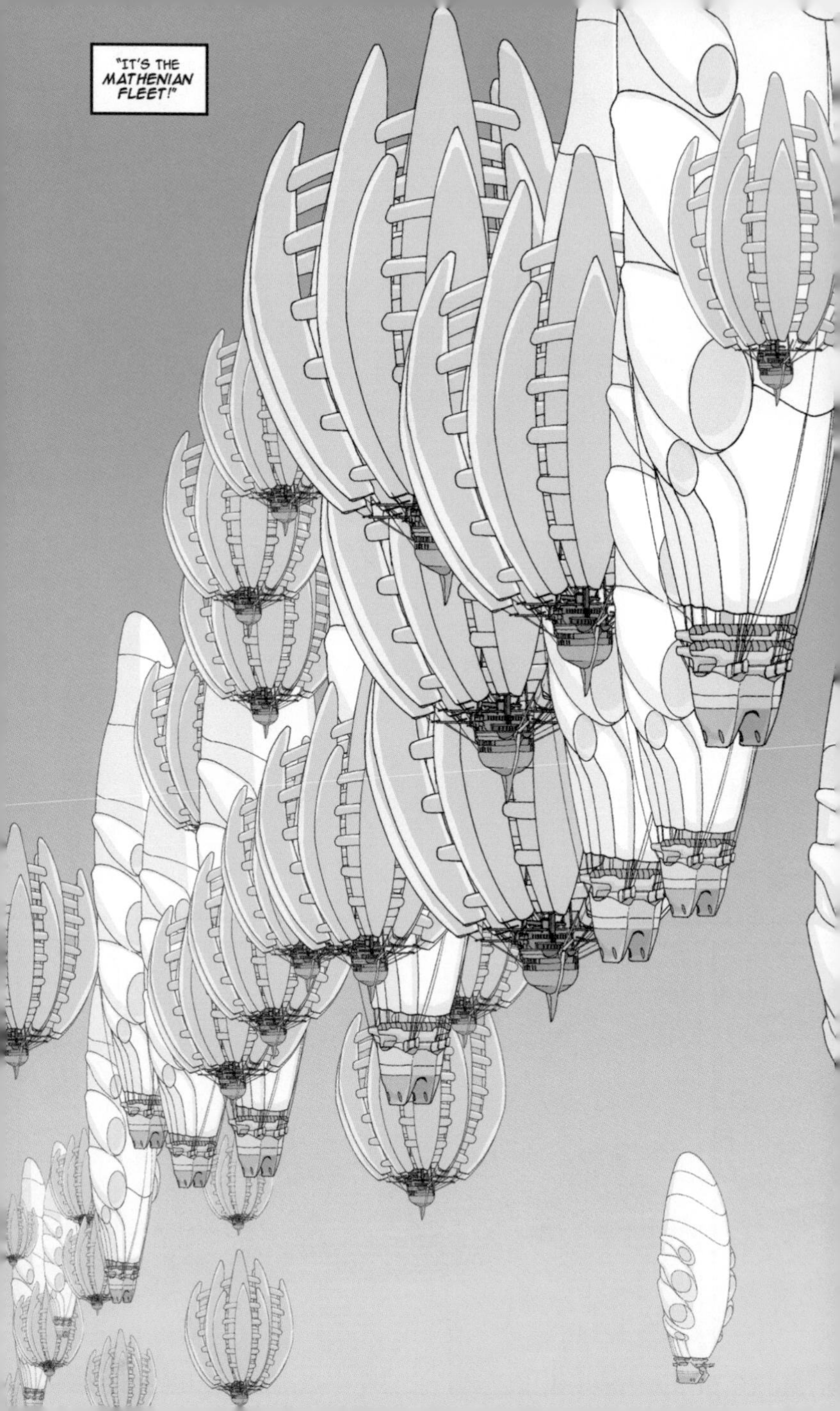
"IT'S THE MATHENIAN FLEET!"

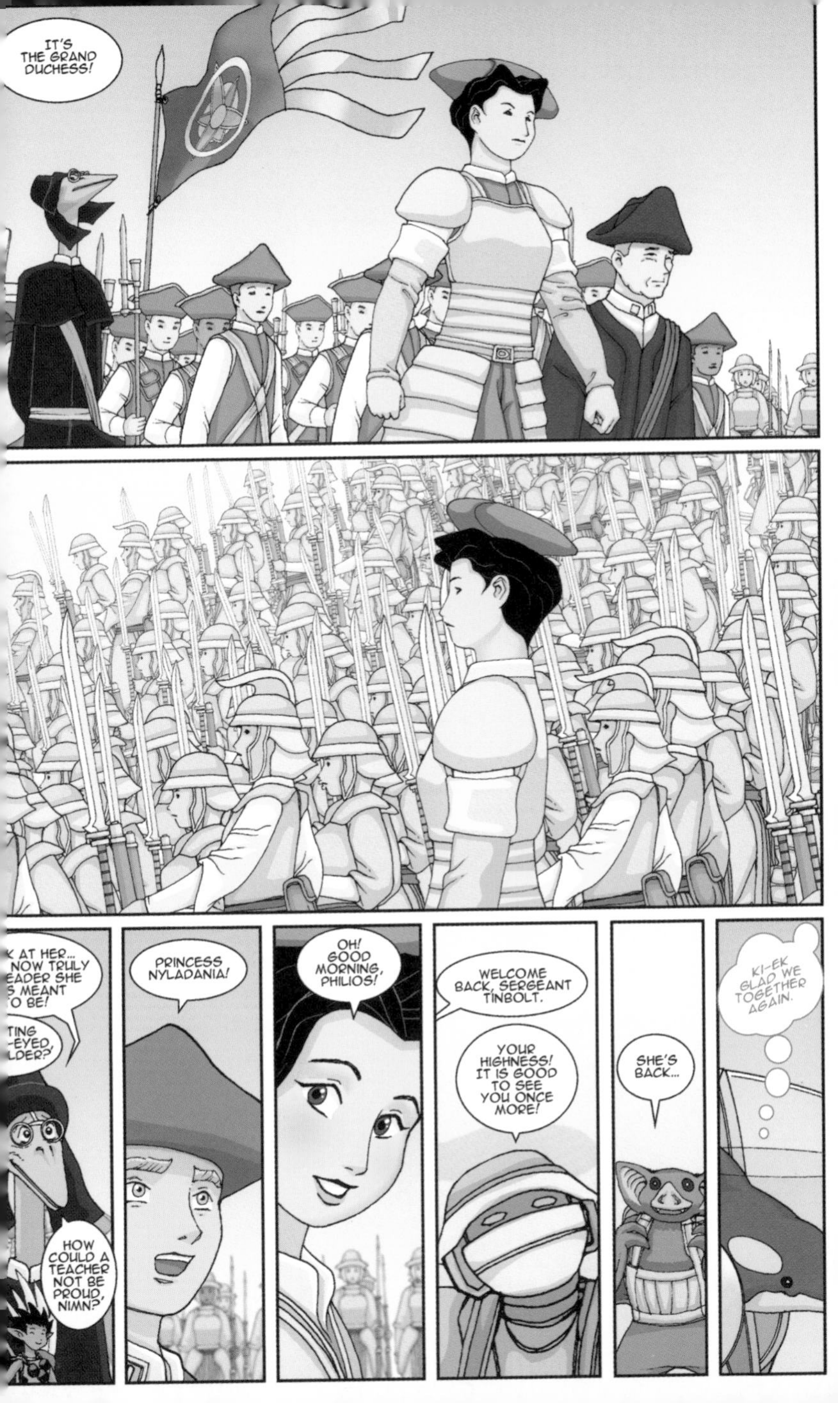
IT'S THE GRAND DUCHESS!
K AT HER... NOW TRULY EADER SHE S MEANT TO BE!
TING -EYED, LDER?
HOW COULD A TEACHER NOT BE PROUD, NIMN?
PRINCESS NYLADANIA!
OH! GOOD MORNING, PHILIOS!
WELCOME BACK, SERGEANT TINBOLT.
YOUR HIGHNESS! IT IS GOOD TO SEE YOU ONCE MORE!
SHE'S BACK...
KI-EK GLAD WE TOGETHER AGAIN.

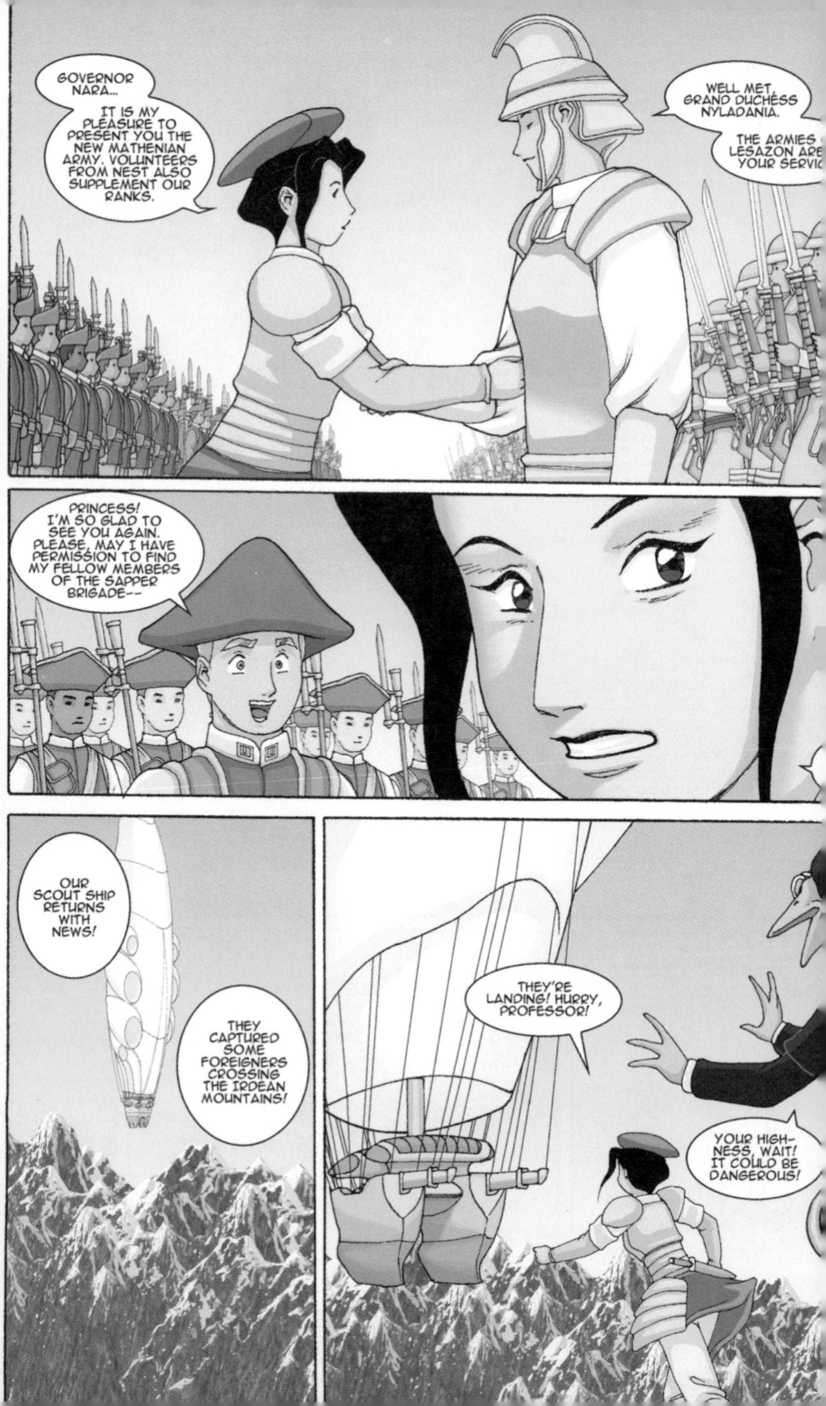
GOVERNOR NARA... IT IS MY PLEASURE TO PRESENT YOU THE NEW MATHENIAN ARMY. VOLUNTEERS FROM NEST ALSO SUPPLEMENT OUR RANKS.
WELL MET, GRAND DUCHESS NYLADANIA.
PRINCESS! I'M SO GLAD TO SEE YOU AGAIN. PLEASE, MAY I HAVE PERMISSION TO FIND MY FELLOW MEMBERS OF THE SAPPER BRIGADE--
OUR SCOUT SHIP RETURNS WITH NEWS!
THEY CAPTURED SOME FOREIGNERS CROSSING THE IRDEAN MOUNTAINS!
THEY'RE LANDING! HURRY, PROFESSOR!
YOUR HIGHNESS, WAIT! IT COULD BE DANGEROUS!

RAJAH AZAN!

GRAND DUCHESS NYLADANIA! IT IS SO GOOD TO SEE YOU ONCE MORE!

Y-YOUR FACE?!

IT'S NOTHING. A SMALL PRESENT FROM THE KROSSIAN ARMY LEADER, GENERAL KAIZLER.

A FEW OF US ESCAPED THEIR SLAVE SHIPS AS SOON AS THEY LANDED AT MALEDON. WE WANDERED FAR INTO THE DESERT OF DRY WATERS. WE WERE CHASED BY THE KROSSIANS...

OOH, LOOK, ARINENNA, LIEUTENANT HERE IS ALL JEALOUS.

DON'T WORRY, DEAR PHILIOS. SHE STILL LIKES YOU. DOESN'T SHE, LAOTIEN?

UHM-HM! THAT'S RIGHT, PHILIOS!

WE MET UP WITH VALUABLE ALLIES.

THEY TAUGHT US SURVIVAL TECHNIQUES WHILE WE FORCE-MARCHED ACROSS THE DESERT OF DRY WATERS...

...AND RESCUED ONE OF OUR OWN WANDERING ACROSS THE WASTELANDS.

WE OWE THE ELFIRIN TRIBE LEO BY CHIEF RABO A GREAT DEBT.

MARRO!

RABO RESISTED THE ELDERS AND TRAINED ME IN THEIR FIGHTING ART.

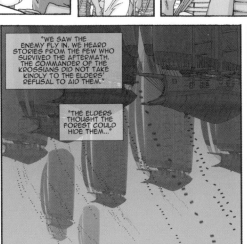

"...OR ALL OF [WH]O WERE [LAS]HED TO [WA]STELANDS [BE]YOND [SHIEL]LINIATH..."

"WE SAW THE ENEMY FLY IN. WE HEARD STORIES FROM THE FEW WHO SURVIVED THE AFTERMATH. THE COMMANDER OF THE KROSSIANS DID NOT TAKE KINDLY TO THE ELDERS' REFUSAL TO AID THEM."

"THE ELDERS THOUGHT THE FOREST COULD HIDE THEM..."

"...BUT THE GENERAL BURNED EVERY ACRE WITH HIS TERRIBLE WEAPONS."

"THERE WAS NO PLACE TO HIDE."

"WE ARE ALL THAT IS LEFT OF THE SHIELLINIATH DWELLERS."

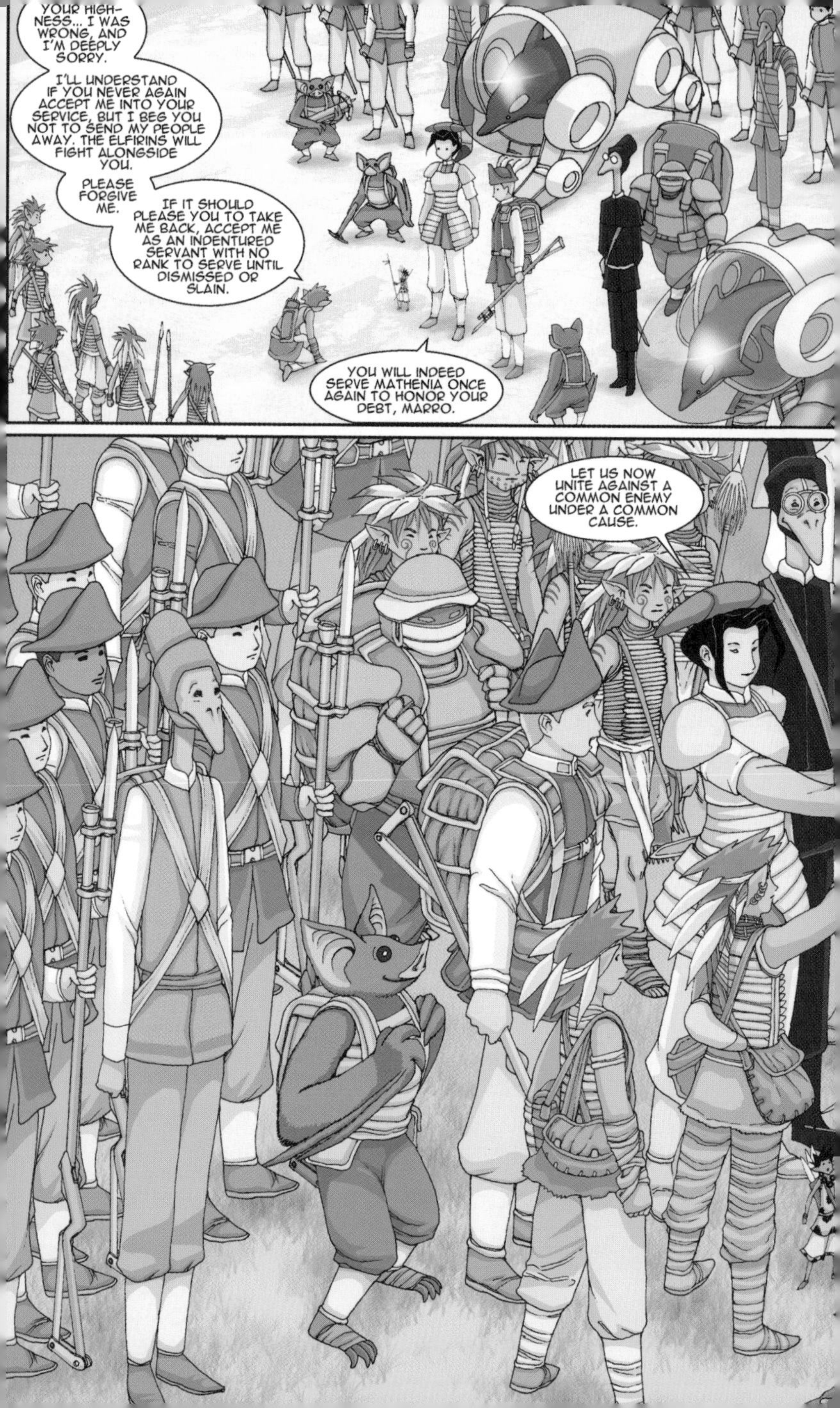
YOUR HIGHNESS... I WAS WRONG, AND I'M DEEPLY SORRY.
I'LL UNDERSTAND IF YOU NEVER AGAIN ACCEPT ME INTO YOUR SERVICE, BUT I BEG YOU NOT TO SEND MY PEOPLE AWAY. THE ELFIRINS WILL FIGHT ALONGSIDE YOU.
PLEASE FORGIVE ME.
IF IT SHOULD PLEASE YOU TO TAKE ME BACK, ACCEPT ME AS AN INDENTURED SERVANT WITH NO RANK TO SERVE UNTIL DISMISSED OR SLAIN.
YOU WILL INDEED SERVE MATHENIA ONCE AGAIN TO HONOR YOUR DEBT, MARRO.
LET US NOW UNITE AGAINST A COMMON ENEMY UNDER A COMMON CAUSE.

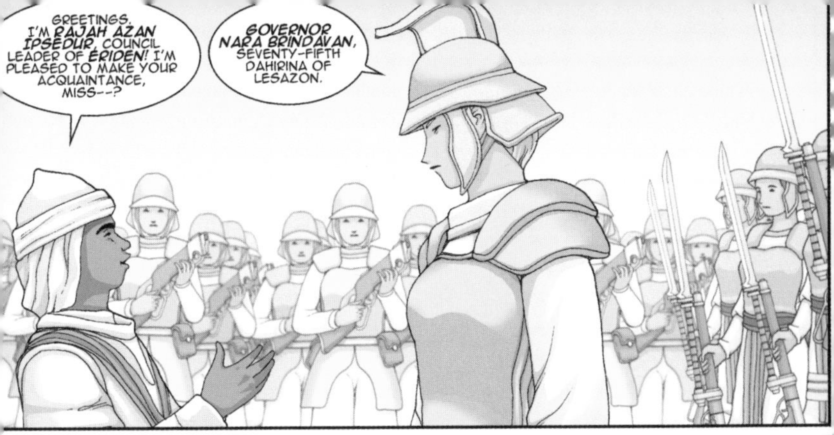
GREETINGS. I'M RAJAH AZAN IPSEDUR, COUNCIL LEADER OF ÉRIDEN! I'M PLEASED TO MAKE YOUR ACQUAINTANCE, MISS--?
GOVERNOR NARA BRINDAVAN, SEVENTY-FIFTH DAHIRINA OF LESAZON.

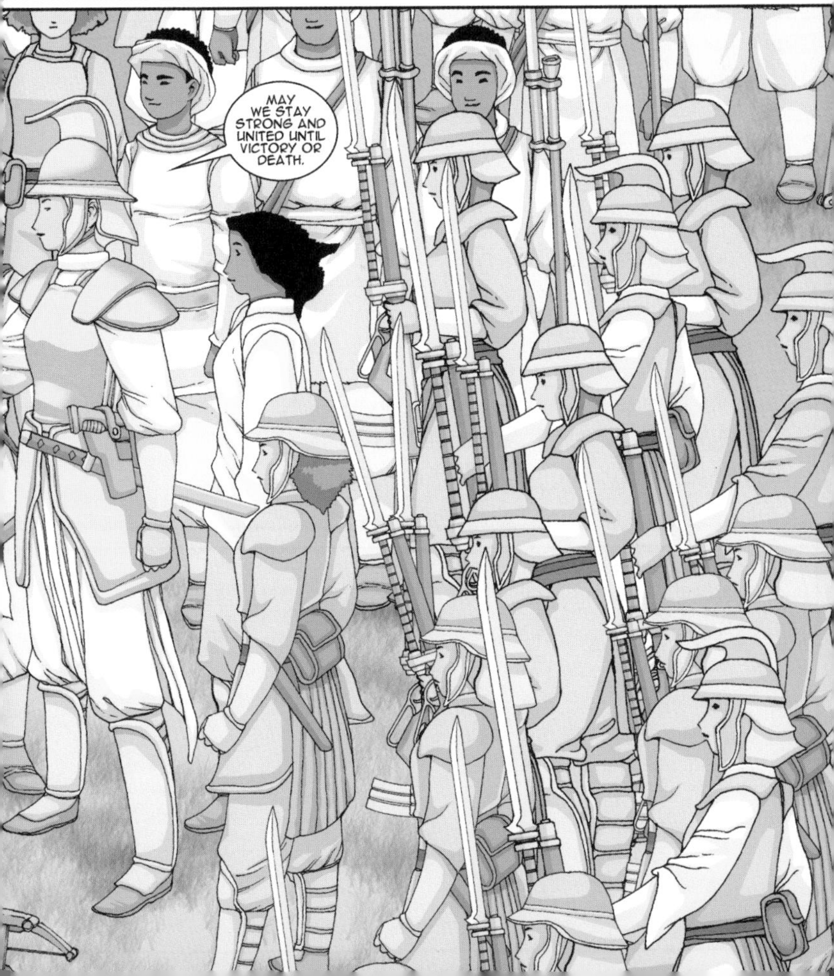
MAY WE STAY STRONG AND UNITED UNTIL VICTORY OR DEATH.

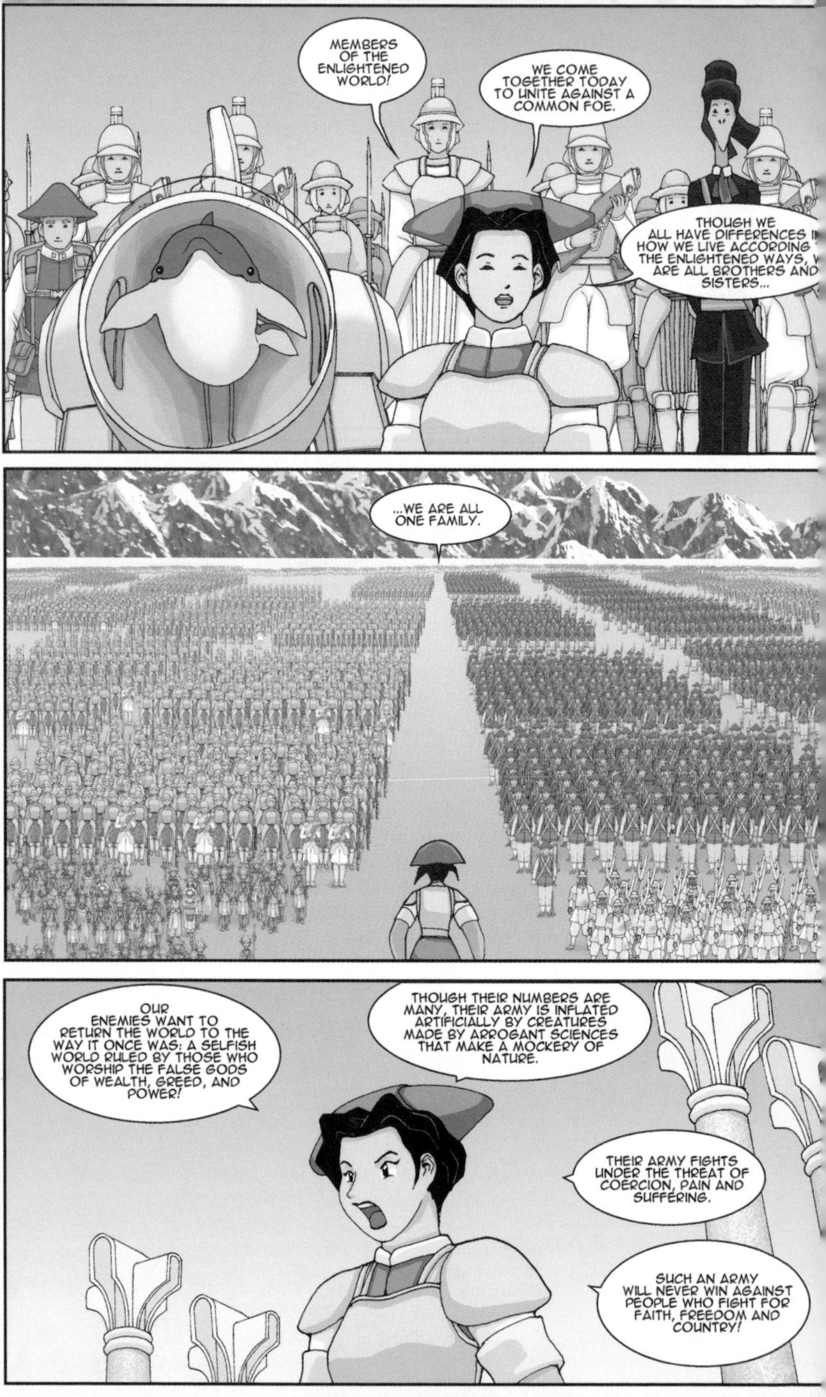
MEMBERS OF THE ENLIGHTENED WORLD!
WE COME TOGETHER TODAY TO UNITE AGAINST A COMMON FOE.
THOUGH WE ALL HAVE DIFFERENCES I HOW WE LIVE ACCORDING THE ENLIGHTENED WAYS, ARE ALL BROTHERS AND SISTERS...
...WE ARE ALL ONE FAMILY.
OUR ENEMIES WANT TO RETURN THE WORLD TO THE WAY IT ONCE WAS: A SELFISH WORLD RULED BY THOSE WHO WORSHIP THE FALSE GODS OF WEALTH, GREED, AND POWER!
THOUGH THEIR NUMBERS ARE MANY, THEIR ARMY IS INFLATED ARTIFICIALLY BY CREATURES MADE BY ARROGANT SCIENCES THAT MAKE A MOCKERY OF NATURE.
THEIR ARMY FIGHTS UNDER THE THREAT OF COERCION, PAIN AND SUFFERING.
SUCH AN ARMY WILL NEVER WIN AGAINST PEOPLE WHO FIGHT FOR FAITH, FREEDOM AND COUNTRY!

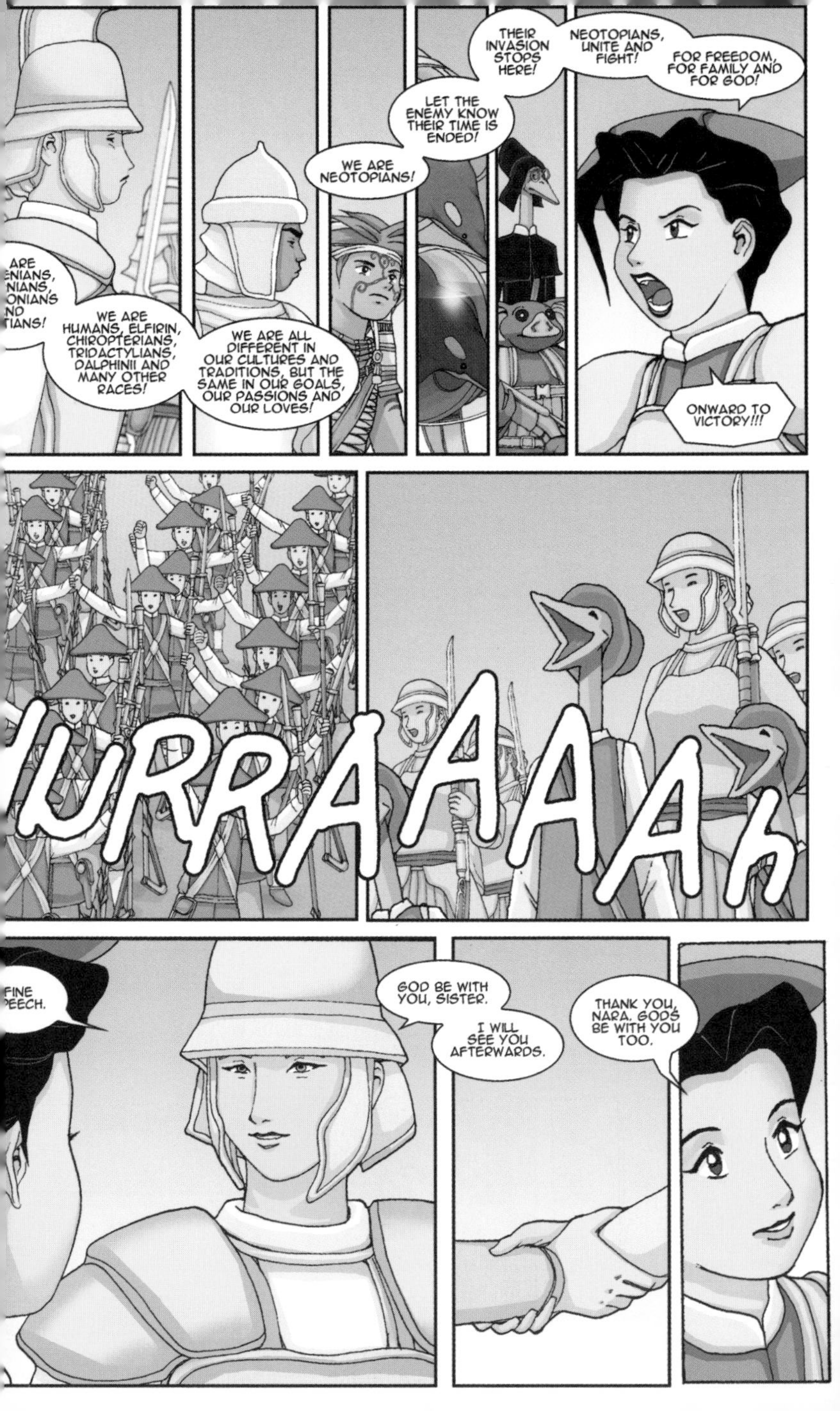
WE ARE HUMANS, ELFIRIN, CHIROPTERIANS, TRIDACTYLIANS, DALPHINII AND MANY OTHER RACES!
WE ARE ALL DIFFERENT IN OUR CULTURES AND TRADITIONS, BUT THE SAME IN OUR GOALS, OUR PASSIONS AND OUR LOVES!
WE ARE NEOTOPIANS!
LET THE ENEMY KNOW THEIR TIME IS ENDED!
THEIR INVASION STOPS HERE!
NEOTOPIANS, UNITE AND FIGHT!
FOR FREEDOM, FOR FAMILY AND FOR GOD!
ONWARD TO VICTORY!!!
URRAAAAAh
GOD BE WITH YOU, SISTER.
I WILL SEE YOU AFTERWARDS.
THANK YOU, NARA. GODS BE WITH YOU TOO.

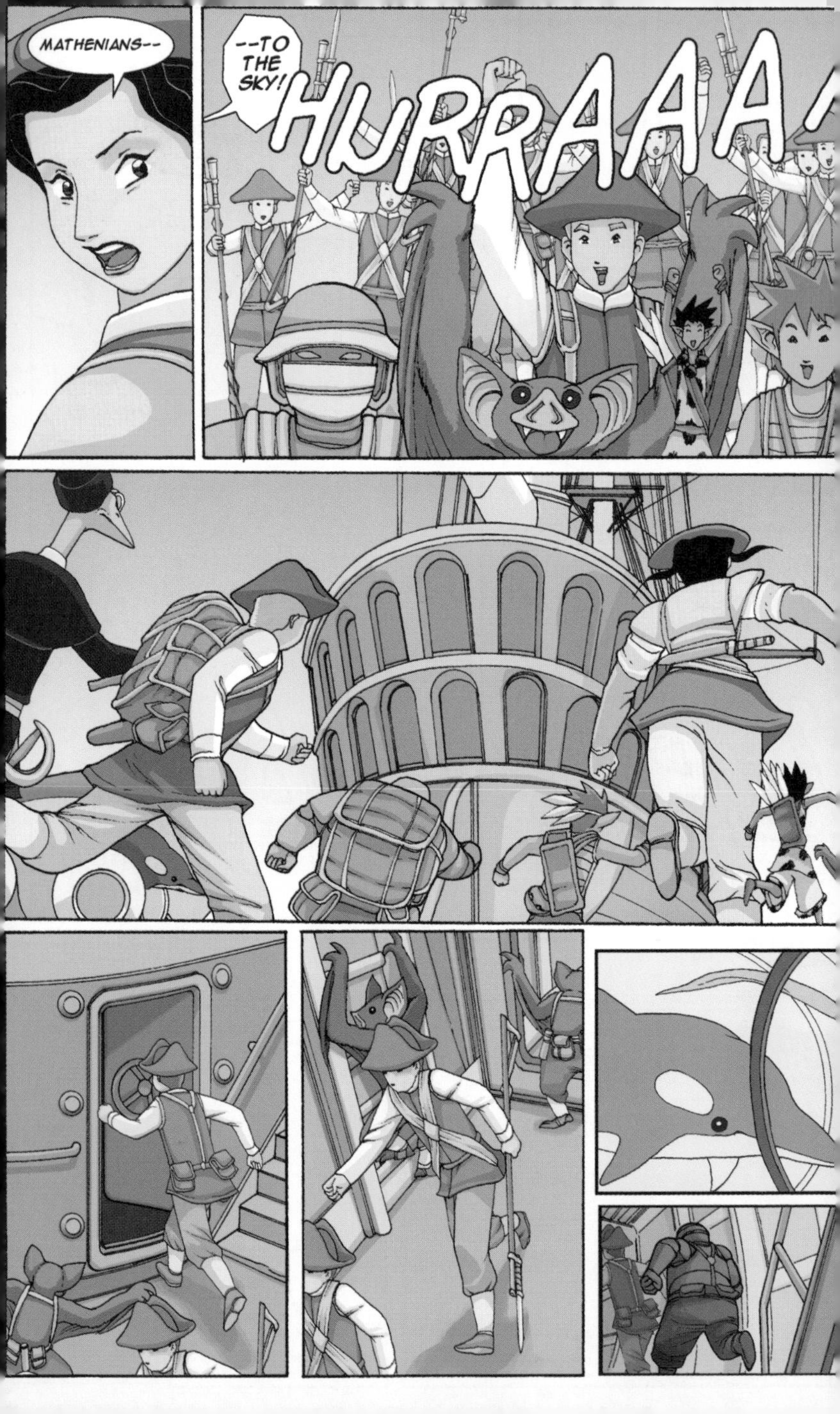
MATHENIANS--
--TO THE SKY!
HURRAAAA

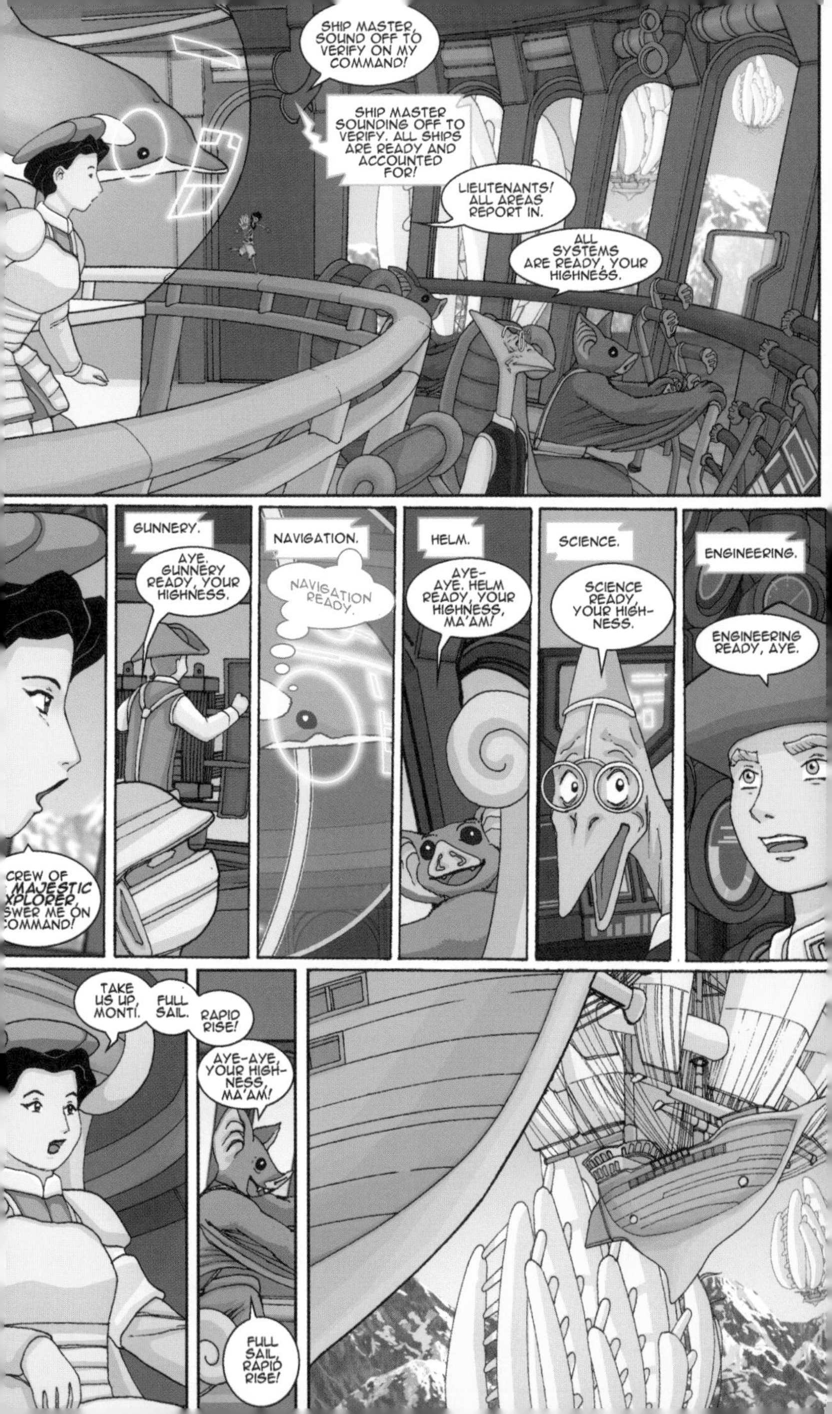
SHIP MASTER, SOUND OFF TO VERIFY ON MY COMMAND!
SHIP MASTER SOUNDING OFF TO VERIFY. ALL SHIPS ARE READY AND ACCOUNTED FOR!
LIEUTENANTS! ALL AREAS REPORT IN.
ALL SYSTEMS ARE READY, YOUR HIGHNESS.
CREW OF MAJESTIC XPLORER, SWER ME ON COMMAND!
GUNNERY.
AYE. GUNNERY READY, YOUR HIGHNESS.
NAVIGATION.
NAVIGATION READY.
HELM.
AYE-AYE. HELM READY, YOUR HIGHNESS, MA'AM!
SCIENCE.
SCIENCE READY, YOUR HIGH-NESS.
ENGINEERING.
ENGINEERING READY, AYE.
TAKE US UP, MONTI.
FULL SAIL.
RAPID RISE!
AYE-AYE, YOUR HIGH-NESS, MA'AM!
FULL SAIL, RAPID RISE!

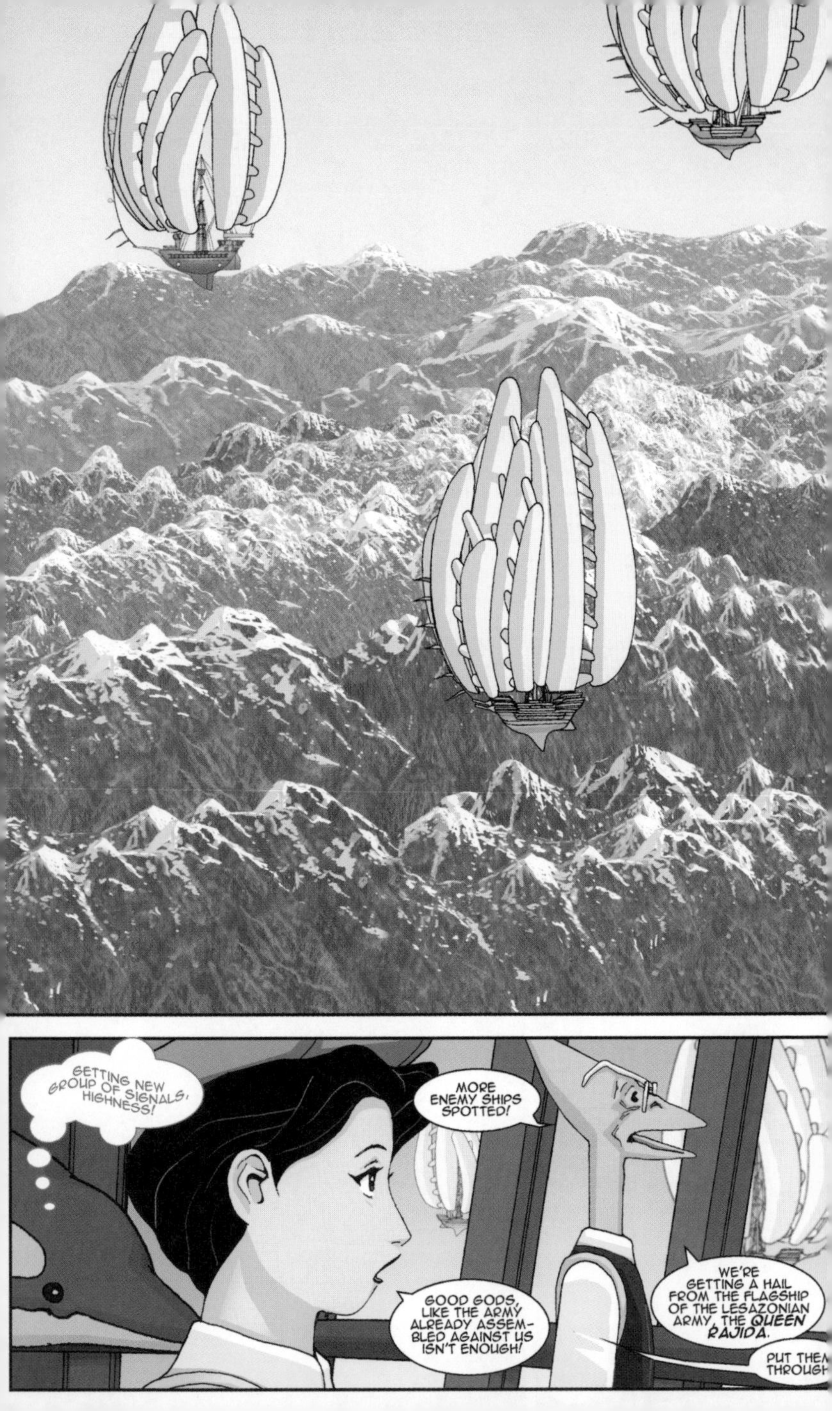
GETTING NEW GROUP OF SIGNALS, HIGHNESS!
MORE ENEMY SHIPS SPOTTED!
GOOD GODS, LIKE THE ARMY ALREADY ASSEM-BLED AGAINST US ISN'T ENOUGH!
WE'RE GETTING A HAIL FROM THE FLAGSHIP OF THE LESAZONIAN ARMY, THE QUEEN RAJIDA.

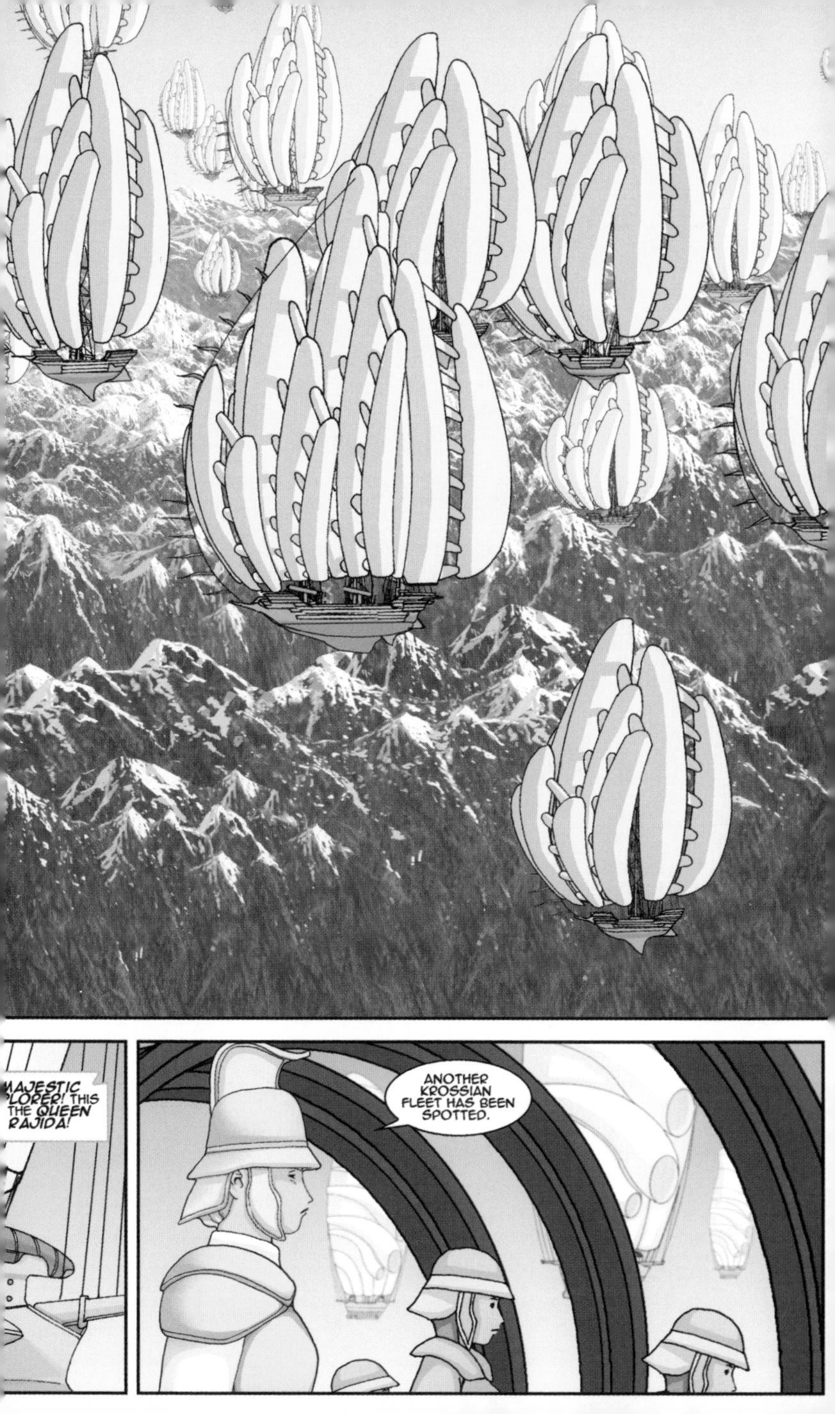
MAJESTIC
LORER! THIS
THE QUEEN
RAJIDA!
ANOTHER KROSSIAN FLEET HAS BEEN SPOTTED.

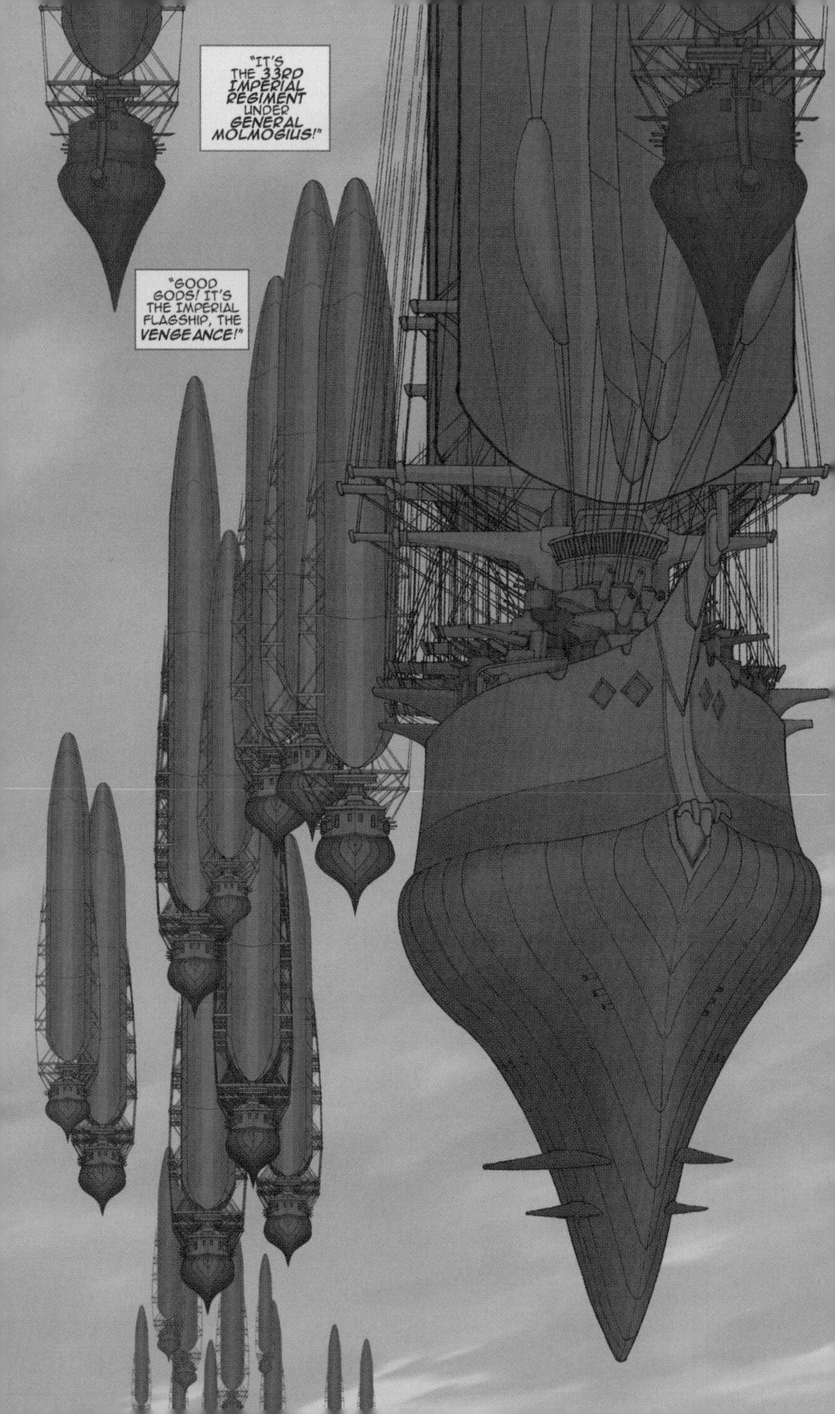
"IT'S THE 33RD IMPERIAL REGIMENT UNDER GENERAL MOLMOGIUS!"
"GOOD GODS! IT'S THE IMPERIAL FLAGSHIP, THE VENGEANCE!"

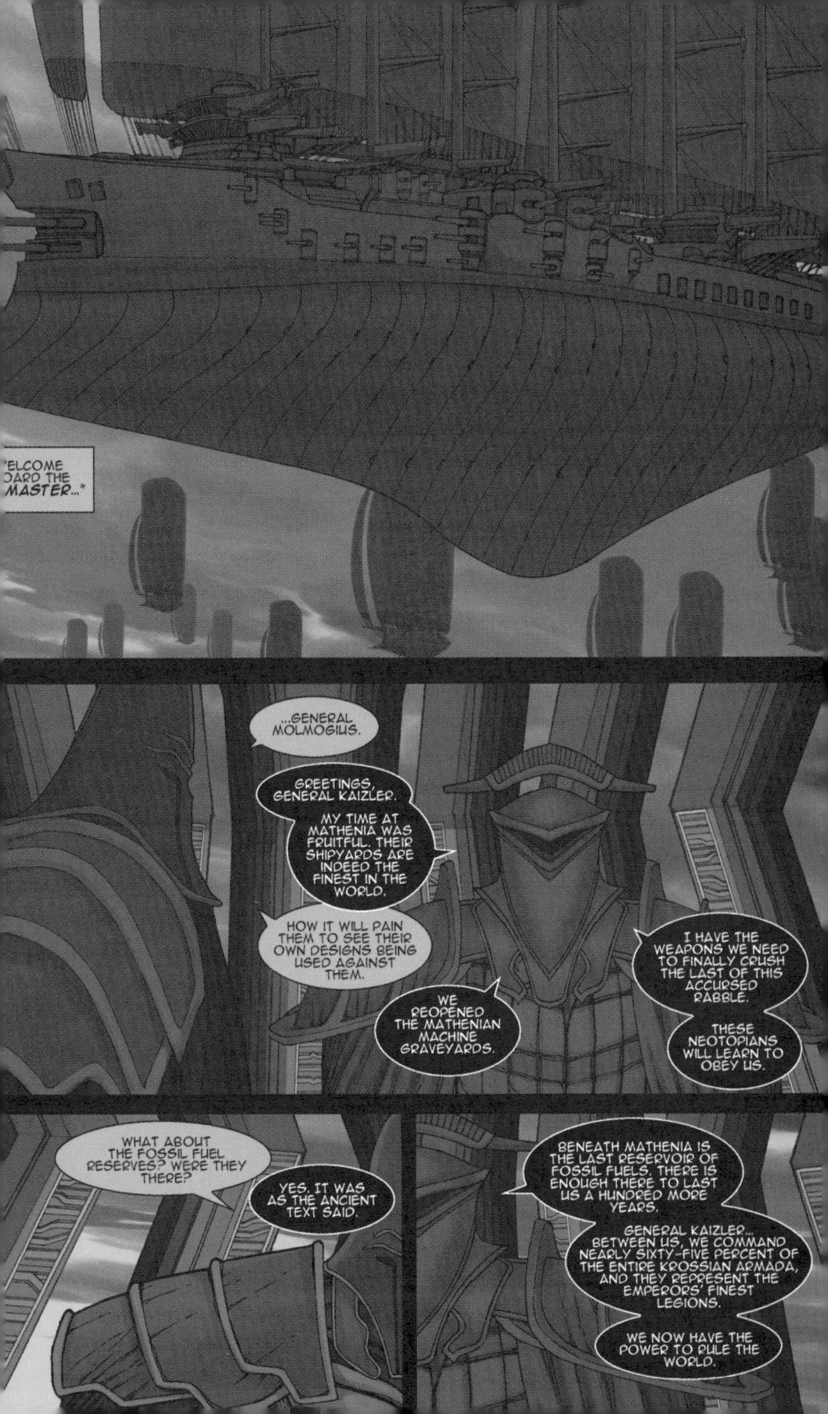

"ELCOME
OARD THE
MASTER..."
...GENERAL MOLMOGIUS.
GREETINGS, GENERAL KAIZLER.
MY TIME AT MATHENIA WAS FRUITFUL. THEIR SHIPYARDS ARE INDEED THE FINEST IN THE WORLD.
HOW IT WILL PAIN THEM TO SEE THEIR OWN DESIGNS BEING USED AGAINST THEM.
WE REOPENED THE MATHENIAN MACHINE GRAVEYARDS.
I HAVE THE WEAPONS WE NEED TO FINALLY CRUSH THE LAST OF THIS ACCURSED RABBLE.
THESE NEOTOPIANS WILL LEARN TO OBEY US.
WHAT ABOUT THE FOSSIL FUEL RESERVES? WERE THEY THERE?
YES. IT WAS AS THE ANCIENT TEXT SAID.
BENEATH MATHENIA IS THE LAST RESERVOIR OF FOSSIL FUELS. THERE IS ENOUGH THERE TO LAST US A HUNDRED MORE YEARS.
GENERAL KAIZLER... BETWEEN US, WE COMMAND NEARLY SIXTY-FIVE PERCENT OF THE ENTIRE KROSSIAN ARMADA, AND THEY REPRESENT THE EMPERORS' FINEST LEGIONS.
WE NOW HAVE THE POWER TO RULE THE WORLD.

GOOD GODS! THEY JUST SWELLED THEIR NUMBERS TO THREE HUNDRED FIFTY WARSHIPS STRONG!

350 KROSSIAN BATTLE CRUISERS AGAINST 25 MATHENIAN FRIGATES AND 40 LESAZONIAN WARBOATS?

THEY'RE TOO MANY.

GOVERNOR-ADMIRAL, WE MUST USE OUR FLYING BOMBS NOW BEFORE THEY COME ANY CLOSER.

PATIENCE, CAPTAIN ARINENNA.

WE WILL USE THEM AT THE RIGHT TIME.

THEY'RE UP TO SOMETHING...

THIS SHOW OF FORCE IS JUST THE BEGINNING...

WE'RE OVER THE HILLS OF BLOOD, PROFESSOR, SIR.

HOLD HERE.

PROFESSOR, SIR, HOW CAN WE FIGHT 350 WARSHIPS WITH 65?

WITH COU AND OF M

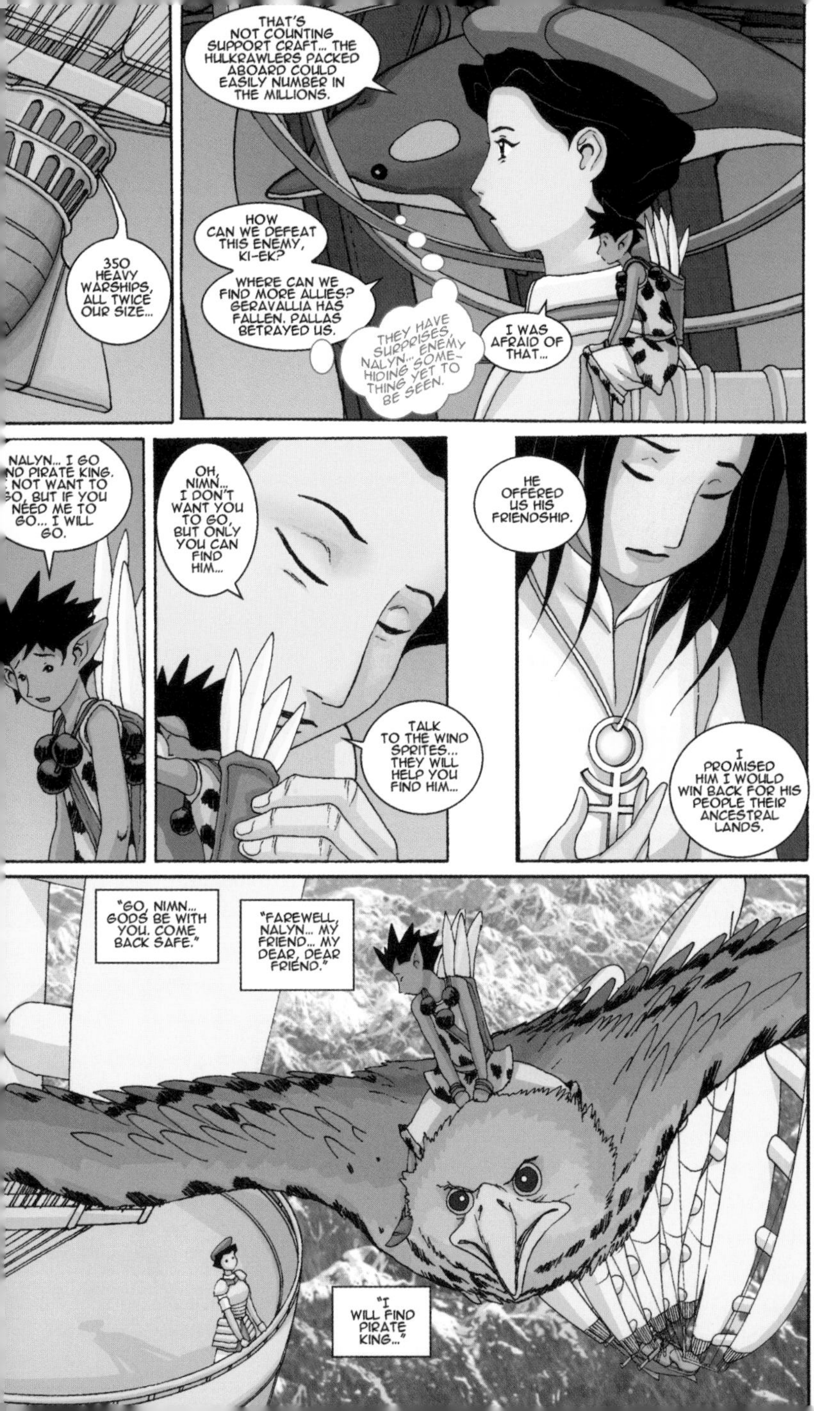
THAT'S NOT COUNTING SUPPORT CRAFT... THE HULKRAWLERS PACKED ABOARD COULD EASILY NUMBER IN THE MILLIONS.
350 HEAVY WARSHIPS, ALL TWICE OUR SIZE...
HOW CAN WE DEFEAT THIS ENEMY, KI-EK?
WHERE CAN WE FIND MORE ALLIES? GERAVALLIA HAS FALLEN. PALLAS BETRAYED US.
THEY HAVE SURPRISES, NALYN... ENEMY HIDING SOMETHING YET TO BE SEEN.
I WAS AFRAID OF THAT...
NALYN... I GO ND PIRATE KING. NOT WANT TO GO, BUT IF YOU NEED ME TO GO... I WILL GO.
OH, NIMN... I DON'T WANT YOU TO GO, BUT ONLY YOU CAN FIND HIM...
TALK TO THE WIND SPRITES... THEY WILL HELP YOU FIND HIM...
HE OFFERED US HIS FRIENDSHIP.
I PROMISED HIM I WOULD WIN BACK FOR HIS PEOPLE THEIR ANCESTRAL LANDS.
"GO, NIMN... GODS BE WITH YOU. COME BACK SAFE."
"FAREWELL, NALYN... MY FRIEND... MY DEAR, DEAR FRIEND."
"I WILL FIND PIRATE KING..."

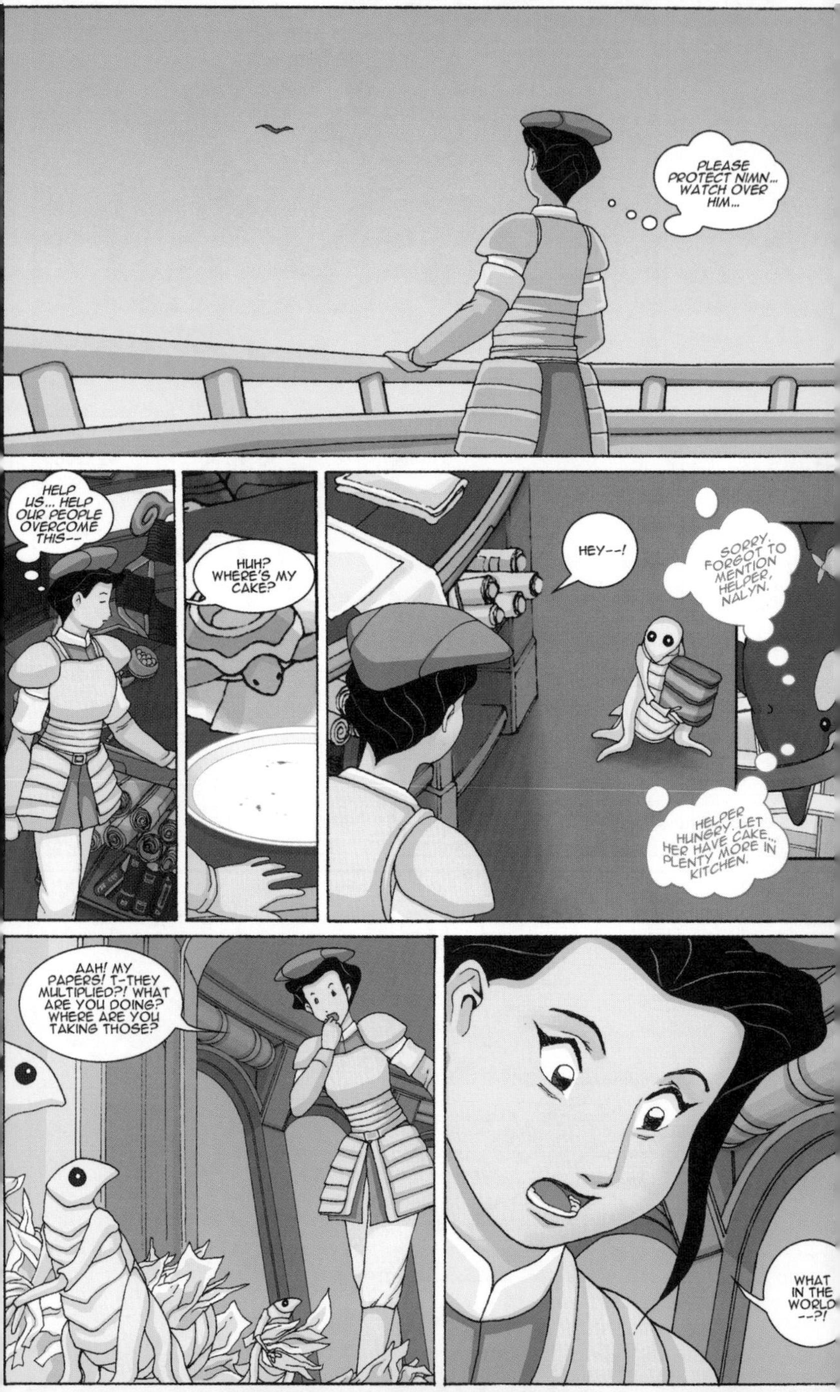
PLEASE PROTECT NIMN... WATCH OVER HIM...
HELP US... HELP OUR PEOPLE OVERCOME THIS--
HUH? WHERE'S MY CAKE?
HEY--!
SORRY. FORGOT TO MENTION HELPER, NALYN.
HELPER HUNGRY. LET HER HAVE CAKE... PLENTY MORE IN KITCHEN.
AAH! MY PAPERS! T-THEY MULTIPLIED?! WHAT ARE YOU DOING? WHERE ARE YOU TAKING THOSE?
WHAT IN THE WORLD --?!

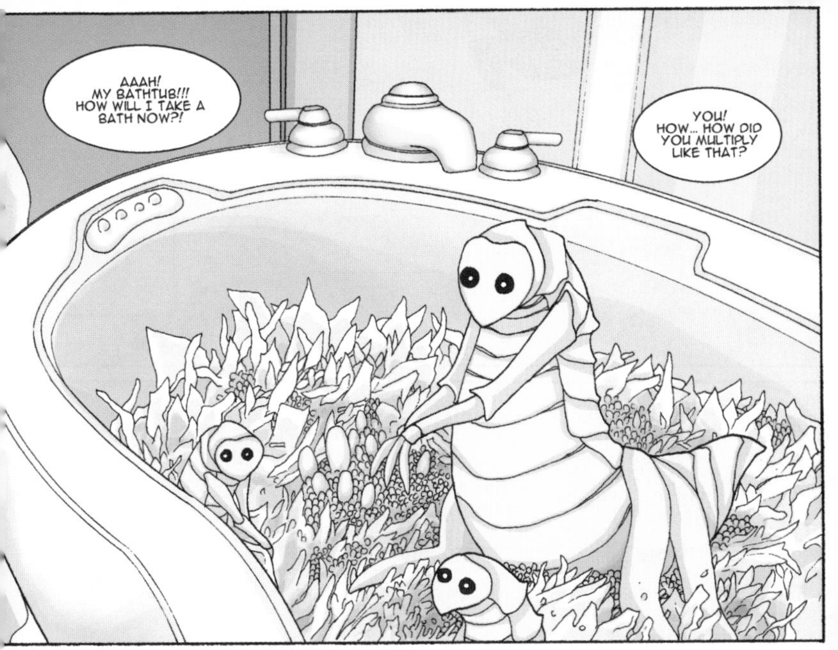
AAAH! MY BATHTUB!!! HOW WILL I TAKE A BATH NOW?!
YOU! HOW... HOW DID YOU MULTIPLY LIKE THAT?

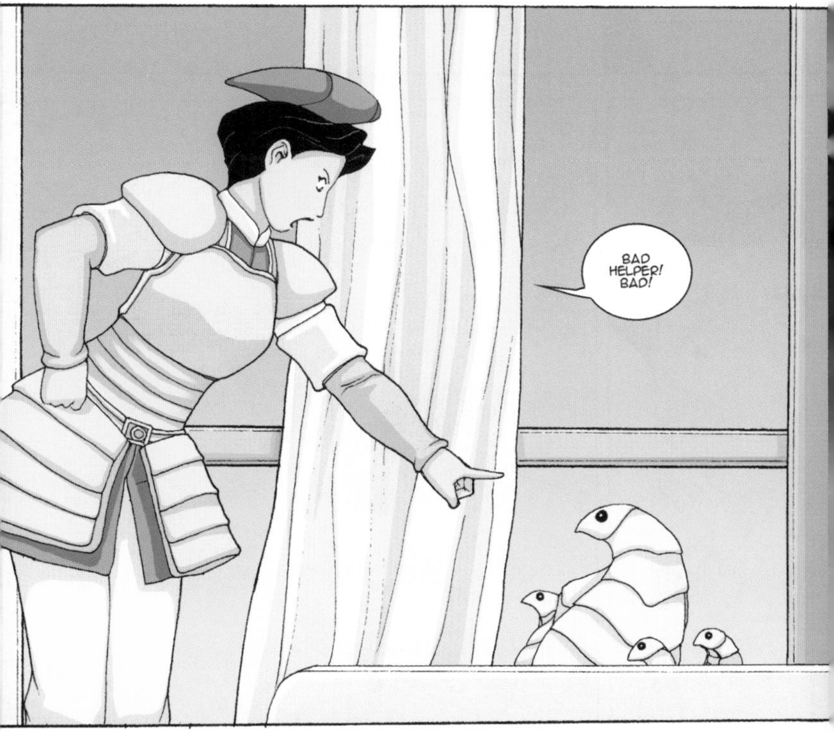
BAD HELPER! BAD!

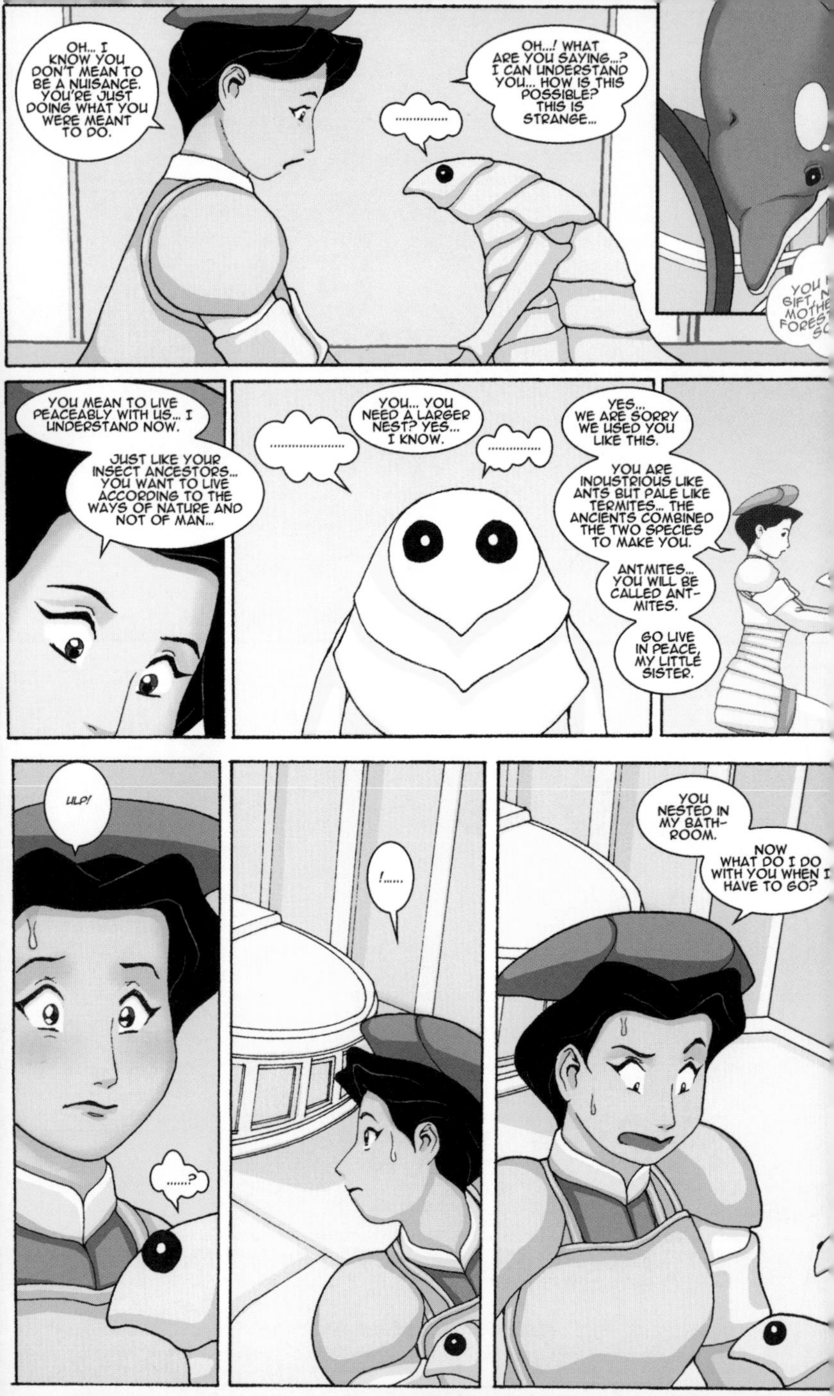
OH... I KNOW YOU DON'T MEAN TO BE A NUISANCE. YOU'RE JUST DOING WHAT YOU WERE MEANT TO DO.
....
OH...! WHAT ARE YOU SAYING...? I CAN UNDERSTAND YOU... HOW IS THIS POSSIBLE? THIS IS STRANGE...
YOU MEAN TO LIVE PEACEABLY WITH US... I UNDERSTAND NOW.
JUST LIKE YOUR INSECT ANCESTORS... YOU WANT TO LIVE ACCORDING TO THE WAYS OF NATURE AND NOT OF MAN...
....
YOU... YOU NEED A LARGER NEST? YES... I KNOW.
....
YES... WE ARE SORRY WE USED YOU LIKE THIS.
YOU ARE INDUSTRIOUS LIKE ANTS BUT PALE LIKE TERMITES... THE ANCIENTS COMBINED THE TWO SPECIES TO MAKE YOU.
ANTMITES... YOU WILL BE CALLED ANT-MITES.
GO LIVE IN PEACE, MY LITTLE SISTER.
ULP!
......?
!......
YOU NESTED IN MY BATH-ROOM.
NOW WHAT DO I DO WITH YOU WHEN I HAVE TO GO?

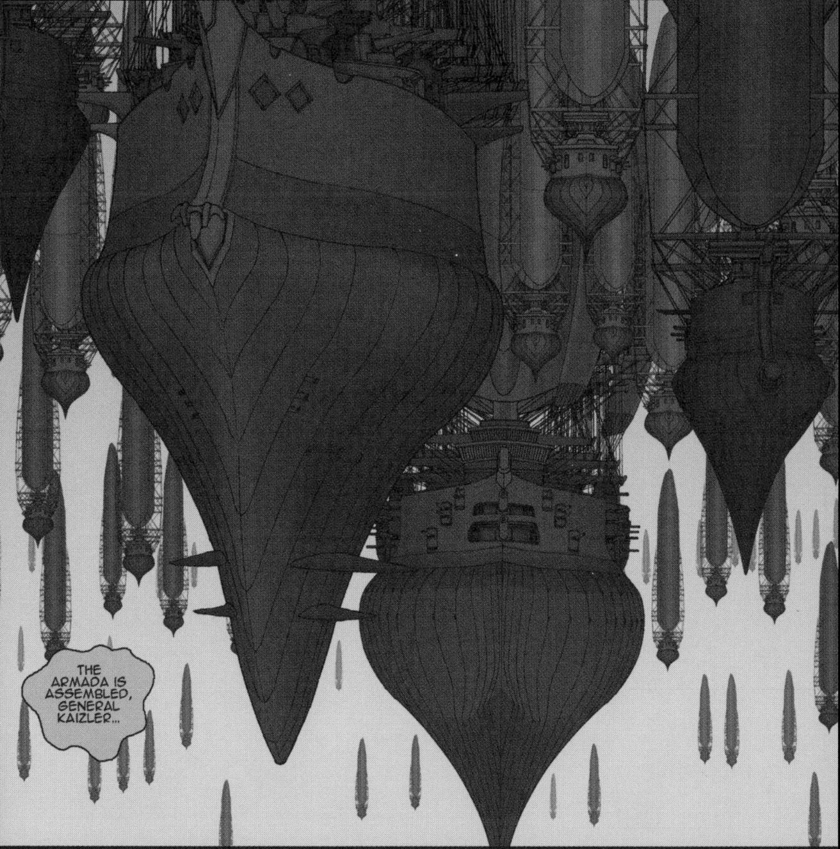
THE ARMADA IS ASSEMBLED, GENERAL KAIZLER...

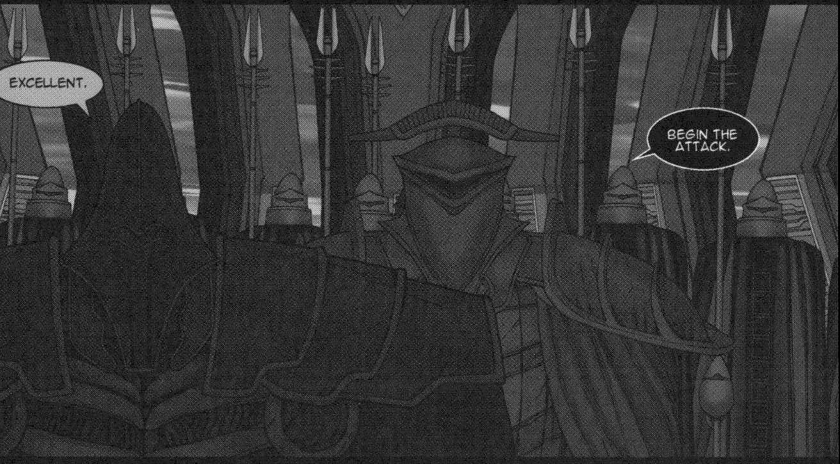
EXCELLENT.
BEGIN THE ATTACK.

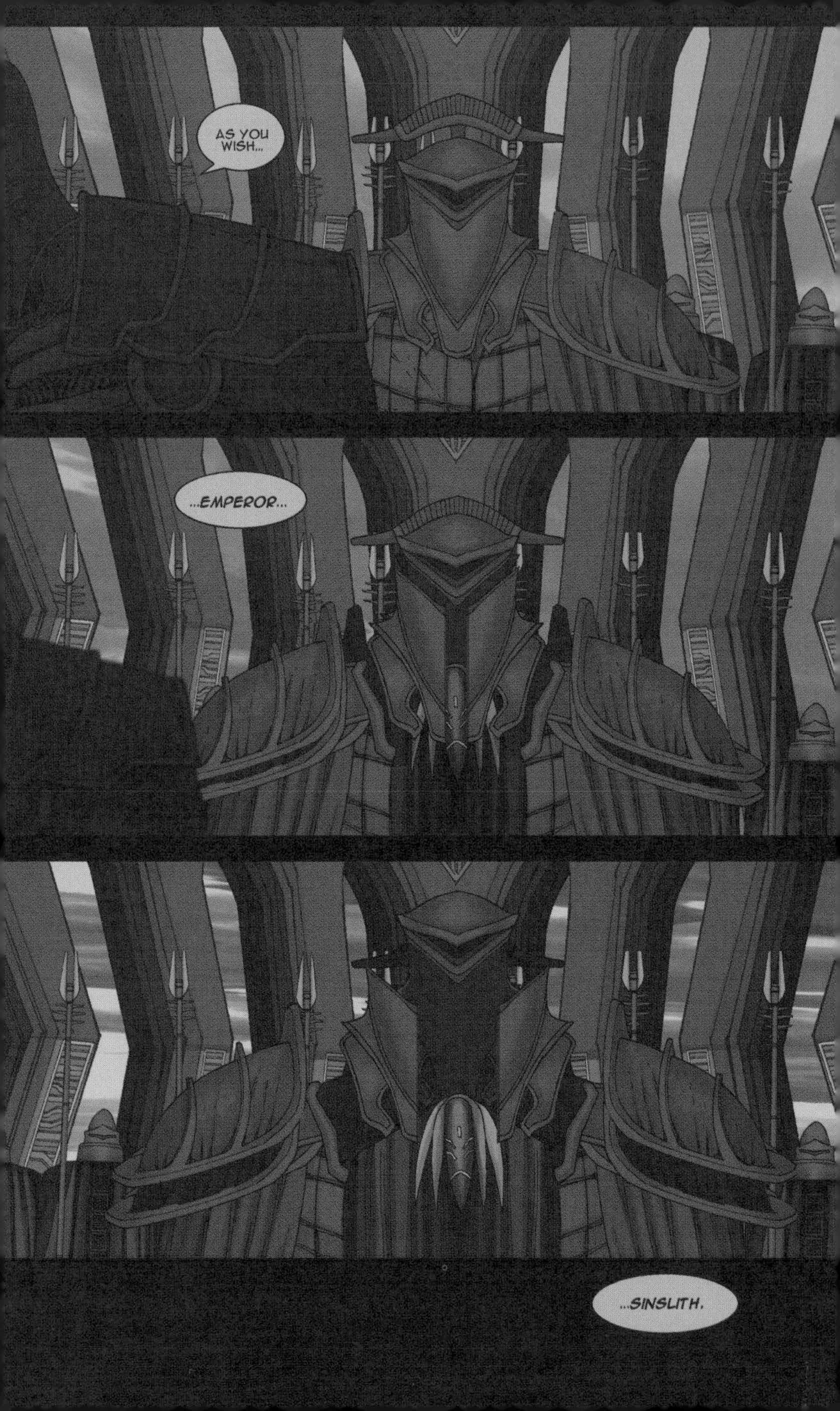
AS YOU WISH...
...EMPEROR...
...SINSLITH.

Next:

The New World

The battle begins!

The Krossians have been busy resurrecting ancient machines. Their fast-flying fighter drones continually pummel the Mathenian float ships, and Sinslith has more surprises in store. He has ordered the disintegrates activated. The ancient sentinels, the protectors of Eriden for nearly a thousand years, reveal their devastating might in the hands of the enemy. The Lesazonian fleet is outmatched, they will need a miracle.

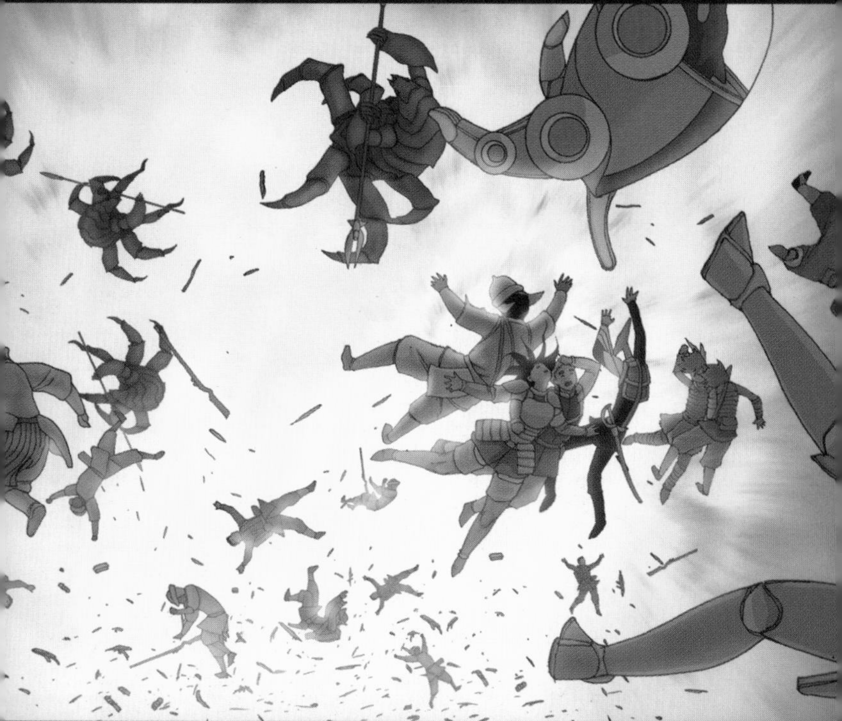

Originally from the
Philippines, Rod Espinosa graduated from Don
Bosco Technical College with a certificate for
Architectural Drafting before going on to the
University of Santo Tomas to earn his degree in
Advertising Arts.

His work with
The Courageous Princess has earned him
nominations for "Best Story for Younger Audiences"
by the prestigious Eisner Awards as well as "Most
Promising Newcomer" and "Best Artist" by the
Ignatz Awards.

His past works include
The Courageous Princess (3 graphic novel
volumes), *Chronicles of the Universe:
The Beginning*, *Battle Girlz* (6-part miniseries),
For*Eternity (4-part miniseries), *Ninja High
School* (artist, 5 episodes), *Ninja High School
Spotlight* and *The Alamo*. He is currently working on
the continuation of *Neotopia*.

This volume collects
Neotopia: The Kingdoms Beyond
episodes 3.1 to 3.5

To learn more about *Neotopia*
and to read notes on the various worlds
as well as special web-exclusive character
diary excerpts, visit us online at

http://www.antarctic-press.com